AF577418

ATLAS OF SOUTH AMERICA

ATLAS OF SOUTH AMERICA

MOSHE BRAWER

SIMON & SCHUSTER

A Paramount Communications Company

New York London Toronto Sydney Tokyo Singapore

Article on Flora & Fauna: Avraham Arbel, Professor of Zoology, Kibbutzim State Teachers College.

Computer generated cartography & shaded relief: Pinhas Yoeli, Professor of Cartography, Tel Aviv University.

Cartographic Editor: Sarah Postavsky

Text Editor: Barbara Ball

Annotated Bibliography: Linda S. Vertrees

Designed and produced by Carta, Jerusalem

The physical maps were partially compiled & drawn with the use of computer generated cartography.

Academic Reference Division
Simon and Schuster
15 Columbus Circle, New York, NY 10023

A Paramount Communications Company

Library of Congress Cataloging-in-Publication Data
Brawer, Moshe, 1919–
Atlas of South America / Moshe Brawer.
p. cm.
Includes bibliographical references.
1. South America--Maps. 2. South America--Economic conditions--Maps. I. Title.
G1700.B7 1991 G&M
912.68--dc20 90-675175
ISBN 0-13-050642-7 CIP
MAP

Picture Credits: Photographs pages 12, 64, 65, 68, 71, 82, 113—Amir Yechiely; pages 74, 99, 103, 130—Didi Menusy; page 79—Shmuel Schatz; page 21 (all four)—Avraham Arbel; page 112—UN 154994/Claudio Edinger; page 27 (upper)—UN 125788; pages 11, 27 (lower), 51—embassy of Peru, Washington, DC; page 41—embassy of Venezuela, Israel; pages 54, 57—embassy of Ecuador, Israel; page 89—embassy of Argentina, Israel; page 100—embassy of Uruguay, Israel; page 43—embassy of Venezuela, Bonn; page 93—Itaipu Binacional; all other drawings and photographs—Carta.
Coins: John M. Kleeberg, The American Numismatic Society.

CONTENTS

ABBREVIATIONS

°C.	degree Celsius
°F.	degree Fahrenheit
ft	feet
GDP	gross domestic product
GNP	gross national product
in	inches
km	kilometers
m	meters
mi	miles
sq	square

COMMON GEOGRAPHICAL ABBREVIATIONS

Av.	Avenue
B.	Bay
C.	Cape
G.	Gulf
I., Is.	Island, Islands
L.	Lake
Mt., Mts.	Mount, Mountains
Nev.	Nevado (snowy)
Pen.	Peninsula
Pt.	Point
Pta.	Punta (Point)
R.	River
Res.	Reservoir
Vol.	Volcano

FLAG COLOR SYMBOLS

black white yellow red blue brown green

THE CONTINENT

SOUTH AMERICA

Area
17,821,028 sq. km.
6,880,706 sq. mi.

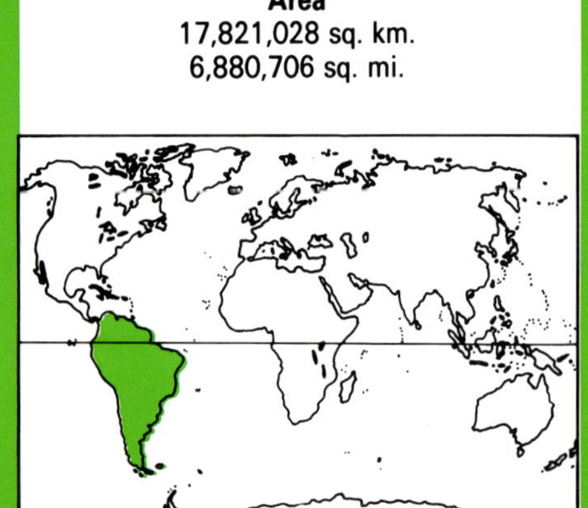

Population
296,789,000 (1990 estimate)

Population in Main Conurbations
São Paulo (Brazil) 15,280,375 (1985)
Rio de Janeiro (Brazil) 10,217,269 (1985)
Buenos Aires (Argentina) 9,766,000 (1985)
Lima (Peru) 5,330,800 (1987)
Santiago (Chile) 4,913,062 (1987)
Bogotá (Colombia) 4,208,000 (1985)

Highest Point
6,960 m. 22,834 ft.
(Mt. Aconcagua, Argentina)

Lowest Point
−40 m. −131 ft.
(Península Valdés, Argentina)

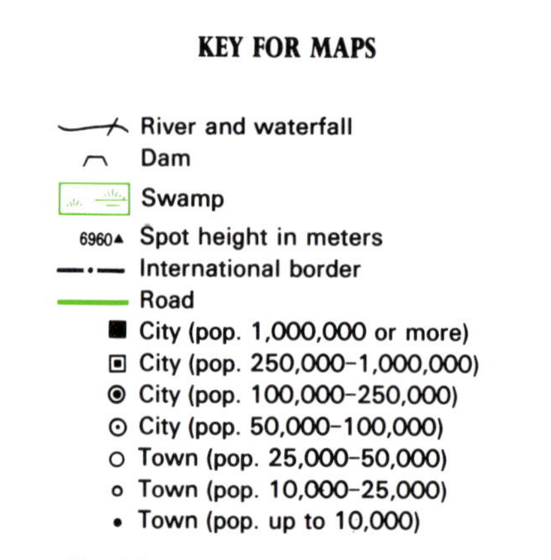

PHYSICAL ENVIRONMENT

South America, which extends over 68 degrees of latitude, from the tropical zone of the Northern Hemisphere across the equator to the vicinity of the sub-Antarctic zone in the south, has a large variety of landscapes that reflect a wide range of combinations of structural characteristics and climatic conditions of its many natural regions. The continent, extending over an area of nearly 17.8 million square kilometers (7 million square miles) or nearly 12 percent of the earth's land surface, is widest in the north (about 5,100 kilometers [3,180 miles]), where its easternmost bulge is only about 2,750 kilometers (1,700 miles) from the coast of West Africa, forming the narrowest part of the Atlantic Ocean. It tapers southward and ends in a spearhead-like peninsula at Tierra del Fuego, facing Antarctica. The continent consists of three main surface divisions: the Andes; the plains of the chief rivers; and the plateaus and highlands of the east.

The Andes, which stretch along the western fringes of the continent from the Caribbean coast to the southern tip of Tierra del Fuego, form a formidable barrier along the entire continent that dominates its drainage pattern and has played a decisive role in the distribution of population and in South America's cultural, economic, and political development. Volcanism is a prominent feature of the Andes; the range has one of the earth's largest concentrations of both active and dormant volcanoes and includes some of the highest and most magnificent volcanic cones.

The river plains extend almost continuously from the Caribbean to the northern edge of the Patagonian Plateau (the valley of the Río Negro). The main arteries of these plains, the rivers Orinoco, Amazon, and Paraguay–Paraná, drain nearly two-thirds (64 percent) of the continent. The Amazon River has the world's largest drainage basin (7 million square kilometers [2.75 million square miles]) and discharge (average 5,520 cubic kilometers [1,327 cubic miles] annually), while the Orinoco (795 cubic kilometers [191 cubic miles]) and Paraná (722 cubic kilometers [174 cubic miles]) are the world's fourth and fifth richest rivers in water volume. These lowlands, which mostly consist of the floodplains of the chief rivers and their tributaries, are covered with a thick mantle of sediments brought down from the Andes and from the eastern plateaus and highlands. The world's most extensive tropical rain forest occupies a large portion of these plains.

The eastern plateaus and highlands, geologically the oldest part of the continent and structurally the most complicated and varied, are made up of the following three parts, separated from each other by penetration of the river plains: the Guiana Highlands in the north; the Brazilian Highlands in the center; and the Patagonian Plateau in the south. The Brazilian Highlands form by far the larger part of the eastern highlands; they include South America's most extensive areas of tabular plateaus and areas elevated by the accumulation of successive lava flows. Unlike the Andes, the highlands on the eastern side of the continent did not (until the nineteenth century) attract much human settlement and activity.

A prominent feature of South America is the manner in which its mountainous rims block much of its interior's outlet to the oceans. As a result, many rivers, including those which form the continent's three predominant drainage systems, rise within short distances of the nearby coast but flow over long distances before reaching the sea.

Another conspicuous feature of South America is the absence of coastal plains, the main exception being near the mouths of the principal rivers. Along the entire western coast, there are hardly any areas that may be described as coastal plains. Where the coast is not lined by cliffs or by mountain slopes and spurs, there are generally only narrow flat coastal strips. There are very few deep indentations and natural harbors along the 5,600-kilometer (3,500-mile) western coast. Only in southern Chile has the submergence of the fringes of the continent produced a fjorded coastal region with numerous small bays, inlets, and islands. Most of the western coast lacks or has a very narrow continental shelf. There are some very deep trenches in the Pacific Ocean bed close to the shore, the deepest of which, more than 8,000 meters (26,000 feet), is situated off the north Chilean coast (Antofagasta). Most of the eastern shores of South America are either not backed by or have only a narrow coastal plain. This is true of the eastern coast of Brazil up to Pôrto Alegre and to a major part of the Argentinian coast. The continental shelf of the eastern coast is broad only in the extreme south, mainly off the shores of southern Argentina (Patagonia). The eastern coast is also not endowed with deep indentations that could be utilized as natural harbors. Most of the large conurbations along the coast grew around these few bays. Coastal plains follow most of the continent's northern shores, although the swampy nature of substantial parts of these have made them unattractive to settlement. Rivers, which drain about half the area of the continent and which carry enormous quantities of water, reach and affect the nature of the sea along the northern coast.

Because of its natural characteristics and resources, South America is considered the continent with the largest potential for further economic development and settlement.

MEXICO
CUBA
HAITI
PUERTO RICO
JAMAICA
DOMINICAN REPUBLIC
BELIZE
HONDURAS
NICARAGUA
DOMINICA
ST. LUCIA
BARBADOS
Caribbean Sea
Punta Gallinas
Aruba
Curaçao
Margarita
TRINIDAD & TOBAGO
North Atlantic Ocean
Barranquilla
Maracaibo
Caracas
Managua
San José
COSTA RICA
Panamá
PANAMA
Ciudad Guayana
San Cristóbal
R. Orinoco
VENEZUELA
Georgetown
Paramaribo
Cayenne
GUYANA
SURINAME
FRENCH GUIANA
Medellín
Bogotá
COLOMBIA
Cali
R. Cauca
R. Magdalena
R. Meta
Llanos
Guiana Highlands
Boa Vista
R. Guaviare
Mitú
Trans Amazon Highway
R. Branco
Macapá
Cocos (Costa Rica)
I. de Malpelo (Colombia)
Quito
ECUADOR
Islas Galápagos (Ecuador)
Guayaquil
R. Putumayo
R. Japurá
R. Negro
Equator
Manaus
Fonte Boa
R. Amazonas
Santarém
Belém
São Luís
Iquitos
R. Juruá
R. Madeira
R. Tapajós
R. Tocantins
Fortaleza
Teresina
C. de São Roque
Natal
Recife
Piura
Punta Aguja
R. Marañón
R. Ucayali
Selvas
R. Purus
BRAZIL
Trujillo
Nev. de Huascarán 6768
Huánuco
Rio Branco
Pôrto Velho
R. Xingu
R. Araguaia
Pôrto Nacional
Brazilian Highlands
R. São Francisco
Aracaju
Salvador
Callao
Lima
Pan American Highway
PERU
Cuzco
R. Madre de Dios
R. Beni
Trinidad
Ica
L. Titicaca
La Paz
Cochabamba
Santa Cruz
Cuiabá
Brasília
Goiânia
Arequipa
Andes
BOLIVIA
Arica
Sucre
Campo Grande
R. Grande
Belo Horizonte
Vitória
Pacific Ocean
Iquique
Gran Chaco
R. Paraguay
R. Paraná
PARAGUAY
Concepción
Agulhas Negras 2787
São Paulo
Rio de Janeiro
Antofagasta
Asunción
Curitiba
San Miguel de Tucumán
Resistencia
Florianópolis
San Félix (Chile)
San Ambrosio (Chile)
Ojos del Salado 6880
R. Salado
R. Uruguay
Serra do Mar
Pôrto Alegre
Cerro Aconcagua 6960
Salto
Córdoba
Valparaíso
Mendoza
Rosario
URUGUAY
Montevideo
Santiago
Buenos Aires
Río de la Plata
Juan Fernández (Chile)
CHILE
ARGENTINA
South Atlantic Ocean
Concepción
Bahía Blanca
Mar del Plata
R. Negro
Puerto Montt
San Carlos de Bariloche
Pen. Valdés
Comodoro Rivadavia
C. Blanco
Patagonia
Falkland Is. (U.K.)
Stanley
1:30,000,000
0 250 500 Km.
0 250 Mi.
Punta Arenas
Tierra del Fuego
C. de Hornos (C. Horn)
South Georgia (U.K.)
90° 80° 70° 60° 50° 40°
20° 10° 0° 10° 20° 30° 40° 50°
100° 90° 80° 70° 60° 50° 40° 30° 20°

THE AMAZON BASIN

DRAINAGE BASINS

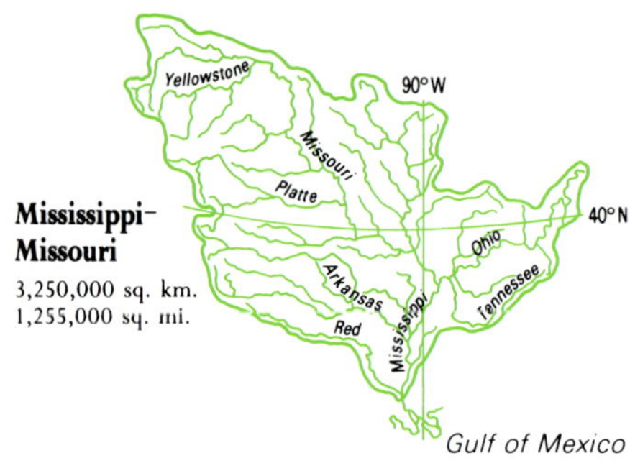

Mississippi-Missouri
3,250,000 sq. km.
1,255,000 sq. mi.

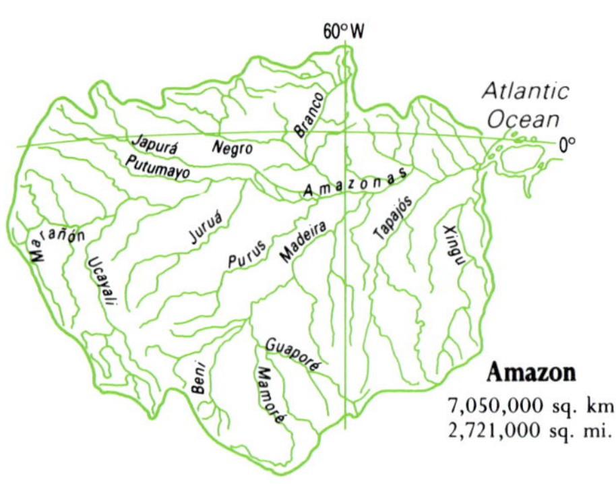

Amazon
7,050,000 sq. km.
2,721,000 sq. mi.

The Amazon Basin is by far the greatest river basin in the world. It drains an area of about 7 million square kilometers (2.73 million square miles), twice the area of the world's second largest basin, that of the river Zaïre (Congo) in Africa. Sloping down eastward from the foot of the Andes in the west, the enormous plains that make up most of the basin area border the Guiana Highlands in the north and the Brazilian Highlands in the south. The basin's lowlands are widest (about 1,400 kilometers [880 miles]) west of the confluence of the Amazon with the Rio Negro and narrowest (about 65 kilometers [40 miles]) near Santarém, where the Guiana and Brazilian highlands come closest. Most of the surface of the Amazon lowlands is an undulating plain, well above the floodplains of the rivers, whose main surface features are river terraces and bluffs which often stand 50 to 60 meters (160 to 200 feet) above the river. This is also by far the richest basin in water resources. The Amazon empties into the sea an average of 5,520 billion cubic meters of water per year (nearly four times that of the Zaïre, the river with the second largest discharge), or 11 percent of all the water drained from the world's continents into the seas. The discharge of the Amazon is highest in July, when the average flow is 216,000 cubic meters per second. It is lowest in November with an average of 73,000 cubic meters per second. The normal width of the channel varies from about 1.6 kilometers (1 mile) to 8 to 10 kilometers (5 to 6 miles). It is generally 6 to 12 meters (20 to 40 feet) deep, but it reaches a depth of nearly 100 meters (300 feet) in its narrow places. When in full flood, the Amazon usually extends over its entire floodplain (as do its tributaries) which at its narrowest parts is only about 30 kilometers (20 miles) wide, but over long stretches of its course is 80 to 100 kilometers (50 to 60 miles) wide. When in flood, the river carries large quantities of silt brought down from the highlands, which it deposits over its floodplain and opposite its mouth in the ocean, causing the discoloration of the seawater to a distance of about 300 kilometers (200 miles) offshore.

The channel of the Amazon has a very low gradient, descending only 170 meters (560 feet) from the foot of the Andes to the ocean over a course of more than 4,000 kilometers (2,500 miles). Over the last 1,400 kilometers (880 miles) of its course from Manaus, it descends only about 30 meters (100 feet). The river meanders over its floodplain, frequently shifting its channel, breaking into several arms, and forming lakes and swamps. The same applies to the courses of most of its tributaries in the lowlands. The Amazon is navigable to small ocean-going vessels (drawing up to 6 meters) up to Manaus and to small ships (drawing up to 4 meters) up to Iquitos in Peru. The Amazon tributaries that come down from the Guiana and Brazilian highlands are interrupted by falls and rapids. In most cases only their courses in the lowlands are navigable.

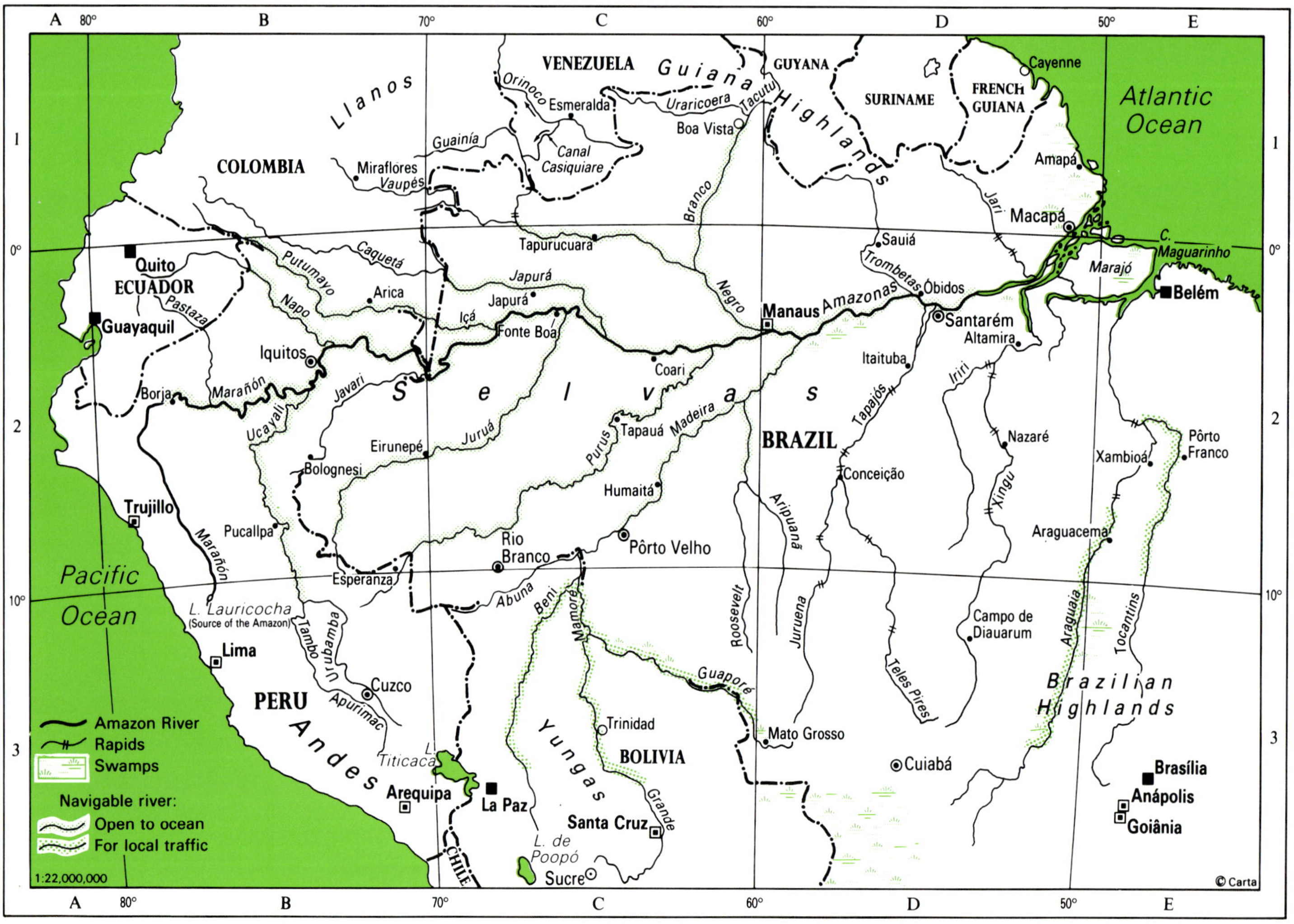

Amazon River
Rapids
Swamps
Navigable river:
Open to ocean
For local traffic
1:22,000,000

© Carta

THE AMAZON FOREST

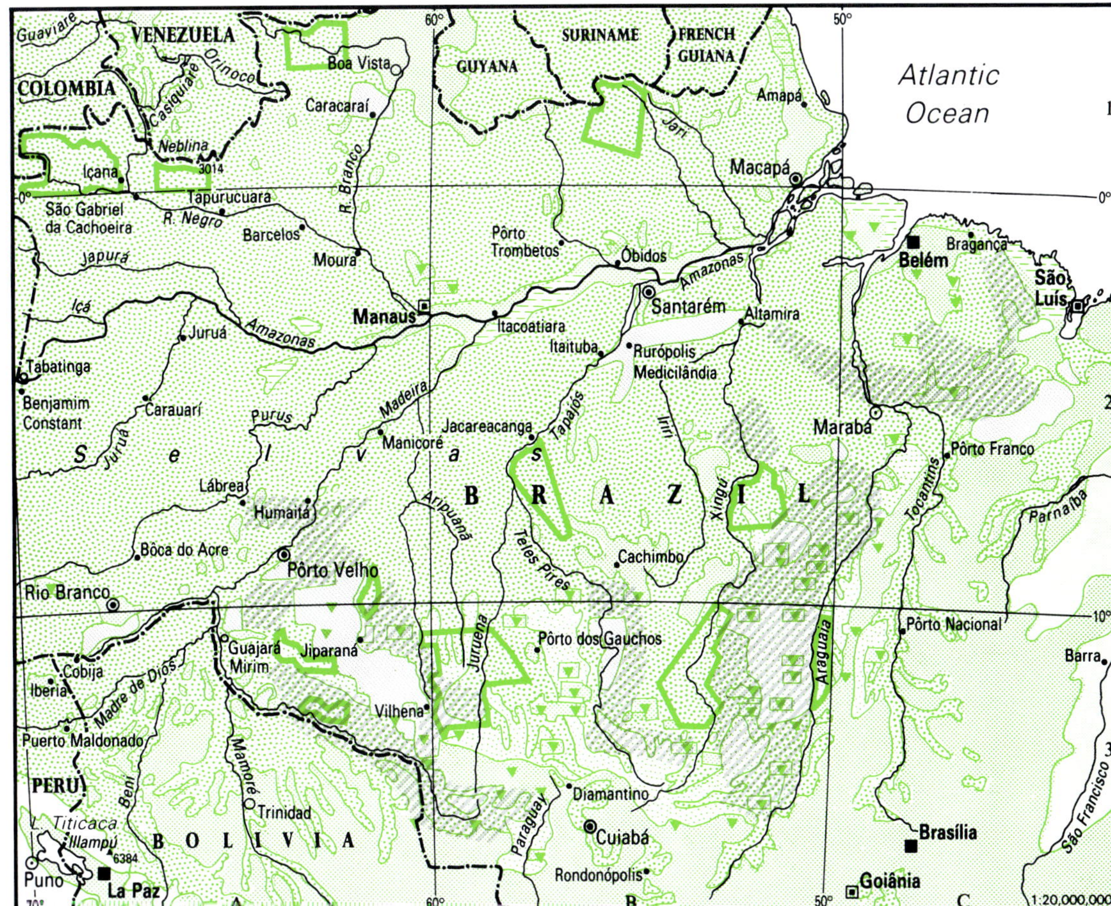

Rio Amazonas

Most of the Amazon Basin is covered with dense tropical rain forest comprised of many different species of trees and shrubs, often hundreds of different species per square kilometer. These are by far the world's most extensive and rich virgin forests. The forests are often less dense and even patchy on the highland fringes of the basin. The prevalent belief that the tropical soils of the Amazon Basin are fertile is, to a large extent, unfounded. The soils over most part of the basin are leached out of valuable mineral content and often coarse. The fertile soils of the basin are mostly confined to the river floodplains where fresh silt is deposited almost annually.

European penetration into the Amazon Basin during the seventeenth and eighteenth centuries led mainly to the establishment of a number of Jesuit missionary stations on the banks of the Amazon and some of its chief tributaries. The Jesuits were engaged in efforts to Christianize the small indigenous Indian tribes and settle them in villages near these stations. The heart of the basin experienced a short economic boom during the second half of the nineteenth and the early twentieth century, when it became the world's source of rubber tapped from naturally grown rubber trees that were found in abundance in part of the rain forest. Large numbers of workers, mainly from northeastern Brazil, were attracted to the rubber-producing area centered in Manaus, which grew from a small settlement to a town of over 50,000. Exports rose from a few tons in the 1850s to 42,000 tons in 1912. The boom ended in the 1920s when large-scale production of rubber from plantations in Southeast Asia (mainly Malaya) made the extraction of rubber from the natural forests unprofitable. Brazil's rubber production diminished to a trickle. Most workers employed in this industry left the region.

Since the 1960s the Amazon lowlands have become one of the main development targets of the Brazilian government. This has been prompted by the desire to realize a long-standing wish to extend effective control over a large part of Brazil's territory, to exploit the vast resources of the region and integrate it into the expanding Brazilian economy, and to solve the problem of overpopulation, unemployment, and poverty in the northeastern region. Brazil is planning to settle in the lowlands 100,000 familes, a large proportion of whom will be engaged in agriculture on land allotted to them mainly along the east-west axis of the Trans-Amazon (Transamazônica) Highway constructed in (1970–1975) across the Amazon Basin. This highway was augmented by a number of additional north-south roads designed to open up wide parts of the Amazon Basin. Planned settlement during the 1970s and early 1980s developed much slower than anticipated and encountered unforeseen difficulties. Unplanned and unsupervised settlement by squatters, speculators, profiteers, and miners (mainly gold prospectors) taking advantage of the development facilities and access created by the government, has proliferated, however. This led to extensive clearing of forest areas and callous disregard of the interests of aboriginal Indian tribes. The progress of economic activites in the Brazilian Amazon has produced growing controversy in Brazil and worldwide; critics point out especially the indifference toward local and global environmental effects caused by massive destruction of the world's principal and largest remaining tropical forest.

THE ANDES

The great Andes mountain system extends for more than 8,900 kilometers (5,500 miles) along the entire length of western South America, from the Caribbean coast in the north to Tierra del Fuego in the south. The Andes form a formidable natural wall separating the narrow western coastal region from the rest of the continent. They are not a continuous mountain chain but a complex of closely joined structural units that may be described as a series of high plateaus surmounted by numerous, much higher peaks. They are formed by folded and faulted structures that have been deeply eroded and partly affected by extensive volcanic activity. The mountain system runs in three main directions: a large arc, extending from the Caribbean coast (according to one view, up to the coast opposite Trinidad, and in another view, only up to northwestern Venezuela) to central Bolivia, the convex side of which faces west and reaches its westernmost section (81° west) in the border area between Peru and Ecuador; a due north-south part from central Bolivia to the Strait of Magellan; and a small, almost due east section in Tierra del Fuego.

Geologically the Andes are the youngest highlands in South America. The eastern side of the Andes is built generally of older rock formations than the western ranges and plateaus. The Andes form part of the belt of high volcanic activity that surrounds the Pacific, with a large number of extinct, dormant, and active volcanoes. The volcanoes and volcanic activity are mainly concentrated in three zones: in southern Colombia and northern Ecuador; in southern Peru, western Bolivia, and northern Chile; and in central and southern Chile. These include some of the world's highest and most impressive volcanic cones, such as Chimborazo (6,267 meters [20,561 feet]) and San Pedro (6,154 meters [20,190 feet]). These zones experience occasional volcanic eruptions and serious earthquakes.

The Andes are widest (about 650 kilometers [400 miles]) in central Bolivia (opposite the Chilean port of Arica) and are narrowest (60-80 kilometers [40-50 miles]) in Patagonia. Climate, which is dependent on latitude, altitude, and topographic position, plays a prominent role in the great variety of landscapes characteristic of the Andes as a whole and of each of their major subdivisions. There are often abrupt changes in the landscape over short distances, mainly due to changes in altitude or the amount of exposure to winds or sun. Even at identical altitudes there are significant differences between the eastern and western ranges or slopes. This is particularly true where the western parts are arid (Peru and northern Bolivia) while the eastern side is well supplied with rain. The respective climatic zones of various parts of the Andes are described in the chapters dealing with each of the Andean countries. The headstreams of most of the major rivers of the continent or of their main tributaries originate in the Andes.

The northern part of the Andes, known as the Colombian Andes, consists of three sets of ranges—the Cordillera Occidental, Cordillera Central, and Cordillera Oriental—separated by deep depressions in which flow the rivers Patia, Cauca (between the Occidental and Central), and Magdalena (between the Central and Oriental). The Cordillera Occidental, which reaches an altitude of 3,900 meters (12,800 feet), is the narrowest of the three cordilleras. It runs almost parallel to the Pacific coast and in the north reaches the Caribbean coast. The Cordillera Central is the highest and most volcanic of the Colombian Andes. Two peaks are Ruiz (5,399 meters [17,716 feet]) and Tolima (5,215 meters [17,110 feet]). This cordillera is short and ends south of the Colombian Caribbean coastal plain, under which it is believed to sink and re-emerge in the Sierra Nevada de Santa Marta (highest peak 5,775 meters [19,000 feet] at Cristóbal Colón) in the extreme north. The Cordillera Oriental is the widest and structurally the most varied. It is made up of chains that enclose internal basinlike plains and plateaus that have become densely populated. Although generally lower than the Cordillera Central, its highest peak, Sierra Nevada del Cocuy, is 5,493 meters (18,000 feet). Branching off the Cordillera Oriental in a northeasterly direction is the Cordillera de Mérida (also known as

Southern part of Mt. Yerupajá

the Venezuelan Andes) which is also made up of small chains separated by depressions. The watershed between the Orinoco basin and the Caribbean runs along this cordillera, ending at the depression of Barquisimeto a short distance from the Caribbean. Southward from the vicinity of the boundary between Colombia and Ecuador the Andes actually consist of two ranges—the Cordillera Occidental and an extension of the Cordillera Central. These cordilleras are separated by a high (about 2,400 meters [8,000 feet]) plateau. Both cordilleras are studded with numerous volcanoes, some of which reach altitudes of over 5,000 meters (16,300 feet), including the world's highest volcano, Chimborazo (6,267 meters [20,561 feet]), and Cotopaxi (5,897 meters [19,347 feet]). The plateau, which is covered by a thick mantle of volcanic materials, is divided into a number of basins. The Peruvian Andes farther south are often described as being composed of three parallel cordilleras similar to those of Colombia. The Cordillera Occidental, in fact, continues southward from Ecuador and runs parallel to the Pacific coast. It rises abruptly in the west to great heights and includes some of South America's highest peaks (Huascarán 6,768 meters [22,205 feet], Yerupajá 6,634 meters [21,750 feet], and Ampato 6,310 meters [20,702 feet]). Beyond this cordillera to the east extends a high level surface, above which rise groups of discontinuous, much higher ranges and peaks. This complex of high surface and mountains is divided by long, deep, north-south valleys of some of the head rivers of the Amazon—the Marañón, Huallaga, Apurimac (Ucayali), and Urubamba—which produce the impression of

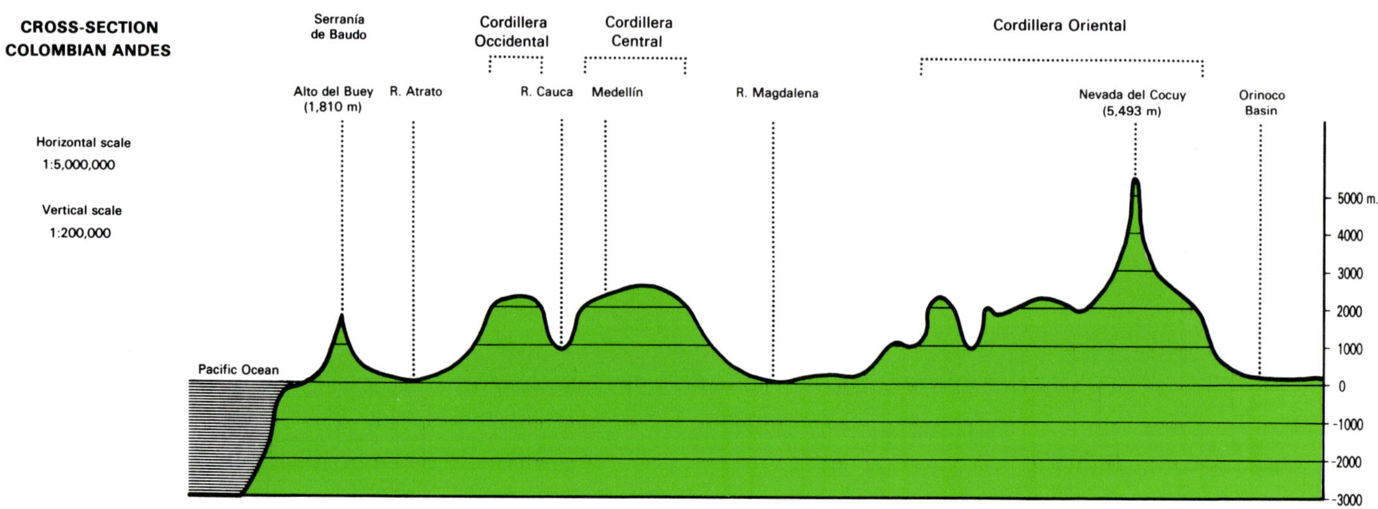

parallel-running cordilleras. The eastern part of these highlands is deeply dissected and slopes precipitously to the Amazon Basin. It is generally known as the Cordillera Oriental. Farther southeast, toward the Bolivian border, it becomes narrower and more mountainous, with peaks of over 6,000 meters (19,700 feet). Mount Illampú just inside Bolivia is 6,485 meters [21,270 feet]) high.

In southern Peru and throughout Bolivia the Andes are much broader (up to a width of 650 kilometers [400 miles]), and the high surface between the western and eastern ranges is much wider. This plateau, 3,400–4,000 meters (11,200–13,100 feet) high, is composed of a series of intermont basins known collectively as the Altiplano. It is an 800-kilometer-(500-mile-) long basin of interior drainage with the world's highest large lake, Titicaca (3,812 meters [12,507 feet]), and a few other smaller lakes. Numerous volcanoes are prominent in the cordillera that encloses the Altiplano. The Altiplano becomes narrower, arid, and less habitable in southern Bolivia and farther south in northern Chile and northeastern Argentina, as the western and eastern cordilleras come closer, until it shrinks into small basins. Southward from about latitude 27° south (north of Valparaíso–Mendoza) the Andes consist of a single cordillera, the southern extension of the unbroken Cordillera Occidental along the entire western coast of the continent. The highest peak in South America, Aconcagua (6,960 meters [22,834 feet]), protrudes near the northern edge of this part of the Andes. Next to it is the famous and most used pass in South America, the La Cumbre pass (3,830 meters [12,560 feet]), through which run the main road and railway between Argentina and Chile.

The southern Andes, known as the Patagonian Andes, are lower and narrower than other parts of the system. Their crests exceed 3,000 meters (10,000 feet), but they become much lower southward, with the exception of a few isolated peaks. Large parts of these Andes are covered with evergreen forests, which disappear in the southernmost section and at Tierra del Fuego, where the snow line descends to less than 700 meters (2,200 feet) above sea level. Glaciers cover substantial areas of the upper areas of the Patagonian Andes. There is also a comparatively large concentration of volcanoes and volcanic activity.

The watershed between the rivers flowing into the Pacific and those to the Atlantic, along the continent's entire length, runs over the Andes. The boundary between Argentina and Chile follows the southern part of this watershed, except in the extreme south near the Strait of Magellan and at Tierra del Fuego. The Andes have been a serious obstacle to communications. There are only a few good passes in the inhabited parts of the continent, and even these rise to altitudes of over 3,000 meters (10,000 feet). Of the few railways that climb the Andes, the Antofagasta–La Paz line (connecting Bolivia with the Chilean coast), the Lima–Cerro de Pasco (between the Peruvian Altiplano and the coast), and the link between Argentina and Chile through the La Cumbre pass are the most important. The Pan-American Highway runs partly through the Andes.

GEOLOGY

The physical structure of South America, with its major surface features, mountain systems, plateaus, river basins, and plains, is the product of a complex of successive geological processes. Endogenic (originating within the earth) and exogenic (originating at or near the surface of the earth) forces continuously at work over the long geological history of the continent brought about many drastic changes in its shape and relief, leading to its present surface and structural characteristics. The geologically oldest parts of the continent consist of three landmasses that today form the Guiana and Brazilian highlands. These three landmasses, known as shields (large rigid areas of the earth's crust, made up of its oldest rocks, which were not affected by later major mountain-building episodes), are the Guiana Shield, the Central Brazilian Shield, and the Eastern Brazilian Shield. A basin known as the Amazon Basin separated the Guiana Shield from the other two shields, which in turn were separated by the ancient Parnaíba-São-Francisco Basin. To the south was another large basin—the Paraná Basin. Both the shields and basins were subject to numerous limited or extensive invasions of the sea and were overlaid by beds of sediment of varying thickness. The basins in particular were filled with very thick beds of sediment brought down from neighboring landmasses and by marine deposits. Such are the origins of some of the main sedimentary rock formations exposed over large areas of the Guiana and Brazilian highlands. Parts of the continent became desert during certain periods of its geological history (there was, for example, an extensive desert south of the Brazilian shields during the Triassic period), causing these and neighboring areas to be overlain by wind-borne (aeolian) sediments. Some sandstone formations covering large areas originated in this way. The surface of the shield and the adjoining basins were also affected by repeated outpours of lava that in some cases spread over large areas and accumulated in great thickness. Outstanding among these is the ancient Paraná Basin, covered with lava deposits which extend over more than one million square kilometers (400,000 square miles), reach a thickness of 1,500 meters (5,000 feet), and are thought to be the largest lava accumulation on earth. The volcanic activity that built up this lava plateau reached its culmination toward the end of the Mesozoic era, when important geological events were also taking place at the western end of the continent, at the Andes.

The geological processes that led to the creation of the Andes began when the Andean Geosyncline (a large linear trough along the margin of a continent) extended along what is now the entire western and part of the northern coast of the continent (from Tierra del Fuego in the south to the island of Trinidad in the north). Large quantities of sediments accumulated over long periods at the bottom of the geosyncline. These sediments reached a thickness of many thousands of meters; at one place, now in the Colombian Andes, sediments were 14,000 meters (46,000 feet) thick. There are indications that movements of the earth's crust leading to the rise of the Andes were active during the early part of the Mesozoic era. It is assumed that the movements started even earlier; however, they were most forceful during the Middle and Upper Tertiary periods, when the uplifting process of the Andes reached its peak, although it actually continued into the Pleistocene epoch. The thick sediments of the Andean Geosyncline when uplifted by movements of the earth's crust were intensely folded and faulted, thus forming the ranges of the Andes. This mountain-building process, accompanied by large intrusions of igneous rock and by much volcanic activity, formed some of the earth's thickest formations of volcanic materials (in Peru and Chile). The Andes assumed most of their present form toward the end of the Tertiary period, when they were already the continuous formidable wall along the entire western fringe of the continent. It was then that the main drainage systems were beginning to develop into their present shape, although at first a huge freshwater lake covered most of the Amazon Basin. One of the last major events affecting the continental surface was the extensive glaciation during the Pleistocene epoch, when glaciers covered much of the Andes from the extreme south to Ecuador. Glacial deposits cover large areas, especially in central and southern Argentina, where they extend to the Atlantic coast. The extensive deposition of sediments in river valleys and lowlands was continued by geological processes of the more recent Quaternary period; the pace of such deposition was often influenced by climatic changes. There has also been much volcanic activity, especially in the Andes, accompanied by deposition of large quantities of volcanic material mainly in intermont basins in the Andes. Some changes in the coastline took place due to uplifting (for example, Patagonia) or subsidence (southern Chile).

STRUCTURAL FEATURES

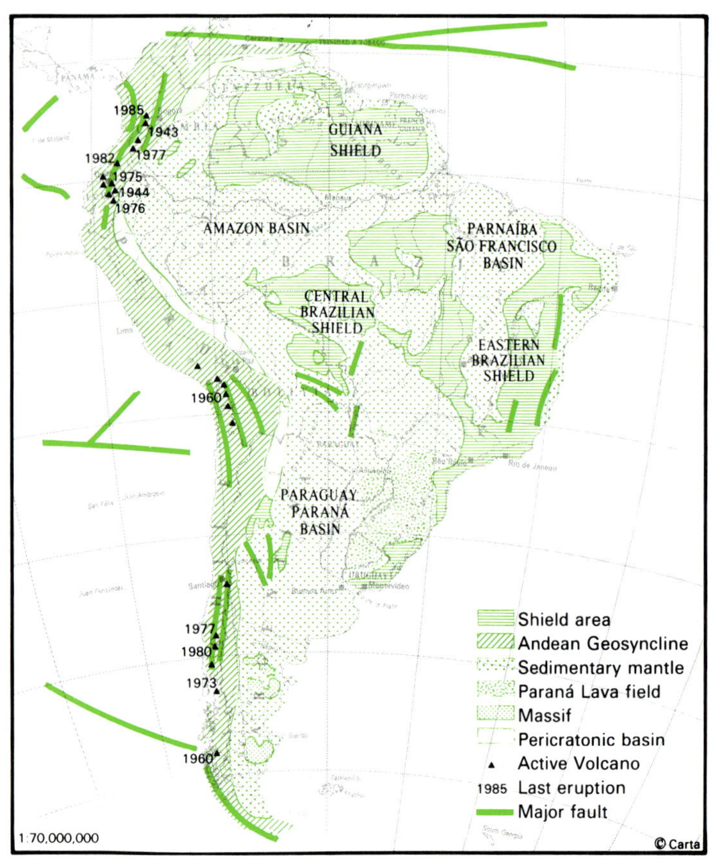

SEISMOLOGY

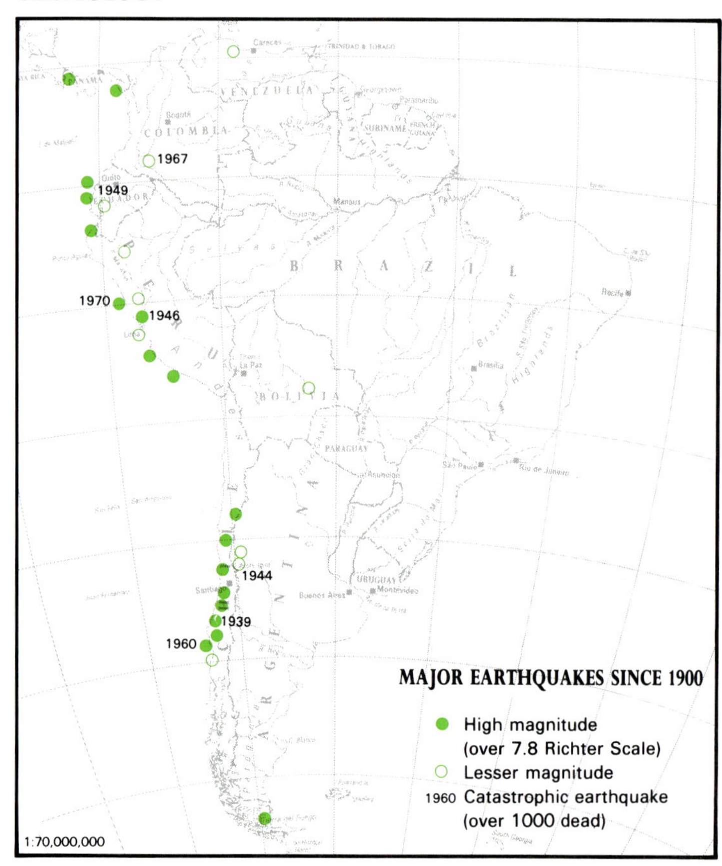

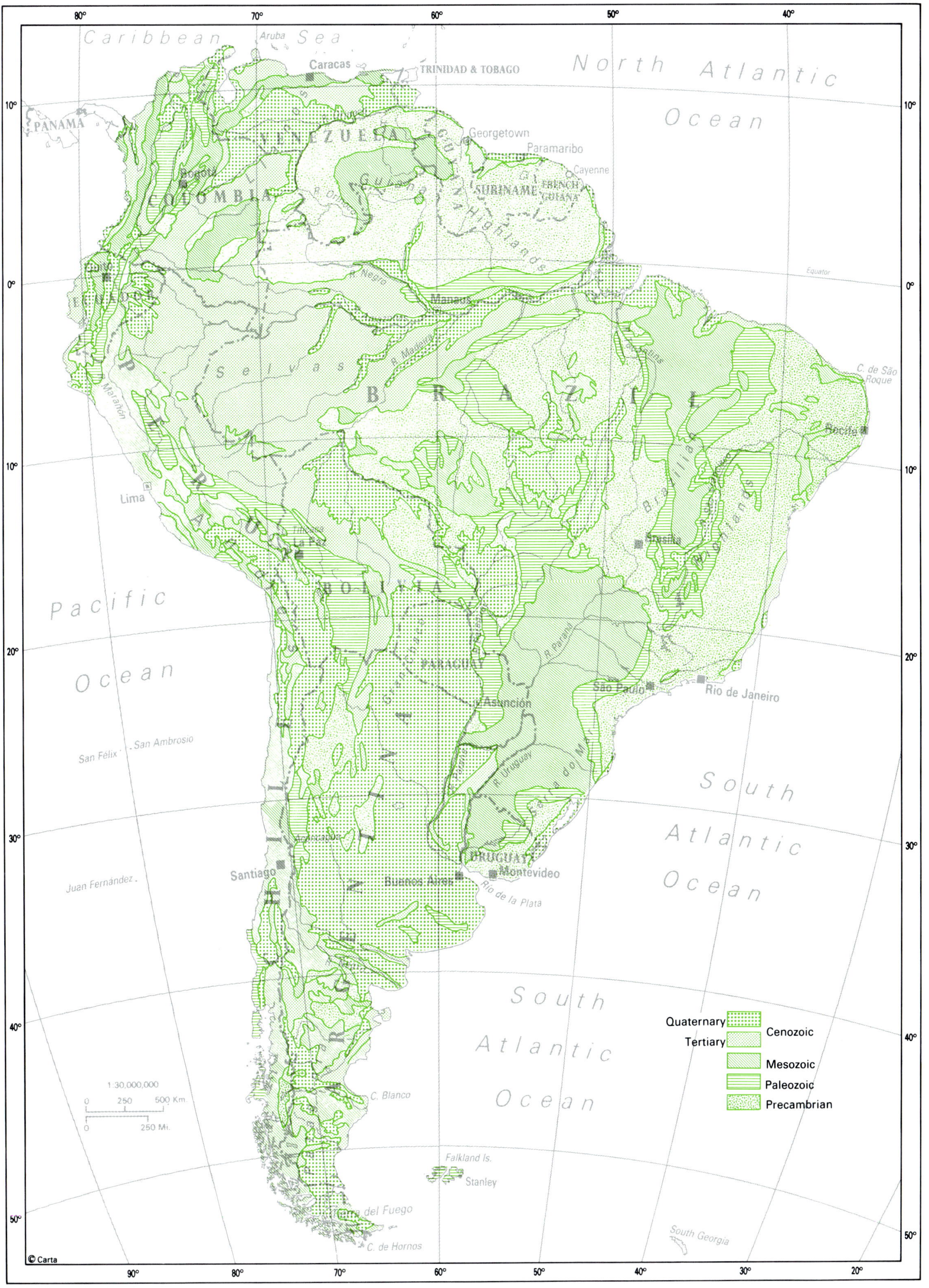
Caribbean Sea
Aruba
Caracas
TRINIDAD & TOBAGO
North Atlantic Ocean
PANAMA
VENEZUELA
Georgetown
Paramaribo
Cayenne
GUYANA
SURINAME
FRENCH GUIANA
Guiana Highlands
Bogotá
COLOMBIA
R. Orinoco
Quito
ECUADOR
Equator
R. Negro
Manaus
Selvas
R. Madeira
BRAZIL
C. de São Roque
Recife
Marañón
PERU
Lima
Titicaca
La Paz
Brasília
Brazilian Highlands
BOLIVIA
Pacific Ocean
PARAGUAY
R. Paraná
São Paulo
Rio de Janeiro
Asunción
San Félix
San Ambrosio
R. Uruguay
Serra do Mar
South Atlantic Ocean
Aconcagua
URUGUAY
Santiago
Montevideo
Buenos Aires
Rio de la Plata
Juan Fernández
CHILE
ARGENTINA
Quaternary
Tertiary
Cenozoic
Mesozoic
Paleozoic
Precambrian
1:30,000,000
0 250 500 Km.
0 250 Mi.
C. Blanco
Falkland Is.
Stanley
Tierra del Fuego
C. de Hornos
South Georgia
© Carta
80° 70° 60° 50° 40°
10° 0° 10° 20° 30° 40° 50°
90° 80° 70° 60° 50° 40° 30° 20°

CLIMATE

The many different climatic conditions that prevail over South America are the result of its extension over a wide range of latitudes and altitudes as well as its shape and structure. It is the only continent in the Southern Hemisphere that extends into the cool temperate zone and comes close to the subpolar region. On the other hand, due to the continent's broad shape in the north, which tapers to a narrow peninsula in the south, most of its area is subject to equatorial and tropical climates. Because of the narrow shape of the southern part of the continent and the fact that there are no areas beyond the moderating effects of the ocean, winter temperatures are much milder than at corresponding middle and high latitudes in other continents. Extremely low temperatures are rare; the average temperature of the coldest month (July) in the extreme south at Tierra del Fuego is 0°C (32°F). Very high temperatures are also rare in South America. The hottest part of the continent in northern Argentina experiences an annual average of less than fifteen days in which temperatures exceed 42°C (108°F). This actually applies to a small area. The average temperature for the hottest month (January) in this part of the continent is 29°C (84°F). The annual range in temperature over most of the continent is small; nowhere does it reach extremes and only in small areas does the range approach 20°C (36°F). Exceptional microclimatic conditions prevail over small areas, with occasional somewhat more extreme temperatures.

Insofar as the effects of altitude on variations in temperature are concerned, the Andes present nearly every type of climatic zone possible, ranging from the hot regions (*tierra caliente*) to the cold treeless zone of the Alpine meadows (*páramos*) and farther up to the permanently snow- and ice-covered (glacial) areas. The altitudes of these vertical climatic zones vary with latitude and position. The snow line is highest in southern Peru and northern Chile, where it is about 5,800 meters (19,000 feet). The fact that it is much higher at this latitude (15°–20° south) than at the equator, where the snow line is at about 4,600 meters (15,000 feet), is attributed to the extreme aridity of the Andes in that part of Peru and Chile. The snow line descends to about 600 meters (2,000 feet) in Tierra del Fuego. There are substantial differences in the altitude of the snow line between west and east and between north- and south-facing slopes. The upper temperature zones largely determine the extent of agricultural activity and of human settlement. Thus, while in southern Peru (around Lake Titicaca) subsistence crops are grown up to an altitude of 3,900 meters (12,800 feet), in southern Chile they can be grown only to an altitude of less than 500 meters (1,500 feet).

The distribution and amount of precipitation are largely determined by the air currents and winds that blow over the continent. These in turn are strongly influenced by the surface relief, mainly the Andes. Ocean currents also have their impact on climatic conditions. The cold Peru current that washes the shores of Peru and northern Chile is largely responsible for the extreme aridity and comparatively low temperatures of this part of the continent. This aridity extends into southern Ecuador and approaches nearer to the equator than anywhere else on earth. The Atacama Desert in the coastal region of southern Peru and northern Chile is one of the world's driest deserts (with an average annual rainfall of less than 10 millimeters [0.5 inch]). The arid zone crosses the Andes in northern Chile into western and then southern Argentina, covering most of Patagonia. Other semiarid and arid zones, much more limited in extent, in northeastern Brazil and part of the coastal area of northern Venezuela, are dry enclaves in regions with a generally adequate supply of rainfall. The western part of the Amazon plain, the northwestern coast of Colombia, the coastal region of Guyana and Suriname, and parts of Chile's southern coast are the wettest parts of the continent, with average annual precipitation exceeding 2,500 millimeters (100 inches). The summer is the main rainy season throughout most of the continent. Large parts of the continent, especially in the tropical regions (with the exception of the arid areas) have no completely dry season or only a short one. Central Chile has rain only in winter, which is also the principal rainy season in southern Chile.

MEAN ANNUAL PRECIPITATION

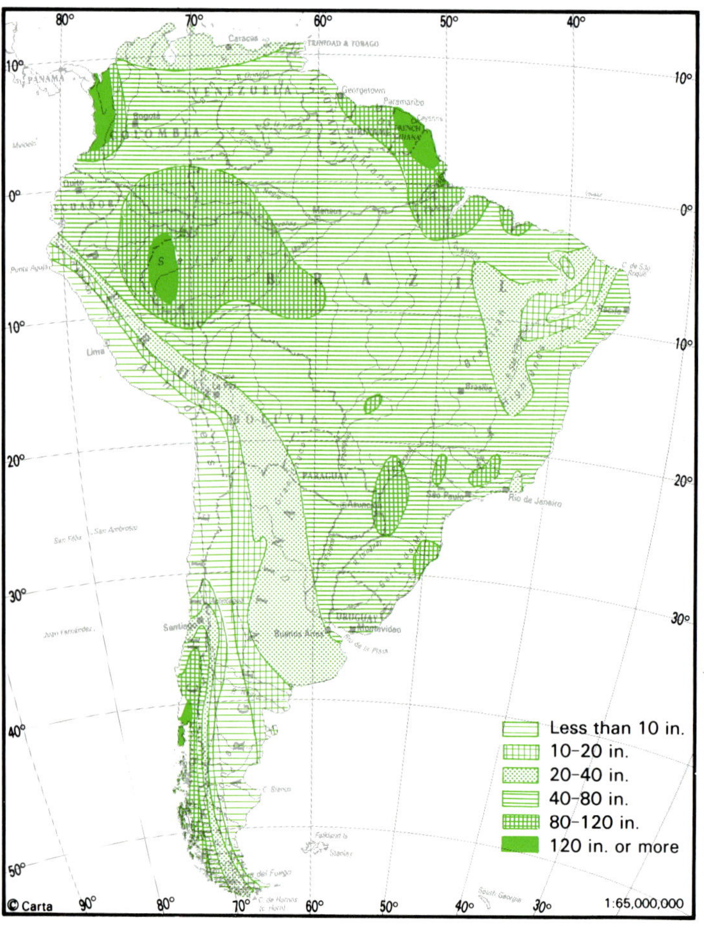

TYPES OF CLIMATE

BY GLENN T. TREWARTHA

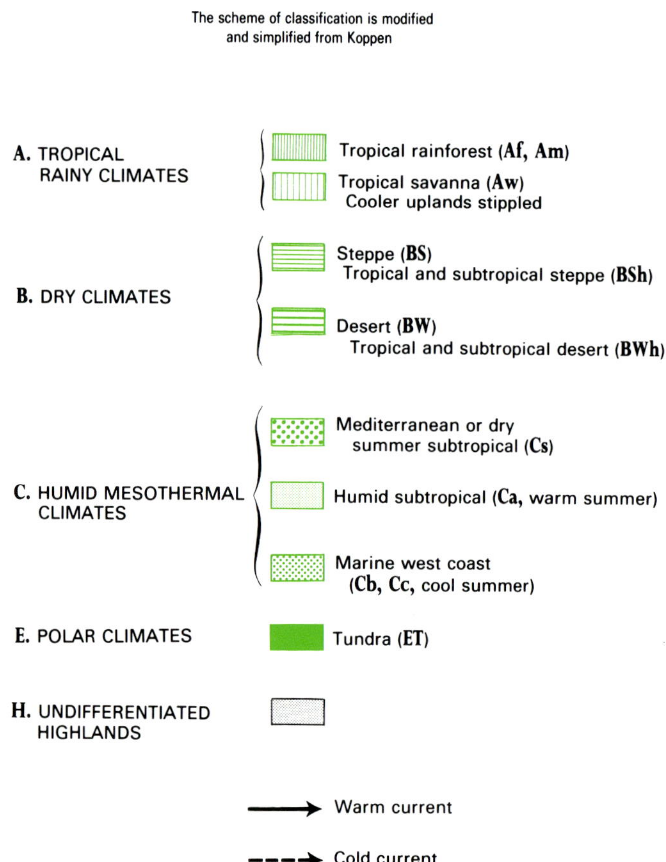

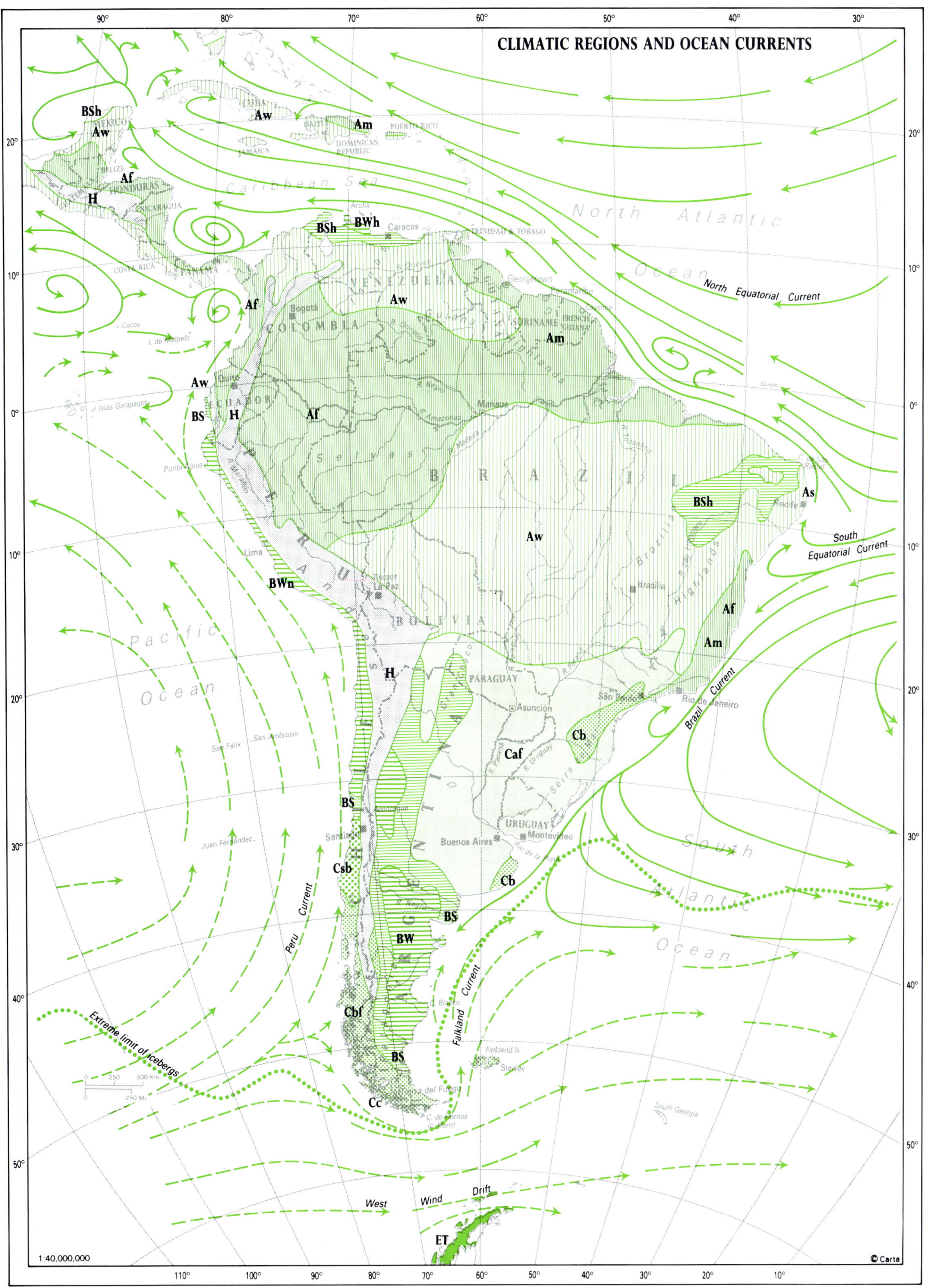
CLIMATIC REGIONS AND OCEAN CURRENTS
North Atlantic Ocean
North Equatorial Current
South Equatorial Current
Brazil Current
South Atlantic Ocean
Pacific Ocean
Peru Current
Falkland Current
West Wind Drift
Extreme limit of icebergs
Caribbean Sea
BSh
Aw
Af
H
Am
BWh
BS
BWn
As
Cb
Caf
Csb
BW
Cbf
Cc
ET
MEXICO
BELIZE
HONDURAS
NICARAGUA
COSTA RICA
PANAMA
CUBA
JAMAICA
HAITI
DOMINICAN REPUBLIC
PUERTO RICO
TRINIDAD & TOBAGO
VENEZUELA
COLOMBIA
GUYANA
SURINAME
FRENCH GUIANA
ECUADOR
PERU
BRAZIL
BOLIVIA
PARAGUAY
CHILE
ARGENTINA
URUGUAY
Caracas
Bogotá
Georgetown
Paramaribo
Quito
Manaus
Lima
La Paz
Brasília
Recife
Rio de Janeiro
São Paulo
Asunción
Buenos Aires
Montevideo
Santiago
Stanley
Falkland Is
South Georgia
Islas Galápagos
I. de Malpelo
Cocos
San Félix
San Ambrosio
Juan Fernández
Selvas
Guiana Highlands
Brazilian Highlands
Andes
Gran Chaco
Tierra del Fuego
C. de Hornos (Cape Horn)
1:40,000,000
© Carta
0 250 500 Km
0 250 Mi
90° 80° 70° 60° 50° 40° 30°
20° 10° 0° 10° 20° 30° 40° 50°
110° 100° 90° 80° 70° 60° 50° 40° 30° 20° 10°

ATMOSPHERIC PRESSURE IN JANUARY

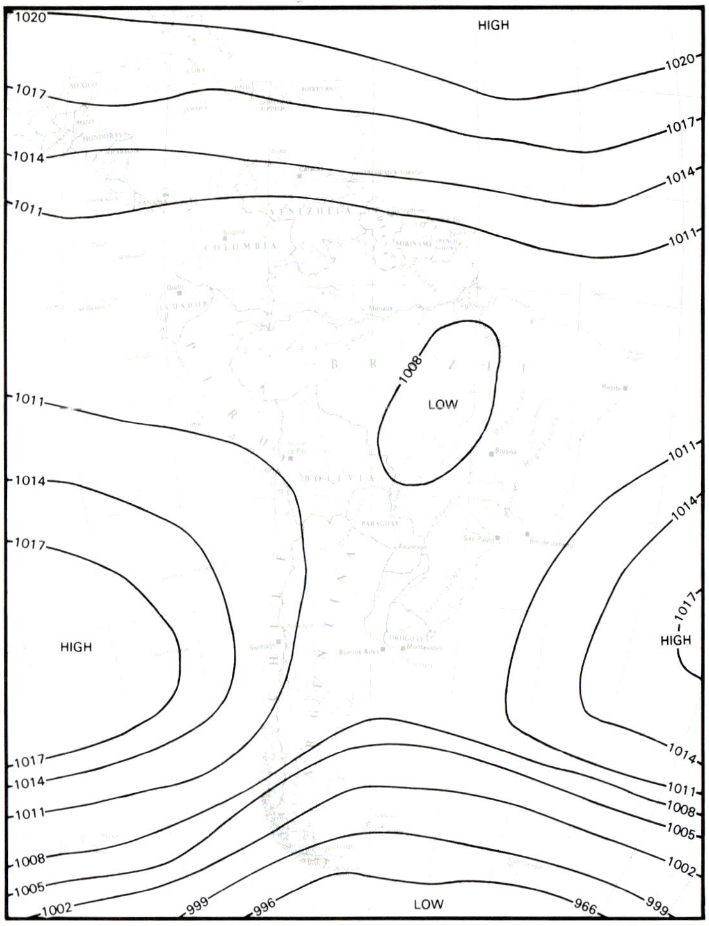

ATMOSPHERIC PRESSURE IN JULY

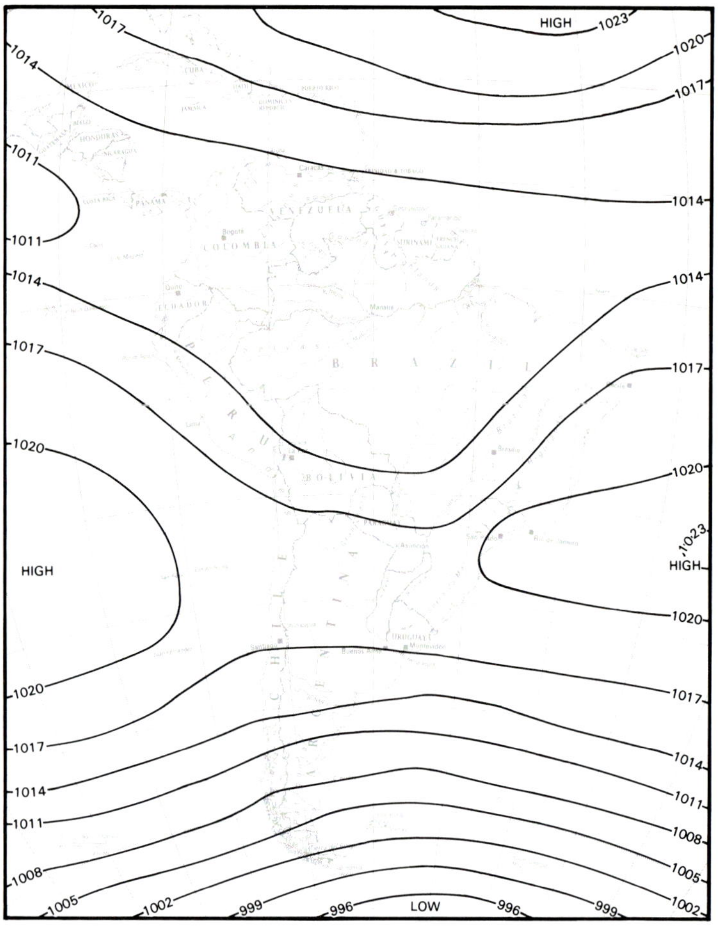

MEAN TEMPERATURE OF JANUARY

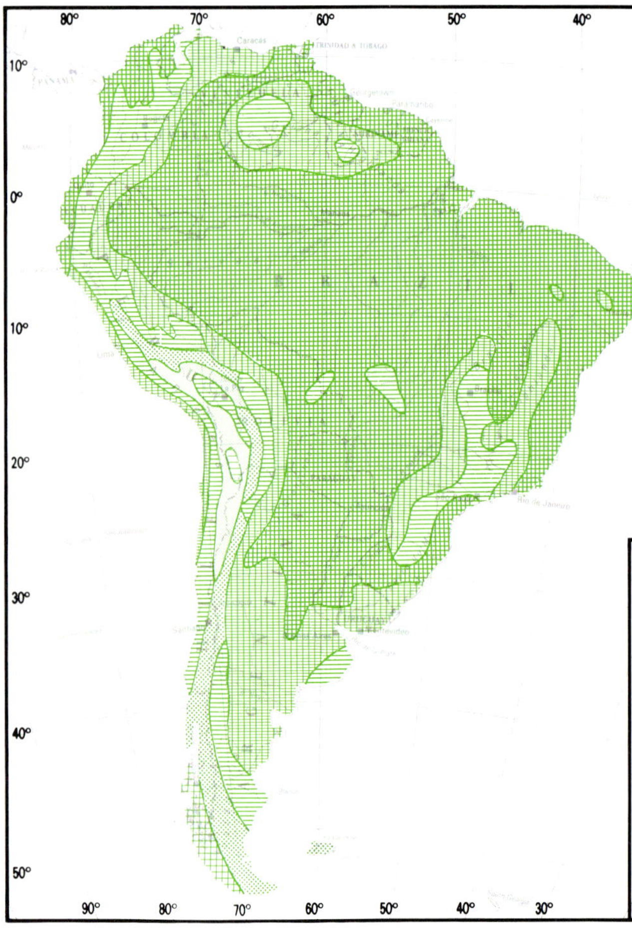

MEAN TEMPERATURE OF JULY

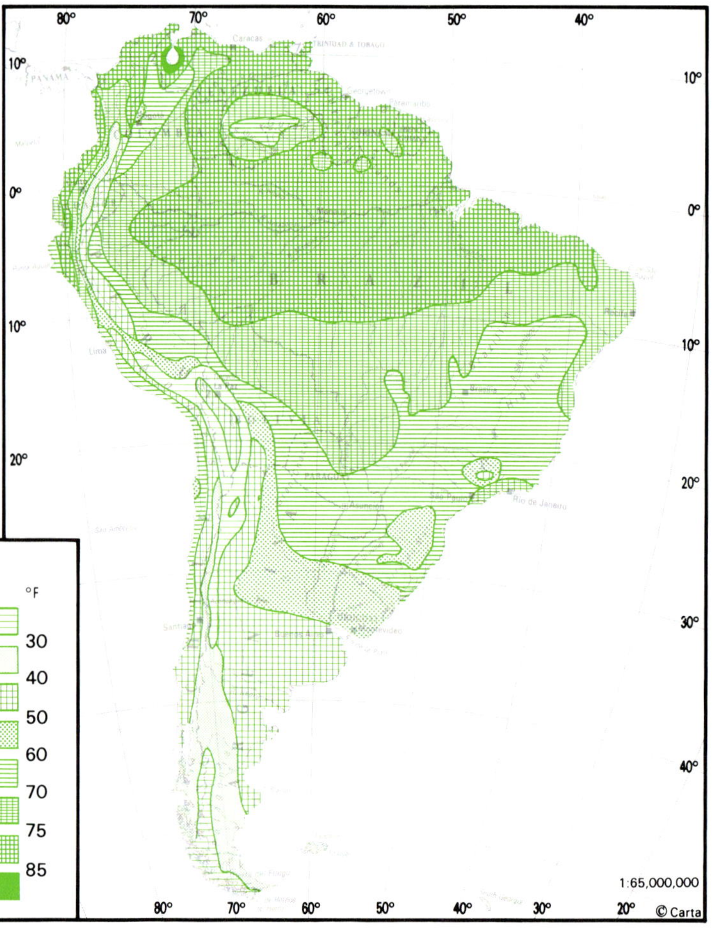

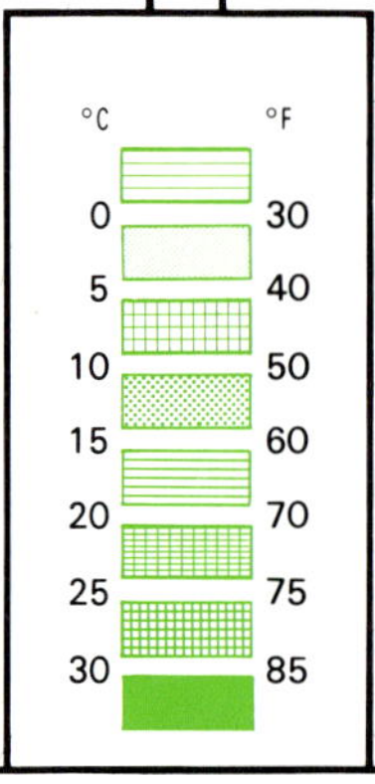

°C	°F
0	30
5	40
10	50
15	60
20	70
25	75
30	85

1:65,000,000

FLORA AND FAUNA

The Neotropical region, or South American region, is one of the six large biogeographic regions in the world. Biogeography is the study of the distribution patterns of the earth's plants and animals. Other regions are, for example, the Ethiopian (Africa) and the Oriental (tropical Asia).

The Neotropical region has the world's richest and most diversified species of flora and fauna. In Brazil, the largest country in this region, about 40,000 super-species of plants are found, most of which do not grow in the Old World. In Central America, there are about 12,000 super-species of plants, 8,000 of which are endemic. The Neotropic has more species of trees than any other biogeographic region and contains the world's largest forest, in the Amazon Basin.

Animal life is also very rich and diversified, with the highest number of species in the world. Among the mammals, 32 families are found in the Neotropical region, six of which are endemic. Some 140 species of bats and 340 species of rodents are found here, more than in any other biogeographic region. The number of endemic species of mammals is greater than any other region. Nearly half the world's fowl is classified within the Neotropical families, and the number of species exceeds that of the Ethiopian (Africa) region. Fish are also in great abundance. In the Amazon Basin, within a radius of 30 kilometers (20 miles) from the Brazilian city Manaus, there are 700 species of fish, more than the total number found in the Neoarctic region (North America).

The large variety of plant and animal species is a result of great climatic and topographical differences, often within a small area, the various influences of some major topographic features—the Andean mountain chain, which extends along the western part of the continent, the Amazon, the largest river in the world in both water discharge and basin size—and the continent's encounter with two oceans—the Atlantic on the east and the Pacific on the west. The long and varied geological and paleoclimatic history has also had its effect.

FLORA

The flora of South America can be divided into four principal regions:

1. *The Caribbean region.* A tropical climate prevails over most of this region. Much of the area is covered with dense forests lush in vegetation. Its desert area is rich in succulent plant species such as cacti, including species of *Agava* and *Yucca.* The forest has several species of trees intertwined with numerous creepers and epiphytes, mostly *Bromeliaceae*, such as *Ananas* (pineapple), and orchids (*Orchidaceae*), for example, vanilla. Also found here are important cultivated plants: maize (corn), cotton, sweet peppers, tobacco, sweet potatoes, beans, avocado, and papaya.

2. *The Brazilian region.* Most of this region is also tropical. Besides the rain forest that covers much of the Amazon Basin, other formations of vegetation are found, resembling different types of small woods, such as the *Llanos, Campos,* and *Caatinga.* As many as 40,000 plant species are known to this region. The largest forest in the world, the virgin forest of the Amazon, is presently undergoing a process of rapid deforestation that is denuding huge areas and diminishing the "green lungs" of South America and of the world at large.

Here, too, many species of creepers (*lianas*) and *epiphytes* are found. Among them are several species of the *Bromeliaceae* (pineapple) family and the *Orchidaceae.* Of the creepers, mention should be made of the *Passiflora* (passion flower), *Philodendron, Monstera,* and *Bougainvillea* species. Upon the region's bodies of water grows the *Victoria regia*, whose enormous leaves attain a size of 2 meters (6.5 feet) in diameter and its flowers, 40 centimeters (16 inches) in diameter. This region has given the world many useful plants, such as the *Hevea brasiliensis* (rubber tree), *Annona* (custard apple), *Jacaranda, Tipuana, Ananas, Theobroma cacao* (cocoa), *Arachis* (groundnuts), and *Manihot* (casaba, tapioca). One of the most important plants is the *Strychnos toxifera*, from which the Indians produce a sharp poison called curare, used in hunting animals.

3. *The Andean region.* Part of this region is tropical and part is temperate. The tropical forest grows in the lowland areas, while in the upper regions the forest disappears and is replaced by grassy plains with misshapen miniature trees. In the north this formation is called the *páramos* while in the south it is known as the *puna.* The Andean peaks are barren of tree vegetation. This region also gave mankind a great number of useful plants, including tomatoes, potatoes, tobacco, bean species, guava (*Psidium guajava), the Cinchona* tree, from whose bark quinine is produced, and the coca tree (*Erythroxylon coca*), form which coca and cocaine are produced. There are many cultivated plants, including *Verbena* (vervain) and *Fuchsia.*

4. *The Pampas region.* The forests which grow in this partially subtropical region, known as *Selvas*, are rich in species (about 15 species of trees per quarter acre). Significant parts of the region consist of grassy plains on which large herds of cattle are raised. These plains extend mainly over southern Argentina and Patagonia. At the western edge of the Pampas is a formation of dense woods called *Monte.* A forest of *Araucaria* (pine) and *Nothofagus* (beech) grows in southern Chile and in Tierra del Fuego. From this area man has acclimatized only a few species, such as the strawberry and the popular *Araucaria* (pine) tree.

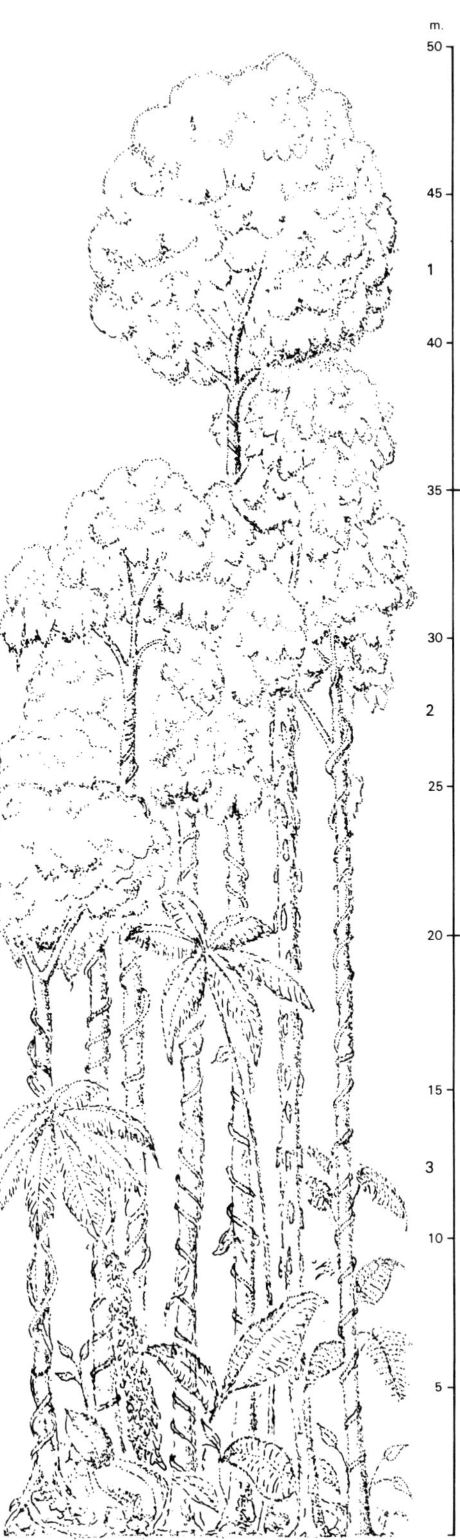

This schematic drawing represents the three stories of vegetation in the tropical rain forest (Selva):

1. This stratum, of trees 30–50 meters (100–165 feet) high, is never continuous and the crowns may be widely separated.

2. In this stratum the crowns are more closely spaced. The trees of 1 and 2 strata together form the forest canopy.

3. This stratum is the densest layer of the forest and most of the space is occupied by trunks, branches, twigs and foliage. The ground surface is covered by a thin layer of dead leaves.

Caribbean Sea
North Atlantic Ocean
Pacific Ocean
South Atlantic Ocean
Rain forest
Mixed forest (deciduous-evergreen)
Savanna
Caatinga
Dry forest and open woodland
Paraná pine forest
Grassland (Pampas)
Desert
Xerophytic associations
Patagonian steppe
Broadleaf and mixed beech forest
Alpine medows (paramos)
Steppe (puna)
Mangrove
Flooded areas and swamps
Vegetation influenced by montane conditions
Caracas
TRINIDAD & TOBAGO
PANAMA
Georgetown
Paramaribo
Cayenne
SURINAME
FRENCH GUIANA
BRAZIL
Manaus
Lima
Brasília
Recife
C. de São Roque
BOLIVIA
PARAGUAY
Asunción
São Paulo
Rio de Janeiro
URUGUAY
Montevideo
Buenos Aires
Rio de la Plata
Santiago
San Félix
San Ambrosio
Juan Fernández
C. Blanco
Falkland Is.
Stanley
C. de Hornos
South Georgia
Equator
1:30,000,000
0 250 500 Km
0 250 Mi
© Carta

ANIMAL LIFE

In the far geological past the continent of South America was connected with other landmasses. According to the continental drift theory, South America was once linked to Africa. However, South America broke away from other landmasses and turned into a large, isolated continent.

The primordial animals that lived during this period developed and formed faunal groups unique to this continent. Among these are various families of marsupials. The *Caenolestidae* (opossum rat) family, with seven species of small marsupials resembling a mouse, inhabits the Andes. The *Didelphidae* (opossum) family has forty species, two of which also inhabit North America. Among the best known are the *Didelphis* and the *Chironectes* (water opossum). A unique faunal order—the *Edenta*—has developed from these primordial animals. The three families which make up this order are scattered throughout the continent. They are the *Dasypodidae* (armadillo) family of about twenty species, the *Myrmecophagidae* (anteater) family of three species, and the *Bradypodidae* (sloth) family of eight species. Many animals belonging to this last group, including the *Megatherium* (giant ground sloth), which was larger than the African elephant, became extinct in later periods.

In the Tertiary period, the so-called "ancient island hoppers" that penetrated South America were mostly rodents and monkeys, which thrived on the isolated continent. From these animals many species developed. Three hundred and forty species of rodents can be found today in South America. Among the largest and most impressive are the capybara (the largest rodent in the world, 1.2 meters in length and weighing 110 pounds), the mara, coypu, cavia (guinea pig), agouti, vizcacha, and the chinchilla.

The monkeys at present include three families: the *Callimiconidae* with one species; the *Callitrichidae* (marmosets) with 15 species of small monkeys; and the *Cebidae* with about 30 species of large and medium-sized monkeys. These are found throughout the continent, mostly in forests.

At the end of the Tertiary period, a land bridge was formed that connected South and North America, and during the Pleistocene epoch many animals migrated to South America. Among the mammals were deer, tapir (*Tapirus*), peccary (*Tayassu*), vicuña, and the guanaco of the camel family, from which developed the llama and alpaca, as well as many carnivores, the most prominent of which are the spectacled bear (*Tremarctos*), coati (*Nasua*), raccoon (*Procyon*), and the kinkajou (*Potos*). Altogether there are in South America today about 600 species of mammals belonging to 32 families.

There are also many variegated species of fish in South America. Among these are the *Arapaima*, the largest edible fish on the continent, which attains a length of 5 meters (15 feet) and a weight of 200 pounds. The piranha (*Serrasalmus*) is a small fish of the Amazon Basin that attains a length of 35 centimeters (14 inches). Piranhas gather in shoals and prey upon anything, including large mammals, even humans. The electric eel (*Electrophorus*) also inhabits the Amazon. It reaches 2 meters (6 feet) in length, and it stuns its prey and enemies with an electric shock. It can create an electrical current of 650 volts and can stun a horse with one shock.

The continent also has several different reptiles. The continent's largest snake, the anaconda (*Eunectes murinus*), a constrictor, lives in rivers and attains a length of 9 meters (29.5 feet). The *Caiman* is a medium-sized crocodile whose species abound in the rivers of the continent. Many venomous snakes are found. Dominant are the species of the colorful and dangerous coral snake (*Micrurus*), forty of which thrive in tropical areas. Prominent among the iguanas is the common type, which lives on trees and attains a length of one meter (3 feet). The *Anolis*, whose species are numerous and are scattered over wide areas of the continent, have mutable colors, much like the chameleon. The marine iguana (*Amblyrhynchus*), which inhabits the Galápagos Islands, is the only sea lizard in the world; it can reach 1.5 meters (5 feet) in length, and it plunges into the sea to eat algae and seaweed. Other species of iguanas are also endemic to the Galápagos Islands, such as the land iguana (*Conolophus*). The islands are also known for the giant tortoise (*Testudo elephantopus*), which attain a weight of 550 pounds.

Bird life of the Neotropic region is richer than in any other biogeographic region. In every biotope there is an abundance of fowl. The forests are rich in numerous species of birds. The best known are the species of the colorful and huge-beaked toucan (*Rhamphastos*). Many parrots inhabit the forests, the most impressive of which are the species of the *Ara* and the *Amazona*, renowned for their bright colors and loud calls. The hummingbirds are the smallest of the fowl. Some 300 colorful species abound in all parts of the continent in a number of variegated biotopes. On the expansive plains of Patagonia and in other places there appears the *Rhea*, resembling a small ostrich, under which order it is classified.

In the southern part of the continent and on the Galápagos Islands live species of penguins. Many birds of prey are found in South America. The most prominent are the *Cathartes* and the caracara (*Polybrus*). The harpy-eagle (*Harpyja*) is the largest predatory bird of the forest; it preys even upon monkeys. Yet the most impressive bird of prey on the continent is the Andean condor (*Vultur gryphus*), whose wing span exceeds 3 meters (10 feet). The sight of the condor soaring over the plains of Patagonia or over an Andean mountain range is indeed majestic, and the bird has become part of the folklore of South America.

Toucan (*Rhamphastos cuvieri*)

Herd of llama in the Andes

Brazilian tapir (*Tapirus terrestris*)

Rhea (*Rhea americana*)

MINERAL RESOURCES

Mineral resources play an important role in the economy of most South American countries. A great variety of mineral deposits found throughout the continent, mainly in the highlands, is exploited and in nearly all cases exported to the industrial countries of North America, Europe, and the Pacific Rim. Precious metals, which were the main attraction for Europeans in the initial stages of Spanish and Portuguese colonization, are still mined in substantial quantities in Peru (gold and silver), Colombia (gold), Brazil (gold and silver), Chile (silver), and Venezuela (gold). However, the continent maintains only a minor position in the production of these metals. Brazil is an important producer of diamonds and gems. Among the metallic minerals, high-quality iron ore and copper top the list. Brazil, which has one of the largest deposits of high-grade (50 to 65 percent) iron ore, is the world's largest exporter and the second largest producer. Venezuela and Chile are also important exporters. Argentina, Colombia, Peru, and Bolivia have iron deposits as well. The continent produced nearly 18 percent of the iron mined in 1987. Chile has the world's largest mines and is the leading copper-producing country. Peru is the only other substantial producer on the continent. Both countries produce nearly 21 percent of the world's copper output (1987). Brazil has the world's second largest output of manganese. Much smaller quantities are mined in Chile. Deposits are known in Bolivia and Ecuador. South America supplies about 13 percent of the world's bauxite. Most of it comes from Brazil and substantial quantities are mined in Guyana and Suriname. Peru is an important producer of zinc and lead, while smaller quantities are mined in Brazil and Bolivia. Brazil and Bolivia are among the large producers of tin (15 percent of world production). Chile is the world's second largest producer of the important metal molybdenum, and Bolivia is the second largest producer of antimony. Both these minerals are also mined in Peru. Bolivia, Brazil, and Peru have a substantial output of tungsten. The many other minerals extracted in South America include chrome (Brazil), mercury (Chile, Colombia), mica (Brazil), and the mineral elements such as beryllium, colombium, tantalum, thorium, and lithium found in Brazil and Argentina. Of the nonmetallic minerals, the large deposits of nitrates in the Atacama Desert in northern Chile (used mainly as fertilizers) were of great importance and were the world's main source of supply during the second half of the nineteenth and first quarter of the twentieth century. The artificial production of this mineral deprived the Chilean deposits of much of their economic value.

Petroleum is the most important of the mineral fuels found in South America, which has in recent years produced about 6 percent of the world's output. Venezuela (ninth among the world's oil-producing countries) produced more than half of the continent's output, which stood at about 179 million tons in 1988 (177 million 1987). The oilfields in and around Lake Maracaibo are the richest and most productive on the continent. Venezuela is also by far the largest oil exporter in South America. Brazil (31 million tons in 1989) and Argentina (23 million tons) come next in output, but both require additional imported supplies to meet their consumption needs. Ecuador is the only South American country, other than Venezuela, which can afford to export a large portion of its oil output (16 million tons in 1988). Colombia, which has a somewhat larger output (17 million tons in 1988), has a much greater local oil consumption. Chile (1.3 million tons in 1988), Bolivia (0.9 million tons) and Peru (0.7 million tons) are much smaller oil producers and depend on imports to meet their requirements. Venezuela and Argentina produce large qantities of natural gas (19.5 billion and 15 billion cubic meters, respectively). Argentina is believed to have the continent's largest known reserves (in Patagonia). Brazil (5.7 billion cubic meters in 1987), Colombia (5.3 billion cubic meters), Chile (4.4 billion cubic meters), Bolivia (2.5 billion cubic meters), Peru (1.1 billion cubic meters), and Ecuador (0.6 billion cubic meters) exploit their natural gas resources, but only Bolivia exports substantial quantities (to Argentina). South America has comparatively small known and exploited coal deposits. Colombia has the largest deposits (14 million tons of output in 1987), followed by Brazil (7 million tons), Chile (1.3 million tons), and then Venezuela and Peru. Chile has lignite deposits. Uranium is found in commercial quantities in Brazil, Chile, and Argentina.

South America's mineral wealth is believed to be much greater than that already known and utilized. Geological research and exploration will no doubt uncover additional mineral resources, especially in the more remote and isolated parts of the continent.

MAIN MINERAL RESOURCES

1987

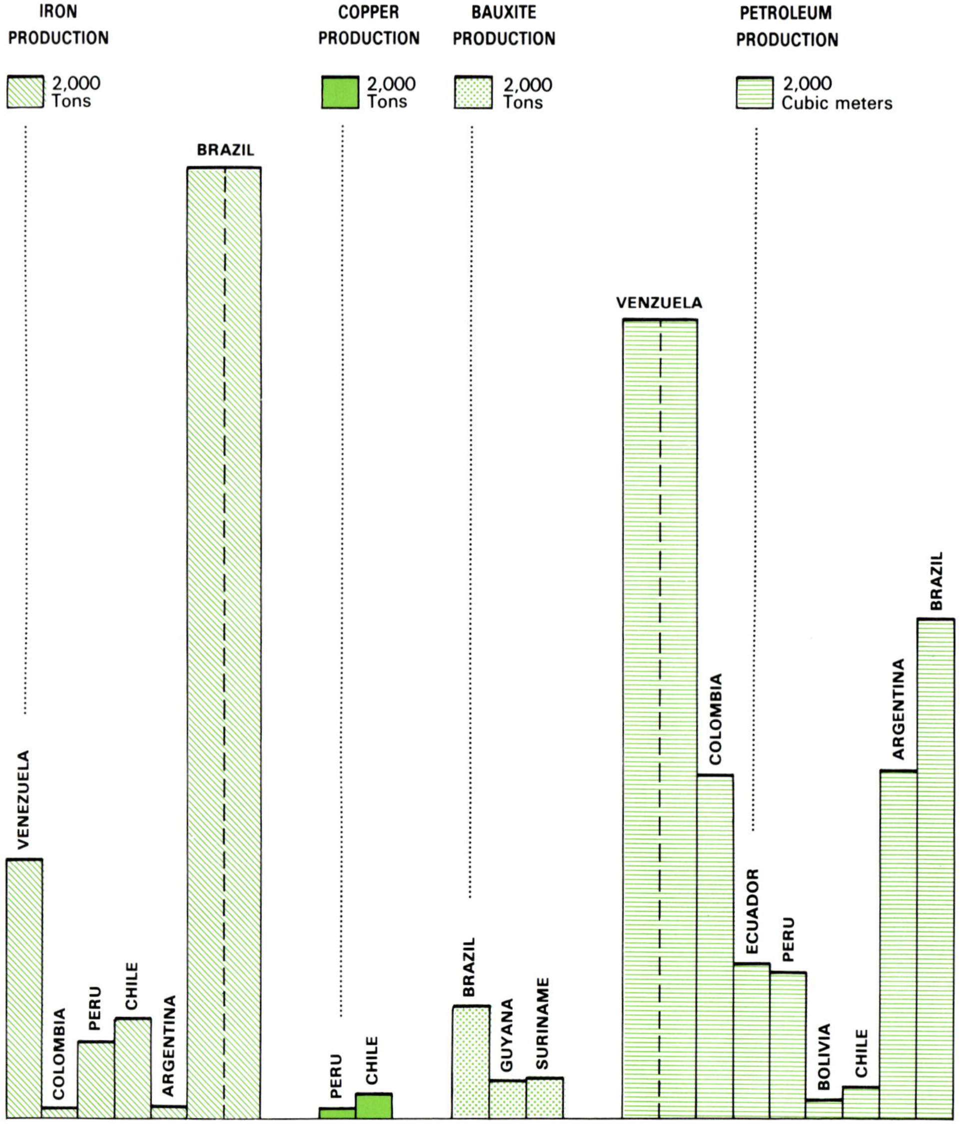

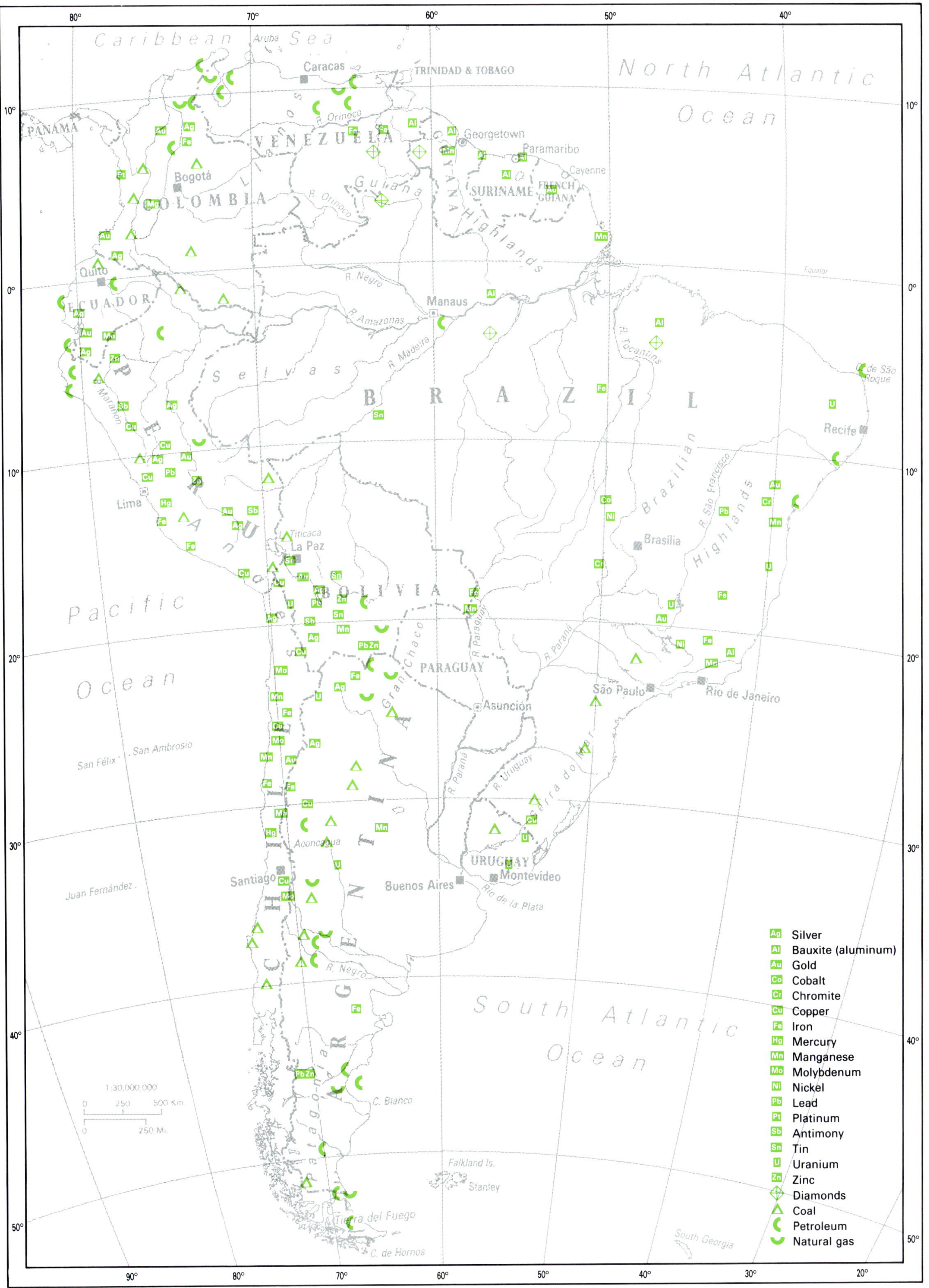
Caribbean Sea
North Atlantic Ocean
Pacific Ocean
South Atlantic Ocean
PANAMA
VENEZUELA
COLOMBIA
ECUADOR
PERU
BRAZIL
BOLIVIA
PARAGUAY
CHILE
ARGENTINA
URUGUAY
GUYANA
SURINAME
FRENCH GUIANA
TRINIDAD & TOBAGO
Caracas
Bogotá
Quito
Georgetown
Paramaribo
Cayenne
Manaus
Lima
La Paz
Brasília
Recife
São Paulo
Rio de Janeiro
Asunción
Santiago
Buenos Aires
Montevideo
Stanley
Aruba
Guiana Highlands
Brazilian Highlands
Selvas
Andes
Gran Chaco
Patagonia
Serra do Mar
Llanos
R. Orinoco
R. Negro
R. Amazonas
R. Madeira
R. Tocantins
R. São Francisco
R. Paraná
R. Paraguay
R. Uruguay
Marañón
Titicaca
Aconcagua
Río de la Plata
C. de São Roque
C. Blanco
C. de Hornos
Tierra del Fuego
Falkland Is.
South Georgia
San Félix
San Ambrosio
Juan Fernández
Equator
1:30,000,000
0 250 500 Km
0 250 Mi.
Ag Silver
Al Bauxite (aluminum)
Au Gold
Co Cobalt
Cr Chromite
Cu Copper
Fe Iron
Hg Mercury
Mn Manganese
Mo Molybdenum
Ni Nickel
Pb Lead
Pt Platinum
Sb Antimony
Sn Tin
U Uranium
Zn Zinc
Diamonds
Coal
Petroleum
Natural gas

POPULATION

South America, whose area covers nearly 12 percent of the earth's surface, had an estimated population of 300 million in 1990, or 5.7 percent of the world total. The population has increased nearly sevenfold since the beginning of the twentieth century, when it was about 45 million, nearly fivefold since 1920, when it was about 61 million, and by 58 percent over the last twenty years.

Since the 1930s natural increase, which reached its peak in the 1950s, has been responsible for the continent's rapid population growth. Immigration, which contributed substantially to growth during the second half of the nineteenth and the first three decades of the twentieth century, has since become insignificant. Natural increase has been on the decline in some countries (Chile, Uruguay, Argentina) since the 1930s and in most other countries since the 1950s or 1960s. At present it is highest in Paraguay (about 3 percent annually) and is still high (over 2 percent annually) in Venezuela, Brazil, Ecuador, Peru, and Bolivia. It is lowest in Uruguay (0.4 percent). The rate of natural increase of the population of European origin is generally lower than that of other races.

The great majority of South America's population is concentrated in comparatively small parts of the continent. Over 80 percent of the continent is only sparsely populated or uninhabited. Parts of the margins of the continent, especially the central section of the eastern coastal regions, are densely inhabited, while most of the interior is sparsely populated. The most densely inhabited country is Ecuador, with 37 persons per square kilometer (95 per square mile), although even here the population is concentrated only in small parts of the country. The most sparsely populated are the three countries of the Guiana coast and highlands (Guyana, Suriname, and French Guiana) with a density of 4, 2, and 1 persons per square kilometer (10, 5, and 2.5 per square mile), respectively.

Nearly 75 percent of the continent's population resides in urban areas. Rapid urbanization has taken place in most countries, especially since the 1940s. The proportion of the urban population in the most urbanized countries has more than doubled over the last fifty years: in Argentina from 41 to 85 percent; in Brazil from 16 to nearly 75 percent; in Chile from 37 to 86 percent; in Uruguay from 38 to 85 percent; and in Venezuela from 19 to 86 percent. Only in four countries (Bolivia, Guyana, Paraguay, and Suriname) is the majority of the population still rural. The continent has three of the world's largest conurbations: São Paulo, with a population of nearly 17 million in 1990; Rio de Janeiro, with over 11 million; and Buenos Aires, with nearly 11 million. Thirteen other cities have a population of over one million.

South America's population is composed of three main racial elements: the American Indians; the aboriginal inhabitants; the Europeans, among whom the Spaniards and Portuguese were predominant until the second half of the nineteenth century, when immigration from other European countries began to considerably exceed that from Iberia, and the Africans, who from the early sixteenth to nineteenth centuries were brought from Africa as slaves. Asians, who first arrived in the continent in the second half of the nineteenth century, are at present comparatively small in number and their presence is limited to small areas. People of mixed European and aboriginal Indian descent—mestizos—had appeared already in the early stages of colonization. Later, a growing number of mixed Europeans and persons of mixed Indian and African descent appeared in some regions. American Indians still form a large part of the population in the three central Andean countries—Ecuador, Peru, and Bolivia—where together with the mestizos they are the great majority. Mestizos also make up the majority of the inhabitants of Venezuela, Colombia, and Paraguay, where there are also substantial minorities of aboriginal Indians. Small tribes can still be found in some areas of the Amazon Basin and Patagonia living lives relatively untouched by the continent's post-Columbian history. Persons of mixed Indian and African descent, known in some parts of South America as zambo, are found mainly in those countries to which large numbers of African slaves were imported, such as Brazil, Venezuela, Colombia,

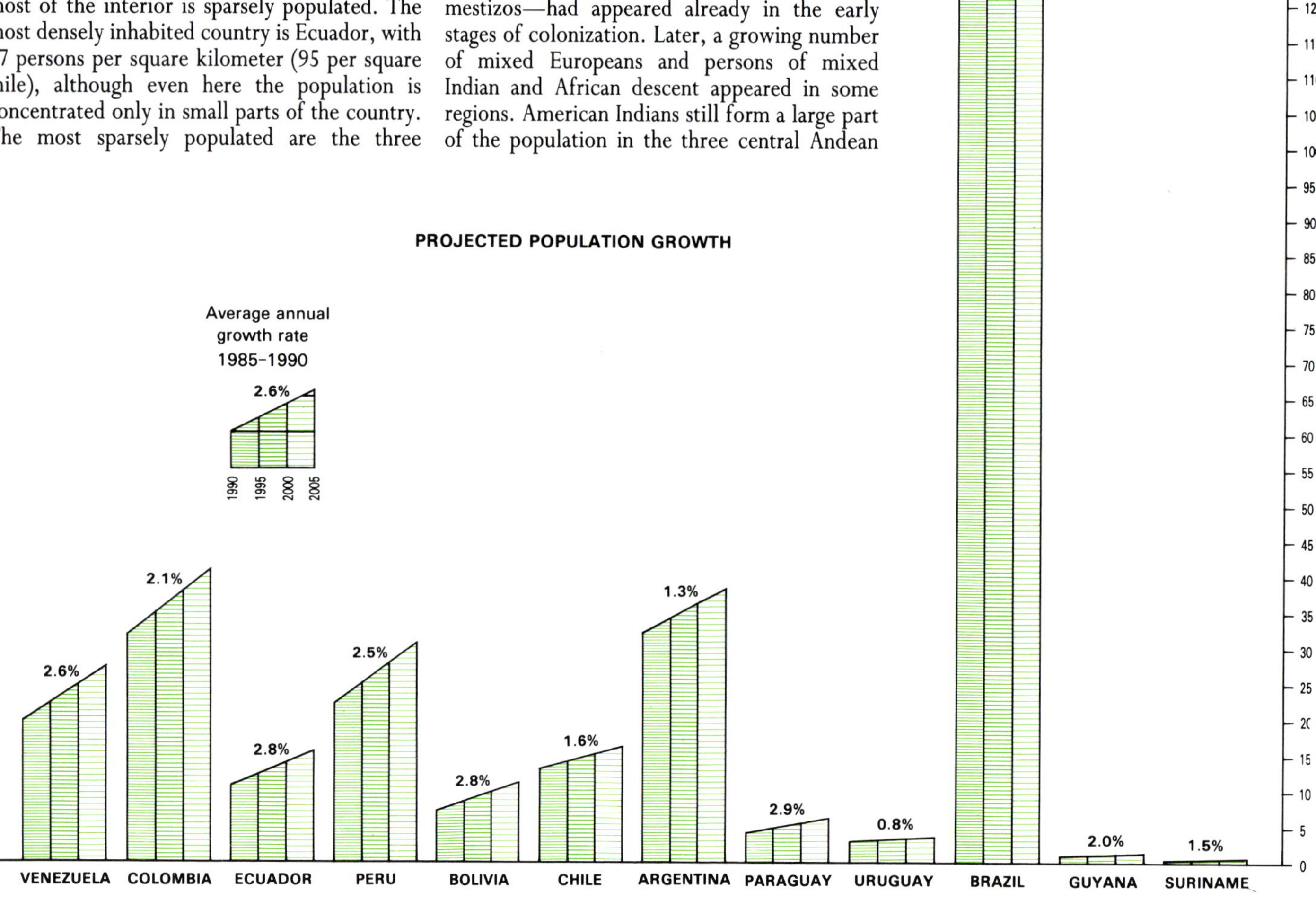

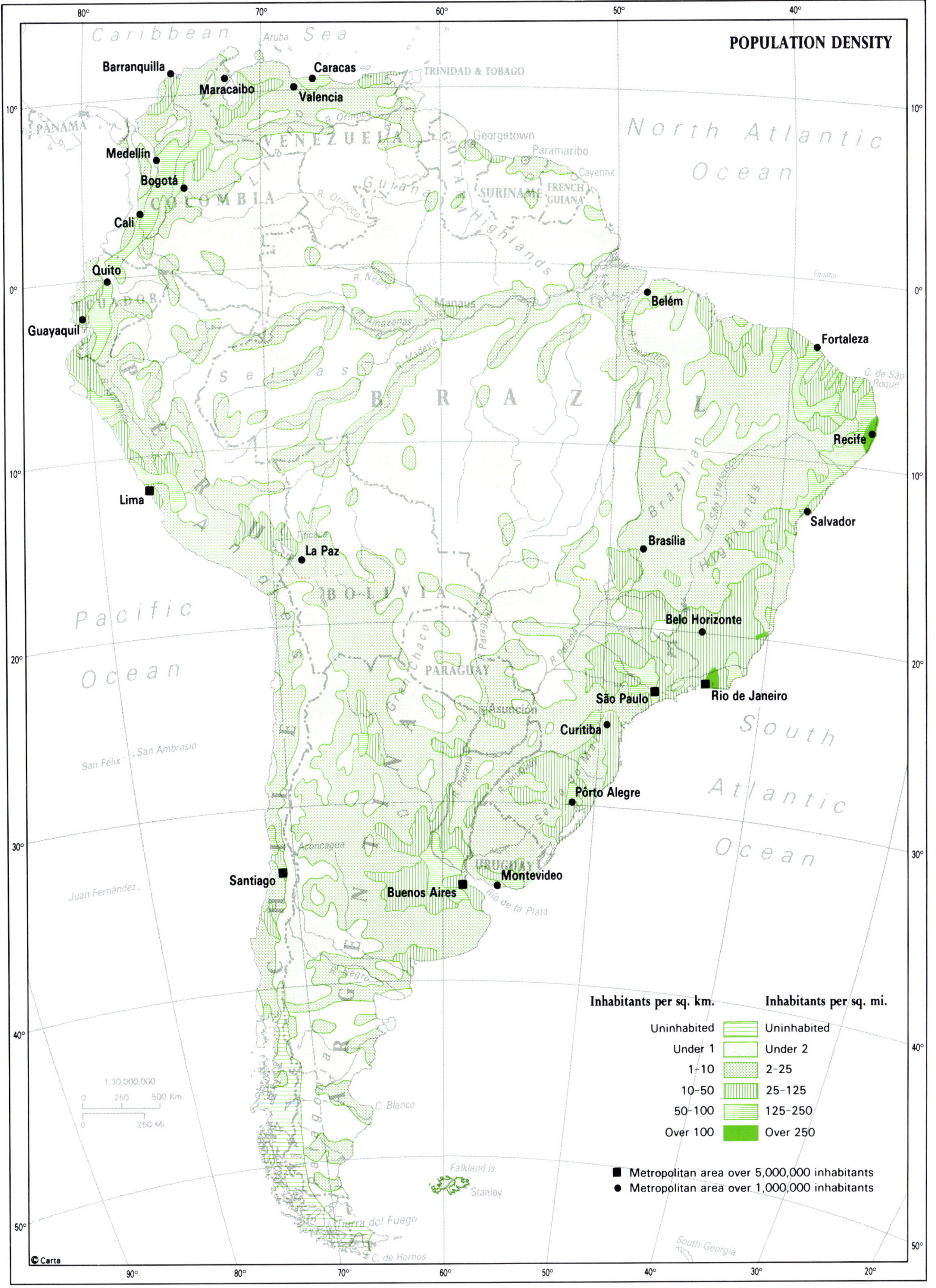
POPULATION DENSITY
Inhabitants per sq. km.
Uninhabited
Under 1
1-10
10-50
50-100
Over 100
Inhabitants per sq. mi.
Uninhabited
Under 2
2-25
25-125
125-250
Over 250
Metropolitan area over 5,000,000 inhabitants
Metropolitan area over 1,000,000 inhabitants
Caribbean Sea
North Atlantic Ocean
Pacific Ocean
South Atlantic Ocean
Barranquilla
Maracaibo
Caracas
Valencia
Medellín
Bogotá
Cali
Quito
Guayaquil
Lima
La Paz
Belém
Fortaleza
Recife
Salvador
Brasília
Belo Horizonte
Rio de Janeiro
São Paulo
Curitiba
Pôrto Alegre
Montevideo
Buenos Aires
Santiago
Asunción
Manaus
Georgetown
Paramaribo
Cayenne
TRINIDAD & TOBAGO
PANAMA
VENEZUELA
COLOMBIA
ECUADOR
PERU
BOLIVIA
PARAGUAY
URUGUAY
BRAZIL
CHILE
ARGENTINA
GUYANA
SURINAME
FRENCH GUIANA
Falkland Is.
Stanley
South Georgia
Tierra del Fuego
C. de Hornos
C. Blanco
Juan Fernández
San Félix
San Ambrosio
1:30,000,000
© Carta

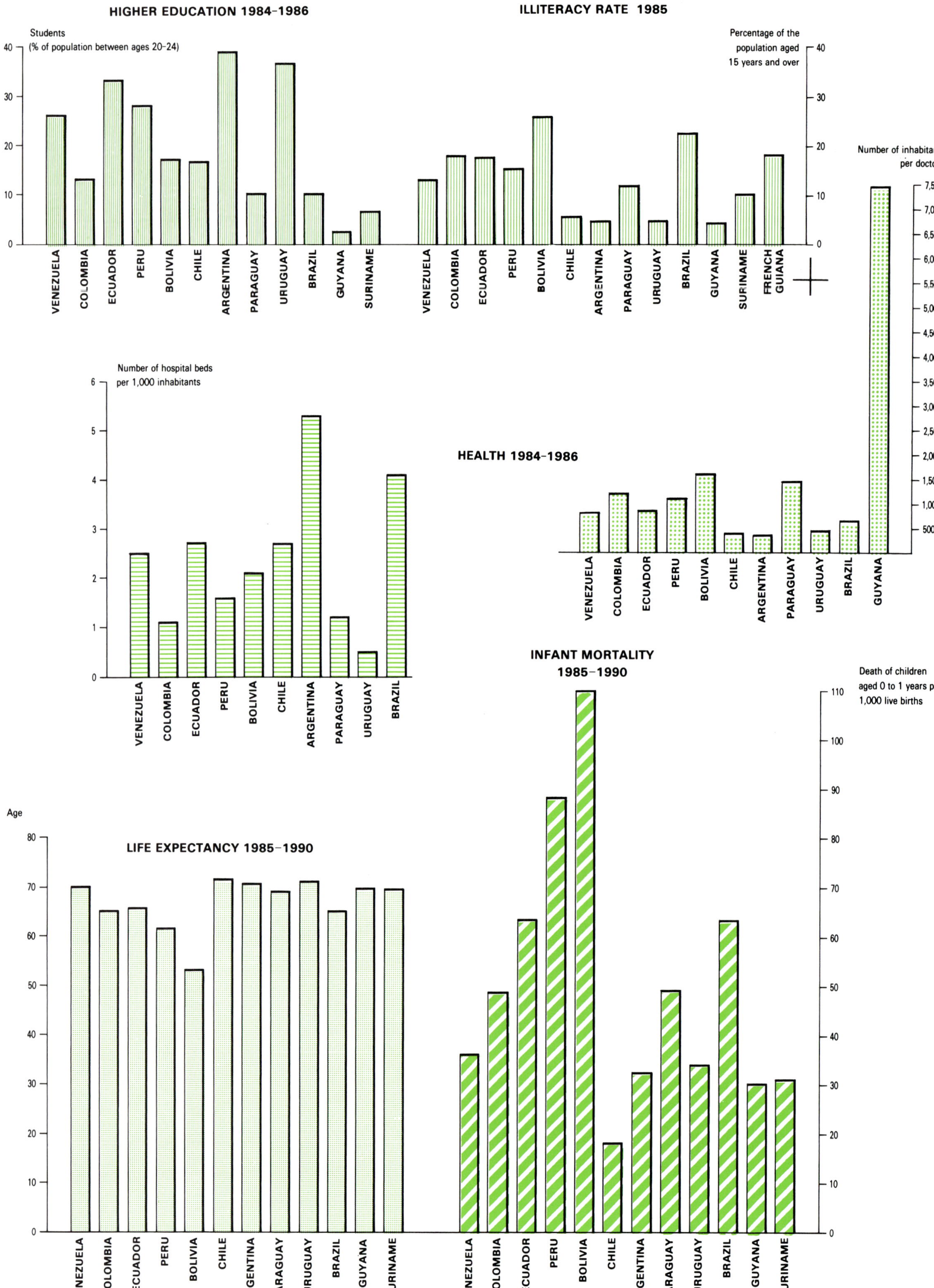
HIGHER EDUCATION 1984-1986
Students
(% of population between ages 20-24)
40
30
20
10
0
VENEZUELA
COLOMBIA
ECUADOR
PERU
BOLIVIA
CHILE
ARGENTINA
PARAGUAY
URUGUAY
BRAZIL
GUYANA
SURINAME
ILLITERACY RATE 1985
Percentage of the
population aged
15 years and over
40
30
20
10
0
VENEZUELA
COLOMBIA
ECUADOR
PERU
BOLIVIA
CHILE
ARGENTINA
PARAGUAY
URUGUAY
BRAZIL
GUYANA
SURINAME
FRENCH GUIANA
Number of inhabitants
per doctors
7,500
7,000
6,500
6,000
5,500
5,000
4,500
4,000
3,500
3,000
2,500
2,000
1,500
1,000
500
HEALTH 1984-1986
VENEZUELA
COLOMBIA
ECUADOR
PERU
BOLIVIA
CHILE
ARGENTINA
PARAGUAY
URUGUAY
BRAZIL
GUYANA
Number of hospital beds
per 1,000 inhabitants
6
5
4
3
2
1
0
VENEZUELA
COLOMBIA
ECUADOR
PERU
BOLIVIA
CHILE
ARGENTINA
PARAGUAY
URUGUAY
BRAZIL
INFANT MORTALITY
1985-1990
Death of children
aged 0 to 1 years per
1,000 live births
110
100
90
80
70
60
50
40
30
20
10
0
Age
80
70
60
50
40
30
20
10
0
LIFE EXPECTANCY 1985-1990
VENEZUELA
COLOMBIA
ECUADOR
PERU
BOLIVIA
CHILE
ARGENTINA
PARAGUAY
URUGUAY
BRAZIL
GUYANA
SURINAME
VENEZUELA
COLOMBIA
ECUADOR
PERU
BOLIVIA
CHILE
ARGENTINA
PARAGUAY
URUGUAY
BRAZIL
GUYANA
SURINAME

Ecuador, Guyana, and Suriname. These are also the countries in certain regions of which most of the Africans (blacks) and mulattos (persons of mixed African and European descent) are concentrated—northeastern Brazil, northwestern Colombia, and western Ecuador, for example. There are hardly any blacks or mulattos in Argentina and Uruguay, where the majority of the population is of European origin. Europeans are also predominant in the southern and southeastern states of Brazil. The small Asian population of the continent (about 0.25 percent) is concentrated mainly in Guyana (Indians), Suriname (Indonesians), and Brazil and Peru (Japanese and Chinese).

Linguistically two languages, Portuguese (Brazil) and Spanish (all other countries except Guyana, Suriname, and French Guiana) dominate the continent and are the official languages of all the states that formed part of the respective colonial empires. Aboriginal Indian languages, mainly of the Quechua and Aymara families, are still spoken by comparatively isolated American Indian communities, mostly in the Andean countries but also in the Amazon and Paraná basins. English is the official language of Guyana, as Dutch is in Suriname, and French in French Guiana. About 93 percent of the continent is Roman Catholic, nearly 4 percent Protestant, about 0.3 percent Muslim, and 0.25 percent Jewish. Native religions are still prevalent among isolated Indian communities in the Andes, the Amazon Basin, the Guiana Highlands, and southern Patagonia.

Andean Indians

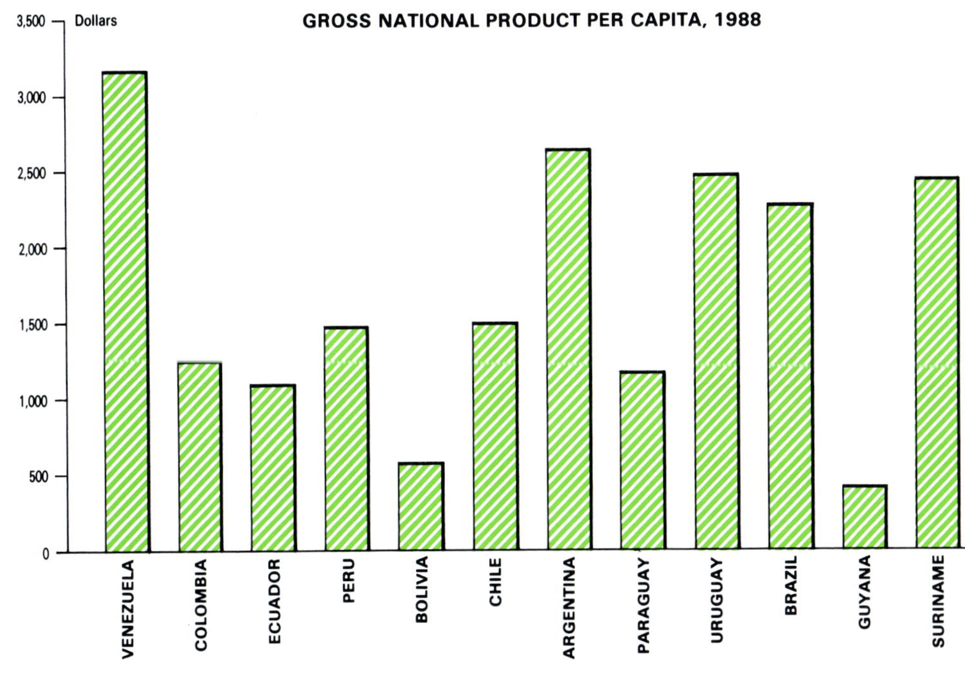

Jungle tribe

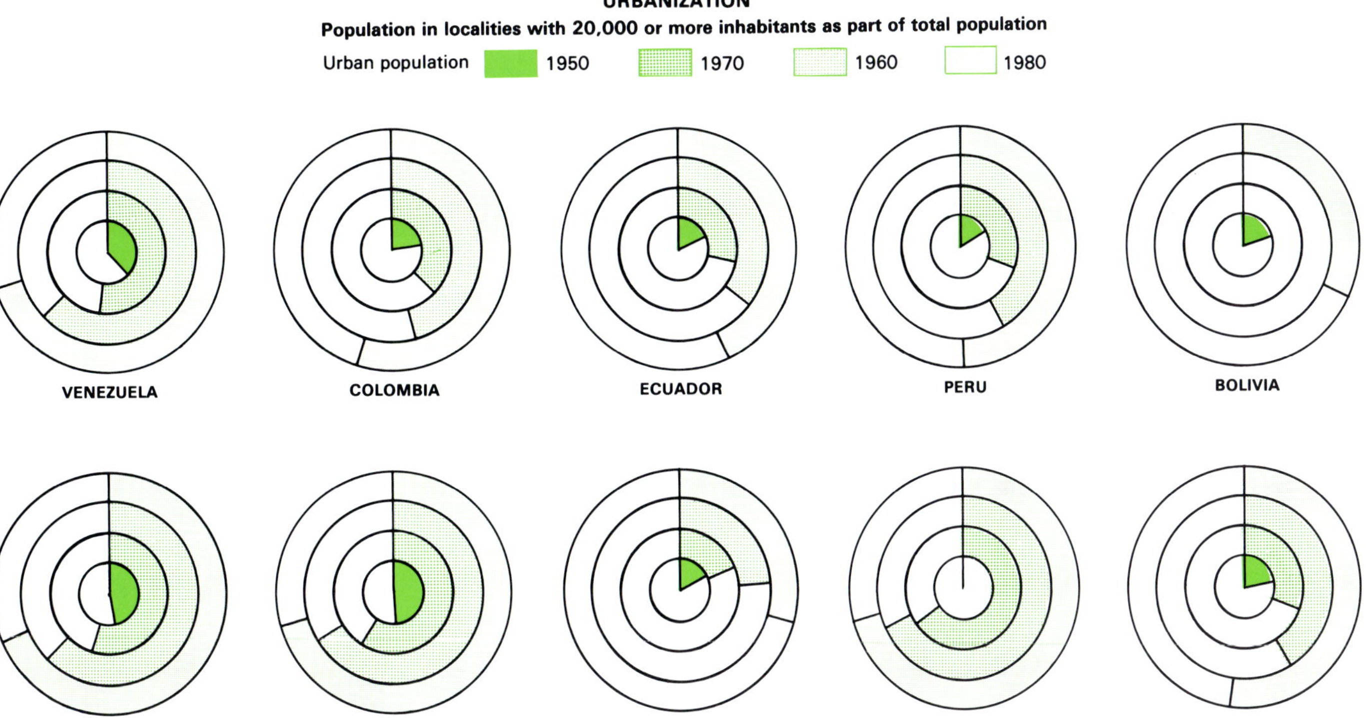

HISTORY

ABORIGINAL SOCIETIES

At the time of the arrival of the first Europeans in the last years of the fifteenth century, the native population of South America, the so-called Indians, was estimated to have numbered 10 to 15 million, more than half of whom lived in the northern and central Andes and adjacent areas. Several waves of American Indians are believed to have immigrated to the Americas from northeastern Asia by way of the Bering Strait. They gradually pushed southward across North and Central America into South America. They were widely scattered in tribal groups over most parts of the continent, and population was sparse except in some basins and valleys of the Andes where more density developed. Although they present wide differences in physical and cultural characteristics, they have certain physical and other features in common that justify the assumption that they belong to the same racial group. The Indians whom the first European explorers and settlers encountered ranged culturally from extremely primitive nomads, such as the tribes in Patagonia, Tierra del Fuego, and the Amazon Basin, to highly advanced communities of the Inca state (in present-day Peru, northern Chile, Bolivia, and Ecuador) and the Chibchas (of present-day Colombia). Many tribes, especially outside the Andean regions, subsisted mainly on food gathering, hunting, fishing, and occasional swidden agriculture (growing mainly manioc). Such tribes, belonging to numerous, widely dispersed groups, inhabited the greater part of the continent. The most advanced tribal societies in the Andes are believed to have had rural communities dependent on agriculture (growing mainly maize) as early as 1000 B.C. The Inca empire, which reached its peak in the fifteenth century and which extended from central Chile to northern Ecuador, represented the most advanced civilization in South America. It developed an economy based on an intensive agriculture, including extensive terracing of mountain slopes and irrigation. This civilization, which developed urban centers, a road network, and a well-organized and efficient administration, achieved remarkable skills in metal refining and metalworking (of copper, gold, and silver), architecture, weaving, pottery, and other arts. The Spanish conquest brought an end to the Inca empire (1532). The inhabitants of the continent did not have any domesticated animals, did not know the wheel, and had no written language.

Quito
R. Putumayo
R. Amazonas
R. Marañón
Moche
Chavín
Huari
Cuzco
Nazca
L. Titicaca
Tiahuanaco
L. Poopó

CULTURES OF THE ANDES

Chavín (1200–200 BC)
Nazca (200 BC – AD 600)
Moche (200 BC – AD 600)
Huari (AD 500–1000)
Tiahuanaco (AD 500–1000)
Inca (maximum extent 1493–1525)

I
1:30,000,000

PRE-COLOMBIAN SOUTH AMERICA

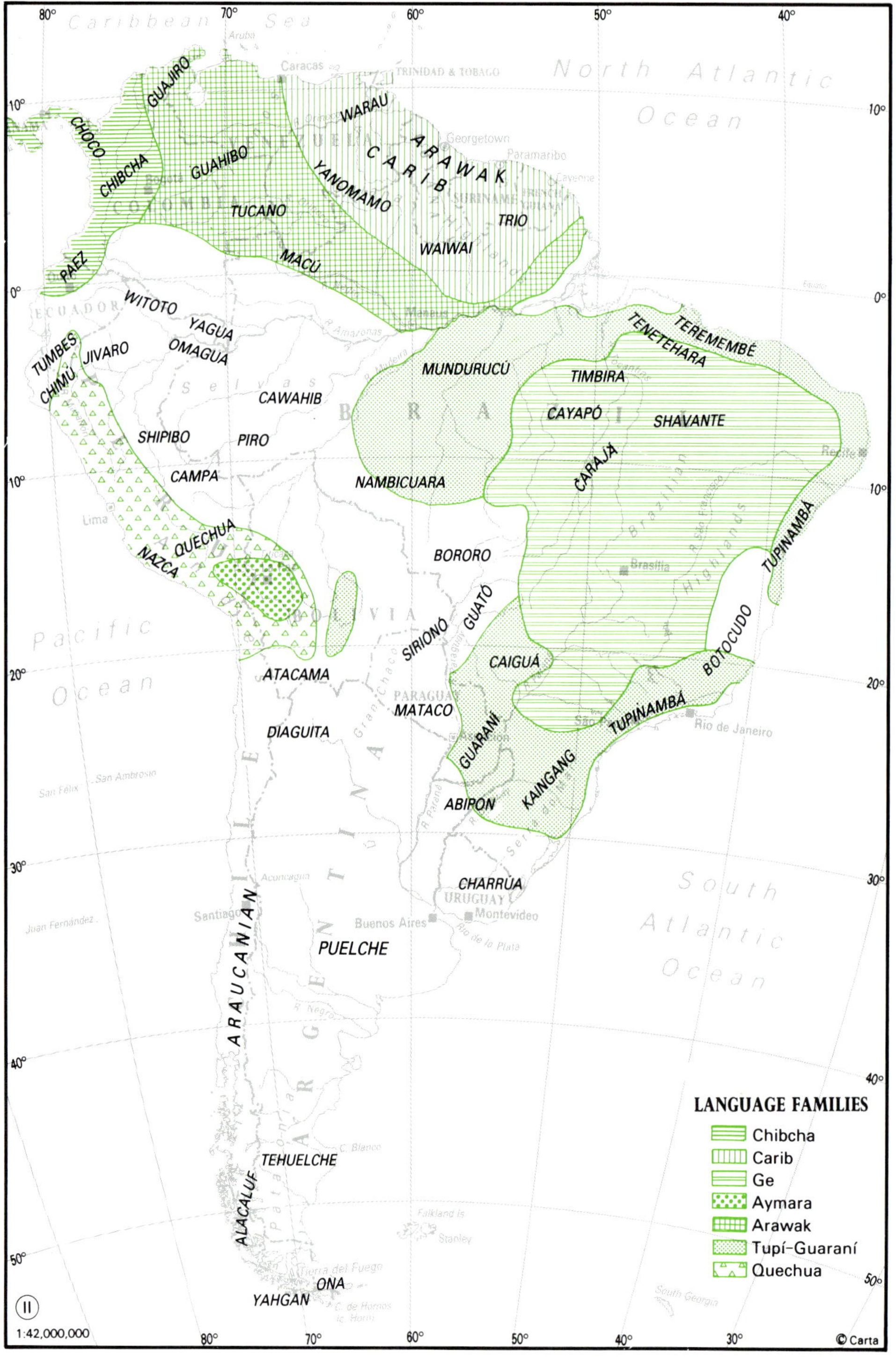

COLONIAL SOUTH AMERICA

Spanish and Portuguese settlement, which actually began in the second quarter of the sixteenth century, was at first mostly limited to coastal regions and along navigable rivers. It later expanded to some basins and valleys in the Andes, where better climatic conditions prevailed and where coveted resources (mainly precious metals) and local labor were more readily available. Gold and silver mining attracted Spanish settlers to Colombia and Peru. These countries were the most important sources of both metals during the sixteenth and seventeenth centuries. Tropical agricultural products, primarily sugar, brought the Spaniards and Portuguese to the northern and northeastern coastal areas. Other colonists seized areas of agricultural land in the Andes and established large estates, using forced local labor. Where native Indians did not meet the labor requirements of the colonists (mainly in the northern and northeastern coastal areas) large numbers of African slaves were imported. It is estimated that from the middle of the sixteenth to the first quarter of the nineteenth century, when the slave trade stopped, an estimated 7 to 8 million African slaves were brought to South America, mainly to Brazil. Disease and oppression brought by colonial rule and immigration greatly reduced the indigenous Indian population in large parts of the continent; in some areas Indians almost disappeared. The number of Europeans who settled in South America during the colonial period (sixteenth to nineteenth centuries) was, according to some estimates, 200,000 to 300,000, including missionaries, army personnel, and government and church officials. These settlers were to a large extent Spanish and Portuguese, as the colonial authorities admitted only small numbers of other European settlers.

The division of South America between Spain and Portugal was originally based on the Treaty of Tordesillas (1494) between both countries. It gave Portugal the right to take possession of the northeastern and eastern coast of Brazil. The actual control and administration of some coastal areas, which began in the second quarter of the sixteenth century, gradually spread inland, although most of the interior of the continent never came under effective control of the Spanish or Portuguese colonial authorities. Lima was for over two centuries the main Spanish administrative center, as capital of the Viceroyalty of Peru, which extended over all Spanish possessions. During the eighteenth century this entity was divided into three main administrative units: the Viceroyalty of New Granada, established in 1717 (Venezuela, Colombia, Panama, and Ecuador); the Viceroyalty of Peru, in 1542 (Peru and Chile); and the Viceroyalty of La Plata, in 1776 (Argentina, Uruguay, Paraguay, and Bolivia). This division remained until the end of the colonial period. Portuguese colonization and domination of Brazil centered at first on Bahia (now Salvador) on the northeastern coast, which was for over two centuries the capital of the colony that became the Viceroyalty of Brazil. The capital was moved in 1762 to Rio de Janeiro. Brazil attracted many Portuguese immigrants during the first half of the eighteenth century, after the discovery of gold in Minas Gerais, which made Brazil for much of the century the world's main source of gold.

The British, Dutch, and French took possession of their small colonies on the continent's northeastern Guiana coast during the eighteenth century, although initial settlement had already been made in the seventeenth century. Final sovereignty and actual settlement came only in the early nineteenth century.

COLONIAL SOUTH AMERICA 16TH TO 18TH CENTURIES

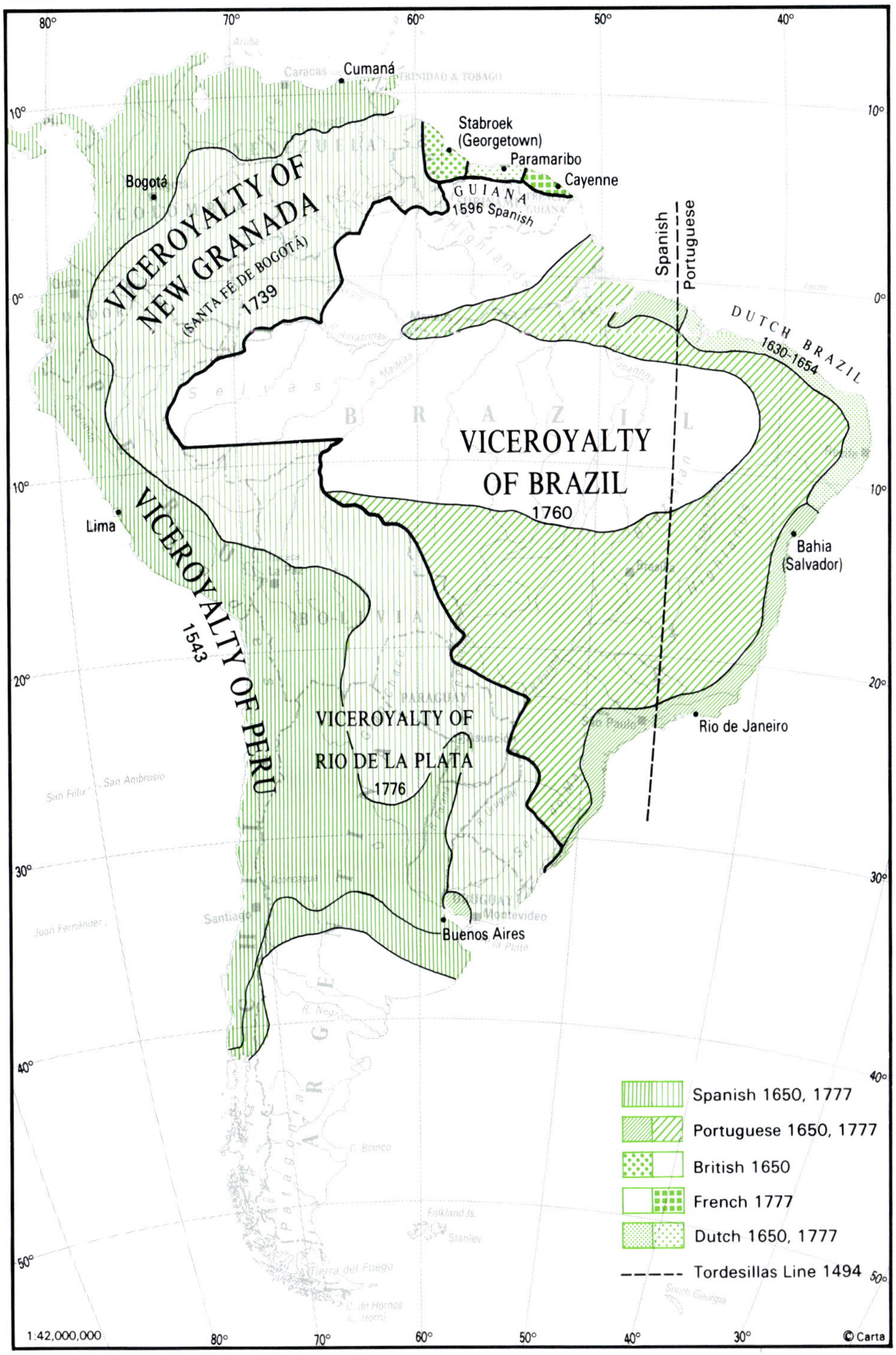

Cumaná
Stabroek (Georgetown)
Paramaribo
Cayenne
GUIANA 1596 Spanish
Bogotá
VICEROYALTY OF NEW GRANADA (SANTA FÉ DE BOGOTÁ) 1739
Spanish | Portuguese
DUTCH BRAZIL 1630–1654
VICEROYALTY OF BRAZIL 1760
Lima
VICEROYALTY OF PERU 1543
Bahia (Salvador)
VICEROYALTY OF RIO DE LA PLATA 1776
Rio de Janeiro
Buenos Aires
Spanish 1650, 1777
Portuguese 1650, 1777
British 1650
French 1777
Dutch 1650, 1777
Tordesillas Line 1494
1:42,000,000
© Carta

Francisco Pizarro

THE FORMATION OF STATES IN SOUTH AMERICA
VENEZUELA
1811/19 independence
Caracas
PANAMA
UNITED REPUBLIC OF
COLOMBIA
1819–1830
Bogotá
Quito
ECUADOR
1828 independence
PERU
1821 independence
Lima
BOLIVIA
1825 independence
La Paz
EMPIRE OF
BRAZIL
1822
Manaus
Recife
Bahia
Brasília
São Paulo
Rio de Janeiro
Georgetown
Paramaribo
Cayenne
BRITISH
DUTCH
FRENCH
GUIANA
PARAGUAY
1811 independence
Asunción
CONFEDERATION OF
ARGENTINA
1810 independence, 1810/16 united province of La Plata, 1825 confederation
CHILE
1810/18 independence
Valparaíso
Santiago
URUGUAY
1825
Montevideo
Buenos Aires
Caribbean Sea
North Atlantic Ocean
Pacific Ocean
South Atlantic Ocean
States Formed under Bolívar's influence
1:30,000,000
© Carta

Simón Bolívar—"El Libertador"

POST-COLONIAL HISTORY

Colonial rule in South America, except in British Guiana, French Guiana, and Suriname, ended during the first quarter of the nineteenth century. The immediate cause of the revolt against Spanish and Portuguese rule was the Napoleonic conquest of the "motherland" and its consequences. However, the ideas emanating from the French Revolution and the Declaration of Independence of the United States had a strong impact on the political aspirations of those who led the struggles for independence. In the first stage seven independent states came into being, but by 1830 their number increased to ten with the breakup of Gran Colombia and the secession of Venezuela and Ecuador (which became independent states) and the agreement between Brazil and Argentina regarding the establishment of Uruguay. The boundaries of the new states, which were largely based on those of the colonial administration, the Spanish and Portuguese viceroyalties and their internal divisions, were not clearly defined and led to much controversy between the new states, resulting in border wars. Most of these boundaries ran through uninhabited or sparsely populated areas, maps were very general and inaccurate (this situation in large continued into the twentieth century), and even information on the nature of the countryside at the frontier zones was scanty and vague. Conflicts concerning boundaries also arose when settlement spread to such areas or when they were found to have important resources. All the new states became formal republics, with constitutions similar, in most cases, to that of the United States; they were headed by a president with wide executive powers and had a legislature composed of two chambers. The only exception was Brazil, which became a monarchy (the Portuguese monarchy spent several years in exile in Brazil during the Napoleonic period). The monarchy ended in 1889.

The colonial rule in the young South American countries was replaced to a large extent by governments, in most cases dictatorial, controlled by the upper classes of the Creoles (locally born of European descent) and mestizos, mainly owners of large estates, wealthy merchants, owners of mines, and senior military personnel. Most states were throughout the nineteenth and much of the twentieth century subject to internal instability and strife between rival political and economic groups or regions (in some cases with secessionist tendencies). Personal enmities also played a part. Changes in regime were often carried out by force, while many such attempts failed. Most South American countries have changed their constitution several times, this being one of the consequences of political instability. Argentina in 1983 reverted to a constitution enacted in 1853 (into which amendments were thrice introduced). Chile was the only country which adhered to its constitution for nearly a century (1833–1925), in the course of which it was amended several times.

The strict restriction on foreign immigration and trade which prevailed throughout the colonial period was lifted following the attainment of independence. It took, however, several decades before the continent attracted immigrants on a much larger scale than before and also for the volume of foreign trade to increase substantially. The trade and importation of slaves decreased considerably in the early nineteenth century, but came to a stop only in the 1830s. Slavery, although gradually on the retreat in most countries since their independence, was not finally abolished before the end of the century (1888). Large-scale European immigration, which changed the character of several South American countries and boosted the economy of most, took place only in the second half of the nineteenth century (mainly from 1870) and the first four decades of the twentieth century. It is estimated that during this period 14 to 15 million European immigrants arrived in South America (many of whom are thought to have left again), mainly from Italy, Spain, and Portugal but also from Germany, France, Russia, and other European countries. Nearly half these immigrants went to Argentina and about one-third to Brazil. The proportion of east and central Europeans among the immigrants increased in the beginning of the century, especially after World War I. Venezuela became a great attraction to European immigrants only after World War II. The Andean countries attracted comparatively fewer European immigrants than the Atlantic states of the continent. Among the former, more immigrants went to Chile, especially during the boom in the nitrate industry toward the end of the nineteenth and in the early twentieth century. The rapid population growth in all South American countries from the beginning of the twentieth century and especially since the 1930s was to a large extent due to natural increase, which was for many years higher than that of any other continent. The economic growth in some regions, such as the rise of the coffee industry in southeastern Brazil, attracted many foreign immigrants as well as internal migration. At the same time, the large European immigration was largely responsible for the economic development, especially the industrialization, of most South American countries.

Substantial progress toward industrialization began in some countries only after World War I and had been accelerated in most only during and after World War II. Industrial production today plays an important role in the economy of all countries. Industrialization is most advanced in Argentina, Brazil, Chile, and Venezuela. Local industrial products are increasingly substituting imported manufactured goods and are taking up a growing share of the continent's exports. Despite the significant increase and changes since the beginning of the twentieth century, exports are still largely comprised of minerals and tropical agricultural products.

The effort toward the establishment of a democratic political system and the elimination of social injustice, which had its roots in some South American countries in their early history as independent states, had very little practical effect throughout the nineteenth and much of the twentieth century. Even in those states in which democratic processes made significant progress, leading theoretically to the establishment of democratic regimes, little success was made in transforming the pravailing social and economic structures and often the regimes did not survive long enough to introduce basic reforms. Only in recent years have democratic regimes gained control in most South American countries (although some still appear fragile) and there are clear indications in most countries of advancement toward a more progressive social and political order.

There are still a number of unsettled territorial disputes between South American countries, although these have not in recent times caused any serious crisis between the states concerned. Claims to large sections of the Antarctic continent and neighboring islands are made by Argentina (between longtitudes 25° and 74° west) and Chile (between longitudes 53° and 90° west). Argentina claims an area of 964,250 square kilometers (376,660 square miles), including the following groups of islands: South Orkneys; South Georgia; South Sandwich; and the Falkland Islands (Malvinas). Chile claims an area of 1,250,000 square kilometers (482,500 square miles), part of which is also claimed by Argentina. Most of the areas claimed are actually held by Britain.

Juan Domingo Perón

SOUTH AMERICA IN THE LATE 19TH CENTURY
Caribbean Sea
Aruba
Caracas
TRINIDAD & TOBAGO
PANAMA
VENEZUELA
R. Orinoco
Georgetown
Paramaribo
Cayenne
BRIT.
DUTCH
FRENCH
SURINAME
GUIANA
Neutral zone 1850-1885
1899
1900
Bogotá
COLOMBIA
Guiana Highlands
North Atlantic Ocean
Quito
ECUADOR
1880
Neutral zone
R. Negro
Manaus
R. Amazonas
R. Madeira
Selvas
BRAZIL
R. Tocantins
C. de São Roque
Recife
Equator
R. Marañón
PERU
Lima
1880
L. Titicaca
La Paz
BOLIVIA
Andes
Brazilian Highlands
R. São Francisco
Brasília
Pacific Ocean
Gran Chaco
R. Paraguay
1870
1880
PARAGUAY
Asunción
R. Paraná
São Paulo
Rio de Janeiro
1874
San Félix
San Ambrosio
CHILE
ARGENTINA
R. Uruguay
Serra do Mar
URUGUAY
Aconcagua
Santiago
Buenos Aires
Montevideo
Río de la Plata
Juan Fernández
South Atlantic Ocean
R. Negro
1881
1899-1902 Chile/Argentina
Patagonia
C. Blanco
Falkland Is.
Stanley
Tierra del Fuego
C. de Hornos
South Georgia
1:30,000,000
© Carta

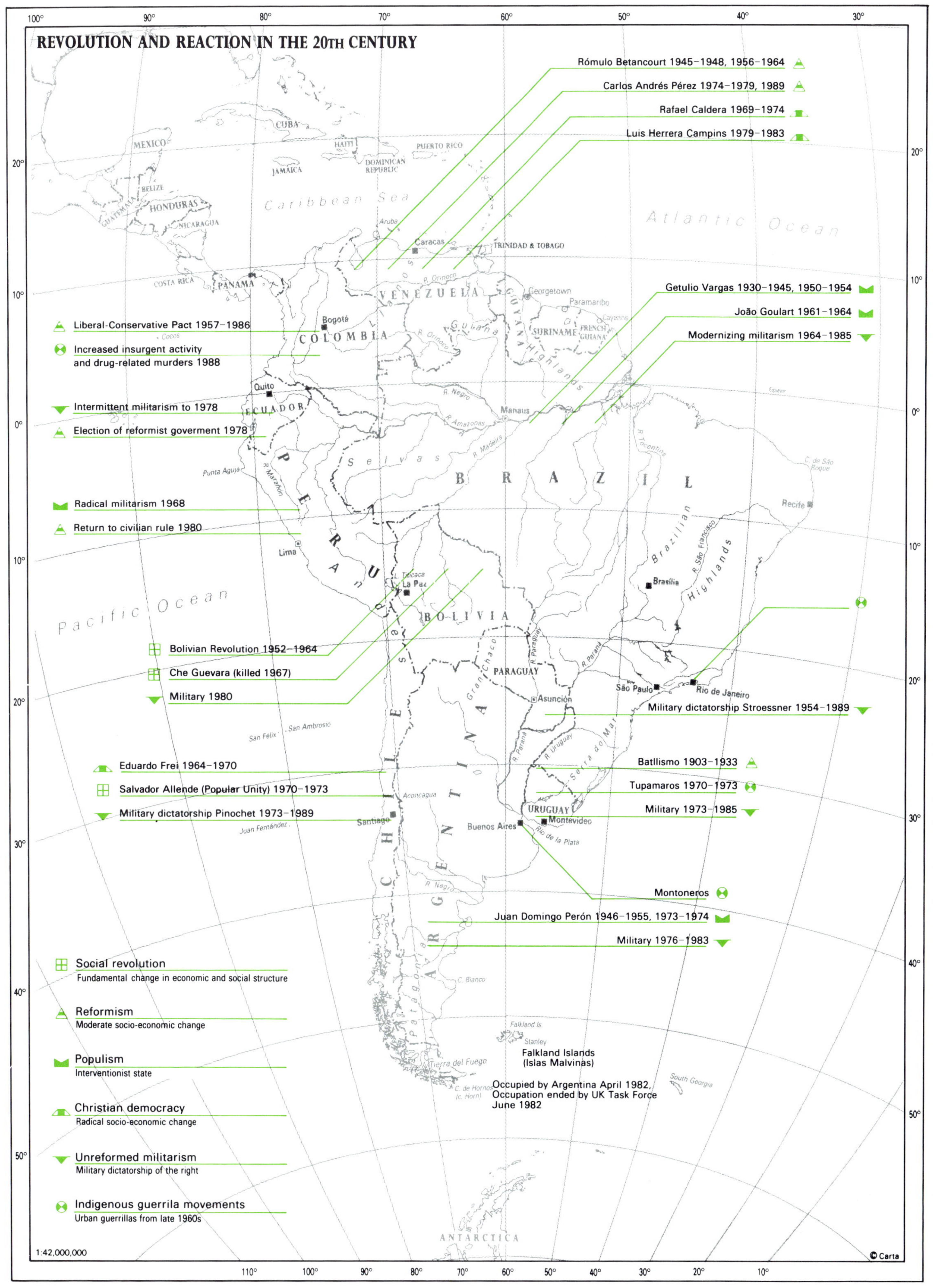
REVOLUTION AND REACTION IN THE 20TH CENTURY
Rómulo Betancourt 1945–1948, 1956–1964
Carlos Andrés Pérez 1974–1979, 1989
Rafael Caldera 1969–1974
Luis Herrera Campins 1979–1983
Getulio Vargas 1930–1945, 1950–1954
João Goulart 1961–1964
Modernizing militarism 1964–1985
Liberal-Conservative Pact 1957–1986
Increased insurgent activity and drug-related murders 1988
Intermittent militarism to 1978
Election of reformist goverment 1978
Radical militarism 1968
Return to civilian rule 1980
Bolivian Revolution 1952–1964
Che Guevara (killed 1967)
Military 1980
Military dictatorship Stroessner 1954–1989
Eduardo Frei 1964–1970
Salvador Allende (Popular Unity) 1970–1973
Military dictatorship Pinochet 1973–1989
Batllismo 1903–1933
Tupamaros 1970–1973
Military 1973–1985
Montoneros
Juan Domingo Perón 1946–1955, 1973–1974
Military 1976–1983
Falkland Islands (Islas Malvinas)
Occupied by Argentina April 1982, Occupation ended by UK Task Force June 1982
Social revolution
Fundamental change in economic and social structure
Reformism
Moderate socio-economic change
Populism
Interventionist state
Christian democracy
Radical socio-economic change
Unreformed militarism
Military dictatorship of the right
Indigenous guerrila movements
Urban guerrillas from late 1960s
1:42,000,000
© Carta
MEXICO
CUBA
HAITI
PUERTO RICO
JAMAICA
DOMINICAN REPUBLIC
BELIZE
HONDURAS
GUATEMALA
NICARAGUA
COSTA RICA
PANAMA
Caribbean Sea
Atlantic Ocean
Pacific Ocean
Aruba
Caracas
TRINIDAD & TOBAGO
VENEZUELA
R. Orinoco
Georgetown
Paramaribo
Cayenne
GUYANA
SURINAME
FRENCH GUIANA
Guiana Highlands
Bogotá
COLOMBIA
Cocos
Quito
ECUADOR
R. Negro
Manaus
R. Amazonas
R. Madeira
Equator
R. Tocantins
C. de São Roque
Selvas
BRAZIL
Punta Aguja
R. Marañón
PERU
Recife
Lima
Brazilian Highlands
R. São Francisco
Brasília
L. Titicaca
La Paz
Andes
BOLIVIA
Gran Chaco
R. Paraguay
PARAGUAY
R. Paraná
São Paulo
Rio de Janeiro
Asunción
San Félix
San Ambrosio
Serra do Mar
R. Uruguay
Aconcagua
URUGUAY
Montevideo
Buenos Aires
Río de la Plata
Santiago
Juan Fernández
CHILE
ARGENTINA
R. Negro
C. Blanco
Patagonia
Falkland Is.
Stanley
Tierra del Fuego
C. de Hornos (C. Horn)
South Georgia
ANTARCTICA

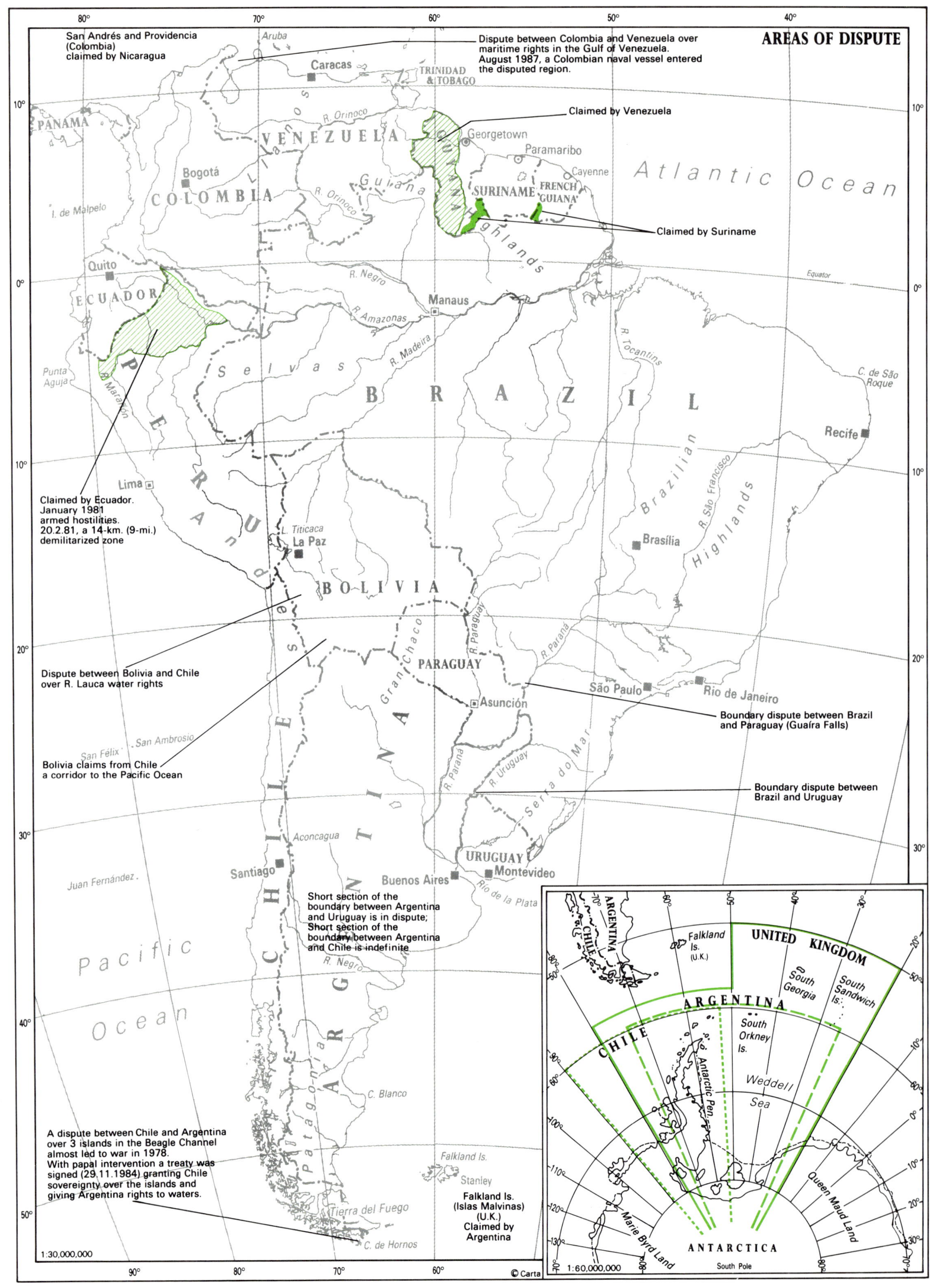
AREAS OF DISPUTE
San Andrés and Providencia (Colombia) claimed by Nicaragua
Dispute between Colombia and Venezuela over maritime rights in the Gulf of Venezuela. August 1987, a Colombian naval vessel entered the disputed region.
Claimed by Venezuela
Claimed by Suriname
Claimed by Ecuador. January 1981 armed hostilities. 20.2.81, a 14-km. (9-mi.) demilitarized zone
Dispute between Bolivia and Chile over R. Lauca water rights
Bolivia claims from Chile a corridor to the Pacific Ocean
Boundary dispute between Brazil and Paraguay (Guaíra Falls)
Boundary dispute between Brazil and Uruguay
Short section of the boundary between Argentina and Uruguay is in dispute; Short section of the boundary between Argentina and Chile is indefinite
A dispute between Chile and Argentina over 3 islands in the Beagle Channel almost led to war in 1978. With papal intervention a treaty was signed (29.11.1984) granting Chile sovereignty over the islands and giving Argentina rights to waters.
Falkland Is. (Islas Malvinas) (U.K.) Claimed by Argentina
Atlantic Ocean
Pacific Ocean
BRAZIL
VENEZUELA
COLOMBIA
ECUADOR
PERU
BOLIVIA
PARAGUAY
ARGENTINA
CHILE
URUGUAY
GUYANA
SURINAME
FRENCH GUIANA
PANAMA
TRINIDAD & TOBAGO
Caracas
Bogotá
Quito
Georgetown
Paramaribo
Cayenne
Manaus
Lima
La Paz
Brasília
Recife
São Paulo
Rio de Janeiro
Asunción
Montevideo
Buenos Aires
Santiago
Aruba
I. de Malpelo
Punta Aguja
L. Titicaca
Aconcagua
San Félix
San Ambrosio
Juan Fernández
C. Blanco
Falkland Is.
Stanley
Tierra del Fuego
C. de Hornos
C. de São Roque
Equator
R. Orinoco
R. Negro
R. Amazonas
R. Madeira
R. Marañón
R. Tocantins
R. São Francisco
R. Paraguay
R. Paraná
R. Uruguay
Río de la Plata
Llanos
Guiana Highlands
Selvas
Andes
Gran Chaco
Brazilian Highlands
Serra do Mar
Patagonia
1:30,000,000
© Carta
UNITED KINGDOM
ARGENTINA
CHILE
Falkland Is. (U.K.)
South Georgia
South Sandwich Is.
South Orkney Is.
Antarctic Pen.
Weddell Sea
Queen Maud Land
Marie Byrd Land
ANTARCTICA
South Pole
1:60,000,000

THE COUNTRIES

VENEZUELA

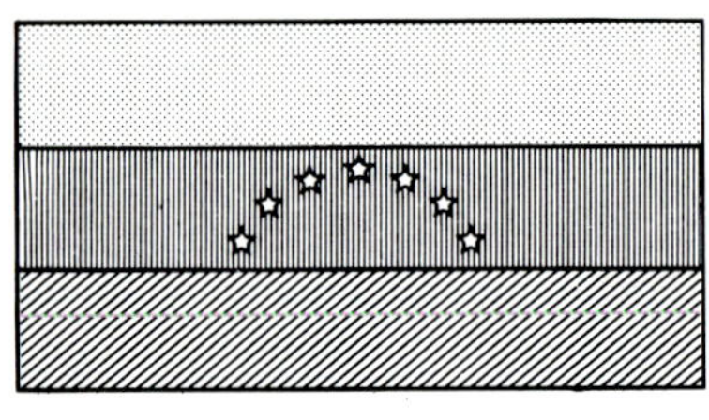

Area
912,050 sq. km.
352,144 sq. mi.

Population
19,735,000 (1990 estimate)

Capital City
Caracas

Gross National Product (GNP) Per Capita
$3,170 (1988)

Population in Main Cities
(1985 estimates)
Caracas 1,246,611 (1987)
Maracaibo 1,260,978
Valencia 1,089,139
Maracay 825,648
Barquisimeto 695,540

Highest Point
5,007 m. 16,427 ft. (Pico Bolívar)

Currency Unit
1 bolívar = 100 céntimos

Density
19.5 persons per sq. km.
50.5 persons per sq. mi. (1985)

Urban-Rural
urban 85.7% rural 14.3% (1985)

Natural Increase
2.6% (1985-1990)

Life Expectancy
69.7 (1985-1990)

Doctors
815 inhabitants per doctor (1986)

Hospital Beds
2.5 per thousand inhabitants (1986)

Infant Mortality
35.9 per thousand live births (1985-1990)

High School Pupils
45.5% of age group 13-18 (1986)

University Students
25.7% of age group 20-24 (1986)

Illiteracy Rate
13.1% (1985)

National Holiday
Independence Day, 5 July

National Anthem
beginning "Gloria al bravo pueblo" ("Glory to the brave people")

Venezuela is the northernmost country of South America, with a long (2,800 kilometer [1,740 miles]) indented coast on the Caribbean Sea. It is bordered on the west by Colombia, on the south by Brazil, and on the east by Guyana. Most of its long land boundaries (5,000 kilometers [3,100 miles]) run through very densely forested areas.

NATURAL REGIONS

Venezuela is made up of four distinct natural regions: the Northern Highlands in the north and west; the Maracaibo Basin in the northwest; the Llanos de Orinoco in the southwest and center; and the Guiana Highlands in the southeast. Of these regions, only parts of the Northern Highlands are densely populated and contain the main urban centers.

The Northern Highlands

This region is a branch of the Andes which turns northeast south of Lake Maracaibo and forms most of Venezuela's northern coastal region. The southwestern part of this region, the Cordillera de Mérida, is a chain of high mountains with the typical structure characteristics of the Andes. It rises to 5,007 meters (16,427 feet) at Pico Bolívar and has a number of permanently snow-covered heights. A number of small intermont basins are still predominantly inhabited by American Indians and mestizos. Farther north, the highlands are lower and more broken, allowing for easier accessibility and transit. A northwestern extension of the main chain, known as the Segovia Highlands, consists mainly of deeply dissected low mountains and hills that cover most of the peninsula between Lake Maracaibo and the Caribbean Sea. This sparsely inhabited region suffers frequently from droughts. The approximately 300-kilometer-long section, generally known as the Central Highlands, from the vicinity of Barquisimeto to Cape Codera, is in fact the central region of Venezuela. It consists of two almost parallel ranges, the northern of which falls abruptly onto a narrow coastal strip along the Caribbean Sea. The ranges, which rise to a height of 2,700 meters (9,000 feet), and the intermont basin—the Valencia Basin—contain the most densely inhabited urban and rural areas of the country. The capital, Caracas, occupies a small river valley on the northern range, 10 kilometers (6 miles) from the Caribbean coast.

The northeastern part of the highlands is separated from the Central Highlands by a wide gap occupied by the Gulf of Barcelona. This is the lowest, most faulted and denuded part of the highlands. It forms the backbone of the Paria and Araya peninsulas and of some neighboring islands. Cumaná, the oldest European settlement on the South American continent (founded 1523), and now the largest urban center in the northeast (250,000 inhabitants), is situated on the fringes of a small basin in these highlands.

The Maracaibo Basin

This basin is a swampy plain, gently rising to the slope of the Andean chains, bordered by the Sierra de Perija in the west, the Cordillera de Mérida in the south and east, and the Segovia Highlands in the northeast. Lake Maracaibo, in the lower part of the basin, occupies approximately one-third of its area. It is connected with the Caribbean Sea by a narrow and shallow natural strait (only 2.5 meters [7 feet] deep during low tide). The strait has been considerably deepened to make it navigable to large steamers. The southern half of the lake contains fresh water but it becomes increasingly brackish in its northern part as it approaches the open sea. Climatically, this basin is the most torrid and oppressive region in South America. It has rich oil resources and for the past 70 years has had some of the most productive oil fields in the Western Hemisphere. It is the main source of Venezuela's mineral wealth, providing about three-fourths of its oil production.

The Llanos de Orinoco

The Llanos is a broad, almost featureless plain between the Northern Highlands and the banks of the river Orinoco. It slopes very gently from an altitude of approximately 200 meters (700 feet) at the foothills of the Andes in the west over a distance of 1,100 kilometers (700 miles) to a swampy delta 200 kilometers (120 miles) wide in the east. Along much of its course the Orinoco flows close to the western and northern margins of the Guiana Highlands. The Orinoco, with a catchment basin of nearly 1.1 million square kilometers (425,000 square miles) and an average annual discharge of nearly 800 billion cubic meters (almost double the average discharge of the Mississippi), is subject to large seasonal fluctuations. During the rainy season, from June to October, the Orinoco and many of its tributaries inundate large parts of the Llanos. Much of the Llanos becomes accessible only after the floods recede in November and December. The Orinoco is navigable for 1,400 kilometers (900 miles), from the Atlantic coast to the Maipures Rapids (south of Puerto Ayacucho), but through its large tributaries, Meta and Apure, it is navigable up to the foothills of the Andes.

The Guiana Highlands

This natural region extends into the neighboring countries of Brazil and Guyana, and covers nearly half the area of Venezuela. It consists of extremely denuded mountains and deeply incised plateaus built mainly of crystalline formations occasionally capped by resistant, old, sedimentary rocks. The highlands rise by escarpments and steep slopes from the Orinoco valley to heights of up to 1,500 meters (5,000 feet) and are characterized by precipitous, deep and narrow river valleys and by mesa-like interfluvial plateaus. Most of the rivers in these valleys are not navigable and are filled with rapids and falls, among which is the highest in the world—the Angel Falls. Some of the mesa-like areas, especially those capped by very resistant rock formations, reach elevations of well over 2,000 meters (6,600 feet). The highest point is Mount Roraima (2,772 meters [9,094 feet]) where the Brazilian, Guyanian, and Venezuelan boundaries meet. The Guiana Highlands are rich in mineral resources. Exploration and exploitation have been hampered by difficulties in access to large parts of this region, due to the nature of the topography and the dense vegetation.

Remote frontier areas with Brazil and Guyana have until recently been outside effective government control.

CLIMATE

Venezuela, extending (approximately) over latitudes 0°20′ and 12°N, has a tropical—hot and humid—climate. However, in actual fact, the climatic patterns are complicated by the

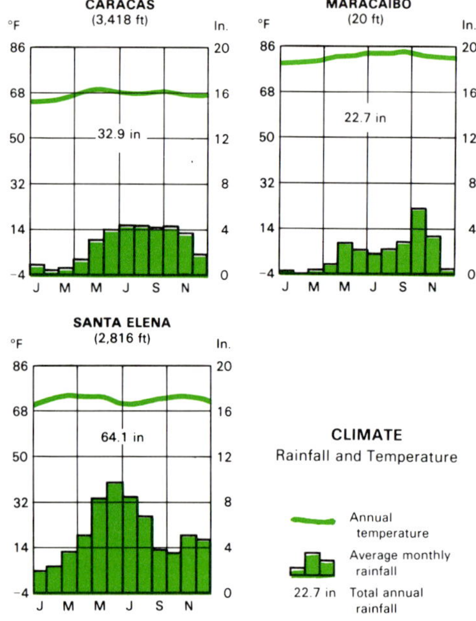

great changes in topographic conditions and altitudes, especially in relation to seasonal variations in predominant winds. The climatic conditions prevailing in each area are clearly reflected by its natural vegetation. The climate of the highland regions is characterized by vertical zones. The lowest of these is the hot zone, or *tierra caliente*, extending upward to an elevation of approximately 1,000 meters (3,300 feet). Above this is the temperate zone, or *tierra templada*, at an elevation of 1,000–2,000 meters (3,300–6,500 feet). Between approximately 2,000 and 3,000 meters (6,500–10,000 feet) is the cool zone, or *tierra fría*. Above that is the zone of high mountain meadows, or *páramos*, which rises to the snow line at approximately 4,500 meters (15,000 feet). While precipitation prevails over most parts of the country, much of the northern coastal areas, parts of the Maracaibo Basin, and some intermont basins and valleys are semiarid. Some of these areas do not get enough rain to support agriculture and are only thinly covered by natural xerophytic vegetation; others suffer occasionally from drought. Thus, while Caracas (altitude approximately 1,000 meters [3,000 feet]) has an average annual rainfall of 800 millimeters (32 inches), the Caribbean port of La Guaira, located only 13 kilometers (8 miles) away, receives only 280 millimeters (11 inches) of rain. Mérida, 1,640 meters high, on the slopes of the Andes (Cordillera de Mérida), receives on the average 1,700 millimeters (68 inches) annually, while Coro, on the northwest coast, gets only 240 millimeters (9.5 inches). The rainy season, longest in the south and somewhat shorter in the north, is from April to November. The heaviest rains usually occur from June to October. Seasonal variations in temperature are small. Temperatures are high all year round in the coastal and low inland areas and are temperate to cool at elevations above 1,000 meters (3,000 feet). The average temperature of the hottest month (July) in Caracas is 20.6°C (69°F) and of the coldest month (January), 18.3°C (65°F), while at the nearby Caribbean port of La Guaira, they are 28.3°C (83°F) and 25.8°C (78.4°F), respectively. At Mérida the averages are 19.3°C (66.7°F) and 17.8°C (64°F), and at Ciudad Bolívar (in the Llanos de Orinoco)—27.2°C (81°F) and 26.1°C (79°F).

POPULATION

The number of inhabitants at the end of 1989 was estimated at 19.3 million; the last census in 1981 totaled 14.5 million. The average annual increase (natural and through immigration) over the period 1980–1987 had been 2.8 percent. In the 1981 census, 69 percent of the population were of mixed race (mestizo), 20 percent white, 9 percent black, and 2 percent Indian. The latter live mainly in valleys and basins in Cordillera de Mérida and in the Guiana Highlands. Nearly 96 percent of the population are Catholic, and 2 percent Protestant. Most of the population is concentrated in a small part of the country, mainly in the central sections of the Northern Highlands where more than 60 percent reside. Density varies from 0.4 persons per square kilometer in the southernmost territory (Amazonas) and 2.2 per square kilometer in the Orinoco Delta, to 1,400 per square kilometer in the Federal District and 310 per square kilometer in the northern state of Carabobo. The average population density for the whole country is 22; only in two states and in the Federal District does it exceed 100 per square kilometer. Venezuela is the most urbanized Latin American nation (86 percent).

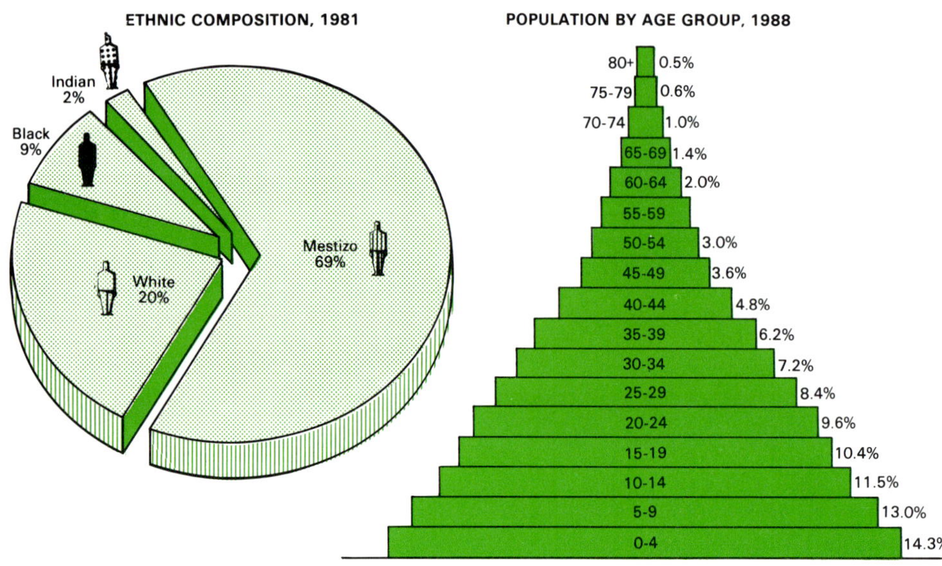

The main urban centers are: Caracas—1.3 million (1989) and 3.3 million in the metropolitan area; Maracaibo—1.3 million; Valencia—1.1 million; Maracay—840,000; Barquisimeto—700,000; Ciudad Guayana—450,000; Petare—380,000; Ciudad Bolívar—270,000; Mérida—260,000; Maturín—250,000; Cumaná—240,000. Fifteen percent of the population are illiterate. The population of Venezuela has grown more than fourfold since World War II. It was estimated at about 1 million in the mid-nineteenth century, 2.4 million in 1920, and 5,034,000 in 1950. The population grew by an average annual rate of approximately 4 percent during the 1950s and 1960s largely because of immigration, mainly from Europe.

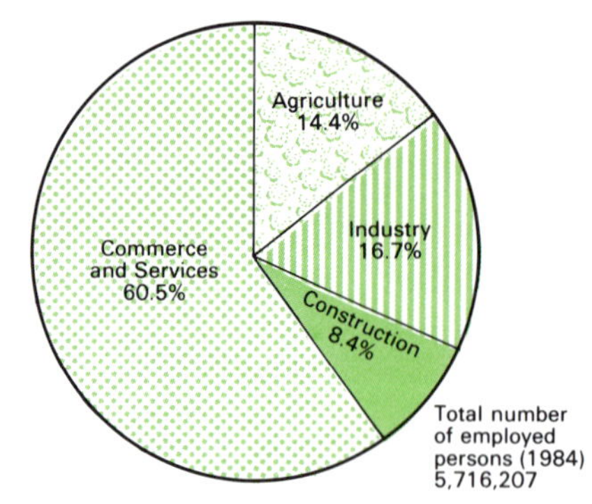

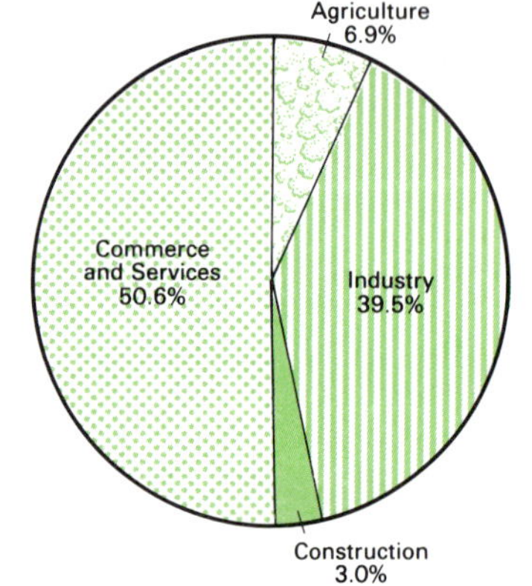

ECONOMY

Venezuela's economy is based largely on the exploitation of its mineral resources—mainly oil, which makes up more than 80 percent (84 percent in 1987) of the country's exports. Industries, especially those based on local mineral resources and other raw materials, play an increasing role in the economic growth of the country. Among the labor force, 15.3 percent are employed in industry, and 12.3 percent in agriculture. The GNP per capita, $3,170 (1988), has been growing in recent years at an average annual rate of 2.2 percent. The country has been suffering from inflation, which in 1987 reached 40.3 percent.

Agriculture

Only 4.1 percent of the area is utilized for agricultural production. This is mainly concentrated in the Northern Highlands and the fringes of the Maracaibo Basin. Most of the areas under cultivation produce foodstuffs for local consumption. Approximately 50 percent of the farmers

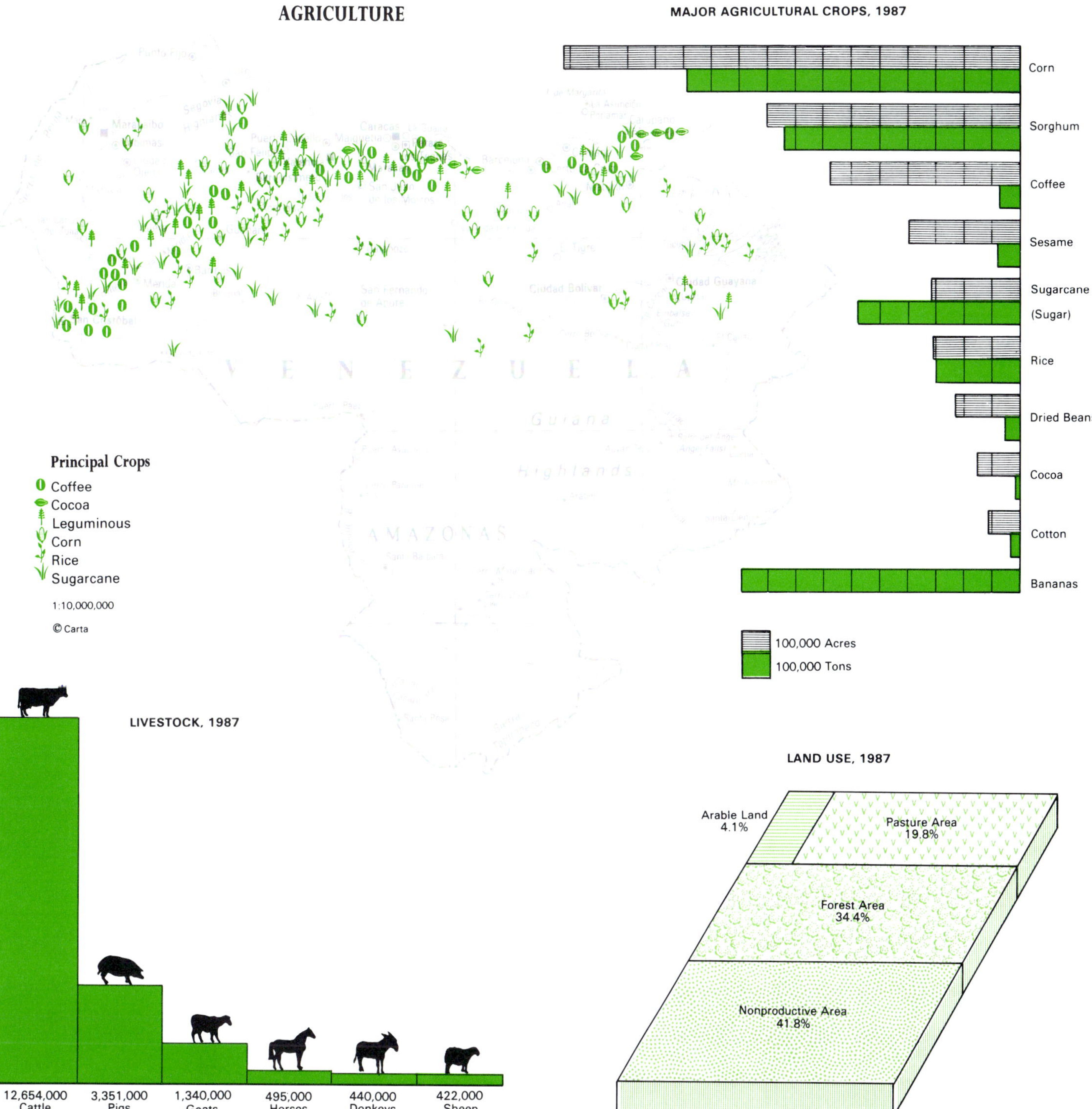

produce mainly for their own consumption. The expansion of agriculture in recent years has not caught up with population growth and increase in demand. The main commercial crops (for export) are coffee, cocoa, and sugarcane. The coffee, which is of high quality, is grown on the slopes of the Cordillera de Mérida and in the central section of the Northern Highlands. The total areas under these crops and their production figures for 1987 were coffee—682,000 acres, 66,000 tons; cocoa—153,000 acres, 14,000 tons; sugarcane—322,000 acres, 7 million tons cane, 584,000 tons sugar. The main field crops are maize (corn)—1,630,000 acres, 1.2 million tons; rice—310,000 acres, 300,000 tons; sorghum—911,000 acres, 850,000 tons. Cotton is grown over 111,000 acres, mainly to supply the local textile industry. Part of the tropical fruit grown is intended for export. The Llanos de Orinoco, with extensive, good-quality grazing areas, is almost entirely used for cattle, goats, and sheep-raising; 19.8 percent of Venezuela's area is classed as permanent pasture. Much livestock is also raised in parts of the Northern Highland region. The total livestock estimated in 1987 was cattle—12,654,000; goats—1,340,000; sheep—422,000; pigs—3,351,000.

Forests and scrublands cover nearly 35 percent of the country. They are most extensive in the Guiana Highlands. The forest resources yield 1,345,000 cubic meters of timber annually and comparatively small quantities of various resins and other products.

Mineral Resources

For over sixty years, Venezuela has been one of the world's largest oil producers. In recent years it has ranked ninth among the main oil-producing countries. Production from wells in the Maracaibo Basin began in 1917 and reached its peak in 1971, when 193 million tons were produced. From the late 1920s to 1970 Venezuela had been the world's largest exporter of oil. Production in 1988 was 93 million tons (an average of 1,825,000 barrels per day). About three-fourths of the production comes from fields in the Maracaibo Basin and many wells in Lake Maracaibo. The rest comes from fields in the lower Orinoco Basin and a number of recently developed offshore wells. There is also a field in the upper Apure valley

INDUSTRY & MINERALS

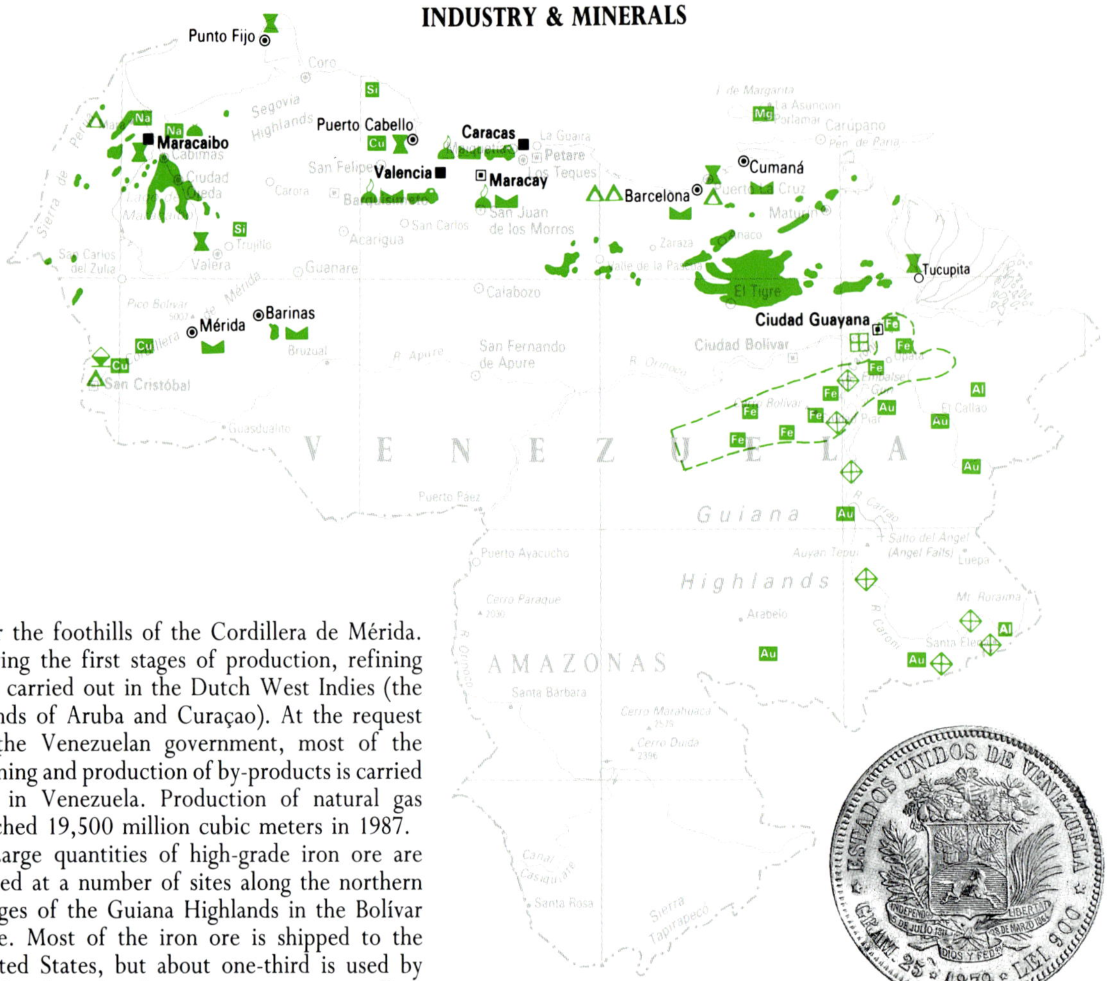

Main Industrial Centers
- Metals
- Oil refinery
- Car assembly
- Textiles
- Chemicals

Mineral Resources
- Al Aluminum
- Si Silicon
- Cu Copper
- Fe Iron
- Mg Magnesium
- Ni Nickel
- Au Gold
- Na Salt (sodium)
- Phosphate
- Oil field
- Coal (carbon)
- Diamonds
- Limit of mineral district

1:10,000,000

near the foothills of the Cordillera de Mérida. During the first stages of production, refining was carried out in the Dutch West Indies (the islands of Aruba and Curaçao). At the request of the Venezuelan government, most of the refining and production of by-products is carried out in Venezuela. Production of natural gas reached 19,500 million cubic meters in 1987.

Large quantities of high-grade iron ore are mined at a number of sites along the northern fringes of the Guiana Highlands in the Bolívar state. Most of the iron ore is shipped to the United States, but about one-third is used by the local steel industry. In 1987, 11.5 million tons were mined. Rich deposits of manganese, nickel, and bauxite exist in the Guiana Highlands where several gold (2,214 kilograms output in 1987) and diamond (215,000 carats) mines are worked. Copper pyrite and asbestos as well as phosphate are mined in this region, and small quantities of coal (57,000 tons in 1986) and asphalt are also produced.

Industry

Industrial development has taken place mostly since World War II, with capital gained largely from oil exports and investments of U.S. companies. Industry is mainly concentrated in and around the urban centers of the north. The manufacture of a wide variety of products and consumer goods, especially food, beverages, clothing, household goods, building materials (mainly cement—5.1 million tons in 1986) meets almost all the domestic requirement. The petrochemical and other industries associated with oil production are mostly concentrated in the Maracaibo Basin and its vicinity. The chemical industry also produces large quantities of fertilizers, ammonia, sulfuric acid, and pharmaceutical products. There are numerous sugar mills (584,000 tons in 1987). The iron and steel (2.3 million and 2.7 million tons, respectively, in 1986) industry, developed to utilize local ore resources, is situated in the lower Orinoco valley in the vicinity of the iron mines. There are several car assembly plants (116,000 cars in 1985). Local ore is used to produce aluminum (400,000 tons in 1986). Other products include paper, rubber, and plastic products, leather goods, and glass and ceramic products.

Five Bolívares, 1879 (depicts Bolívar)

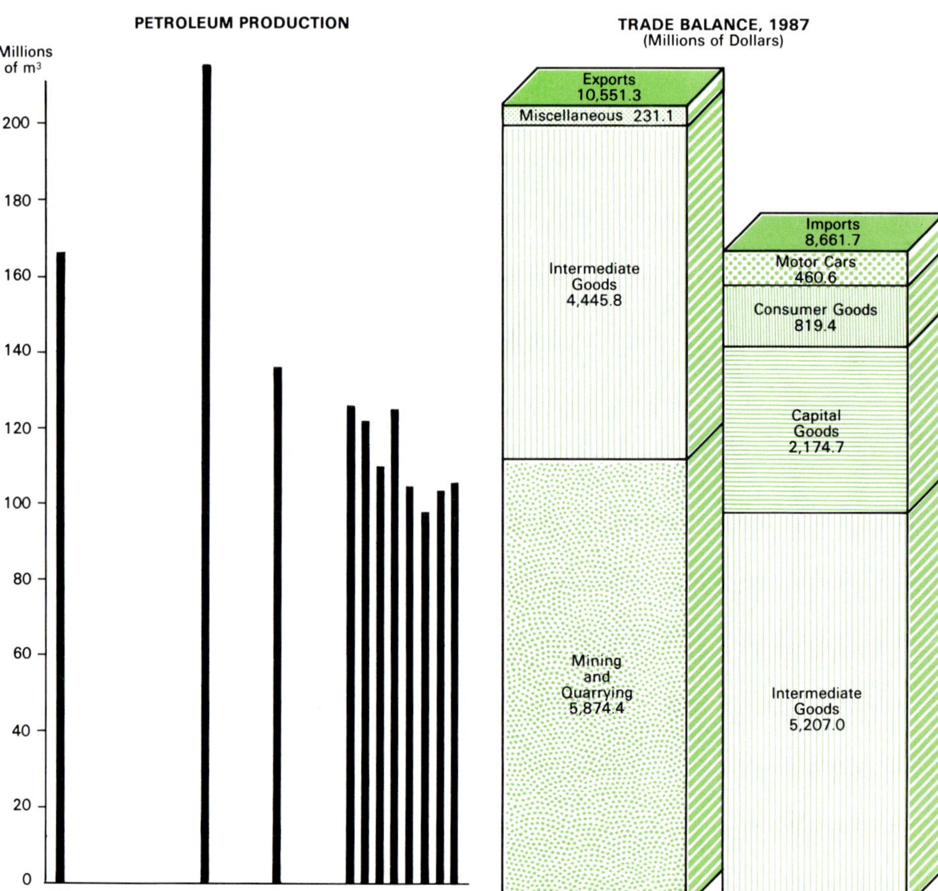

MARACAIBO BASIN

Until 1918, the lowlands that surrounded Lake Maracaibo were one of the most neglected and sparsely inhabited areas of northern Venezuela, despite their convenient accessibility from the Caribbean coast. The torrid climate and oppressive humidity that characterize this basin, enclosed on three sides by high ranges of the Andes, made it unattractive to European settlers. Most of its inhabitants were miserably poor, aboriginal Indian fishermen, whose villages were built on piles over shallow parts of the lake. There were a few plantations of sugarcane and cocoa. Then came the discovery of some of the world's richest oil fields in the northeastern parts of the basin. Within a decade, the basin became the source of Venezuela's wealth and a focus of much economic activity. It has since become one of the country's most flourishing regions, having attracted many industrial and agricultural enterprises apart from the extensive activities directly connected with the exploitation of the oil and natural gas resources. Maracaibo, which was a small market township at the northern outlet of the basin, with a few thousand inhabitants at the turn of the century, has grown into an industrial center with a population of over 1.3 million.

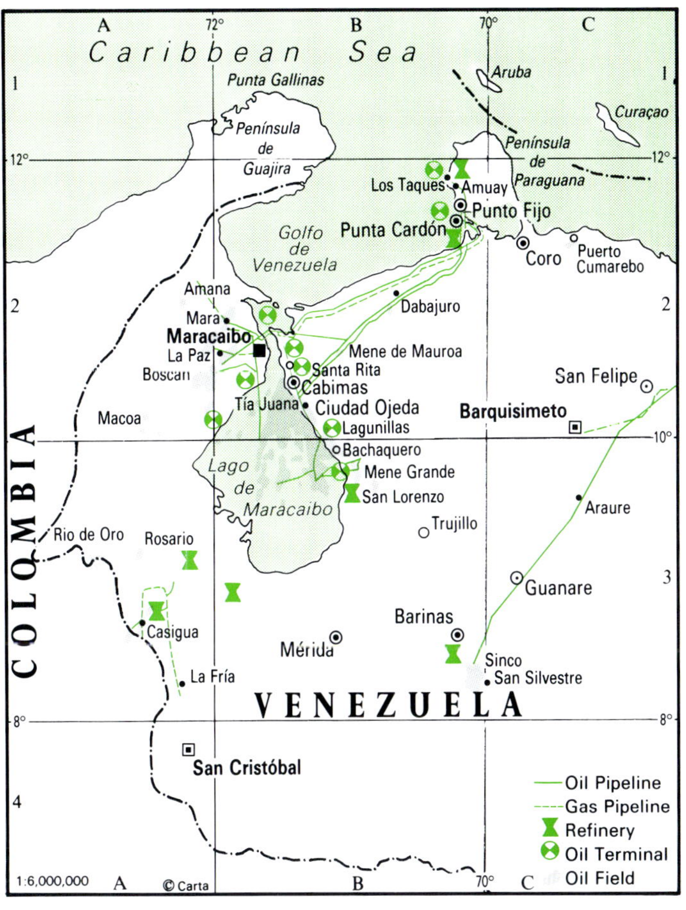

Oil derricks in Maracaibo Basin

Trade

Trade is mainly with the United States, which provided 47 percent of the country's imports and took 51 percent of the exports in 1985. Other important trading partners have been West Germany, Canada, and Italy.

Tourism: 317,000, mainly from the United States, visited Venezuela during 1986.

HISTORY

Northern Venezuela was sparsely inhabited by small, scattered Carib and Arawak tribes when the first Europeans (Spaniards) explored the coastal areas and established their first settlements early in the sixteenth century. Christopher Columbus sailed along the northeast coast of Venezuela during his third voyage to America in 1498. Although of the same racial and linguistic group, there were conspicuous differences in the physical features and lifestyles between the natives of the coastal and lowland areas and those of the highlands. The latter enjoyed higher technical and cultural achievements. The first Spanish settlements, which have survived to the present day, are Cumaná (1523) and Coro (1527). The name "Venezuela" (Little Venice) was given to the northwestern part of the country by the first Spanish explorers, headed by Alonso Ojeda (1499), who, near the banks of Lake Maracaibo, encountered Indian villages whose houses were built on piles over the water. The use of this name was later gradually applied to much larger areas. The presence of placer gold in the beds of some of the streams in the central sections of the Northern Highlands attracted many Spaniards, especially during the second half of the sixteenth century. The first European settlers in the Caracas valley were gold miners. Many of the miners turned to agriculture when it became apparent that the gold resources were scant. The great majority of the Spanish settlers were males, many of whom took native Indian wives, thus laying the foundation for a large mestizo population. Epidemics, brought by the Europeans, and brutal enslavement depleted the native Indian population. Valencia and Barquisimeto, which later became the centers of a rich agricultural district, were founded in 1555, and Caracas in 1567. Big estates were established during the second half of the sixteenth and early seventeenth centuries by Spaniards, mainly officers and officials who took possession of extensive areas of good agricultural lands. Large sugar plantations, on which local Indian, and later African, slaves were employed, were established on some of these estates. Spanish settlement farther inland in the northern and eastern parts of the Llanos de Orinoco began only in the seventeenth century and was very slow. Barcelona was founded in 1671, Maturín in 1710, and Angostura, later renamed Ciudad Bolívar, in 1764. Most of the Llanos remained sparsely inhabited by Indians and settlers of mixed race into the twentieth century, while much of the Guiana Highlands remains uninhabited to this day. The discovery of oil has brought in the 1920s a large influx of people to the Maracaibo Basin. The development of oil and iron resources and industries in the lower Orinoco valley has attracted many settlers to this region in recent decades.

The area of present-day Venezuela was part of the Spanish Viceroyalty of Granada (which also extended over Colombia, Ecuador, and Panama) during the period prior to independence. The Northern Highlands, in which the great majority of the population lived, formed part of the administrative subdivision (originally formed in 1550) called "Captaincy General of Caracas." Venezuela was one of the first areas in Latin America in which an independence movement became active and gained much support among the population. Simón Bolívar,

Administrative Division

States	Capitals	area sq mi	area sq km	population (1987 estimate)
Anzoátegui	Barcelona	16,700	43,300	820,300
Apure	San Fernando de Apure	29,500	76,500	239,000
Aragua	Maracay	2,700	7,014	1,196,800
Barinas	Barinas	13,600	35,200	428,500
Bolívar	Ciudad Bolívar	91,900	238,000	895,600
Carabobo	Valencia	1,795	4,650	1,443,500
Cojedes	San Carlos	5,700	14,800	178,300
Falcón	Coro	9,600	24,800	599,000
Guárico	San Juan de Los Morros	25,091	64,986	457,100
Lara	Barquisimeto	7,600	19,800	1,155,400
Mérida	Mérida	4,400	11,300	580,300
Miranda	Los Teques	3,070	7,950	1,837,800
Monagas	Maturín	11,200	28,900	475,500
Nueva Esparta	La Asunción	440	1,150	254,600
Portuguesa	Guanare	5,900	15,200	553,900
Sucre	Cumaná	4,600	11,800	705,500
Táchira	San Cristóbal	4,300	11,100	800,900
Trujillo	Trujillo	2,900	7,400	526,200
Yaracuy	San Felipe	2,700	356,400	
Zulia	Maracaibo	24,400	63,100	2,071,100
Other federal entities				
Amazonas	Puerto Ayacucho	67,900	175,750	76,900
Delta Amacuro	Tucupita	15,500	40,200	89,500
Dependencias Federales	—	50	120	1,000
Distrito Federal	Caracas	745	1,930	2,530,000
Total		***352,144**	**912,050**	**18,273,400**

*Detail does not add to total given because of rounding.

who led the struggle for liberation in South America against Spanish colonialism, was born and raised in Caracas, where he initiated his political activities. During the first phase of independence (1821–1830), Venezuela was part of Gran Colombia, a state which extended over the area of the colonial Viceroyalty of Granada. Contrary to Bolívar's plans and aspirations for the creation of a United States of South America, Venezuela declared in 1830 its independence from Gran Colombia. Boundary disputes with all its land neighbors, some of which still remain unresolved, followed the lines of independence.

From the declaration of independence (1830) to 1959, with the exception of short intervals, Venezuela was actually ruled by dictators, many of whom were heads of military juntas. Only since 1959 has the country been run by civilian, democratically elected presidents. Venezuela was a poor, backward, and largely uninhabited country until the 1920s when, as a result of the discovery of rich oil resources, it entered a period of rapid economic development. The main growth and expansion of the population and the rise in economic and cultural activities have taken place since World War II.

Three of Venezuela's dictators were outstanding: General José Antonio Páez, who ruled from 1830 to 1849 and was responsible for the country's secession from Gran Colombia; General Antonio Guzmán Blanco, who seized power in 1868 after several years of bitter internal strife following the transformation of Venezuela into a federation of 20 states (1864), and who was deposed in 1889; and General Juan Vicente Gómez, who ruled from 1908 to 1935 and who was responsible for the initiation and development of the oil industry.

Venezuela's constitution has undergone numerous changes, mostly in order to legalize the aspirations of various military dictators, in some cases with the aim of restoring democratic rule. Such a democratic liberal constitution was adopted in 1946, but was abolished two years later when the army again seized control. The present democratic constitution was enacted in January 1961. The oil companies were nationalized in 1976.

GOVERNMENT AND POLITICS

Venezuela is a federation of 20 states, each of which has a legislative assembly and a governor. The states exercise limited internal autonomy. There are also two territories (the almost uninhabited region of the south and east), a Federal District, and federal dependencies (72 islands in the Caribbean Sea). The states are divided into districts (156) and municipalities (613), the territories and Federal District into departments (9). The president, who has broad powers and a qualified veto over congressional decisions, is elected by popular vote for a five-year period. The Congress consists of a Senate (50 members) and a Chamber of Deputies (201 members), also elected for a five-year period. Each state and the Federal District are represented in the Senate by two members. Other members include the ex-president and representatives of the minorities and the judiciary. The Chamber of Deputies is elected by proportional representation. The present president—Carlos Andrés Pérez (of the Acción Democrática)—was elected in December 1988 and took office in February 1989. The political scene has been dominated in recent years by three main parties: Acción Democrática—AD (a Venezuelan version of a social democratic party), which in the last general elections held in December 1988 won 97 and 23 seats in the Chamber of Deputies and in the Senate, respectively; the Comité de Organización Política Electoral Independiente—COPEI (the social Christian party), with 67 and 22 seats; and Movimiento al Socialismo—MAS (Movement toward Socialism), a left-wing party, with 18 and 3 seats. Two small parties are also represented: the New Generation Democracy, whose seats number 6 in the Chamber of Deputies and 1 in the Senate; and the Radical Cause, with 3 seats only in the Chamber of Deputies.

CARACAS

Venezuela's capital has over the last half century been one of the most rapidly growing and transforming metropolitan centers of South America. Perched upon a high rift valley, 920 meters (3,000 feet) above sea level, and adjoining slopes, 11.2 kilometers (7 miles) south of the Caribbean coast, Caracas is located in one of the geographically, topographically, and climatically most attractive regions, where a large conurbation has developed in modern times. Caracas is embraced by mountains into which its outlying suburbs and satellite towns have spread. The metropolitan area extends over approximately 400 square kilometers (150 square miles) with a population of 3.2 million (of which Caracas covers 80 square kilometers [30 square miles] with 1.3 million inhabitants), including 4 urban parishes of the Federal District (of which it is the core) and 5 municipalities in the neighboring state of Miranda.

The city was founded by Spanish settlers led by Diego de Losada in 1567 in what was a very fertile valley inhabited by Caracas Indians. Caracas was named Santiago de León Caracas, but by the nineteenth century, Caracas preserved only the name of the natives whom its founders encountered there. Although it became a colonial administrative center of the region as early as 1577 and the capital of independent Venezuela in 1831, its growth was slow. Two devastating earthquakes, in 1755 and 1812, and the ravages of the war for independence greatly deterred its development. In 1771 it had a population of 18,500 and in 1800, nearly 40,000. By 1926 it had 135,000 inhabitants and by 1941—269,000. Its rapid growth and expansion occurred after World War II. In 1950 it had 495,000 inhabitants, in 1961—787,000 (the metropolitan area exceeded 1.3 million), and in 1971—1,036,000 (the metropolitan area, 2.2 million).

The pattern of the city and the dominant architecture was typical Spanish colonial up to the 1870s when French influence brought about a gradual change in the appearance of much of the city. However, the great transformation and modernization of Caracas began only in the 1920s, and even more so from the 1940s. Almost the entire valley became urbanized with new development projects, and the city spread over adjacent hills and slopes and into neighboring narrow valleys and ravines. A new business center with modern tall buildings replaced the old center. At the same time, the large influx of the poor, attracted from the backward rural areas, resulted in the appearance of large slums. These slums have been, to a large extent, gradually cleared since the 1960s and replaced by extensive housing projects.

Caracas and its environs are Venezuela's main industrial center. At one time, in the early 1970s, more than half of Venezuela's industrial establishments were concentrated there. A wide range of industries are represented, ranging from food, clothing, and household products to chemicals, building materials, metallurgy, automotive assembly, and electronics.

Caracas is also an important center of higher learning and scientific research. A modern university complex sprang up after the 1940s at the southern outskirts of Caracas. Of the three main universities, the Universidad Central de Venezuela is one of the oldest in South America (established in 1725). The city's impressive cathedral, built 1664-1674, underwent extensive reconstruction and renovation during the twentieth century.

Thirty-two story skyscrapers in Caracas symbolize modernity

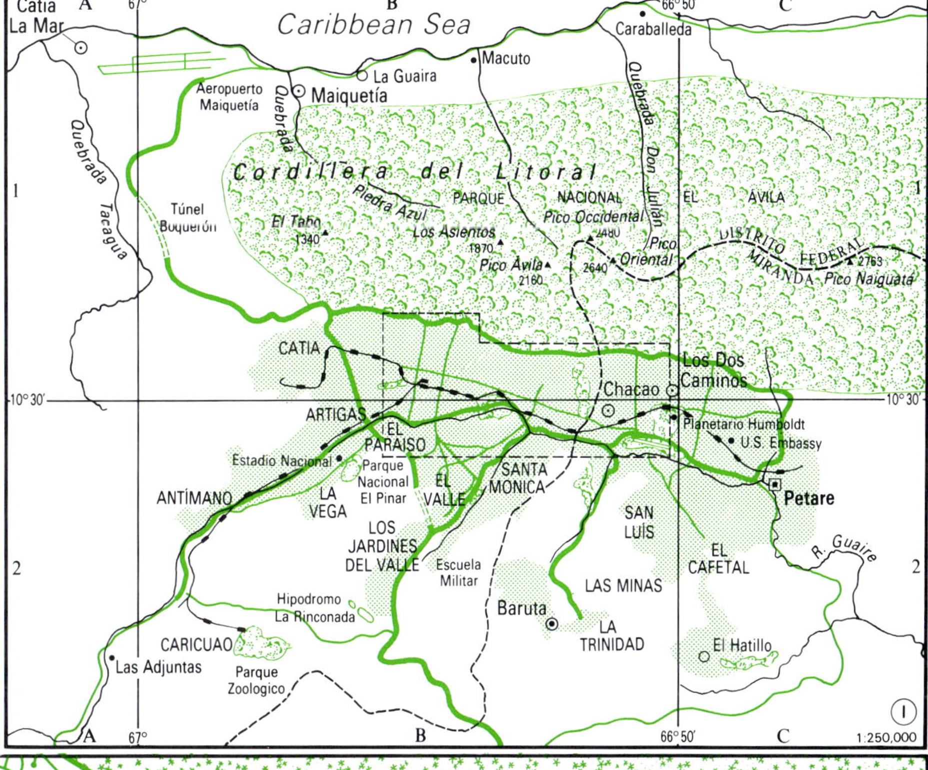

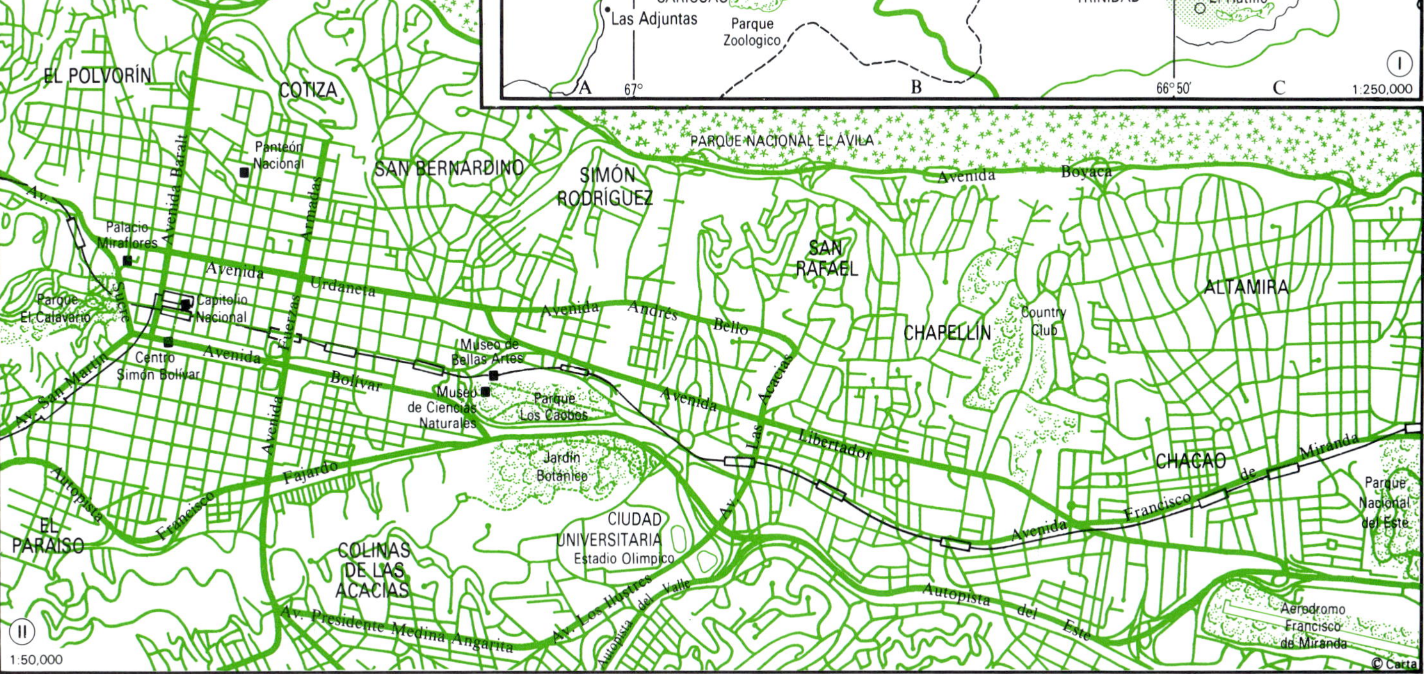

COLOMBIA

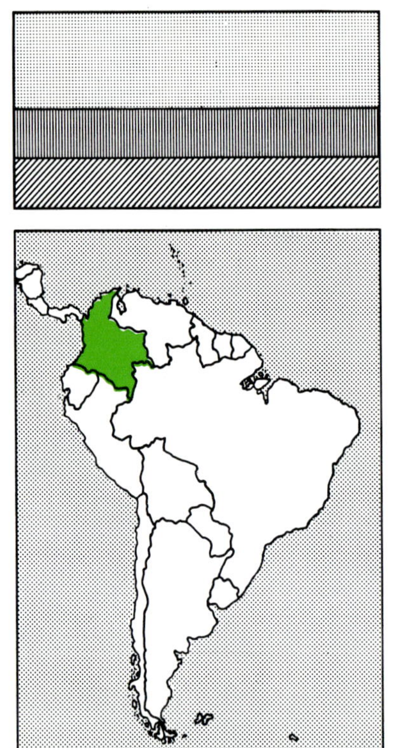

Area
1,141,748 sq. km.
440,831 sq. mi.

Population
31,820,000 (1990 estimate)

Capital City
Bogotá

Gross National Product (GNP) Per Capita
$1,240 (1988)

Population in Main Cities
(1985 estimates)
Greater Bogotá 4,208,000
Medellín 2,095,147
Cali 1,400,828
Barranquilla 1,137,150
Bucaramanga 595,006

Highest Point
5,800 m. 19,020 ft.
(Pico Cristóbal Colón)

Currency Unit
1 peso = 100 centavos

Density
24.7 persons per sq. km.
64.0 persons per sq. mi. (1986)

Urban-Rural
urban 69.9% rural 30.1% (1985)

Natural Increase
2.1% (1985-1990)

Life Expectancy
64.8 (1985-1990)

Doctors
1,200 inhabitants per doctor (1984)

Hospital Beds
1.7 per thousand inhabitants (1984)

Infant Mortality
48.6 per thousand live births (1985-1990)

High School Pupils
55.3% of age group 13-18 (1986)

University Students
13.1% of age group 20-24 (1986)

Illiteracy Rate
17.7% (1985)

National Holiday
Independence Day, 20 July

National Anthem
beginning "O gloria inmarcesible, júbilo immortal"
("O unwithering glory, immortal joy")

Colombia is the only South American country with ports and long coasts on both the Atlantic (Caribbean coast, 1,760 kilometers [1,100 miles]) and Pacific (1,459 kilometers [900 miles]) oceans. Extending over both sides of the equator and the Andes, from sea level to permanently snow-covered peaks of nearly 5,800 meters (19,000 feet), Colombia has a wide variety of landscapes, climatic conditions, peoples, and types of settlement and economic activity. It has in recent years been the focus of international interest because of its large illegal production and trade in narcotics.

Colombia borders Venezuela and Brazil in the east, Ecuador and Peru in the south, and Panama in the northwest. Its island possessions include the Malpelo, opposite its Pacific coast, and several small islands, coral reefs, islets and sandbanks (San Andrés, Providencia, Serrana, Serranilla, and Roncador) in the Caribbean Sea.

NATURAL REGIONS

Colombia is made up of two major physical regions: the Andes, with its large valleys and basins in the west; and the broad lowlands, which extend over almost two-thirds of the country in the east. The population is concentrated in the valleys and basins of the mountain region, while the lowlands are sparsely inhabited. The physical structure of the mountain region and the direction of its main ranges and valleys are a dominant factor in the distribution of the population, with orientation toward the Caribbean (rather than the Pacific) coast, where most of the country's ports are located.

The Andes

The mountain region consists of three ranges of the Andes: Cordillera Occidental, Cordillera Central, and Cordillera Oriental, all of which have a general south-north direction. The Serranía de Baudo is a short, comparatively low range along the northern portion of Colombia's Pacific coast, which extends from just north of Buenaventura into southwestern Panama. It is a very rugged range with deeply incised, narrow, and steep river valleys, mostly barren rock surface, and sharp ridges, some of which rise above 1,500 meters (5,000 feet). These mountains, which are almost uninhabited, are covered partly by dense forests. The parallel coast, mostly lined with high cliffs, has only a few small settlements.

The Andes proper in southern Colombia consist of two parallel high ranges (the highest peak is 4,760 meters [15,620 feet]) separated by a narrow high plateau. This is the narrowest part of the mountain region, only 200 kilometers (125 miles) wide. A short distance north of Pasto, the Andes diverge into three ranges and fan out, making the mountain region at the latitude of Medellín much broader—600 kilometers (370 miles). North of Pasto, the easternmost of the three ranges—the Cordillera Oriental—takes a northeasterly direction, diverging into two ranges in the vicinity of the southwestern corner of Venezuela. The Cordillera de Mérida turns eastward from the Cordillera Oriental to form the northern highland region of Venezuela. The Cordillera Central is the highest and most formidable of the Andean ranges in Colombia, with several peaks rising above the snow line. Pico Cristóbal Colón, in the extreme north, is the highest peak at 5,775 meters (19,000 feet), and among the number of active volcanoes the highest is Tolima, at 5,215 meters (17,110 feet); it last erupted in 1829. While the range's southern half forms a continuous wall of high ridges with steep eastern and western slopes, the northern part is broken, much lower, and slopes gently into the lowlands that border the Caribbean coast. Only in the extreme north, in the Sierra Nevada de Santa Marta, does it rise again above the snow line with the strong relief characteristic of the high Andes. The Cordillera Central, which is approximately 65 kilometers (40 miles) wide, has many small, populated valleys at different altitudes; taken as a whole, however, the range is only sparsely inhabited.

The Cordillera Occidental is much lower and narrower. Its highest peaks rise only to about 3,000 meters (10,000 feet). Even in its

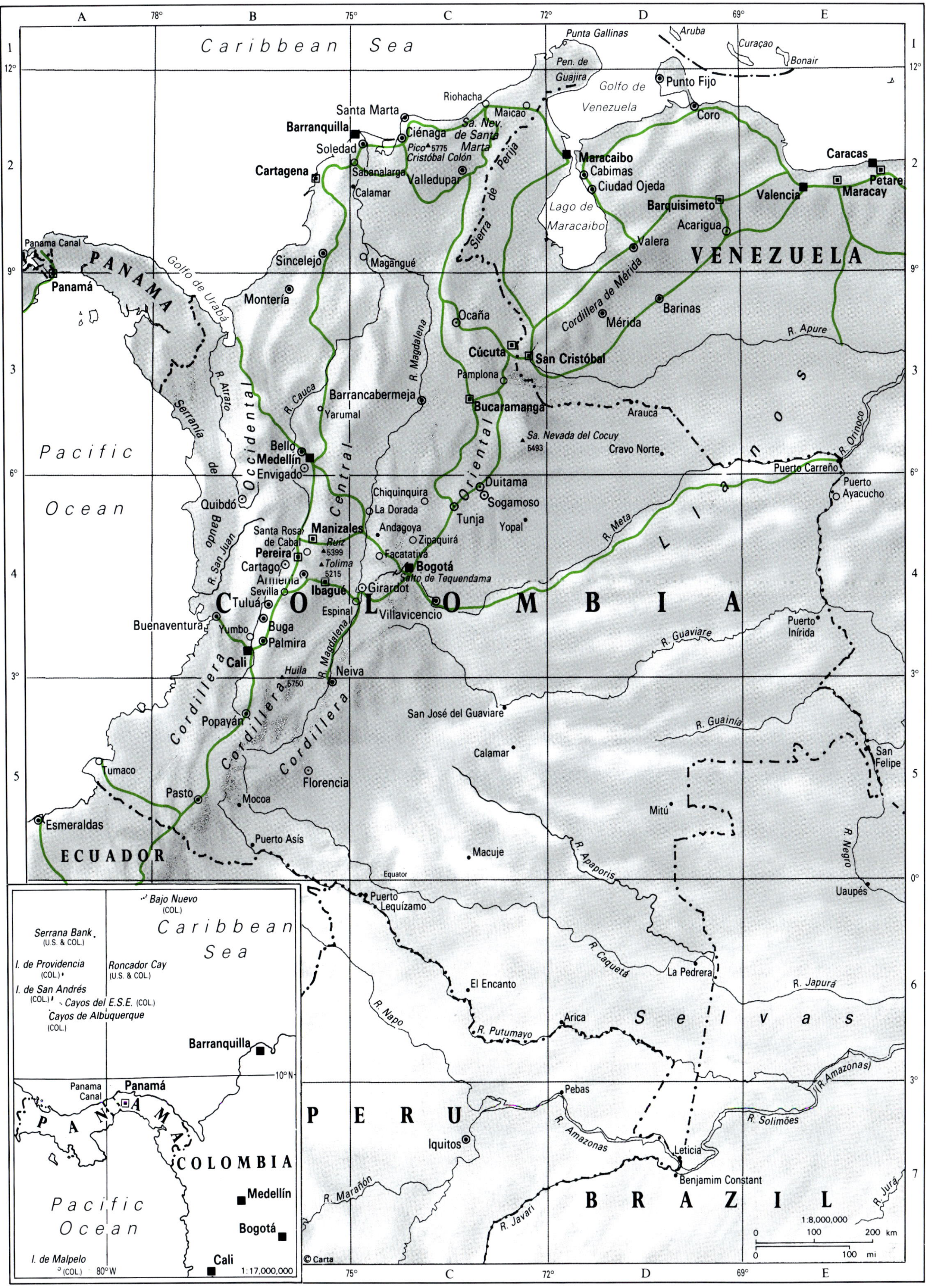

Caribbean Sea
Pacific Ocean
COLOMBIA
VENEZUELA
PANAMA
ECUADOR
PERU
BRAZIL
Llanos
Selvas
Bogotá
Medellín
Cali
Barranquilla
Cartagena
Santa Marta
Cúcuta
Bucaramanga
Manizales
Pereira
Ibagué
Neiva
Pasto
Popayán
Villavicencio
Leticia
Caracas
Maracaibo
Valencia
Barquisimeto
Panamá
Golfo de Venezuela
Lago de Maracaibo
Golfo de Urabá
Cordillera Occidental
Cordillera Central
Cordillera Oriental
R. Magdalena
R. Cauca
R. Orinoco
R. Meta
R. Guaviare
R. Caquetá
R. Putumayo
R. Amazonas
1:8,000,000
1:17,000,000
© Carta

Tequendama Falls, 1948

high southern part, it has convenient passes. The range descends gently to the Caribbean coastal plain, where it becomes partly submerged under thick beds of sediment deposited by the rivers draining the Colombian Andes. A deep and mostly narrow valley, drained by the river Cauca, runs between the Occidental and Central ranges. In the south, a number of high basins form a transitional structure between the high Andean plateau of Ecuador and southern Colombia and the Cauca valley, which extends for nearly 800 kilometers (500 miles) northward to the Caribbean lowlands. Like the Cordillera Central, the Cordillera Occidental has only small valleys, in which most of the population lives. The Cauca and some adjoining valleys constitute one of the most densely inhabited parts of the country, with two of Colombia's four large conurbations, Medellín and Cali.

The Cordillera Oriental has a much more complex and varied structure. It consists of short, noncontinuous ridges that follow a north-south direction, with some ridges running nearly parallel. This is particularly so in the middle part of the range, from the vicinity of Bogotá northward, where it reaches its maximum width of 225 kilometers (140 miles). The Cordillera Oriental rises well above the snow line (the highest peak is slightly over 5,490 meters [18,000 feet]), and extensive areas are snow-covered the year around. Another feature of the Cordillera Oriental is a number of high basins, three of which are comparatively large, resembling intermont plateaus. The capital, Bogotá, stands in one of these basins, the gently sloping surface of which is 2,440–2,740 meters (8,000–9,000 feet) high, which places the basin within a cool climatic zone. Below the level of the basins and high valleys, the Cordillera Oriental descends in steep, deeply dissected slopes. This is a rugged zone that leads down to the adjacent lowlands. The rivers here flow through narrow, precipitous valleys where they often form high falls. Among the most famous and beautiful of these falls are the Río Bogotá (120 meters [400 feet]) and the Tequendama, near Bogotá. The Magdalena is Colombia's main river, which drains most of the mountain region. The Cauca runs into it upon reaching the Caribbean lowland. The Magdalena is shallow, however, with many sandbars, and is navigable by small steamer only up to Neiva. Farther upstream navigation is obstructed by rapids. The Magdalena valley for much of its length is narrow and enclosed by steep slopes. Where it broadens, or where valleys of main tributaries converge with it, the population is comparatively dense. Settlement and agricultural activity has spread to some parts of the lower, more gentle, and easily accessible slopes overlooking the Magdalena valley.

The Lowlands

The lowlands along the Caribbean coast in the north consist mainly of a low-lying flat plain formed by the extensive deposition and accumulation of sediments carried down by the Cauca, Magdalena, and a few smaller rivers. This alluvial plain is interspersed with hills, descending spurs of the Andes, that extend in a south-north direction. The central part of these lowlands, especially around the mouth of the Magdalena, is one of the most densely inhabited areas of Colombia.

The extensive lowlands of the east, which cover nearly two-thirds of Colombia, belong to two large drainage basins, that of the Orinoco in the north and the Amazon in the south, and to two natural landscape regions, the Llanos in the north and the Selvas in the south. The westernmost fringes and some outlying spurs of the Guiana Highlands and of the Andes extend into the eastern lowlands. These give the vast undulating plain most of its topographical variety and its elevated areas, which rise well above the wide floodplains of the great rivers that cross it. The rivers are a dominant feature of both the physical and human landscapes of the region. Almost the entire population of the lowlands is settled on or near river banks. Rivers, some of which are navigable up to the eastern foot of the Andes, provide the main, if not the only, access to most parts of the lowlands.

Most of the Llanos is covered by scrubwoods, with dense gallery forests along the rivers. The southern half of the lowlands is almost entirely covered by equatorial rain forest with the characteristics of the Selvas, which dominates the vast Amazon plain.

CLIMATE

The basic characteristics of a wet tropical climate prevail over Colombia. Most of the country lies in the Northern Hemisphere but its southern part extends into the Southern Hemisphere, and each side of the equater has its corresponding seasons. The summer is the principal rainy season. The eastern lowlands and the Caribbean and Pacific coastal lowlands have tropical and equatorial climates with high temperatures and humidity throughout the year and abundant precipitation of over 1,000 millimeters (40 inches). There is no completely dry season, although the north and northwest have a comparatively drier winter.

In the mountainous region, climatic conditions are much more complex and varied. These variations depend on altitude, topographic position, and extent of exposure to prevailing winds and the sun. There are often extreme differences over short distances, especially with regard to precipitation. Slopes facing rain-bearing winds are amply supplied with rainfall, while the adjacent sheltered slopes and valleys have a dry climate. But climatic differences, which are reflected in the natural vegetation and which determine types of agricultural activity, are related mainly to the vertical zoning of the Colombian Andes, where natural conditions provide the full range of climates, from the torrid equatorial type to the permafrost of areas above 4,750 meters (15,000 feet). There are five vertical zones. The *tierra caliente* (hot zone) ranges from sea level to approximately 1,000 meters (3,300 feet). Here temperatures are high throughout the year, with small seasonal variations. The average temperatures of the hottest (December and January) and coolest (July) months at sea level are 28°C (82°F) and 27°C (80.5°F), respectively.

The next zone, the *tierra templada* (temperate zone), extends to an altitude of 2,000 meters (6,500 feet). Temperatures are lower, especially toward the higher altitudes, and precipitation is higher. In this zone is Colombia's second largest city, Medellín (1,500 meters [4,950 feet]), where the average temperatures for the hottest (June) and coldest (November) months are 21.7°C (71°F) and 20.6°C (69°F), respectively. The average annual rainfall is 1,400 millimeters (56 inches).

This is followed by the *tierra fría* (cool zone), ranging from 2,000 meters (6,500 feet) to 3,000 meters (10,000 feet). This is a much cooler area. The capital Bogotá (2,660 meters [8,730 feet]) is situated in the upper part of this zone, considered the most comfortable of Colombia's climates. The average temperatures for the hottest (March) and coolest (January) months are 15°C (59°F) and 14°C (57°F), respectively. The average annual rainfall is 1,050 millimeters (42 inches). Pasto, at about the same altitude (2,590 meters [8,500 feet]) in the south, has similar temperatures but less rainfall (800 millimeters [32 inches]). A large proportion of the population resides in this zone, especially in the high basins and valleys of the Cordillera Oriental.

The next zone, the lower part of which is only sparsely populated, is the *tierra helada*, or *páramos* (cold treeless zone), which extends to the snow line (3,000–4,500 meters [10,000–15,000 feet]). The average temperatures of the warmest and coolest months, at an altitude of 3,500 meters (11,400 feet) on the Cordillera Oriental (in the vicinity of Bogotá), are 11.5°C (53°F) and 10°C (50°F), respectively.

The upper zone is the *tierra nevada* (the snow-covered zone).

It should be emphasized that high maximum temperatures above 38°C (100°F) are common in the deep sheltered valleys.

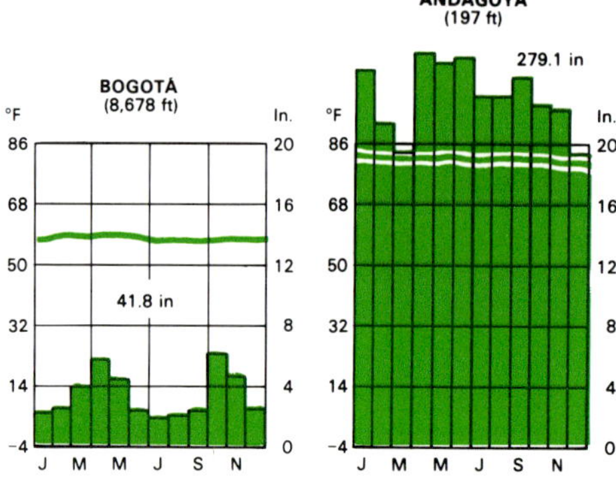

POPULATION

According to official estimates, the population numbered 31.5 million in 1990. It was 27.9 million at the 1985 census and has been growing at an average annual rate of nearly 2 percent over

FROM TIERRA CALIENTE TO TIERRA NEVADA

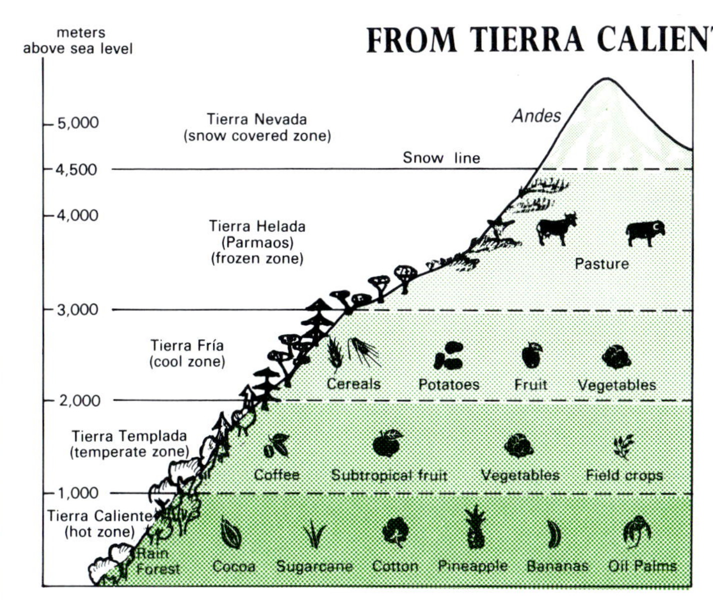

The Andes are divided climatically into five vertical zones, as reflected in the natural vegetation and types of agricultural activity. Much of the lower zone, the *tierra caliente* (hot zone), is covered by dense tropical forests. The main crops grown in this zone are cocoa, sugarcane, cotton, tropical fruit (pineapple, bananas), and oil palms. The next zone, the *tierra templada* (temperate zone), grows mainly coffee, the primary agricultural export of Colombia. Most subtropical fruit, vegetables, and field crops (rice) are also grown in this zone. This is followed by the *tierra fría* (cool zone), which produces much of the local food supply—cereals, potatoes, fruit, and vegetables. Next is the *tierra helada*, or *páramos*, a treeless zone whose vegetation of shrubs and herbs gradually becomes more scant and finally disappears toward the upper limit. The lower part of this zone is used as pasture, mainly for sheep and goats. The upper zone is the *tierra nevada* (the snow-covered zone), where permanent snow and glaciers are formed.

the last decade. The population has more than tripled over the last 50 years, mainly by natural increase but also by European immigration. It was 8.7 million in 1938 and 13.5 million in 1958.

Estimates of the racial composition of the population vary widely. The people of mixed European and American Indian race (mestizo) form the largest group, with estimates ranging from 45 to 68 percent of the population; people of pure European descent—20 to 25 percent; mixed European-African and Indian-African (mulatto)—14 to 20 percent; aboriginal Indians—5 to 7 percent; and blacks—5 to 8 percent. The proportions of these racial groups differ widely from one part of the country to the other. The percentage of blacks and mulattos (descendants of slaves) is much higher in the Caribbean lowlands and in the Cauca and Magdalena valleys. The proportion of mestizos is higher in the densely inhabited parts of the Cordillera Oriental. The unmixed Indian population partly resides in the high valleys of the Andes (Cordillera Central and Cordillera Oriental), where in some areas of the *páramos* zone they are the only inhabitants. These Indians are mostly descendants of the Chibcha tribes that inhabited the mountainous region when the first Europeans arrived. Other remaining Indian tribes dwell in the eastern lowlands, where in some areas they are still the only inhabitants. Native languages still predominate among groups of aboriginal Indians in some areas—Chibcha in the Andes and several other languages and dialects in the eastern and northern lowlands.

Almost the entire population (over 95 percent) is Roman Catholic, and nearly 1 percent is Protestant. Native religions are still prevalent among Indian tribes, especially in isolated areas in the eastern lowlands. Among some Indian communities, native beliefs and practices are maintained alongside an adherence to Christianity.

Most of Colombia is sparsely populated. The average population density for the country is 27 inhabitants per square kilometer (69 per square mile). Comparatively small parts are densely inhabited: the high basins of the Cordillera Oriental, especially that of Bogotá; parts of the Cauca and Magdalena valleys; and parts of the Caribbean lowlands. The great majority of the population lives in the temperate (*tierra templada*) and cool (*tierra fría*) climatic zones. In the eastern lowlands, the average population density is less than 1 person per square kilometer (2.5 per square mile), while most of the lowlands' Amazon basin (over 400,000 square kilometers [160,000 square miles]) has less than 0.2 persons per square kilometer (0.5 per square mile). The portion of the urban population is more than 70 percent, having increased rapidly over the last 40 years. It was 39.6 percent in 1951 and 52 percent in 1964. Conspicuous is the share in the population growth rate of the capital Bogotá, from 3.8 percent in 1938 to 16 percent in 1988, and that of Colombia's 16 large cities, from 16.6 percent in 1938 to 39 percent in 1988. Colombia has four conurbations of more than 1 million inhabitants: Bogotá—4.5 million (1989); Medellín—2.2 million; Cali—1.6 million; and Barranquilla—1.2 million. Three cities have more than half a million inhabitants: Bucaramanga—650,000; Cartagena—580,000; and Cúcuta—500,000. Other large cities include: Pereira—420,000; Manizales—360,000; Ibagué—320,000; Pasto 270,000; Palmira—240,000; Santa Marta—230,000; Neiva—210,000; Armenia—200,000; and Ciénaga—200,000. Twelve more cities have a population of 100,000-200,000. About 17 percent of the population is illiterate.

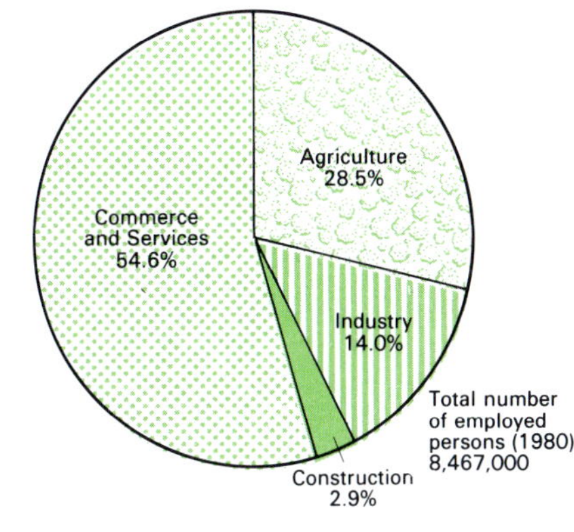

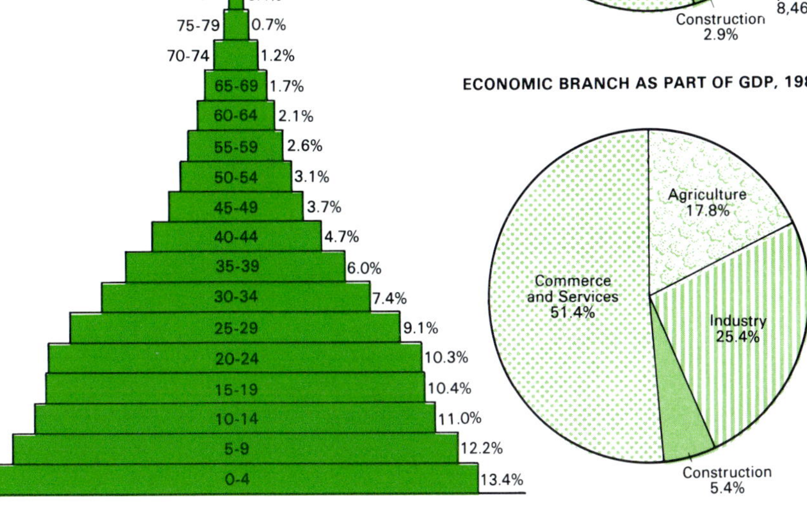

ECONOMY

Colombia's economy is based mainly on agriculture, the exploitation of mineral resources, and industry. Coffee plays a dominant role in agriculture, Colombia being the world's second largest producer. It is South America's leading producer of gold, nickel, and coal. Most of the country's land, water, and forest resources are not utilized. The GNP per capita was $1,240 in 1988 ($1,129 in 1986). The inflation rate was 24 percent in 1987. Colombia is one of the world's largest producers of coca and cannabis for the illegal international drug trade. It is alleged that drug exports in recent years have earned Colombia more in revenue than any other product.

The unemployment rate was 12 percent in 1987. It is higher in the main conurbations.

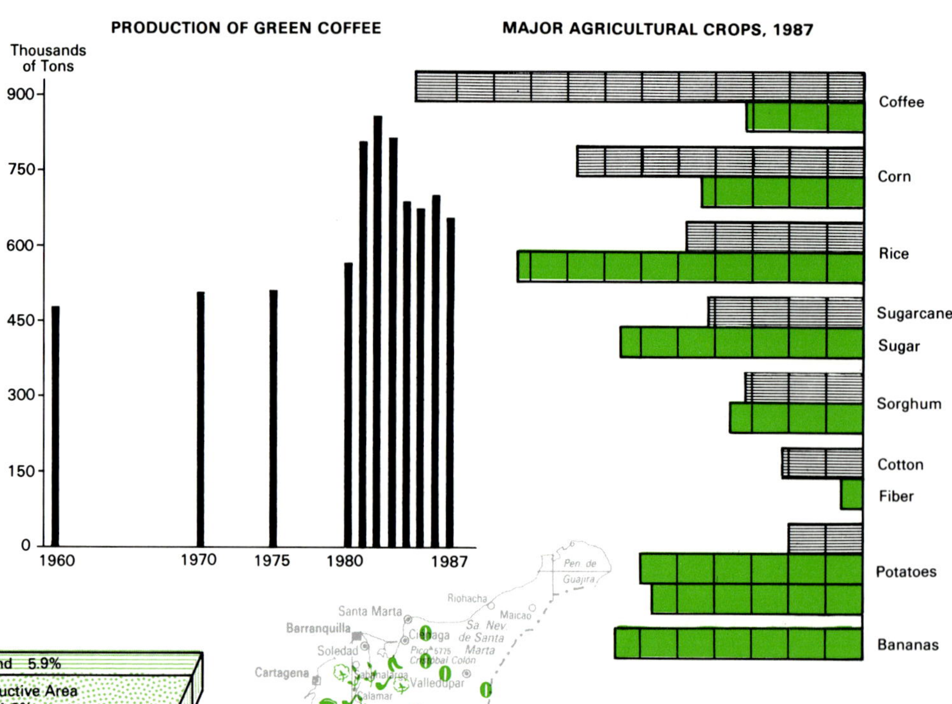

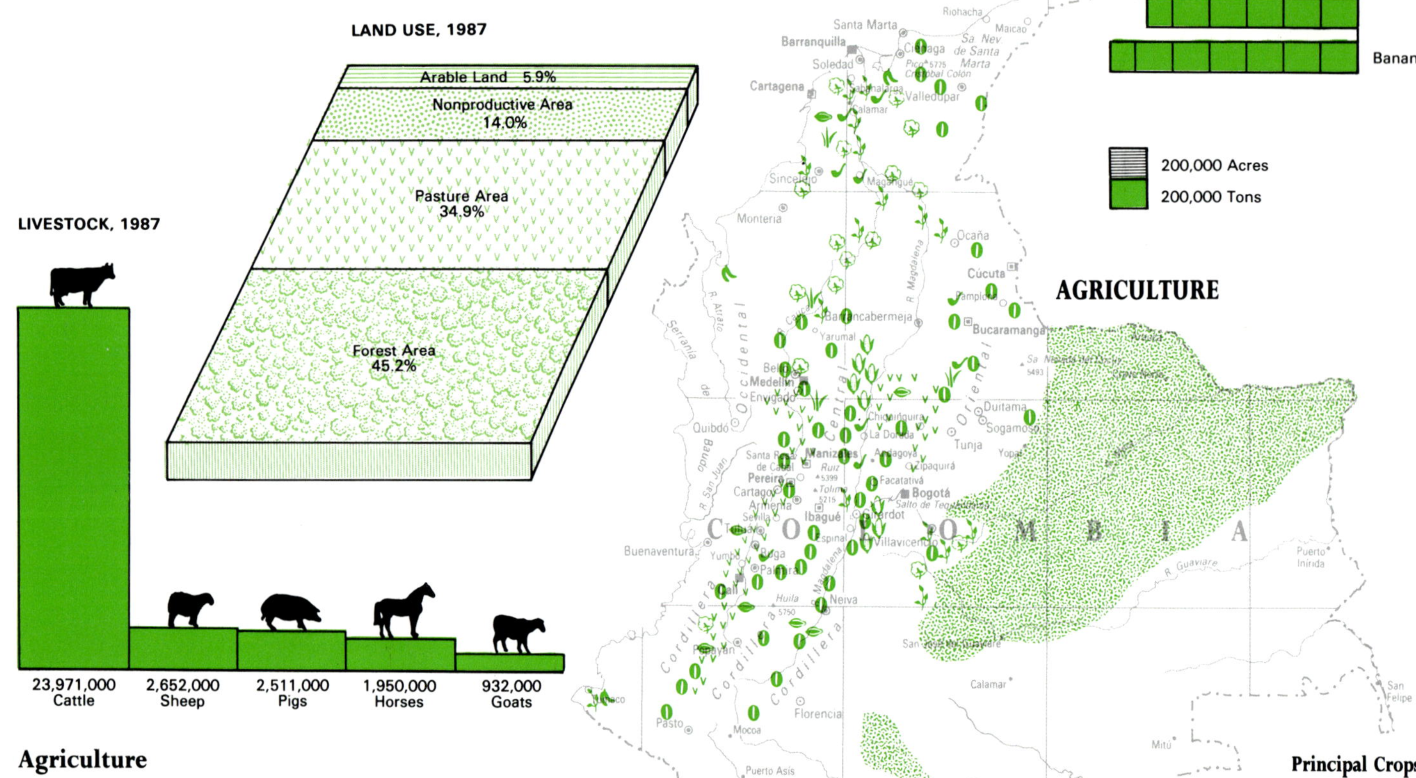

Agriculture

Only 6 percent of Colombia's area is cultivated, and arable land estimated to be at least 20 percent of the country's total area. Thirty-five percent could be used as permanent pasture. Forty-five percent of the country is covered by forest and scrubwood. Agriculture contributes about 25 percent of the local product and nearly 75 percent of the exports (excluding cocaine and cannabis). Coffee has been by far the most important commercial crop since the beginning of the twentieth century. It is grown mostly on small farms in the temperate zone of the Andes. There are approximately 300,000 coffee-growing farms, extending over a total area of 2.5 million acres, producing 654,000 tons of mostly high-quality coffee. Coffee provided one-third of all (legal) exports in 1987. Next in importance as export crops are bananas—1.3 million tons in 1987; cotton—427,000 acres, 114,000 tons of fiber; sugarcane—840,000 acres, 1.5 million tons of sugar; cocoa—252,000 acres, 51,000 tons; oil palms, 146,000 tons of oil; pineapple—228,000 tons; and flowers. Since the 1960s the government has encouraged the expansion of export production of several crops. As a result, the production of rice increased from 421,000 to 1.7 million tons between 1960 and 1980, and that of soybeans from 14,000 to 131,000 tons. The main crops for domestic consumption are corn (maize)—1.55 million acres, 888,000 tons; rice—960,000 acres, 1.9 million tons; sorghum—652,000 acres, 718,000 tons; potatoes—400,000 acres, 2.4 million tons; manioc—398,000 acres, 1.4 million tons; and tobacco—52,000 acres, 35,000 tons (1987 figures).

The vast forests of the eastern lowlands and the Andes yield 17.5 million cubic meters of timber annually as well as several types of resins. The share of the workforce in agriculture has declined from 54 percent in 1951 to 29 percent in 1988. The area under cultivation has more than doubled over the same period.

Livestock production, mostly on large estates, is concentrated mainly in and around the upper Magdalena and Cauca valleys, in the vicinity of Medellín, and at the western fringes of the Colombian Llanos. Animal products figure prominently in agricultural exports. Twenty-four million cattle, 2.7 million sheep, 2.5 million pigs, nearly 2 million horses, and 932,000 goats were raised in 1987.

Mineral Resources

Gold (placer), found in several valleys of the mountainous region, was largely responsible for bringing the Spaniards to Colombia during the first stages of colonization. The sites of many of the first permanent Spanish settlements were chosen for their proximity to gold. Many of the African slaves brought to Colombia were employed in gold mines. Gold, both placer and vein, is mined in many valleys, mainly in the Cordillera Central and Cordillera Occidental. Most mines are small, and the most important are located in the Antioquía district. Production was 26,300 kilograms (853,470 ounces) in 1987. There are also several platinum mines (mainly in the San Juan valley), which produced 448 kilograms (15,800 ounces) in 1987; silver mines (in the Antioquía district and the Cordillera Oriental) which produced 4,742 kilograms (167,280 ounces); and emerald mines, mainly northeast of Bogotá. Other minerals produced are nickel (north of Medellín)—19,000 tons; iron—508,000 tons; sulfur—41,000 tons; phosphate—23,000 tons; and rock salt—228,000 tons (an additional 517,000 tons of salt were produced from the sea) (1987 figures). There are also deposits of copper, lead, manganese, and mercury. Colombia has the largest coal deposits in South America; 14.6 million tons were produced in 1987. Colombia's oilfields produced 17.4 million tons of oil in 1988 (an average of 451,000 barrels per day in 1989). Scattered over wide areas, the main oilfields are near the Venezuelan frontier in the northeast and in the central and lower Magdalena valley. Natural gas fields in the Guajira peninsula produced 5,280 million cubic meters of gas. Hydroelectric power stations produce 70 percent of the country's electricity.

Industry

Colombia has a variety of industries, engaged mainly in processing agricultural, mineral, and forest products and in supplying domestic demand for a wide range of consumer goods, machinery, vehicles, tools, building materials, chemicals, wood products, and paper. Industrial development began after World War I, when the coffee export boom created much surplus capital. A general rise in the standard of living stimulated domestic demand for many manufactured commodities. Between 1919 and 1945 the number of industrial plants grew from 121 to 7,850 and the number of workers rose from approximately 1,500 to 135,000. The number of plants had doubled by the mid-1980s, and their average size had grown considerably. About 20 percent of the workforce is employed in industry (nearly 2 million workers in 1988). The main industries are textiles (using local cotton and wool), apparel and footwear, food processing, tobacco, iron and steel (partly using local coal and iron ore, 607,000 tons of steel in 1987), metal products, automobile assembly (52,000 vehicles in 1987), chemicals (fertilizers), oil refining and petrochemical products, cement, wood pulp, and paper. The illegal drug industry has processing plants and is believed to employ thousands of workers.

About 70 percent of the country's industry is concentrated in and around the three main urban centers—Bogotá, Medellín, and Cali. Barranquilla and its vicinity are another industrial center. The large iron and steel plant in the Cordillera Oriental, 260 kilometers (160 miles) north of Bogotá, was built near iron and coal resources.

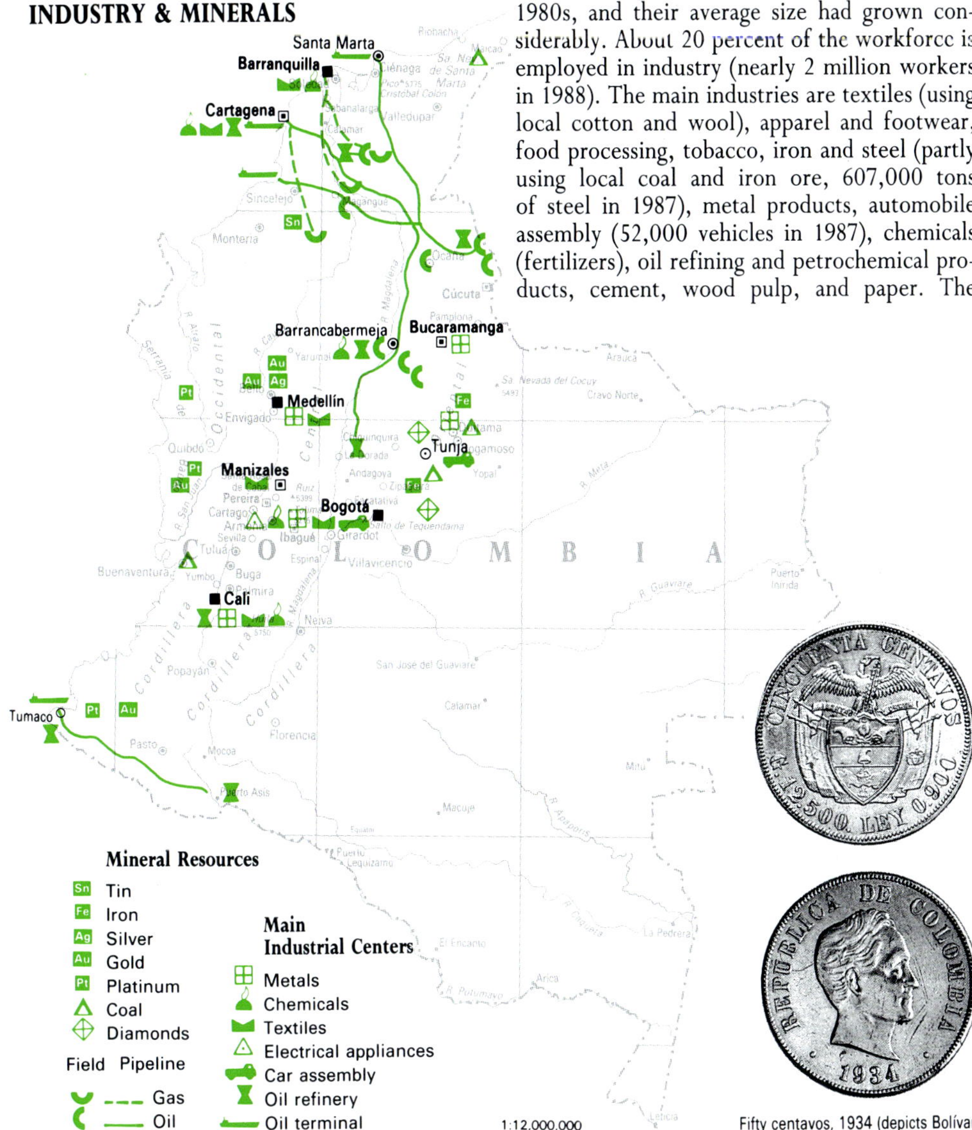

Fifty centavos, 1934 (depicts Bolívar)

Trade

The country's main trading partners are the United States (36 percent of exports and 38 percent of imports in 1988); West Germany (18 and 8 percent); Japan (5 and 11 percent); and France (3 and 4.4 percent).

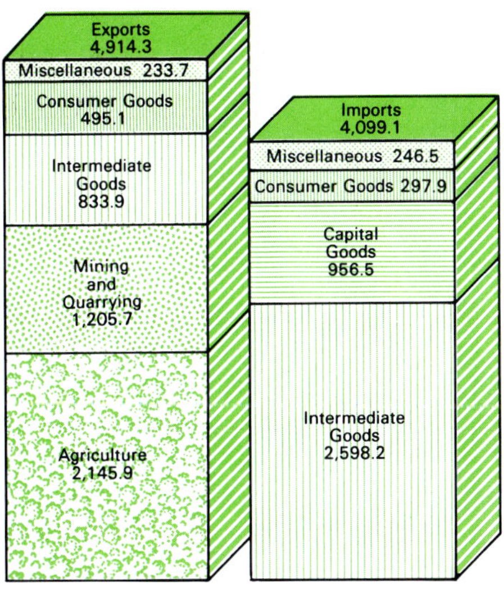

HISTORY

Many different Indian tribes lived in what is now Colombia when the first Spaniards settled on the Caribbean coast early in the sixteenth century. The largest and most widespread were the Chibchas, the majority of whom were sedentary and practiced subsistence agriculture. They were concentrated mainly in the highland basins and valleys of the Cordillera Oriental. Various small tribes, mostly nomadic, lived in the Caribbean lowlands, the Atrato and San Juan valleys, and near the Pacific coast. Small tribes in the eastern lowlands were the most primitive; many of these maintained their isolation well into the twentieth century.

The first Spanish settlement was established in 1510 on the coast of the Gulf of Urabá (Caribbean Sea) but was abandoned after a few years. Santa Marta and Cartagena (founded in 1525 and 1533, respectively) were the earliest permanent settlements. Bogotá was founded in 1538, followed by more than 20 other settlements by the middle of the sixteenth century. About the same time, Spaniards moving northward from Peru reached southern Colombia and founded Pasto and Popayán. Spanish settlement grew and expanded during the seventeenth century, stimulated by the sources of gold and silver. Gradually, an increasing number of settlers turned to agriculture. Large estates were established using the Indians and later Africans for forced labor. As in most other countries of South America, Spanish settlers were mainly males who took native Indian wives. By the end of the seventeenth century the population in the European settlements was largely mestizo. Colombia was part of the territory known as New Granada, which also extended over present-day Panama, Venezuela, and Ecuador. This territory was at first under the control of the Viceroyalty of Peru, but in 1740 it became the Viceroyalty of New Granada. The population of Colombia was estimated at approximately 800,000 in 1770. It is believed to have crossed the 1-million mark early in the nineteenth century. In 1811 the population in parts of Colombia rose up against Spanish colonial rule. A period of armed struggle followed. "Greater (Gran) Colombia," whose independence was declared in 1819, extended over the former Viceroyalty of New Granada. It dissolved in 1830, when Venezuela and Equador declared their independence. Colombia and Panama became the Republic of New Granada in 1831. Political and economic rivalry between the different social groups plunged the country into a long period of internal instablility with intermittent civil wars and dictatorships. This continued into the twentieth century. In an attempt to overcome the regional conflict and dissension, the country was given a new constitution and, in 1863, turned into a federation of nine states called the United States of Colombia. A new constitution, which came into force in 1886, abolished the federation and divided Colombia into departments with some local autonomy. In 1903 Panama withdrew from Colombia and declared its independence.

The production of high-grade coffee, which began to play an important role in the country's economy in the 1880s, expanded rapidly in the early twentieth century, becoming Colombia's principal source of wealth. The growing profits from coffee had a decisive impact on the economic and political development of modern Colombia.

Colombia's population, which numbered about 3 million in 1870, grew to 4.1 million by 1905 and to nearly 6 million by 1918. Natural increase has been largely responsible for population growth.

GOVERNMENT AND POLITICS

Colombia is divided administratively into 23 departments, four intendancies, and five commissariats. The intendancies and commissariats of the sparsely inhabited territories of the eastern lowlands are directly administered by the central government. The departments are headed by governors appointed by the central government, but their administration has limited local autonomy, especially in financial matters. The country is governed by a president with wide executive powers who is elected by direct popular vote to a single four-year term. The president appoints the government. The bicameral legislature is composed of a 114-member Senate and a 199-member House of Representatives, both of whose members are elected by the people to a four-year term.

Two main parties—the Liberal Party and the Conservative Party—dominate internal politics. Regional rivalries, focused on the large conurbations, mainly Bogotá, Medellín, and Cali, are important aspects of political life. After a long period of internal strife and instability, the two major parties agreed in 1957 to govern alternately for four-year periods and maintain political equality throughout the administration. This arrangement has operated since the presidential elections of 1958, except for the period from 1970 to 1978, when two successive presidents were leaders of the Conservative Party. The other, much smaller, parties are the New Liberals (a faction which seceded from the Liberal Party) and the Patriotic Union (an extreme left-wing movement formed by a coalition between a former underground organization, the Revolutionary Armed Forces of Colombia, and the Colombian Communist Party). Armed leftist terrorist organizations are active in some areas. The organizations that control most of the illegal production and trade in drugs (cocaine, marijuana) are very influential in some centers and have their own armed forces that have carried out many terrorist acts.

In the elections held on March 11, 1990, César Gavira Trujillo was elected president, and the composition of the Senate was as follows: Liberal Party (PL)—72; Conservative Party (PC)—41; and Patriotic Union (UP)—1. In the House of Representatives, the Liberal Party secured about 60 percent of the 199 seats.

BOGOTÁ

Bogotá is the capital of Colombia and of one of the country's most populated departments (provinces), Cundinamarca. Bogotá lies in the heart of a conurbation whose population approached 5 million in 1990, or about 16 percent

Administrative Division

Commissariats	Capitals	area sq mi	area sq km	population (1983 estimate)
Amazonas	Leticia	42,342	109,665	18,000
Guainía	San Felipe	27,891	72,238	11,000
Guaviare	Guaviare	16,342	42,327	37,000
Vaupés	Mitú	25,200	65,268	
Vichada	Puerto Carreño	38,703	100,242	14,000
Departments				
Antioquía	Medellín	24,561	63,612	4,081,700
Atlántico	Barranquilla	1,308	3,388	1,379,100
Bolívar	Cartagena	10,030	25,978	1,076,800
Boyacá	Tunja	8,953	23,189	1,100,400
Caldas	Manizales	3,046	7,888	870,600
Caquetá	Florencia	34,349	88,965	302,300
Cauca	Popayán	11,316	29,308	821,700
César	Valledupar	8,844	22,905	542,600
Chocó	Quibdó	17,965	46,530	253,500
Córdoba	Montería	9,660	25,020	861,900
Cundinamarca	Bogotá	8,735	22,623	*1,288,000
Huila	Neiva	7,680	19,890	272,900
La Guajira	Riohacha	8,049	20,848	510,200
Magdalena	Santa Marta	8,953	23,188	610,100
Meta	Villavicencio	33,064	85,635	384,800
Nariño	Pasto	12,845	33,268	947,000
Norte de Santander	Cúcuta	8,362	21,658	878,300
Quindío	Armenia	712	1,845	352,700
Risaralda	Pereira	1,598	4,140	630,800
Santander	Bucaramanga	11,790	30,537	1,367,600
Sucre	Sincelejo	4,215	10,917	398,400
Tolima	Ibagué	9,097	23,562	1,128,900
Valle	Cali	8,548	22,140	2,848,600
Intendancies				
Arauca	Arauca	9,196	23,818	82,000
Casanare	Yopal	17,236	44,640	
Putumayo	Mocoa	9,608	24,885	79,000
San Andrés and Providencia	San Andrés	17	44	30,000
Special District				
Bogotá		613	1,587	4,483,300
Total		****440,831**	**1,141,748**	**27,663,200**

* Population for the city of Bogotá is included with the special district.
**Detail does not add to total given because of rounding.

Bogotá's cathedral at Plaza de Bolívar

of the country's inhabitants. Over the last three to four decades it has been one of the fastest-growing conurbations. Its population has actually quadrupled since 1960, when it stood at 1.2 million. The area was the main center, called Bacatá, of the Chibcha Indians when the Spaniards arrived and conquered it in 1538. This was an expedition under the command of Gonzalo Jiménez de Quesada, who set out from the Caribbean coast along the Magdalena valley into Colombia's interior. The Spanish settlement of Santa Fé de Bacatá was established on the site. The present name is a distortion of the original Indian name.

The city is situated on the eastern fringes of a large and fertile basin in the Cordillera Oriental, at an altitude of 2,660 meters (8,730 feet). Much of it is built on a surface that slopes westward from the foot of the range that rises above to the east and gives the surrounding landscape a distinct beauty. Difficult access to the city from the coast and other centers of settlement greatly impeded its development until its isolation was gradually overcome by modern means of transportation at the end of the nineteenth century. In 1740 it became the capital of the newly formed Viceroyalty of New Granada and, in 1819, of the independent Gran Colombia, a confederation that was later reduced to the size of present-day Colombia.

The main part of Bogotá is laid out in a gridiron pattern, with the older part forming its government and business center. It is a mixture of old and new, with squares (plazas) dominated by seventeenth-century churches and colonial-style buildings that represent some of the finest premodern architecture in South America side by side with modern office buildings and skyscrapers. South of the center are extensive poor and slum areas, while to the north are mainly the wealthier businesses, residential areas, and suburbs. Bogotá has several universities (the oldest and most prestigious is Universidad de Santo Tomás, founded in the seventeenth century), other institutions of higher learning, museums, and art galleries. There are also a number of attractive parks and beautiful scenic sites in and around the city.

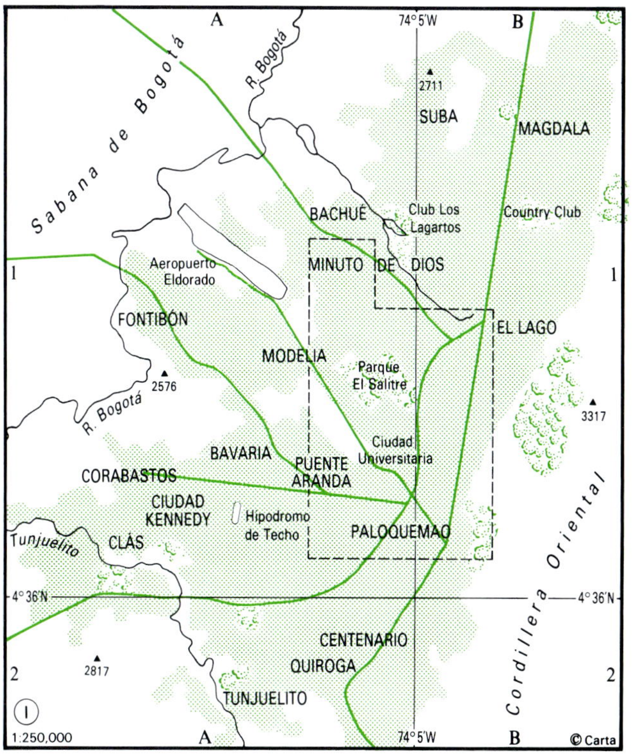

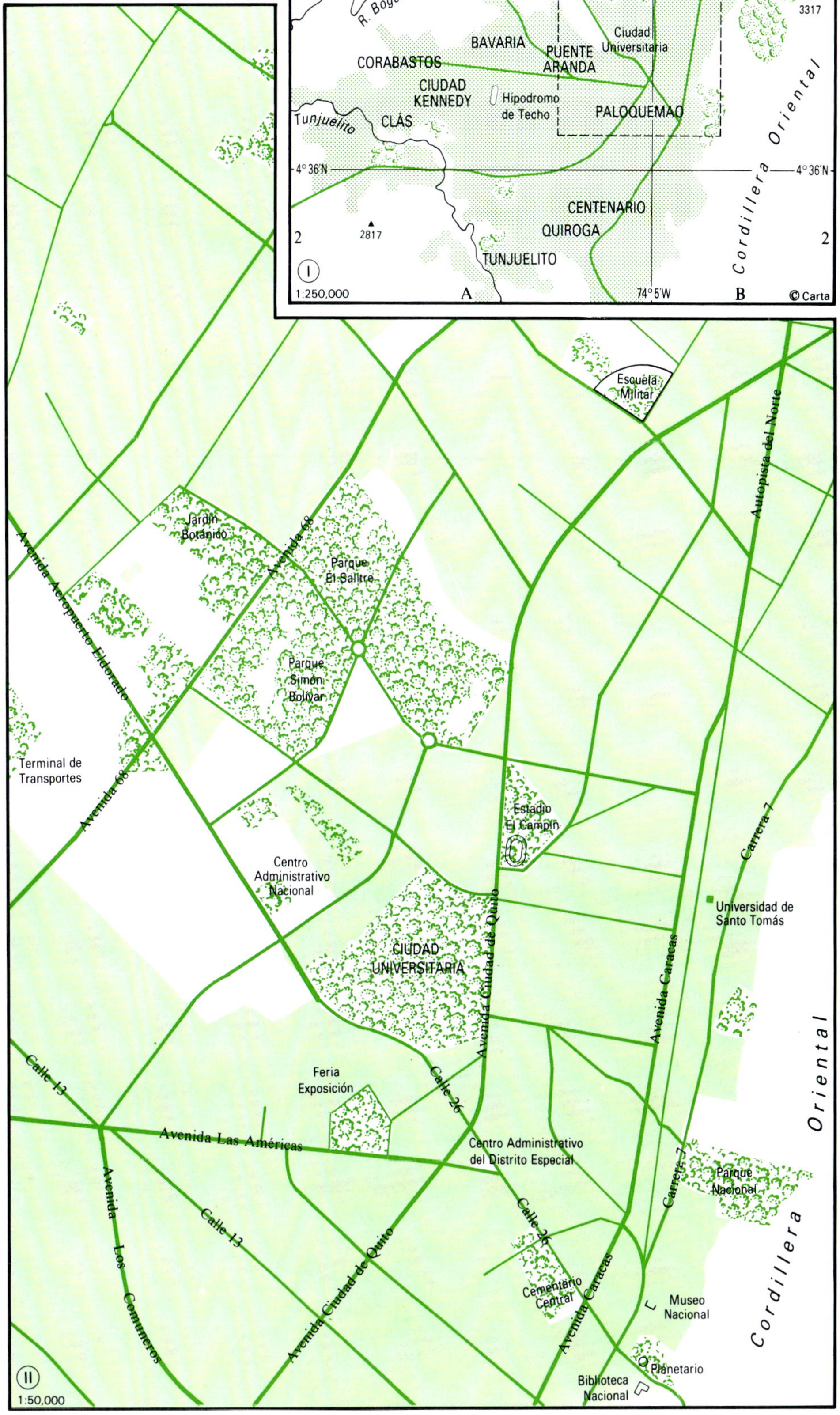

ECUADOR

Area
269,178 sq. km.
103,930 sq. mi.

Population
10,782,000 (1990 estimate)

Capital City
Quito

Gross National Product (GNP) Per Capita
$1,080 (1988)

Population in Main Cities
(1987 estimates)
Quito 1,137,705
Guayaquil 1,572,615
Cuenca 201,490
Riobamba 149,800
Machala 144,396

Highest Point
6,267 m. 20,561 ft. (Chimborazo)

Currency Unit
1 sucre = 100 centavos

Density
35.8 persons per sq. km.
92.8 persons per sq. mi. (1986)

Urban-Rural
urban 52.8% rural 47.2% (1986)

Natural Increase
2.8% (1985-1990)

Life Expectancy
65.4 (1985-1990)

Doctors
850 inhabitants per doctor (1985)

Hospital Beds
1.7 per thousand inhabitants (1986)

Infant Mortality
63.4 per thousand live births (1985-1990)

High School Pupils
54.7% of age group 13-18 (1985)

University Students
33.1% of age group 20-24 (1984)

Illiteracy Rate
17.6% (1985)

National Holiday
Quito's Independence Day, 10 August

National Anthem
Slave, O Patria
(Hail, O Fatherland)

Ecuador is the smallest of the Andean countries. It has the highest average population density in South America and the highest percentage of native Americans. As its name indicates, Ecuador (equator in Spanish) extends over both sides of the equator. It is bordered in the north by Colombia and in the east and south by Peru (a disputed boundary). The Galápagos Islands are a province of Ecuador located 1,040 kilometers (650 miles) off Ecuador's Pacific coast.

NATURAL REGIONS

The country consists of three distinct geographical regions: the Pacific coastal lowlands in the west; the highlands (Andes) in the center; and the eastern lowlands (Oriente). The last, which forms nearly half the country's area, is only sparsely populated. The coastal lowlands are the most populated and economically the most important part of Ecuador; this has been the case only since the end of the nineteenth century. Until then, especially before the arrival of the Europeans and during the colonial period, the great majority of the population lived in the highlands.

The Coastal Lowlands

The coastal lowlands are in general relatively flat, interspersed with low hills that are spurs of the Andes. The most prominent is a line of hills reaching an altitude of approximately 750 meters (2,500 feet) that extends to the coast at Guayaquil. Huge alluvial fans line the eastern part of the coastal lowlands along the foot of the Andes and give the landscape a hilly character. The northern part of the coastal lowlands is covered by a tropical rain forest, while in the south there is a rapid transition to the arid conditions that prevail also over the coastal region of Peru.

The coastal lowlands are the most productive part of Ecuador, especially insofar as agricultural exports are concerned. However, only the central part, the Guayas and Los Ríos provinces, has a comparatively dense rural population.

The Highlands

Two parallel ranges, a southern extension of the Colombian ranges—the Cordillera Occidental and the Cordillera Central—make up the highland region. The two ranges are separated by a succession of ten main basins that form part of a long, deep rift valley. The intense volcanic activity characteristic of this rift valley has produced the discontinuities that resulted in a series of basins. Rising alongside the basins are thirty volcanoes, many of them active, with some of the world's highest, largest, and most beautiful snow-capped volcanic cones. These include Mount Chimborazo (6,267 meters [20,561 feet]) and Cotopaxi (5,897 meters [19,347 feet]), the world's highest active volcano. Most of the basin floors are covered with a thick mantle of volcanic material (mainly ash and decomposed or eroded lava). The base elevation of these basins varies from approximately 750 meters (2,500 feet) to 2,900 meters (9,500 feet). The mountain slopes enclosing them are generally steep and often rugged. Most of the basins are densely inhabited; in some, the population is almost entirely Indian and in others, Indian and mestizo. Most of the rural population practices subsistence agriculture. In the higher basins the main crop is potatoes, grown up to an altitude of approximately 3,400 meters (11,000 feet). Corn (maize), wheat, barley, and various vegetables are grown in the lower basins. The higher basins and adjacent slopes are used mostly for pasture. The most inhabited and productive basins are those of Quito in the north and Cuenca in the south.

With the exception of these basins and some adjoining valleys, the two ranges of the cordillera (Andes) are only sparsely populated wherever topographic, soil, and climatic conditions allow cultivation and animal husbandry. Many of the peaks in both ranges rise to over 4,000 meters (13,000 feet), and some are higher than the snow line, 4,500–4,800 meters (15,000–15,700 feet). Large parts of the lower slopes, especially in the north, are covered by forests; these thin out toward the south and gradually change to scrub in the drier areas and in the deep, sheltered slopes and valleys.

The Eastern Lowlands

The eastern lowlands are part of the Amazon Basin. An undulating plain slopes gently eastward and is drained mainly by the Putumayo (which flows along part of the boundary with Colombia), Napo, and Pastaza rivers and their tributaries. This region is covered almost entirely by dense tropical rain forest. Most of it is uninhabited; settlement is confined to the foot of the Andes and to small areas along the banks of the main rivers, where some agriculture is practiced. The rivers are the main or only means of access to most parts of this region. The main rivers are navigable to small craft up to the foot of the Andes.

CLIMATE

Climatic conditions generally reflect the country's equatorial latitude and local vertical altitudes. There are almost no seasonal variations in temperature. The average temperatures of the hottest and coolest months at Quito (2,850 meters [9,350 feet]) are 12.7°C (54.9°F) and 12.5°C (54.5°F), respectively, and at Guayaquil (sea level) 27.2°C (81.0°F) and 24.5°C (76.0°F). Seasonal differences are reflected mainly in variations in rainfall. There is no dry season in the extreme north, where maximum rainfall occurs twice (March–April; September–November). This changes gradually to southward, until there is a single rainy season, from November to June, which becomes shorter farther south (January to May in Guayaquil). In the coastal lowlands the average annual precipitation decreases southward, from more than 1,700 millimeters (68 inches) in the north, to 1,000 millimeters (40 inches) at Guayaquil, and to 200 millimeters (8 inches) farther south.

The vertical zones are similar to those of other Andean countries. The *tierra caliente* (hot zone) extends to an upper limit of 1,000 meters (3,300 feet). Most of this zone is in

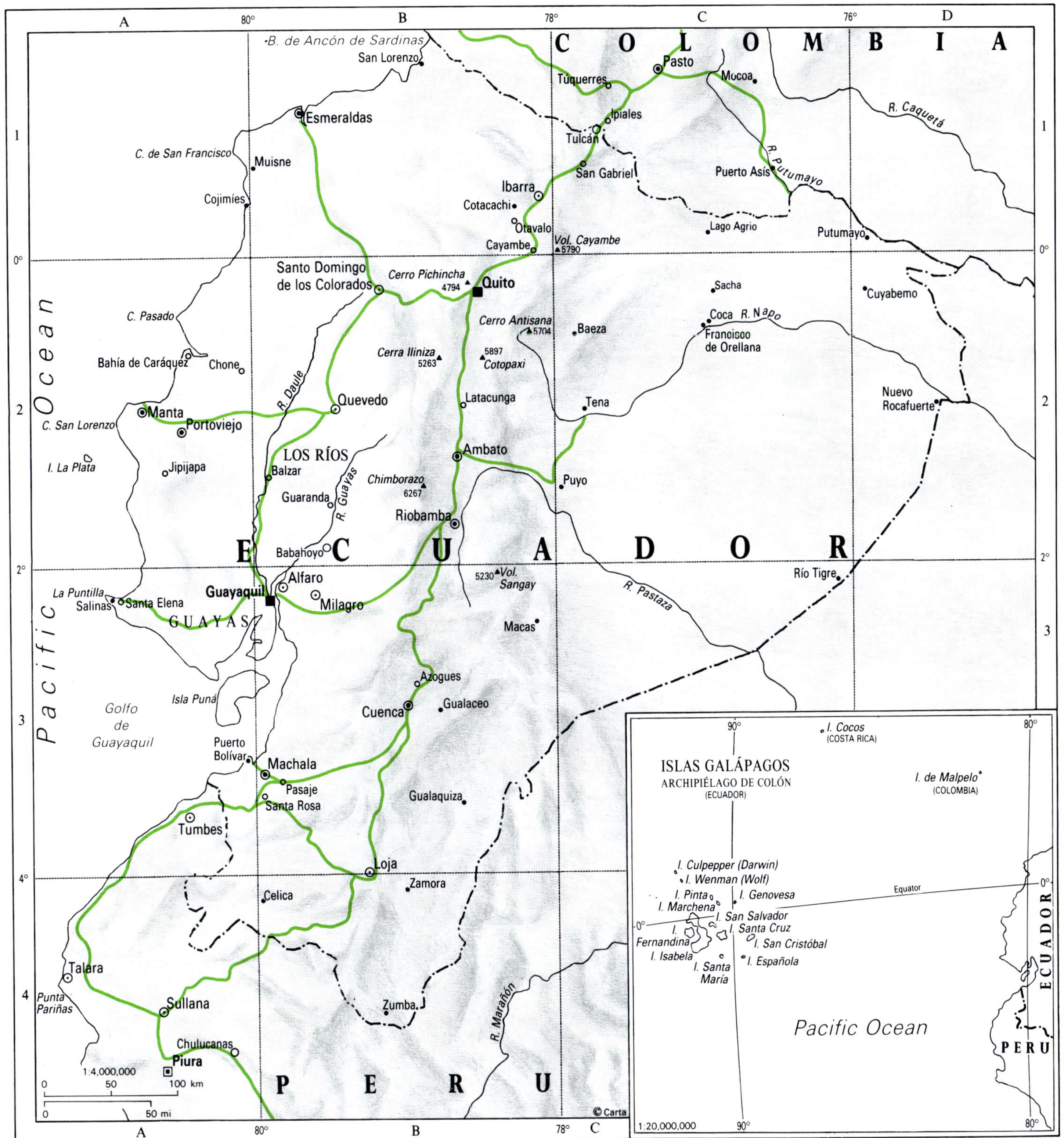

THE GALÁPAGOS ISLANDS (Archipiélago de Colón)

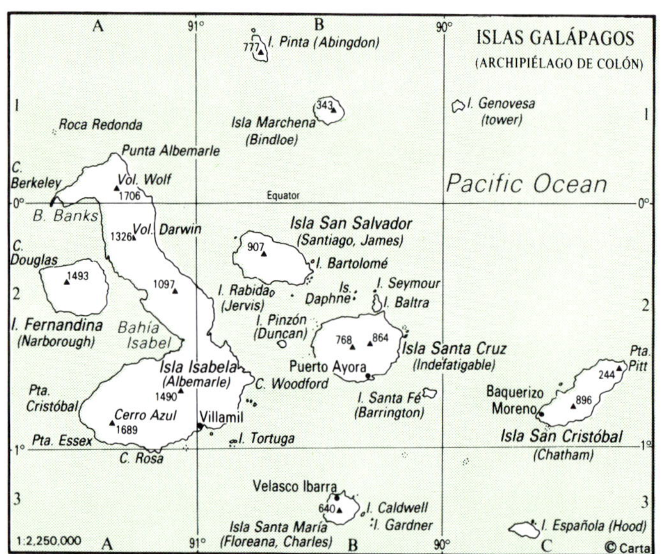

The Galápagos are a group of twelve volcanic islands and numerous islets and rocks 1,040 kilometers (650 miles) off the Pacific coast of Ecuador. They form the country's twentieth province, known as the province of Colón. The area of the islands is 7,994 square kilometers (3,086 square miles). Only two are inhabited—Isabela (Albemarle), the largest of the group, and San Cristóbal (Chatham). The population was nearly 8,000 in 1987. The islands are hilly, rising to a height of 1,500 meters (5,000 feet), and there are several active volcanoes.

The Galápagos are famous for their unique fauna and flora, which include species not found elsewhere. Best known are the huge tortoise (*galápago* in Spanish) and some species of lizards. Charles Darwin visited the islands in 1830. It was here that he made the major portion of his observations that led to his theories on evolution and the *Origin of the Species*. Many scientists have since carried out research on the islands. When the islands were discovered by Spanish sailors early in the sixteenth century they were uninhabited. The islands were given English names by British sailors, who visited in the seventeenth century.

Land iguana

Giant tortoise

Frigatebird

the coastal and eastern lowlands. The *tierra templada* (temperate zone), ranging from 1,000 to 2,000 meters (3,300 to 6,500 feet), extends over some intermont basins, valleys, and slopes of the Andes. The *tierra fría* (cool zone), from 2,000 to 3,000 meters (6,500 to 10,000 feet), is the climatic zone of most of the basins and densely inhabited valleys of the mountain region, including the capital Quito and the other important urban centers of Cuenca and Riobamba. The *páramos* (cold treeless zone), which extends to the snow line (3,000–4,600 meters [10,000–15,000 feet]), is partly utilized as a grazing area for sheep. Its lower part is sparsely populated by small Indian villages.

GUAYAQUIL (20 ft) — 38.8 in

QUITO (9,446 ft) — 43.9 in

POPULATION

Ecuador's population was estimated at 10.7 million in 1989. The average annual rate of natural increase has been 2.8 percent over the last decade, the highest of any country in South America. The population has increased nearly tenfold since the beginning of the twentieth century (when it was estimated at 1.1 million). The increase was most rapid over the last 40 years, from slightly more than 3 million in 1950, to 4.5 million in 1962, and to 6.5 million in 1974. The average annual growth rate was highest in the 1960s when it was 3.3 percent. Immigration then played only a marginal role in population growth.

Native Americans are believed to make up 40 to 60 percent of the total population; mestizos, 40 to 50 percent; blacks and mulattos, 5 to 10 percent; and unmixed Europeans, 5 to 10 percent. The official national language is Spanish, but nearly 30 percent of the people speak aboriginal languages. The Indians are concentrated mainly in the highland region, where they form the great majority of the population. They are descendants of the Quechua and affiliated tribes and speak Quechua, the language of nearly a quarter of the population. Descendants of the Chibcha tribes live in the northern and northeastern part of the country. The primitive tribes of the Amazon Basin inhabit the sparsely populated eastern region. Nearly the entire population is Catholic. The Indian tribes of the eastern region practice their native religions.

About 52 percent of the population lives in the coastal lowlands, with an average population density of nearly 80 persons per square kilometer (200 per square mile). The most densely inhabited province is Guayas (which includes the conurbation of Guayaquil) with 130 persons per square kilometer (330 per square mile). Forty-five percent of the population resides in the highland region, which has an average population density of 70 persons per square kilometer (175 per square mile). Here, the small province of Tungurahua is the most densely inhabited, with 124 persons per square kilometer (317 per square mile). Slightly more than 3 percent of the population lives in the eastern lowlands, which has an average density of only 2.5 persons per square kilometer (6 per square mile). The development of oilfields and agriculture over the last 25 years has resulted in a significant increase in population in the eastern region (from 75,000 in 1962 to 340,000 in 1988). The average population density for

Ecuador as a whole is 37 persons per square kilometer (95 per square mile). The proportion of the population that lives in urban areas is 53 percent; it was 35 percent in 1962.

Ecuador has two large conurbations: Quito, the capital, with a population of 1.2 million (1988), and Guayaquil, the main port and economic center, with 1.6 million. Both have grown rapidly since World War II. Their respective populations were 210,000 and 260,000 in 1950, 355,000 and 511,000 in 1962, and 565,000 and 861,000 in 1974. Other urban centers are much smaller: Cuenca—210,000; Riobamba—155,000; Machala—150,000; Portoviejo—145,000; and Ambato—125,000. The illiteracy rate is 17 percent.

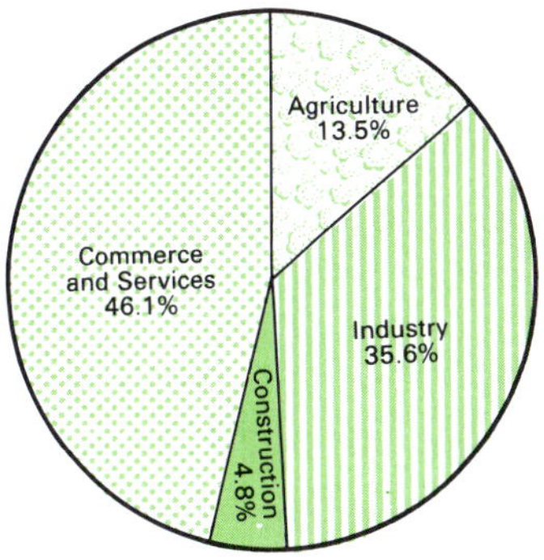

POPULATION BY AGE GROUP, 1988

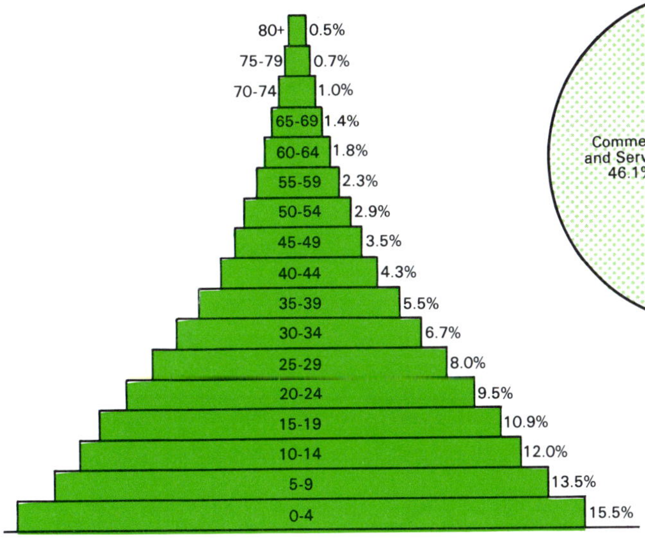

Age group	Percent
80+	0.5%
75-79	0.7%
70-74	1.0%
65-69	1.4%
60-64	1.8%
55-59	2.3%
50-54	2.9%
45-49	3.5%
40-44	4.3%
35-39	5.5%
30-34	6.7%
25-29	8.0%
20-24	9.5%
15-19	10.9%
10-14	12.0%
5-9	13.5%
0-4	15.5%

EMPLOYMENT BY ECONOMIC BRANCH, 1982

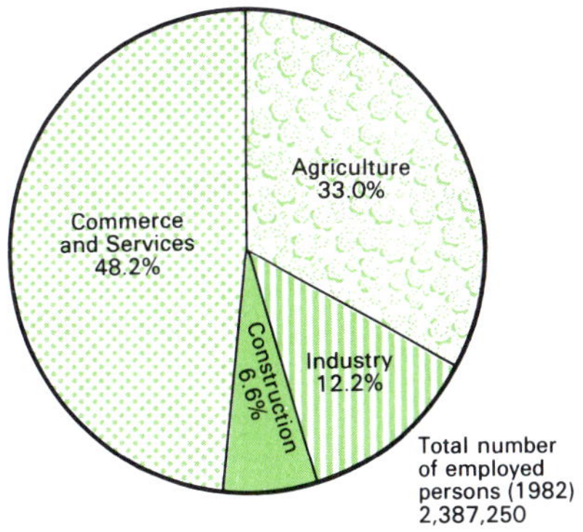

Agriculture 33.0%
Commerce and Services 48.2%
Construction 6.6%
Industry 12.2%
Total number of employed persons (1982) 2,387,250

ECONOMIC BRANCH AS PART OF GDP, 1984

Agriculture 13.5%
Commerce and Services 46.1%
Construction 4.8%
Industry 35.6%

ECONOMY

Main Industrial Centers
Chemicals
Textiles
Oil refinery
Oil terminal

Principal Crops
Wheat
Corn
Citrus
Cotton
Sugarcane
Bananas
Rice
Cocoa
Coffee
Coco

Mineral Resources
Gold
Gas field
Oil field
Oil pipeline

1:5,000,000

Esmeraldas
Quito
Lago Agrio
Sacha
Ambato
Guayaquil
Santa Elena
Cuenca
ECUADOR

LAND USE, 1987

Arable Land 8.9%
Pasture Area 17.2%
Nonproductive Area 31.3%
Forest Area 42.6%

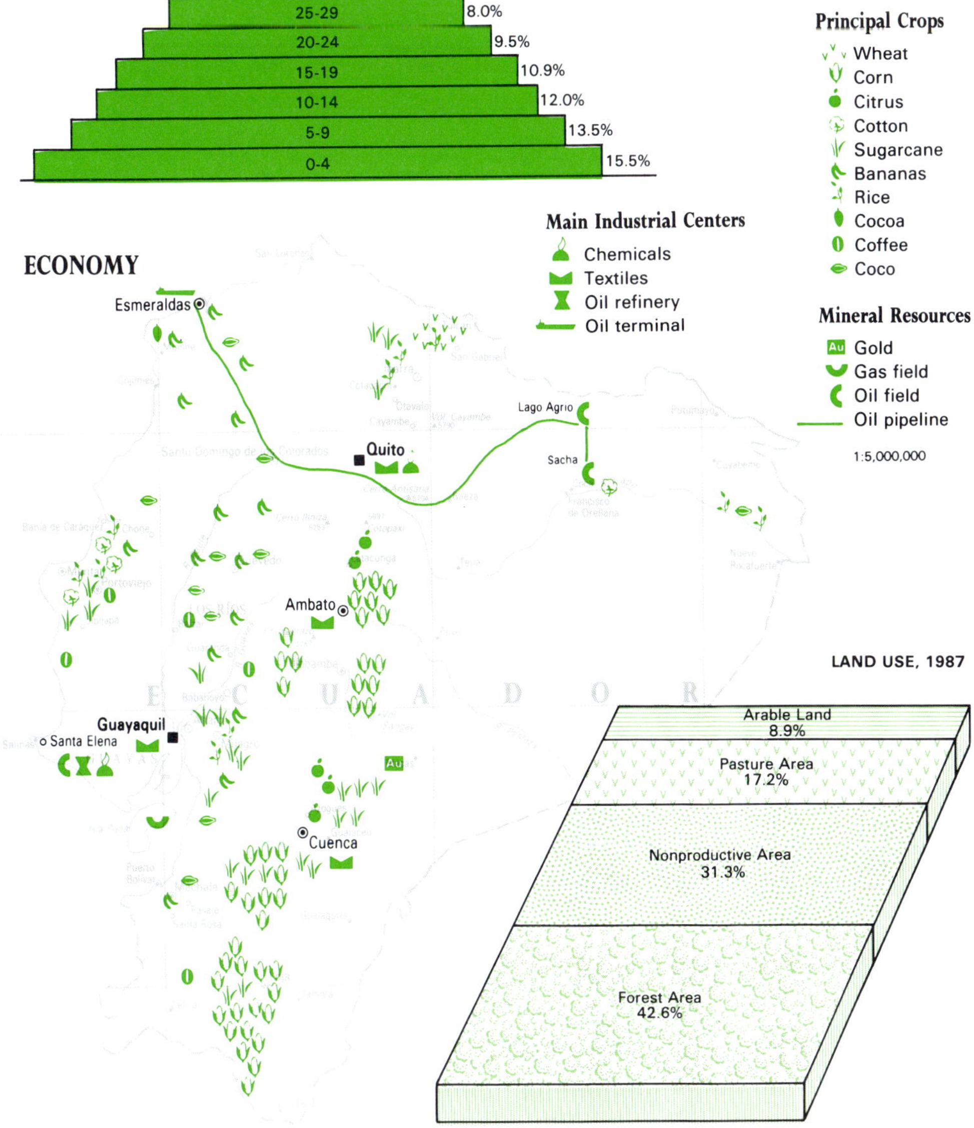

ECONOMY

Ecuador's economy is based on agriculture, fishing, and mining. The exploitation and exporting of oil have played a dominant role in the country's economy since the early 1970s. Over the last century, economic development depended on the exports of first cocoa and then bananas, of which Ecuador was the world's largest exporter for several decades. Agricultural exports came mainly from the coastal lowlands. Illegal production of drugs has in recent years become an important source of income.

The GNP was $1,080 per capita in 1988. It has grown in recent years at an average annual rate of nearly 2 percent. The inflation rate was 32.4 percent in 1987.

Agriculture

Ecuador is predominantly an agricultural country, despite the fact that oil has become its main source of revenue and industry has expanded substantially. Agriculture employs 32 percent of the workforce. The area under cultivation is 6.4 million acres, nearly 9 percent of the country's area. Permanent pasture covers 17 percent of the total area and forests nearly 43 percent. In the highlands subsistence agriculture and the production of staples for the urban areas are predominant; the main crops are corn, wheat, barley, potatoes, pulses, and various vegetables. The total areas under cultivation for these crops and the yields for 1987 were as follows: corn 502,000 acres, 330,000 tons; barley—100,000 acres, 43,000 tons; wheat—65,000 acres, 20,000 tons; and potatoes—100,000 acres, 397,000. Rice, grown in the coastal lowlands over a total of 346,000 acres produced 417,000 tons. In the coastal lowlands tropical crops are grown for export. Since the late 1940s, bananas have been the main commercial crop of this region. Production rose from 9,000 tons in 1925, to 600,000 tons in the early 1960s, to 1.4 million tons in the mid-1970s, and to 2.3 million tons in 1984. It was nearly 2 million tons in 1987. Cocoa is grown on 726,000 acres, producing 85,000 tons of cocoa beans (1987). The large-scale production of cocoa for export began in the 1870s. Exports were 11,000 tons in 1880 and had reached 40,000 tons by 1910. Ecuador was the world's largest exporter between 1910 and the mid-1920s. Cocoa is grown mainly in the vicinity of Guayaquil. Production of coffee for export began in the late 1920s. The area under cultivation by the usually small coffee plantations is 857,000 acres, with a production of 118,000 tons (1987). Other products are sugar—222,000 acres, 275,000 tons; tobacco—5,000 acres, 4,000 tons; cotton—45,000 acres, 1,300 tons of fiber; citrus—140,000 tons; pineapple—75,000 tons; and mango—30,000 tons (1987 figures). Tropical plantations and subsistence agriculture on a much more limited scale are found in the eastern lowlands.

Ecuador's forests produced 8.7 million cubic meters of timber in 1986. Livestock, raised mainly in the highland region, included 3.8 million cattle, 2.1 million sheep and 4.2 million pigs in 1987.

Fishing has expanded rapidly since the mid-1960s when the annual catch was about 50,000 tons. It was over one million tons in 1987.

MAJOR AGRICULTURAL CROPS, 1987

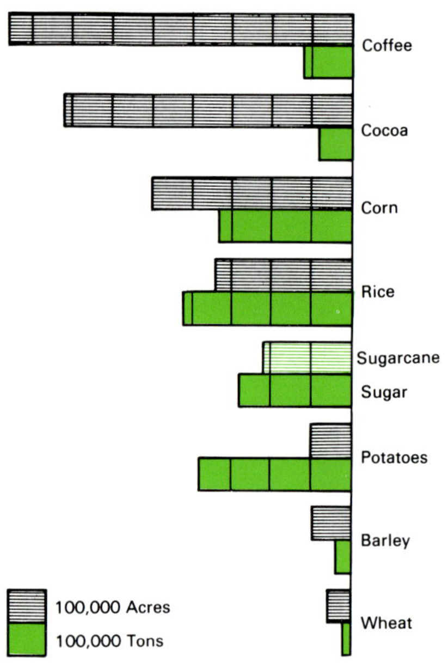

TRADE BALANCE, 1986
(Millions of Dollars)

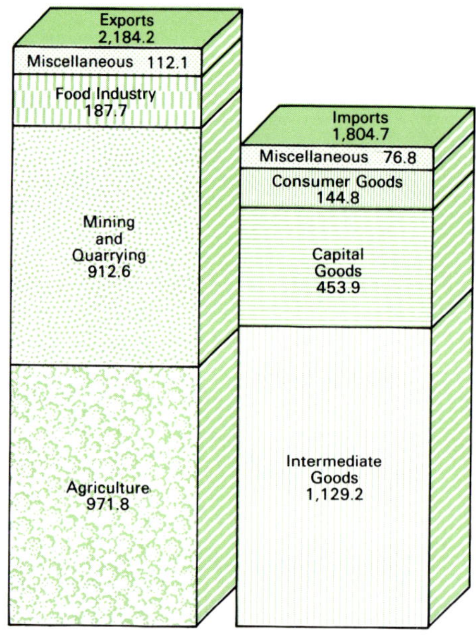

Mineral Resources

Oil and natural gas are the main mineral resources. Large-scale oil production began in 1972 from fields in the northwestern corner of the eastern lowlands (Lago Agrio). The oil is carried through a pipeline that crosses the Andes to the Pacific port of Esmeraldas, where a refinery operates. Production rose from 191,000 tons in 1970 to 9 million tons in 1976, 10.8 million tons in 1980, and to 15.8 million tons in 1988 (an average of 309,000 barrels per day). Pruduction of natural gas totaled 608 million cubic meters in 1986. Sulfur (4,000 tons) and small quantities of gold (placer, 31 kilograms in 1985), silver (62 kilograms), copper (100 tons), and zinc are produced. The country is known to have deposits of uranium, iron ore, lead, and coal.

Industry

Until the 1950s Ecuador had few industries, and these were engaged mainly in processing agricultural products and the manufacture of textiles, leather products, and some consumer goods. The manufacture of straw hats (Panama hats) was the main export industry. Industry has been developing and expanding since the late 1950s and especially since the mid-1970s. In addition to much wider activities in processing agricultural, marine, and forest products, there are modern textile, chemical, petrochemical, electronic, steel, shipbuilding, and building-material industries. Guayaquil and its environs is the main industrial center, with Quito next in importance. Nearly three-quarters of Ecuador's industry is concentrated in these conurbations. The industrial branch employs 13 percent of the workforce. Hydroelectric stations produced 81 percent of the country's electric power in 1987.

Trade

The main trading partners are the United States, which takes 54 percent of the exports and provides 33 percent of the imports; Japan—2.5 and 12 percent; and West Germany—2 and 10 percent.

HISTORY

The coastal region and the high Andean basins of what is now Ecuador were inhabited by Indian tribes when the first Europeans reached the area's Pacific coast in 1526. The Inca empire extended over the highland region to an area north of Quito. The first Spanish settlement in Ecuador was established in 1534 at Quito on the site of an important Inca town of the same name. Another settlement was established four years later near the mouth of the river Guayas on the site of Guayaquil. Expeditions initiated by Francisco Pizarro, who discovered and conquered Peru, founded the settlements and extended Spanish rule over the highland basins and coastal lowlands. Ecuador was part of the Viceroyalty of Peru until 1740, when it was transferred to the Viceroyalty of New Granada (together with Colombia and Venezuela). With hardly any gold or silver, Ecuador did not attract many European settlers during the Spanish colonial period, which lasted until 1822. Large fertile areas and the availability of local Indian labor did lead to the establishment of large Spanish estates, however. The Spaniards who came to this country were nearly all males who took local Indian wives, thus engendering the large mestizo population.

The first uprising against Spanish rule took place in 1809, but only in 1822 did Ecuador gain independence as part of the federation of Gran Colombia, from which it withdrew in 1830. A long period of internal strife and instability followed, caused mainly by struggles between conservative and liberal elements, clerical and anticlerical movements, and large landowners and owners of small farms or plantations. The country was run by dictators, and the army played an important role in internal politics. During the first century of its independence, Ecuador had changed its constitution 13 times and only a few of its presidents had managed to serve a full four-year term.

The economic development associated with the cocoa boom at the end of the nineteenth and the first quarter of the twentieth century helped to improve and stabilize the country's administration, despite the frequent turnover in rulers—18 presidents between 1897 and 1934 and 25 presidents between 1934 and 1988.

Ecuador extended over an area of 706,000 square kilometers (275,000 square miles), 2.5 times its present area, when it established its independence. It then bordered on Brazil, Colombia, and Peru, but had boundary disputes with all. It first had to cede territory to Colombia, then to Brazil and, finally, most of its share in the Amazon Basin (eastern lowlands) to Peru, by which it was badly defeated in a short war during 1941–1942.

GOVERNMENT AND POLITICS

The country is divided into twenty provinces (ten in the highland region, five in the coastal lowlands, four in the eastern lowlands, and the Galápagos Islands). Each province is administered by a governor appointed by the central government. Each province is divided into a number of cantons, each with an elected cantonal council. Under the present constitution, which came into force in 1979, the country is governed by an executive president with wide powers who, together with a vice president, is elected for a single four-year term. The government is appointed by the president. There is a unicameral legislature, the National Congress, whose 71 members are elected for a four-year term. Twelve members are elected nationally and 59 by provinces. Rodrigo Borja Cavallos, member of the Democratic Left (ID), was elected president in May 1988 and took office three months later. The composition of the National Congress after the January 1988 elections was as follows: the Democratic Left (ID)—27 seats; Popular Democracy (DP, center left)—8 seats; Social Christian Party (PSC, center right)—7 seats, Roldosist Party (PRE, left)—6 seats; and Concentration of Popular Forces (CEP)—6 seats. The remaining 17 seats were won by small parties. The leftist faction won the last presidential and congressional elections after a long period during which the right controlled the country.

One sucre, 1896 (depicts Sucre)

1967

Administrative Division

Regions Provinces	Capitals	area sq mi	area sq km	population (1986 estimate)
Coastal				
El Oro	Machala	2,281	5,908	406,822
Esmeraldas	Esmeraldas	5,854	15,162	297,376
Guayas	Guayaquil	8,256	21,382	2,485,763
Los Ríos	Babahoyo	2,459	6,370	533,685
Manabí	Portoviejo	6,990	18,105	1,039,408
Eastern				
Morona-Santiago	Macas	10,200	26,418	85,619
Napo	Tena	20,200	52,318	151,745
Pastaza	Puyo	11,687	30,269	38,531
Zamora-Chinchipe	Zamora	7,102	18,394	59,113
Sierra				
Azuay	Cuenca	3,124	8,092	513,343
Bolívar	Guaranda	1,599	4,142	164,741
Cañar	Azogues	1,344	3,481	198,322
Carchi	Tulcán	1,446	3,744	143,274
Chimborazo	Riobamba	2,338	6,056	369,229
Cotopaxi	Latacunga	2,007	5,198	312,671
Imbabura	Ibarra	1,921	4,976	281,032
Loja	Loja	4,429	11,472	404,036
Pichincha	Quito	6,404	16,587	1,710,275
Tungurahua	Ambato	1,201	3,110	374,322
Island Territory				
Galápagos Islands	Puerto Baquerizo Moreno	3,086	7,994	7,954
Total		***103,930**	**269,178**	**9,577,261**

*Detail does not add to total given because of rounding.

Quito, showing characteristic architecture

QUITO

Quito, capital of Ecuador and of Pichincha, the country's most populous Andean province, is situated 183 kilometers (116 miles) from the Pacific coast at an altitude of 2,850 meters (9,350 feet) just south of the equator. It has a pleasant climate that can be described as "permanent spring." It has hardly any seasonal variations in temperature, with an average daily maximum of approximately 20°C (68°F) the year around. The city, one of the oldest in South America, is built in a small basin on the lower slopes of Cerro Pichincha, a volcano that last erupted in 1666. It was the capital of the ancient kingdom of Quitu and for several decades, prior to its occupation by the Spaniards in 1534, was a second (northern) capital of the Inca empire. The city's official name, as given by the Spaniards, is Villa de San Francisco de Quito. Greater Quito, with a population of 1.3 million in 1989, is Ecuador's second largest city. Its population has more than doubled over the last twenty years. It is the political, administrative, and cultural capital but has lost its primary economic position to Guayaquil, with which it has had a railway link since 1908. Quito, more than any other South American capital, has preserved its colonial atmosphere, with squares, fountains, public buildings, and houses built in the typical Spanish or Moorish style. Most attractive is the main square, Plaza Mayor, with its seventeenth-century cathedral, government palaces, municipal hall, and other buildings. In 1535, the Spanish Franciscan monks established an art school in Quito and later founded a movement to foster art that left its mark on a wealth of colonial-era churches, cloisters, and mansions in the old quarter. A public university was established in the city in 1787 and a Catholic university in 1946. Quito is well known for its many small workshops producing native arts and for its outdoor Indian markets. With its rapid growth, the city has extended into the rural surroundings and has also become a modern industrial center.

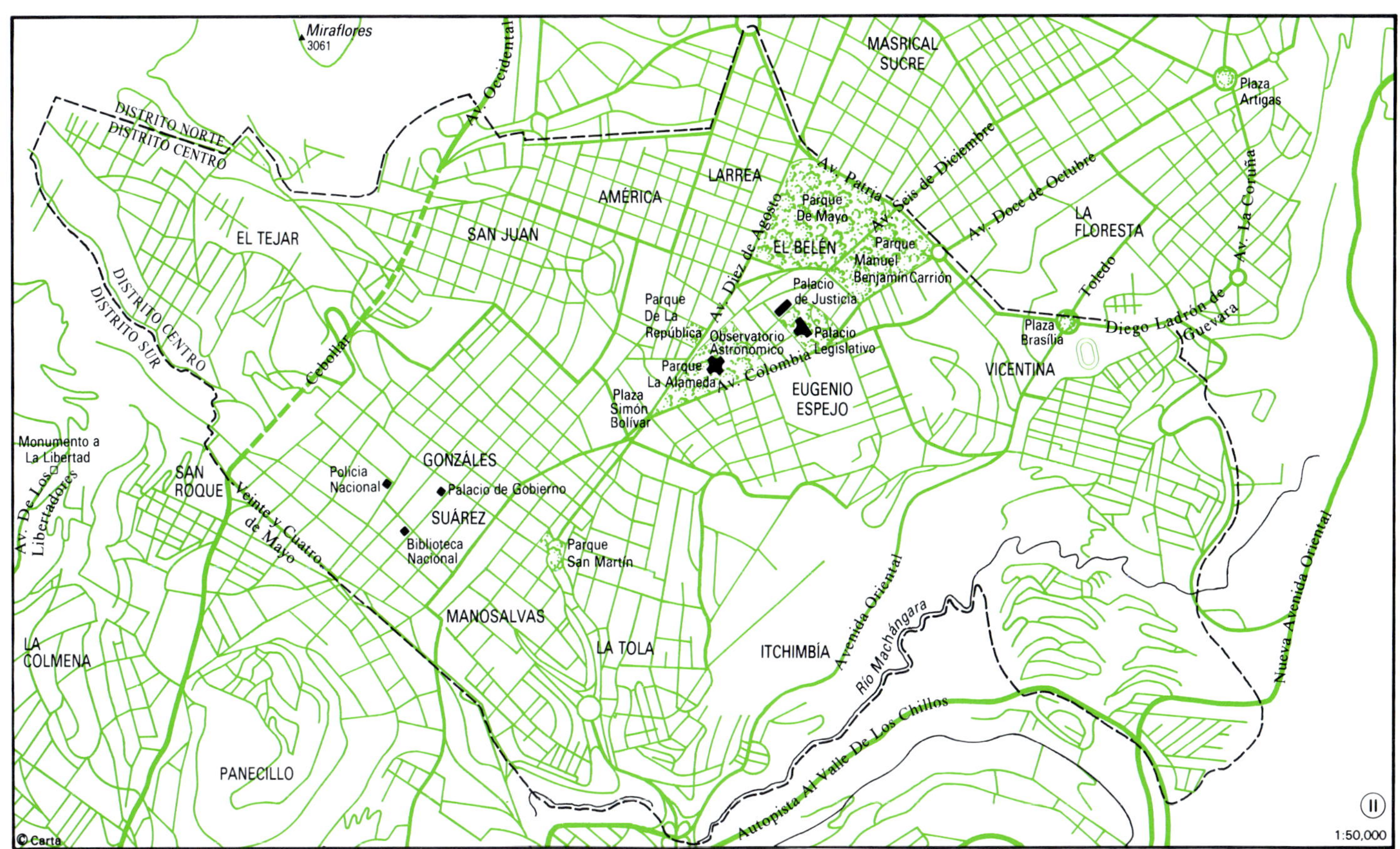

PERU

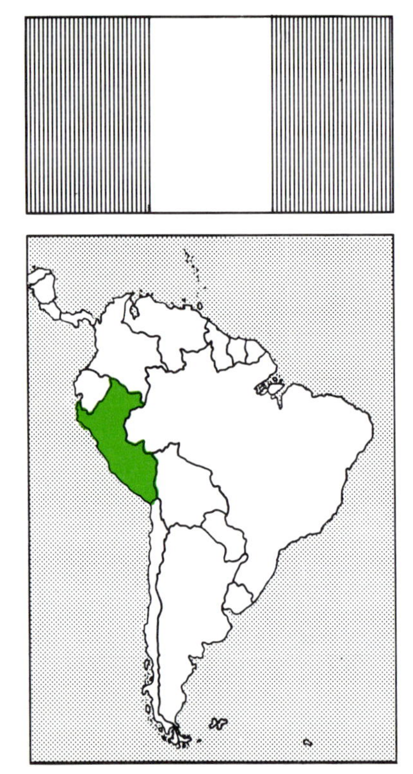

Area
1,285,216 sq. km.
496,225 sq. mi.

Population
22,332,000 (1990 estimate)

Capital City
Lima

Gross National Product (GNP) Per Capita
$1,470 (1987)

Population in Main Cities
(1985)
Greater Lima 5,330,800 (1987)
Arequipa 531,800
Callao 515,200
Trujillo 438,700
Chiclayo 347,700

Highest Point
6,768 m. 22,205 ft. (Huascarán)

Currency Unit
1 inti=100 céntimos

Density
15.7 persons per sq. km.
40.7 persons per sq. mi. (1986)

Urban-Rural
urban 70.2% rural 29.8% (1985)

Natural Increase
2.5% (1985-1990)

Life Expectancy
61.4 (1985-1990)

Doctors
1,111 inhabitants per doctor (1984)

Hospital Beds
1.6 per thousand inhabitants (1985)

Infant Mortality
88.2 per thousand live births (1985-1990)

High School Pupils
72.3% of age group 12-16 (1986)

University Students
27.7% of age group 20-24 (1986)

Illiteracy Rate
15.2% (1985)

National Holiday
Independence Days, 28-29 July

National Anthem
beginning "Somos Libres, seámoslo siempre"
("We are free; Let us remain so forever")

Peru, the largest in area of the Andean countries, was the cradle of the most advanced indigenous civilizations and most powerful empire in pre-Columbian South America—that of the Incas. Peru was also the focus of Spanish colonial domination for its first two hundred years of rule. What has remained of pre-Columbian America with regard to people, culture, and settlement is perhaps better represented in Peru than in any other country. The country has a 2,400-kilometer- (1,500-mile-) long coast on the Pacific Ocean and borders Colombia and Ecuador (with which it has boundary disputes) on the north, Brazil and Bolivia on the east, and Chile on the south. It is the only country that borders all the other Andean states.

NATURAL REGIONS

Three main natural regions are distinguishable: the coastal zone (costa); the highlands (Andes or sierra); and the eastern hills and lowlands.

The Coastal Zone

The coastal zone is an arid, mostly hilly region between the Pacific shore, much of which is bordered by high cliffs, and the Andes farther east. In the north, it is characterized by a low, extremely faulted plateau, a substantial part of which is an almost flat, arable land where water for irrigation is available. The central part, which extends from the vicinity of Trujillo to Ica, is narrower and more rugged. Here, spurs of the Andes extend to the coast and end in high cliffs. These spurs are separated by deep narrow valleys in which small rivers, some of them seasonal, flow. The beds of these valleys are covered with a thick mantle of sediment that forms a fanlike flat area at the outlet to the coast. When irrigated, the valleys can be agriculturally utilized. Because of the nature of the terrain and its aridity, settlement is almost entirely confined to river valleys and small sections of the coast, mostly near the mouths of rivers.

The southern part of the Peruvian coastal zone is very similar in structure to that of northern Chile. A narrow coastal mountain range rises steeply just behind the shore. This area is composed mainly of a very rugged surface, much of which is covered by bare hard rocks with deeply incised narrow gorges. Troughlike basins running parallel to this range separate it from the Andes. These flat-bottomed basins are covered with a thick mantle of sediment in which rivers have cut deep valleys. Agricultural settlements that irrigate and cultivate small areas of these valleys are actually oases in this desertlike environment. Unlike other parts of the coastal belt, most of the population in the south resides along its eastern margins, away from the coast and close to the foot of the Andes.

The Highlands

The highlands (Andes) in Peru are generally considered to consist of two parallel ranges, the Cordillera Occidental and the Cordillera Oriental, extending in a northwest to southeast direction. Valleys and basins, which follow the same direction and in the south broaden into the Altiplano (with Lake Titicaca and a few smaller lakes), are generally cited as the structural features that separate the western range from the eastern one. The structure here is, in fact, complicated. Both the western and eastern ranges, with peaks rising to over 6,000 meters (20,000 feet), are not continuous. They are in most cases arranged in echelon form between the rows of peaks that make up each range. Some of these ranges deviate from the general orientation of the Andes. The line dividing the Pacific and Atlantic watersheds runs along the Cordillera Occidental. The line enters northern Peru (and southern Ecuador) to within 100 kilometers (62 miles) of the Pacific coast. The high peaks and slopes are permanently snow-covered, with some remnants of glaciers. The snow line in central Peru is at an elevation of approximately 4,900–5,200 meters (16,000–17,000 feet). The eastern slopes of the western ranges are generally much more dissected and eroded than the western slopes because of the aridity of the Climate on the side facing the Pacific. Volcanoes, active and

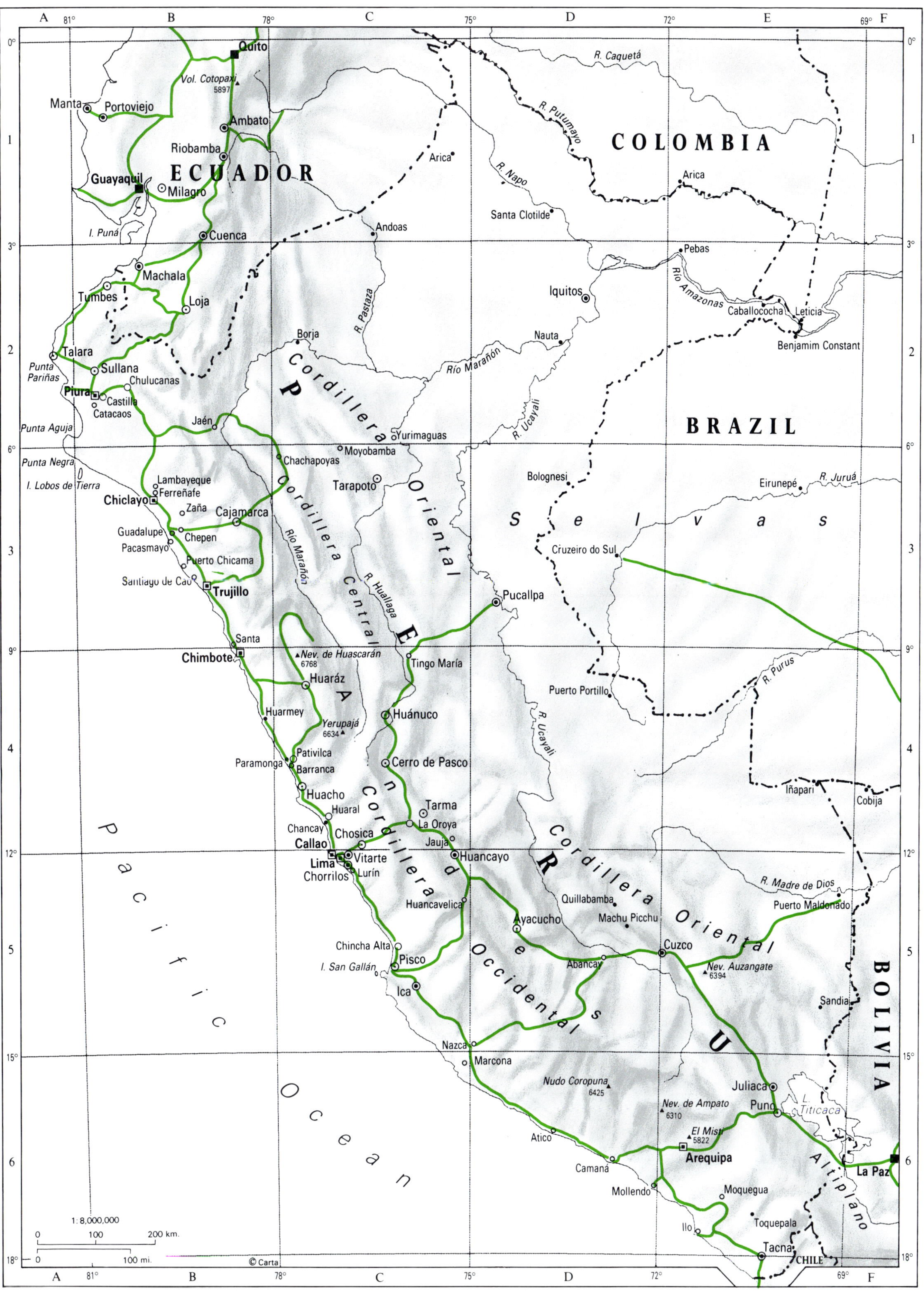

COLOMBIA
ECUADOR
BRAZIL
BOLIVIA
CHILE
PERU
Pacific Ocean
Selvas
Cordillera Oriental
Cordillera Central
Cordillera Occidental
Cordilleras Andes
Altiplano
Quito
Vol. Cotopaxi 5897
Manta
Portoviejo
Ambato
Riobamba
Guayaquil
Milagro
I. Puná
Cuenca
Machala
Tumbes
Loja
Talara
Punta Pariñas
Sullana
Piura
Castilla
Catacaos
Chulucanas
Punta Aguja
Jaén
Punta Negra
I. Lobos de Tierra
Lambayeque
Ferreñafe
Chiclayo
Zaña
Cajamarca
Guadalupe
Pacasmayo
Chepen
Puerto Chicama
Santiago de Cao
Trujillo
Santa
Chimbote
Nev. de Huascarán 6768
Huaráz
Huarmey
Yerupajá 6634
Paramonga
Pativilca
Barranca
Huacho
Huaral
Chancay
Callao
Lima
Chorrillos
Chosica
Vitarte
Lurín
Chincha Alta
Pisco
I. San Gallán
Ica
Nazca
Marcona
Atico
Camaná
Mollendo
Ilo
Tacna
Moquegua
Toquepala
Arequipa
El Misti 5822
Nev. de Ampato 6310
Nudo Coropuna 6425
Puno
L. Titicaca
Juliaca
La Paz
Cuzco
Nev. Auzangate 6394
Sandia
Abancay
Ayacucho
Huancavelica
Huancayo
Jauja
La Oroya
Tarma
Cerro de Pasco
Huánuco
Tingo María
Pucallpa
Quillabamba
Machu Picchu
Puerto Maldonado
R. Madre de Dios
Iñapari
Cobija
Puerto Portillo
R. Purus
R. Ucayali
Cruzeiro do Sul
Bolognesi
Eirunepé
R. Juruá
Yurimaguas
Moyobamba
Chachapoyas
Tarapoto
Río Marañón
R. Huallaga
Borja
R. Pastaza
Andoas
Arica
R. Napo
R. Putumayo
R. Caquetá
Santa Clotilde
Iquitos
Nauta
Pebas
Río Amazonas
Caballococha
Leticia
Benjamim Constant
1: 8,000,000
0 100 200 km.
0 100 mi.
© Carta
A B C D E F
81° 78° 75° 72° 69°
0° 3° 6° 9° 12° 15° 18°

dormant, are confined mainly to the southern part of the highlands (south of latitude 14°). High, cone-shaped volcanoes, mainly along the fringes of the basins, are a conspicuous part of Peru's Andean landscape that extends to the boundaries with Bolivia and Chile. One of the most prominent is El Misti (5,822 meters [19,101 feet]). Many of the basins and valleys in the south are deeply covered with lava and other volcanic material.

The basins and valleys wedged high between the Peruvian Andes are the intermont high level surface over which, historically, the majority of Peru's population has been concentrated. Most of these basins and valleys, which lie at altitudes of between 3,000 and 4,600 meters (10,000 and 15,000 feet), are broad and covered with a mantle of sediment washed down from the neighboring mountains. They are crossed by rivers whose sources are in the Cordillera Occidental or in the basins themselves and which are, in fact, the tributary headwaters of the Amazon. These include the river Marañón (considered the upper part of the Amazon) and its large tributary, Ucayali. Some small basins are closed and have only internal drainage. The Altiplano of the southern Peruvian Andes (which extends into Bolivia) is made up of some basins and valleys of the high level surface, including Peru's share in Lake Titicaca, with its densely inhabited environs. Only the lower basins and valleys of the high level surface are climatically within the zone suitable for agriculture. The altitude of most of this surface is outside the limit of cultivation or is marginal for some crops, such as potatoes (which can be grown here up to 4,000-4,300 meters [12,000-13,000 feet]), barley (up to 3,700-4,000 meters [12,000-13,000 feet]), and corn (up to 3,350 meters [11,000 feet]). Much of the high level surface is used mainly as pasture for sheep, goats, alpacas, and llamas.

The rivers that descend from the basins and valleys of the high level surface through the cordillera have cut very deep and narrow gorges. This makes passage extremely difficult through the lower parts of the mountains and to the bottoms of many of the gorges. The sharpest descents and roughest surfaces are on the eastern slopes of the Cordillera Oriental, where the powerful erosive processes of the rivers are reinforced by heavy rains. The extremely dissected and rugged nature of these slopes has been a serious obstacle to communication between the inhabited areas of the highlands and the eastern lowlands.

The Eastern Lowlands

The eastern lowlands are generally divided into the *selva alta*, the higher hilly areas at the foot of the Andes, and the *selva baja*, the lower areas farther east (especially in the northeast) that slope toward the boundaries with Colombia and Brazil. The *selva alta* is dominated by low, gently sloping eastern spurs of the Andes (370-910 meters [1,200-3,000 feet]) with broad valleys that have potentially arable land. There is a gradual transition to the *selva baja*, a much lower undulating plain where the relief is dominated by a dense network of rivers and river terraces. It slopes gently northeastward from approximately 370 meters (1,200 feet) to 90-120 meters (300-400 feet). The eastern lowlands are covered with dense tropical rain forest. Over large areas the forest is so dense that access is possible only via the rivers. The density of the forest diminishes toward the extreme southeastern corner of this region. The eastern lowlands of Peru are, in fact, part of the western margin of the huge Amazon plain. Small ocean-going steamers can sail up the Amazon into eastern Peru to Iquitos, the country's main river port.

CLIMATE

Peru has a wide variety of climatic conditions that change with the region, altitude, and topographic position. Over short distances there can be considerable differences in temperature and precipitation. The annual range of temperatures, especially in the highlands, increases southward; however, it is smaller than the average diurnal range. Also, to southward there are small differences in the ranges of altitudinal zones, with a gradual rise in the upper limits of each, especially those of the *páramos* (cold zone) and the snow line. Thus, while the snow line is at about 4,500-4,900 meters (15,000-16,000 feet) in northern Peru, it reaches 5,200-5,800 meters (17,000-19,000 feet) in the extreme south. This rise in the snow line with increasing distance from the equator is due mainly to the increase in aridity toward southern Peru.

The coastal region, which is the *tierra caliente* (hot zone) of western Peru, and the western slopes of the Andes are arid. Desert conditions prevail over the southern part of this region, where the average annual rainfall is less than 25 millimeters (1 inch). The average temperatures for the hottest (January-February) and coolest (June-July) months in the coastal region in the north (Trujillo) are 25.1°C (77.2°F) and 17.2°C (63°F); in the center (Lima), 23.5°C (74.3°F) and 16.1°C (61°F); and in the south (Mollendo), 21.5°C (70.7°F) and 15.2°C (59.4°F). The average annual rainfall is 30 millimeters (1.2 inches), 45 millimeters (1.8 inches), and 18 millimeters (0.7 inches), respectively. Conditions are similar in the *tierra templada*, or temperate zone (900-2,100 meters [3,000-7,000 feet]) and the *tierra fría*, or cool zone (2,100-3,350 meters [7,000-11,000 feet]) on the western face of the Andes, with lower temperatures (corresponding to altitude) and slightly higher rainfall. Thus, at Arequipa (2,500 meters [8,050 feet]), the average temperatures for the hottest and coolest months are 14°C (57°F) and 11°C (52°F). The average annual rainfall is 105 millimeters (4.2 inches). The anomalously low temperatures for this latitude of the coastal region are due to the cold ocean currents off the Peruvian shore, which are also largely responsible for the region's aridity.

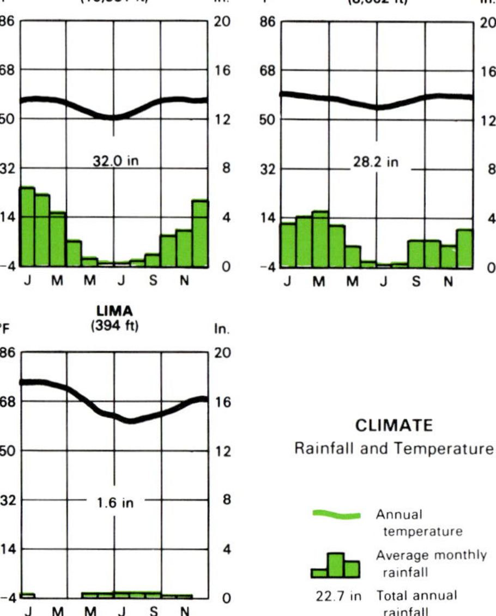

The basins and valleys of the inner parts of the highlands, the areas in which most of the population is concentrated, are climatically the upper part of the *tierra fría* and the lower part of the *páramos* (3,350-4,600 meters [11,000-15,000 feet] in the north; 3,700-5,800 meters [12,000-19,000 feet] in the south). Here temperatures are lower and rainfall more abundant. Rain occurs mainly during the summer (October to March). The average temperatures for the warmest (January) and coolest (July) months at Cuzco (3,350 meters [11,000 feet]) are 13.3°C (56°F) and 10°C (50°F), and at Cerro de Pasco (4,350 meters [14,270 feet]), 6.7°C (44.1°F) and 4.7°C (40.5°F). The average annual rainfall at these two locations is 800 millimeters (32 inches) and 850 millimeters (34 inches), respectively. Temperatures are much higher in the eastern region, which includes climatically the *tierra caliente* and *tierra fría* of the adjacent slopes of the Andes. The rainy season is much longer, extending from September to June. Rainfall is especially heavy in parts of the eastern flanks of the Andes, where it may reach 4,000 millimeters (160 inches) annually. The average temperatures for the hottest and coolest months at Iquitos (in the northeast) are 26°C (78°F) and 23.4°C (74.1°F), with an average annual rainfall of 2,600 millimeters (104 inches).

POPULATION

Estimated at 22 million in 1990, Peru's population has more than tripled over the last 50 years (it was slightly more than 7 million at the 1940 census) and more than doubled over the last 30 years (10.4 million at the 1961 census). The average annual rate of increase over the last decade has been 2.6 percent. The ethnic composition of the population is estimated as follows: Indians of "pure" descent—45-47 percent; mestizos—32-37 percent; unmixed Europeans—12-15 percent; blacks and mulattos—about 2 percent; and Asians (Japanese and Chinese)—about 1 percent. In the basins and valleys of the highlands, the population is predominantly Indian. Spanish is spoken by about two-thirds of the population. The majority of the Indians still speak Quechua (about 27 percent of the population) and Aymara (about 5 percent). Spanish and Quechua are the official languages. About 93 percent of the population is Roman Catholic. Native religions are still predominant among some Indian populations in remote and isolated valleys and in the forests of the eastern region.

Most of Peru is only sparsely populated, with large areas in the Andes and eastern lowlands almost uninhabited. The average population density for the country as a whole is 17 inhabitants per square kilometer (43 per square mile). Only a comparatively small part

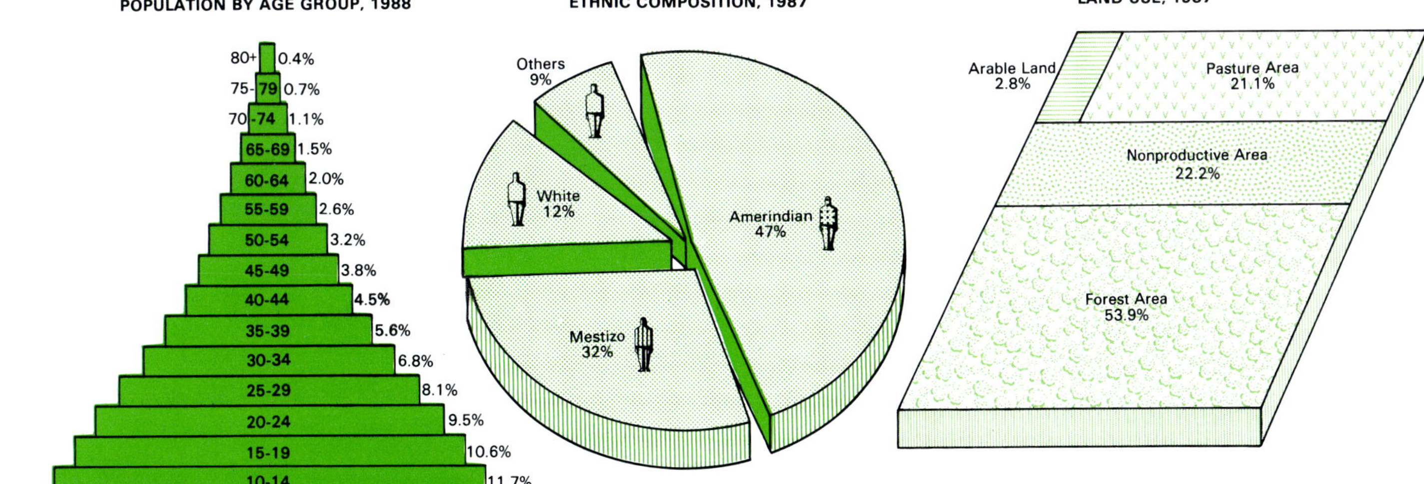

of the country—the coastal region and the high level surface of the Andes—has a dense population. The most densely inhabited district (department) is that which surrounds the capital Lima, with 180 persons per square kilometer (450 per square mile), followed by the departments of Lambayeque, with the capital Chiclayo (52 per square kilometer [133 per square mile]) and La Libertad, with the capital Trujillo (50 per square kilometer [128 per square mile]) in the northern part of the coastal region. In the highlands, the department of Cajamarca has the densest population (34 persons per square kilometer [87 per square mile]). In the eastern region the average population density is 2.5 persons per square kilometer (6.3 per square mile). Extensive internal migrations and demographic changes have taken place since the beginning of the twentieth century. Many people migrated from the higher and poorer settled areas of the highlands to the coastal region and the eastern lowlands. Toward the end of the nineteenth century about 70 percent of the Peruvians lived in the highlands, 25 percent in the coastal region, and 5 percent in the eastern lowlands. The figures for 1940 were 64, 30, and 6 percent, and for 1975, 40, 49, and 11 percent, respectively. Only about one-third of the population lives in the highlands, and more than half dwells in the coastal region (early 1990s). About 71 percent of the population is urban, 25 percent of which lives in the conurbation of Lima (which includes the capital, its port Callao, and a number of satellite towns). The main urban centers (with estimated population figures for 1987) are Lima—420,000 (the conurbation—5.5 million); Arequipa (main center of the south)—600,000; Trujillo (main port of the north)—500,000; Chiclayo—400,000; Callao (port of Lima and central Peru)—320,000; Piura—300,000; Cuzco—260,000; and Iquitos (the main center and river port of the eastern region)—250,000. About 20 percent of the population is illiterate.

ECONOMY

Mining, agriculture, industry, and fisheries are the main components of the Peruvian economy. While the development of mining and industry

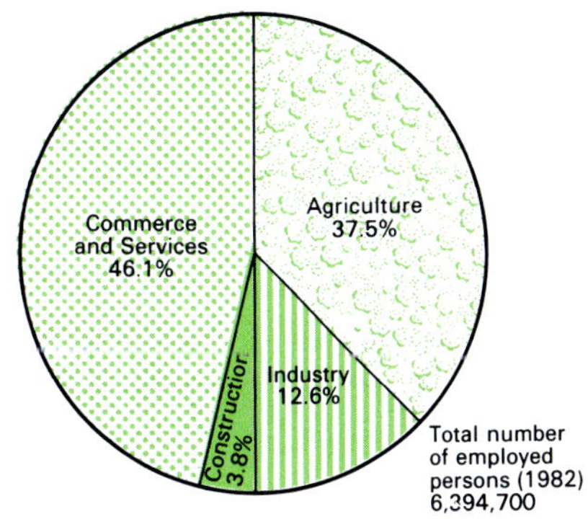

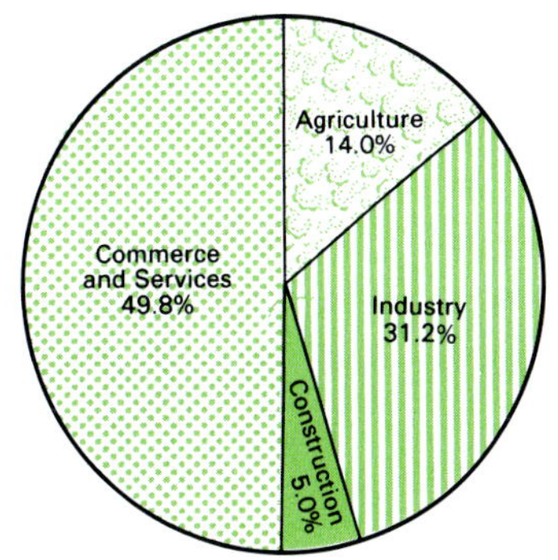

over the past three decades has been very substantial, that of agriculture, especially for the domestic market, has been slow. The GNP was $1,470 per capita in 1987 and has grown in recent years at an annual rate of approximately 8 percent. The unemployment rate was 8.2 percent in 1987. Underemployment, however, is very widespread and, in the mid-1950s was estimated to affect 51 percent of the workers. The inflation rate was 114 percent in 1987. Tourism is assuming a growing importance in Peru's economy.

Agriculture

Since the 1950s agriculture's share in the GNP and in the workforce has been declining. Although the area under cultivation has expanded, production, especially for the domestic market, has failed to meet the needs of the increasing population. Whereas only 2.8 percent of Peru's area is agriculturally utilized, the proportion arable land is estimated to be much greater. Of the total area, 21 percent is permanent pasture and 54 percent is covered by forests and brush. The main commercial crops in 1987 were coffee—350,000 acres, 97,000 tons (grown mainly in the lower part of the *tierra templada* on the eastern slopes of the Andes); sugarcane—128,000 acres, 566,000 tons of sugar; cotton—341,000 acres, 87,000 tons of fiber; rice—580,000 acres, 1.187 million tons; and cocoa—11,000 tons (all of which are grown mainly in the coastal region under irrigation and in the eastern lowlands). The production for local consumption, much of which is grown by peasants who still practice subsistence agriculture, includes potatoes—524,000 acres, 1.68 million tons (grown up to an altitude of approximately 4,300 meters [14,000 feet]); corn (maize)—1.35 million acres, 919,000 tons (up to 3,350 meters [11,000 feet]); barley—287,000 acres, 119,000 tons (up to 4,000 meters [13,000 feet]); wheat—250,000 acres, 124,000 tons (up to 3,700 meters [12,000 feet]); manioc—400,000 tons; sweet potatoes—124,000 tons; and vegetables and fruit. Agriculture is concentrated mainly in the valleys of the coastal region, in the basins and valleys of the high level surface of the Andes, and at the western margins of the eastern region. Of the total workforce, 35 percent is employed in agriculture (1988); the portion was 58 percent in 1958.

The forests yield nearly 8 million cubic meters of wood annually, including a substantial proportion of valuable hardwoods.

Pastoralism plays an important role in the *páramos* zone and in the high valleys and basins of the Andes. The total number of livestock in 1987 included cattle—4 million; sheep—13.5 million; goats—1.7 million; alpacas—1.2 million; llamas—0.7 million; and vicuña—25,000. Large quantities of wool are produced, part of which is used in local handicrafts and industry.

Fisheries

An insignificant industry until the late 1950s, fishing has since grown into a major economic activity. Peru has one of the world's largest fishing zones, rich in a wide variety of fish and other marine life. The annual catch exceeded 10 million tons in the late 1960s and early 1970s (the world's largest at that time). It dropped substantially in the mid-1970s, due mainly to

AGRICULTURE

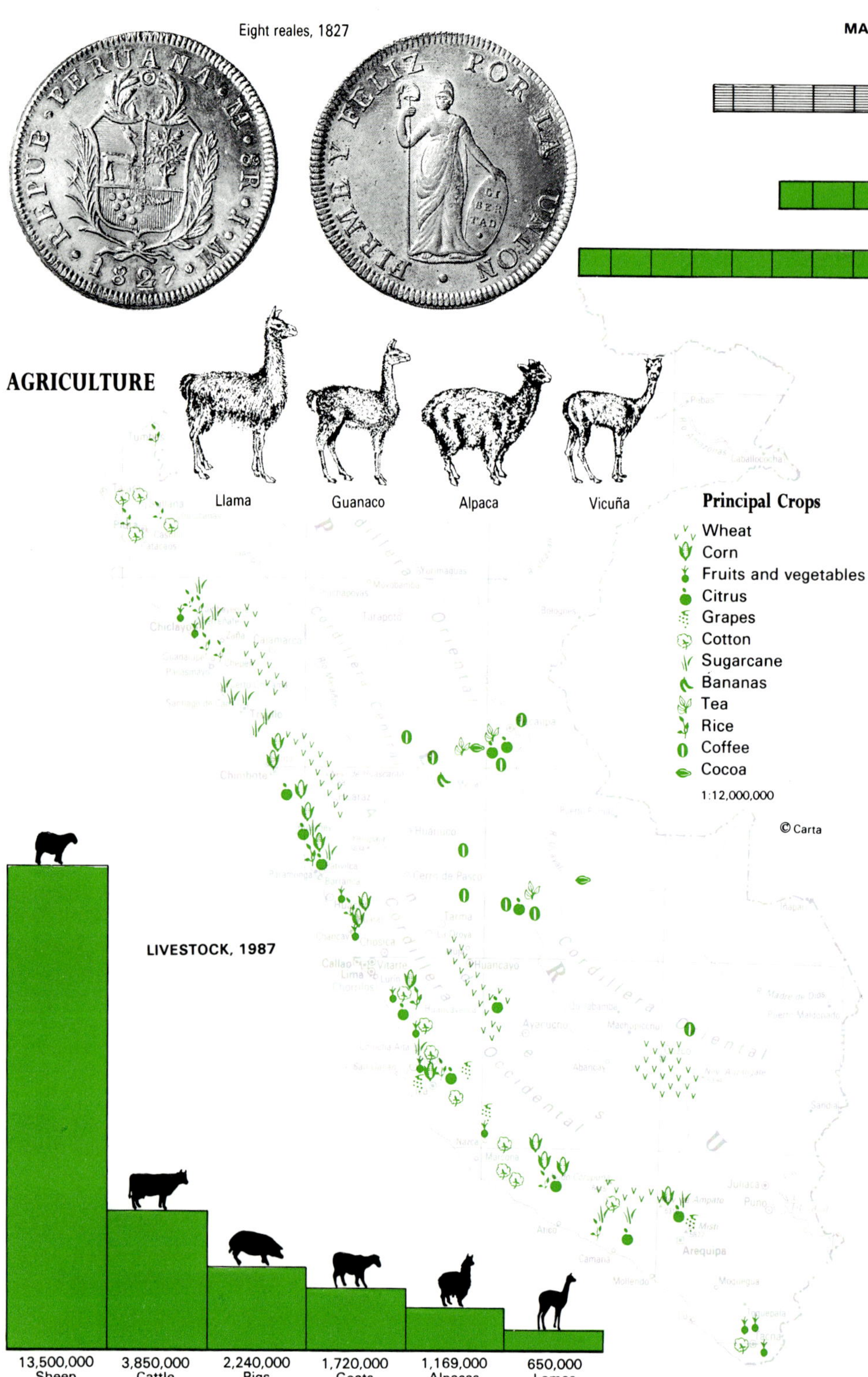

overfishing, and has not recovered since. The catch was 4.3 million tons in 1987 (5.6 million tons in 1986). Large quantities of fish meal are produced.

Mineral Resources

Peru produces and exports 28 different minerals, which are mined mainly in the central and southern parts of the highlands and the coastal region. The mines have provided a major part of Peru's exports for over 350 years. The most important mines are in the vicinity of Cerro de Pasco and La Oroya (northeast of Lima) and Arequipa and Toquepala (in the extreme south). Some mines are located at altitudes of over 4,900 meters (16,000 feet). The most important product is copper—396,000 tons (1987), followed by zinc—593,000 tons, lead—192,000 tons, silver—2,013,000 kilograms, gold—10,800 kilograms, iron (mined in the coastal region)—3.3 million tons, tin—5,300 tons, molybdenum—1,000 tons, tungsten—742 tons, antimony—194 tons, bismuth—605 tons, vanadium, mercury, uranium, sulfur, phosphate, and salt. Small quantities of coal (150,000 tons in 1987), used mainly for smelting, are mined at several locations on the western fringes of the Andes.

Peru's main oilfields are on the western fringes of the northern part of the lowlands. The oil is conveyed by pipeline to Talara in the extreme northern coastal region, where it is refined and partly exported. Peru's first oilfields were discovered in the vicinity of Talara, where some fields are still productive. There are also some offshore oil wells. Production was 7 million tons in 1988 (an average of 105,000 barrels per day in 1989). Natural gas production was 1,140 million cubic meters (in the central part of the lowlands).

Guano was exported in large quantities in the nineteenth century, when it was in ample supply along rocky stretches of the coast and on offshore islets. Since the beginning of the twentieth century, guano has lost most of its export value.

Industry

Modern industries developed mainly after World War II. Prior to that time, Peru's industry was engaged mainly in preliminary processing of mineral products, processing of agricultural products, and the manufacture of textiles and leather products. Between 1950 and 1980 the contribution of industry to the domestic product increased from 13.6 percent to 24.5 percent. Industrial development over the last 40 years embraced a wide range of industries. In addition to much more technologically advanced and in most cases complete processing of mineral products, a modern iron and steel industry (with the main plant in Chimbote) has developed. Other manufacturing includes engineering products, shipbuilding, assembly of motor vehicles, electronic products, chemicals (including fertilizers), pharmaceuticals, textiles, rubber and plastic products, building materials (1.6 million tons of cement in 1987), foodstuffs, and tobacco products. The number of workers employed in industry has risen from just under 100,000 in 1952 to 742,000 in 1988 (19 percent of the total workforce). About 70 percent of Peru's industry is concentrated in the Lima metropolitan area.

Trade

Peru's main trading partners are the United States, which in 1987 provided 18 percent of the imports and in 1985 took 31 percent of the exports: Japan—7 and 8 percent; Germany—8 and 5 percent; and Argentina—5 and 1 percent.

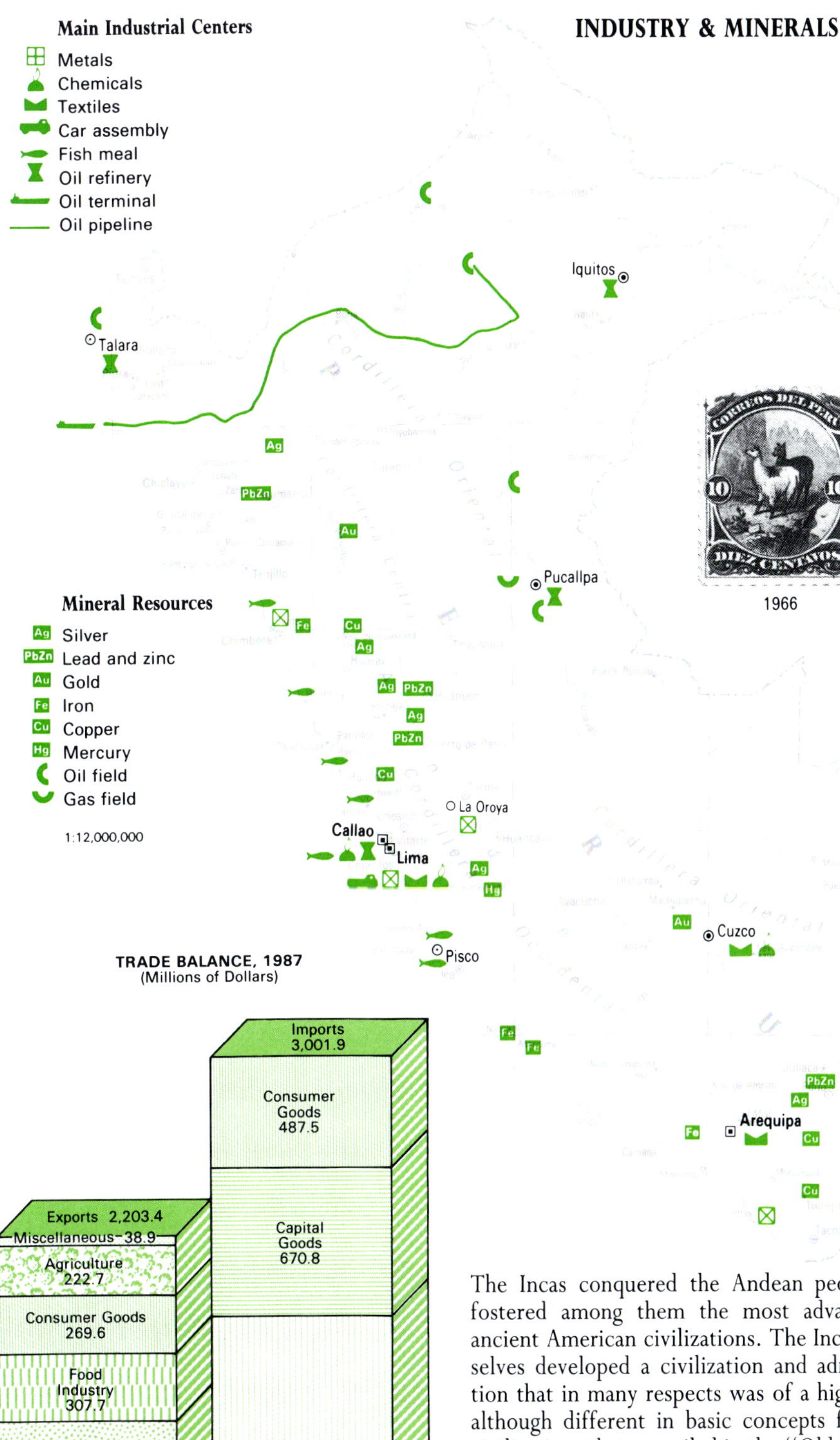

HISTORY

For at least 300 years before the arrival of the first Europeans (Spaniards), most of Peru (excluding the eastern lowlands) was the heart of the Inca empire that extended from present-day northern Ecuador to central Chile. The area from which the empire developed was centered in the basins and valleys of Cuzco. The Incas conquered the Andean people and fostered among them the most advanced of ancient American civilizations. The Incas themselves developed a civilization and administration that in many respects was of a high order, although different in basic concepts from the civilizations that prevailed in the "Old World." The Inca empire ended with the conquest of its heartland and capital Cuzco (1531–1533) by the Spaniards under Francisco Pizarro. Lima was founded in 1535 and became the focal point of Spanish expansion and domination of western South America. It soon became the capital of the Viceroyalty of Peru, which, until the mid-eighteenth century, extended from the Caribbean to La Plata. In their quest for wealth, Spanish officials and settlers forced great numbers of the native Indians off their land to work in gold and silver mines in the highlands and on large estates (haciendas) in which European crops and livestock were introduced. This, together with severe oppression and epidemics, caused extensive depopulation in areas that had been densely inhabited by the Indians. It is estimated that by the end of the sixteenth century the Indian population of Peru was reduced to about one-third of what it had been at the beginning of the century. During the seventeenth century Peru was the world's second most important producer of silver (for 20 years it was the largest producer). Indians who attempted to rebel or to evade exploitation and forced labor were executed. The establishment of the viceroyalties of New Granada (1739) in the north and La Plata (1776) in the south greatly reduced the extent and power of the colonial administration centered in Lima.

Peru declared its independence in 1821, following an uprising by local European (Creole) inhabitants against the Spanish colonial rule, which came to an end only in late 1824. A long period of instability followed, during which the country was governed by a succession of generals. A short confederation with Bolivia (1836–1839) was broken up by rebellion. The longest reigning president during the nineteenth century was General Ramón Castilla (1845–1851 and 1855–1862). Peru went to war with Spain (1864–1871); during the fighting Callao was damaged by heavy bombardment from the sea. In 1879 Peru, together with Bolivia, fought a four-year war with Chile over possession of the nitrate-rich northern part of the Atacama desert. The defeat of the Peruvian army led to the occupation of Lima by the Chilean army and to loss of territory. The border dispute with Chile was settled only in 1929. In the late nineteenth century, construction of a railway connecting the mining centers of the highlands with the coast, coupled with large foreign capital investments, brought extensive development to Peru. With economic development came a power struggle between the conservative Creole (European) upper class and the liberal elements pressing for social and economic changes. During the first half of the twentieth century, Peru had eighteen presidents (five were deposed and four resigned), many of whom assumed dictatorial powers. A boundary dispute with Colombia was settled in 1932 by the withdrawal of Peru from a large area in the Amazon plain. A boundary dispute with Ecuador was settled after a short war in favor of Peru (1942), but the dispute was revived in 1981.

A liberal president (Fernando Belaúnde-Terry), elected in 1963, introduced reforms to improve the social and economic conditions of peasants and workers; these brought about some fundamental changes in the position of the masses. The main reforms, however, were instituted by the head of a junta, General Juan Velasco Alvarado, who deposed Belaúnde-Terry in 1968. Alvarado initiated a far-reaching program of agrarian reform and nationalized the major mining companies, industries, railways, banks, and other vital public services. He was deposed after seven years in power by a member of the same junta, General Francisco Morales Bermúdez Cerruti. Fernando Belaúnde-Terry was reelected president in 1980 with the restoration of free democratic elections.

GOVERNMENT AND POLITICS

The country is divided into 24 departments, which are subdivided into 179 provinces. The constitutional province of Callao has some of the functions and rights of a department. Each

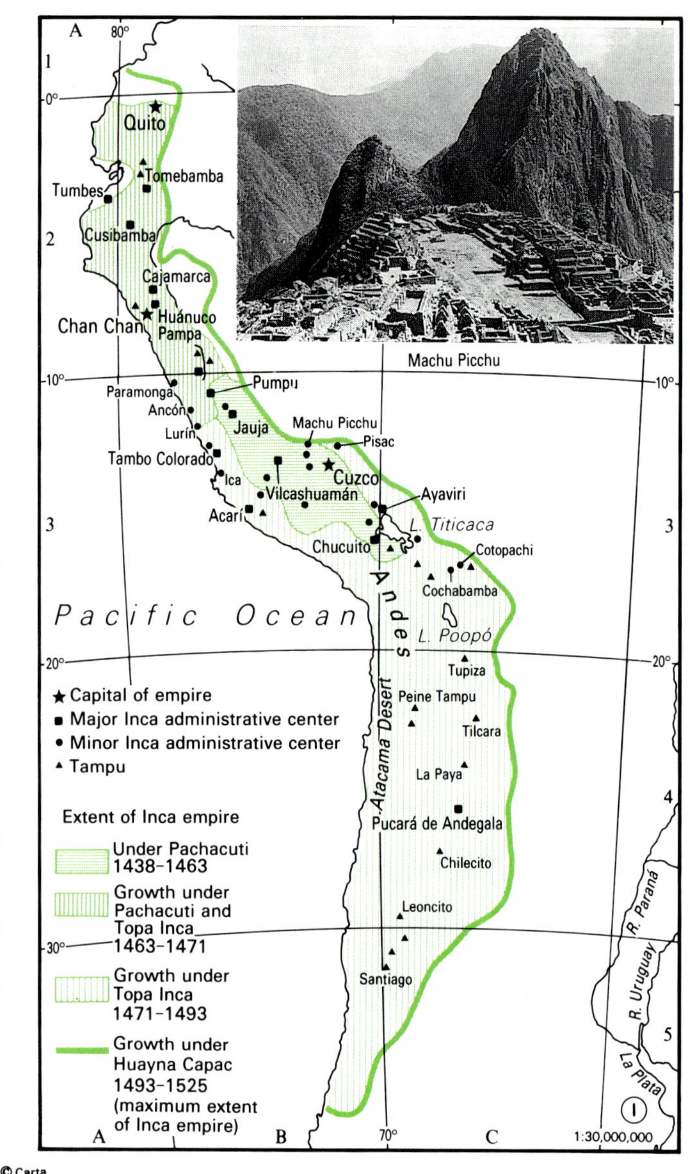

THE INCA EMPIRE

The Inca empire was the largest and most advanced empire on the American continent before its discovery by Europeans. At its height, the empire extended from northern Ecuador to central Chile and from the Andes to the coast. The Incas were originally a Peruvian highland tribe who spoke a Quechua language. According to a mythological account, they came from the south and settled in the Cuzco basin, to which they were at first confined. Apparently the Incas expanded their rule on neighboring tribes about 1100 A.D., when governed by the first nonlegendary ruler. The empire reached its peak in the fifteenth century. By the time of the Spanish conquest, it was already torn by internal strife.

The supreme ruler of the empire, the Sapa Inca, held complete power over his subjects and their land. It was, however, a benevolent and paternalistic rule, organized on the basis of family groups (ranging from ten to several thousand) administered as communities. Work and food supply were closely regulated. There was no poverty or hunger. Food production (mainly maize, potatoes, and quinoa), yielded surpluses which were stored in warehouses for distribution to any part of the empire where crops had failed. The Incas expanded the arable area and food production by means of building terraces, irrigation, and control of water supply. The family's land and property were regarded as their own as long as they used them. Inca achievements in textiles (alpaca wool and cotton), pottery, monumental building, and bridge construction, were remarkable. They had no knowledge of the wheel or iron, but produced bronze from tin and copper. They had no written language. One of the primary administrative problems was communication. Their capital Cuzco lay astirde a four-way junction, with bridges across deep valleys and sections cut from solid rock. Since they had no vehicles or domesticated animals, travel was only by foot. About 200 Spaniards, under the command of Francisco Pizarro, managed to destroy the Inca empire within two years (1531–1533).

province is divided into districts (1,764 altogether).

Under the constitution that came into force in 1980, Peru is governed by a president with wide executive powers who is elected by popular vote for a five-year term. The president appoints the government. The bicameral legislature consists of a Senate (60 members) and Chamber of Deputies (180 members); legislators are also elected for a five-year term.

The parties that have dominated the political arena in recent years are Alianza Popular Revolucionaria (APRA, or American Popular Revolutionary Alliance, a leftist party founded in the 1930s whose activities for many years were suppressed); Izquierda Unida (IU, or United Left); Convergencia Democrática (CD, or Democratic Convergence); Acción Popular (AP, or Popular Action Party); Izquierda Nacional (National Left); the Peruvian Party; and several radical communist organizations, one of which, the "Shining Path," has military underground units carrying out acts of violence, mainly in southern Peru.

Alberto Keinyo Fujimori, who was elected president in June 1990, took office the following month. He was the leader of the newly formed Cambio 90 (Change 90) movement.

Administrative Division

Departments	Capitals	area sq mi	area sq km	population (1987 estimate)
Amazonas	Chachapoyas	15,945	41,297	311,800
Ancash	Huaraz	14,158	36,669	936,600
Apurímac	Abancay	7,934	20,550	361,400
Arequipa	Arequipa	24,528	63,528	884,200
Ayacucho	Ayacucho	17,058	44,181	553,000
Cajamarca	Cajamarca	13,486	34,930	1,200,000
Cuzco	Cuzco	29,471	76,329	980,600
Huancavelica	Huancavelica	8,139	21,079	371,400
Huánuco	Huánuco	13,088	33,897	571,600
Ica	Ica	8,205	21,251	508,200
Junín	Huancayo	15,944	41,296	1,037,500
La Libertad	Trujillo	8,973	23,241	1,150,900
Lambayeque	Chiclayo	5,304	13,737	854,600
Lima	Lima	13,058	33,821	6,116,700
Loreto	Iquitos	146,342	379,025	605,900
Madre de Dios	Puerto Maldonado	30,271	78,403	44,500
Moquegua	Moquegua	6,065	15,709	123,400
Pasco	Cerro de Pasco	9,356	24,233	264,800
Piura	Piura	14,055	36,403	1,374,200
Puno	Puno	27,947	72,382	984,500
San Martín	Moyobamba	20,197	52,309	414,500
Tacna	Tacna	5,881	15,232	188,300
Tumbes	Tumbes	1,827	4,732	131,700
Ucayali	Pucallpa	38,931	100,831	211,700
Constitutional Province				
Callao	Callao	57	148	545,100
Total		***496,225**	**1,285,216**	**20,727,100**

*Detail does not add to total given because of rounding.

LIMA

Lima is the capital of Peru and of its most populous department (province). The city lies at the heart of the largest conurbation on the western side of South America, whose population is approaching 6 million (estimated 5.9 million in 1990). The municipal area of Lima has only 430,000 inhabitants, but the conurbation, which includes the port of Callao 13 kilometers (8 miles) away and a large number of satellite towns, mainly to the south, forms a very densely populated and continuous built-up area. It is, in fact, a huge oasis in the very arid Peruvian coastal area (with less then 50 millimeters [2 inches] of average annual rainfall) hedged between the Pacific coast and the foot of the Andes. Nearly 26 percent of Peru's population resides in this conurbation, which over the last 40 years has been one of the most rapidly growing urban areas in South America. Its population was about 900,000 in 1950, 1.2 million in 1960, and 3 million in 1970.

The site, on the southern banks of the Río Rimac, 13 kilometers (8 miles) from the coast, was chosen in 1535 by Francisco Pizarro because of the adequate supply of water from the river, the irrigated agriculture in the area, a headland, and an adjoining elongated island along the nearby coast, which provided good anchorage and protection for ships. Callao, which was built on this headland, is Lima's harbor. The site is also advantageous for access inland. The Spaniards made it the capital of most of their colonial possessions in South America and only toward the end of the colonial period was its dominance confined to the Viceroyalty of Peru. The Spanish city was laid out in a rectangular pattern around a central square (plaza), a pattern that the old city retains to this day, although much of the original city was ruined by an earthquake in 1746. The city and conurbation has been growing rapidly since the beginning of the twentieth century, first in the south, where settlements that grew into towns became the first suburbs of Lima, then westward into the open area separating Lima from Callao. Many old colonial-style buildings have been preserved in the older part of the city, which now forms Lima's center. These include the cathedral, churches, government buildings, and private mansions. Some of the towns in the southwestern part of the conurbation, such as Miraflores, are wealthy residential suburbs and seaside resorts. But much of the conurbation consists of very densely inhabited slums, squatter settlements, and residential suburbs of the poorer classes.

Lima dominates Peru's economic and cultural life. It has five national universities (including the Universidad Mayor de San Marcos, founded in 1551, which is the oldest in the Americas) and seven private universities, attended by a total of more than 150,000 students, and institutions of higher learning for various professions, the arts, music, and languages. There are also many museums and galleries. Many of Peru's industries are situated in greater Lima. The conurbation's rapid growth has produced acute problems of supplying water and food, which have to be brought from afar.

Plaza de Armas

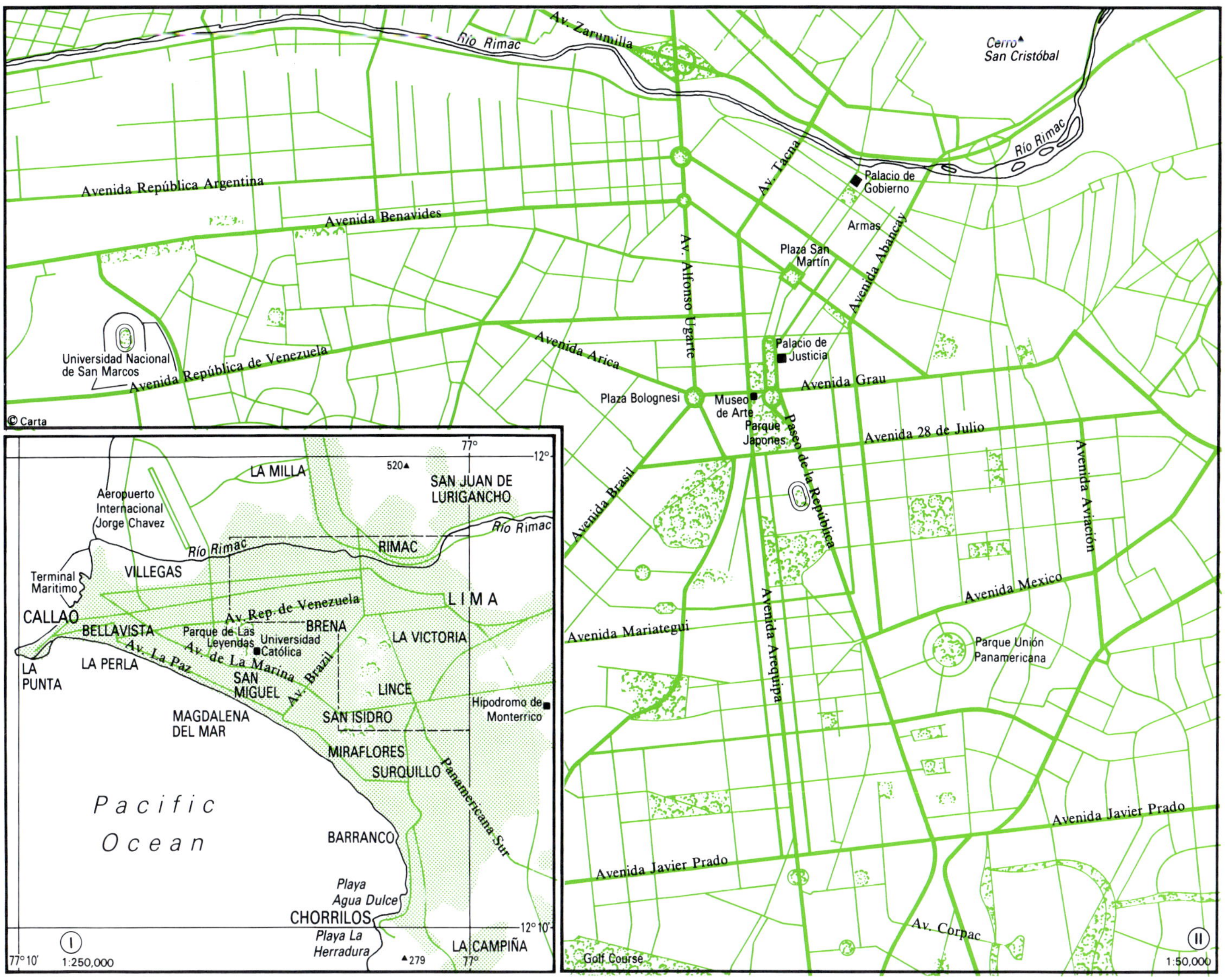

Río Rimac
Av. Zarumilla
Cerro San Cristóbal
Avenida República Argentina
Avenida Benavides
Av. Tacna
Palacio de Gobierno
Armas
Avenida Abancay
Plaza San Martín
Av. Alfonso Ugarte
Universidad Nacional de San Marcos
Avenida República de Venezuela
Avenida Arica
Palacio de Justicia
Avenida Grau
Plaza Bolognesi
Museo de Arte
Parque Japonés
Paseo de la República
Avenida 28 de Julio
Avenida Brasil
Avenida Aviación
Avenida Mexico
Avenida Mariategui
Avenida Arequipa
Parque Unión Panamericana
Avenida Javier Prado
Av. Corpac
Golf Course
II
1:50,000
© Carta

LA MILLA
520
77°
12°
SAN JUAN DE LURIGANCHO
Aeropuerto Internacional Jorge Chavez
Río Rimac
RIMAC
Terminal Marítimo
VILLEGAS
CALLAO
LIMA
Av. Rep. de Venezuela
BRENA
BELLAVISTA
Parque de Las Leyendas
Universidad Católica
LA VICTORIA
LA PUNTA
LA PERLA
Av. La Paz
Av. de La Marina
Av. Brazil
SAN MIGUEL
LINCE
Hipodromo de Monterrico
MAGDALENA DEL MAR
SAN ISIDRO
MIRAFLORES
SURQUILLO
Panamericana Sur
Pacific Ocean
BARRANCO
Playa Agua Dulce
CHORRILOS
Playa La Herradura
12°10'
LA CAMPIÑA
279
77°10'
I
1:250,000

BOLIVIA

Area
1,098,581 sq. km.
424,164 sq. mi.

Population
7,314,000 (1990 estimate)

Capital City
La Paz (administrative) Sucre (judicial)

Gross National Product (GNP) Per Capita
$570 (1988)

Population in Main Cities
(1986 estimates)
La Paz 1,033,000
Santa Cruz de la Sierra 458,000
Cochabamba 330,000
Oruro 184,000
Sucre 89,000

Highest Point
6,919 m. 22,700 ft. (Ancohuma)

Currency Unit
1 bolivian=100 centavos

Density
6.0 persons per sq. km.
15.6 persons per sq. mi. (1986)

Urban-Rural
urban 48.4% rural 51.6% (1986)

Natural Increase
2.8% (1985-1990)

Life Expectancy
53.1 (1985-1990)

Doctors
1,580 inhabitants per doctor (1985)

Hospital Beds
2.1 per thousand inhabitants (1984)

Infant Mortality
109.9 per thousand live births (1985-1990)

High School Pupils
37.0% of age group 14-17 (1984)

University Students
17.2% of age group 20-24 (1985)

Illiteracy Rate
25.8% (1985)

National Holiday
National Festival, 5-7 August

National Anthem
beginning "Bilivianos, el hado propicio coronó nuestros volos anhelos" ("Bolivians, propitious fate crowned our outcries of yearning")

Bolivia is the larger and more populated of two landlocked countries (the other is Paraguay) in South America. The country has a largely indigenous Indian population that has preserved its native languages and much of its traditional way of life. Bolivia is the poorest of the veteran South American countries. It borders Peru and Chile in the west, Brazil in the east, and Paraguay and Argentina in the south.

NATURAL REGIONS

Structurally and climatically, Bolivia consists of two main regions: the highlands and the eastern lowlands, divided between the Amazon and Paraná basins.

The Highlands

The highlands of Bolivia consist of three distinct parts: the Cordillera Occidental; the Altiplano; and the Cordillera Oriental. The Cordillera Occidental is part of the Andean range that extends along the western fringe of South America. It features many active volcanoes, part of a line of volcanoes that runs from southwest Peru to Chile. There is a distinct climatic difference between the northern and southern parts of the Cordillera Occidental; the latter are arid and almost uninhabited. In the north, some high valleys, with altitudes of up to 4,200 meters (14,000 feet), are inhabited by Indians who engage in subsistence agriculture (mostly irrigated) and pastoralism. With peaks of more than 6,500 meters (20,000 feet), steep slopes, and much volcanic activity, the Cordillera Occidental is the least inhabited part of the Bolivian Highlands.

The Altiplano is a high plateau, 3,600–3,900 meters (12,000–13,000 feet) above sea level, which lies between the Occidental and Oriental ranges. Its broadest point is over 320 kilometers (200 miles) north of Lake Poopó, where the Andes reach their greatest width, approximately 650 kilometers (400 miles). The Altiplano is divided into a number of basins by spurs of the Andes. The northernmost of these basins, which extends into Peru, is partly occupied by Lake Titicaca, at 3,812 meters (12,507 feet) the world's highest large lake. Most of the population around Lake Titicaca is engaged in subsistence agriculture, growing mainly potatoes, corn (maize), quinoa (a small edible herb), and some vegetables. The density of the rural population decreases farther south in more arid basins that are partly covered by shallow, saline lakes or marshes. The marshy and saline shores of Lake Poopó (3,690 meters [12,120 feet]), whose depth is only 3 meters (10 feet), are uninhabited, as are the surroundings of the arid saline swamps and salt pans farther south, Salar de Coipasa and Salar de Uyuni.

The capital, La Paz, the highest (3,630 meters [11,900 feet]) large city in the world, is situated in a valley southeast of Lake Titicaca below the rim of the Altiplano. Part of the population of the Altiplano has since before the arrival of the Europeans been engaged in mining activities concentrated around two main centers—Corocoro and Oruro. These areas were important sources of silver in the Spanish colonial period.

The structure of the Cordillera Oriental is more varied and complex, with distinctly different landscapes and habitats in the northeast, which follows a northwest to southeast direction, and the south, which follows a north to south direction. The northeastern part rises abruptly to great heights above the Altiplano (the Titicaca Basin and La Paz Valley) and has snow-capped peaks of over 6,400 meters (21,000 feet). The descent from this part of the Cordillera Oriental to the eastern lowlands is generally abrupt. The eastern slopes are densely covered by forests and are known as the Yungas, the wettest part of the Bolivian Andes.

The southern part (from the vicinity of Santa Cruz) rises abruptly from the Altiplano in a precipitous escarpment but has a less rugged upper surface that slopes gently toward the eastern lowlands. This high level surface of 3,600–4,300 meters (12,000–14,000 feet) is surmounted by a number of short ranges with higher peaks. Known as the Puna (not to be confused with the vegetation type puna), this moderately high surface relief is dissected by a number of rivers that drain parts of the Altiplano and the Cordillera Oriental into the Paraguay River and the Paraná Basin. Natural conditions in the basins and valleys of the Cordillera Oriental are much more favorable to human settlement than those of the Cordillera Occidental and Altiplano. These basins are much lower (2,000–2,800 meters [6,000–9,000 feet]) and are better supplied with water. The most densely inhabited rural areas of Bolivia are in the main basins of this region, the most important of which are the basins of Cochabamba, Sucre, and Tarija. Agriculture is much more intensive and varied. The Cordillera Oriental also has a number of important mining centers. Potosí the highest (4,200 meters [13,780 feet]) and oldest center, was the richest source of silver in the early stages of Spanish colonial rule. Although tin is the main product of the mines of the Cordillera Oriental, lead, zinc, copper, silver, antimony, tungsten, and small quantities of gold are also extracted. Mining communities, mainly of native American Indians, are a prominent feature in the human landscape of this region.

The Eastern Lowlands

In the eastern lowlands, there are distinct differences between the natural features of the northeast and those of the southeast. In the northeast the Llanos de Mamoré, which slopes gently to the Amazon Basin, is well watered by rain and rivers and has rich natural vegetation, while in the southeast the Gran Chaco, which slopes toward the Pilcomayo and Paraguay rivers, is semiarid, with dry scrub and savanna and occasional gallery forests along the rivers. The eastern lowlands are sparsely populated. The discovery of oil and natural gas, the development of roads between Santa Cruz (the region's main urban center) and the urban centers of the Altiplano, and government-backed settlement have resulted in a significant increase in population in this region since the 1950s. The eastern lowlands are Bolivia's main source of tropical agricultural products.

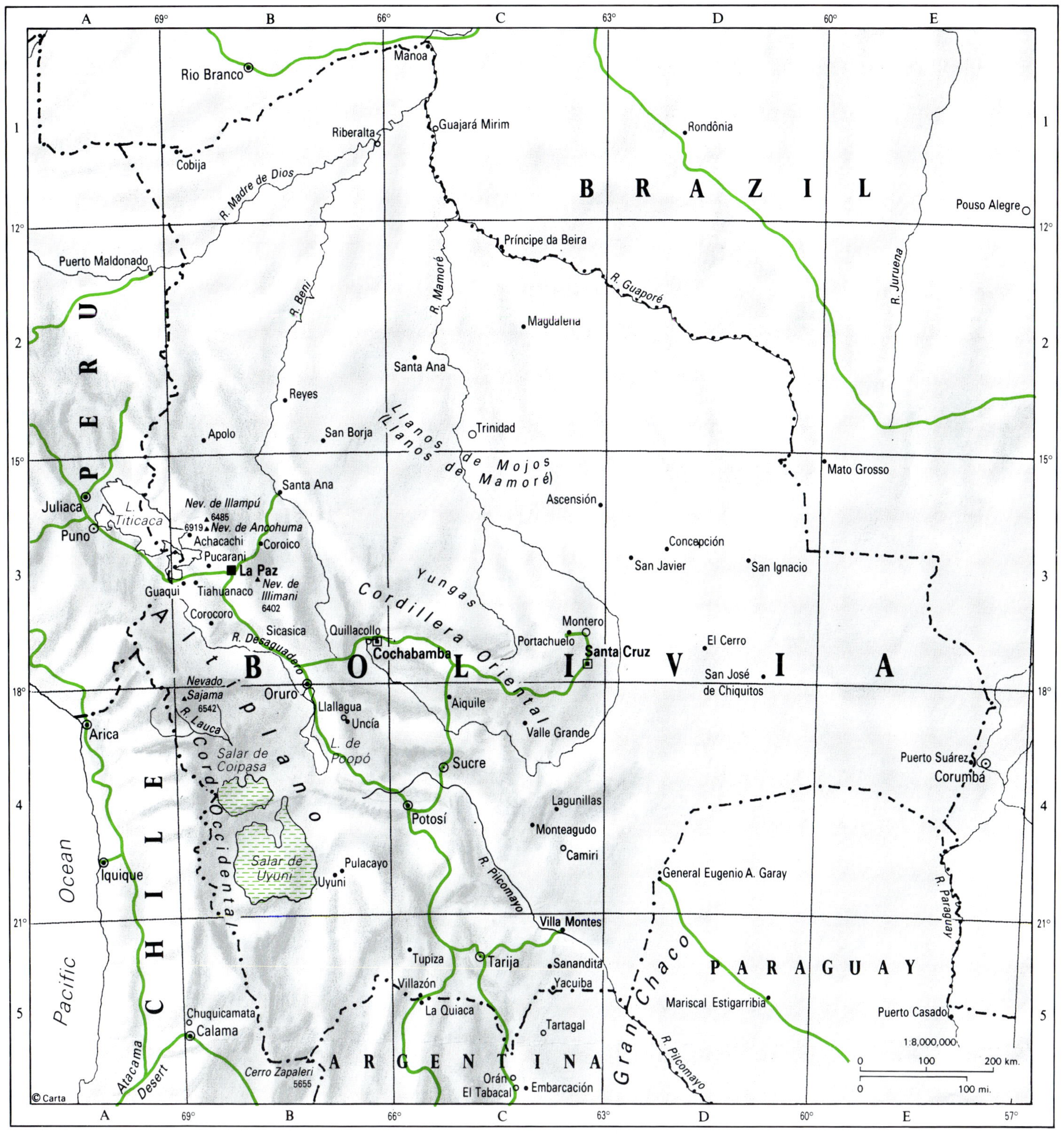

LAKE TITICACA

Because of its location and environmental influence, Lake Titicaca since prehistoric times has been one of the main focuses of human settlement in South America. The remains found at Tiahuanaco near the southeastern end of the lake attest to the previous existence of one of the oldest civilizations known in the Americas, preceding that of the Aymara and Inca. The first Europeans (Spaniards) who reached the lake found its surroundings to be one of the most densely populated areas in South America. It continued so until the nineteenth century. The area around the lake is still densely populated.

The highest large lake in the world (3,812 meters [12,507 feet]), it is 200 kilometers (125 miles) long, with a maximum width of 110 kilometers (69 miles), maximum depth of 280 meters (918 feet), and an area of 8,300 square kilometers (3,240 square miles). It is a fresh-water lake fed by a number of rivers coming mainly from the Cordillera Real (part of the Cordillera Oriental) near its eastern shores. The surplus waters of the lake are drained by Río Desaguadero into the shallow brackish waters of Lake Poopó. The temperature of the lake varies little through the year (10°–12°C [50°–53.6°F]). Under the influence of the lake, temperatures in the surrounding area do not drop at night nor in winter as much as they do at similar altitudes on the Altiplano. Thus, wheat and maize (corn) can be grown to a higher altitude (3,900 meters [12,800 feet]) around the lake than in other parts of the Altiplano. Lake Titicaca includes many small bays and headlands along its shores as well as small islands. The lake has an extensive fleet of motorboats carrying goods and passengers, especially between the Peruvian and Bolivian ports.

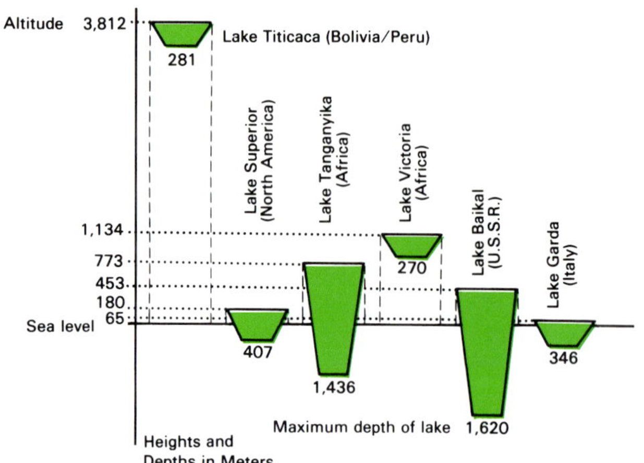

Reed fishing boat on Lake Titicaca

CLIMATE

Altitude and the changes in annual precipitation toward the southwest dominate the climate of Bolivia. Widely varying conditions can often be seen over short distances. Average seasonal temperature ranges are generally smaller than the average diurnal ranges. The average temperatures of the coldest (June/July) and warmest (November) months at La Paz (3,630 meters [11,900 feet] above sea level) are 6.4°C (43.5°F) and 11°C (51.8°F), respectively; at Cochabamba (2,580 meters [8,450 feet]), 14°C (57.2°F) and 20°C (68°F); and at Santa Cruz (640 meters [2,100 feet]), 18.2°C (65°F) and 24.2°C (75.6°F). The average seasonal range is approximately 6°C (11°F) whereas the diurnal range is 11°–16°C (20°–29°F).

Lake Titicaca, with a nearly constant water temperature of 10.5°C (51°F) throughout the year, has a moderating influence on its surroundings; winter temperatures in its environs are slightly higher than those at similar altitudes elsewhere on the Altiplano. The southern areas that form the Bolivian part of the Gran Chaco have the highest temperatures in South America, with highs of over 40°C (104°F) and an average of 28°C (82.5°F) and 22°C (72°F) for the hottest and coolest months.

The rainy season lasts from approximately October to March and is longer in the north. The southwestern part of Bolivia is arid, and agriculture there is largely dependent on irrigation. The northeastern flanks of the Cordillera Oriental and the northern part of the lowlands have abundant rainfall (an annual average of over 1,500 millimeters [60 inches]).

The extreme south is semiarid, with an average annual rainfall of 500 millimeters [20 inches]) and frequent drought. The northern part of the eastern lowlands and the adjacent lower slopes of the Cordillera Oriental are covered by dense evergreen forests. The vegetation of the Bolivian Chaco is that of a dry savanna with scrublands, thorny bushes, and high grasses. The average annual precipitation at La Paz is 565 millimeters (22.6 inches), at Cochabamba—460 millimeters (18.5 inches), at Villazón (in the extreme south)—270 millimeters (11 inches), and at Salar de Uyuni—less than 100 millimeters (4 inches).

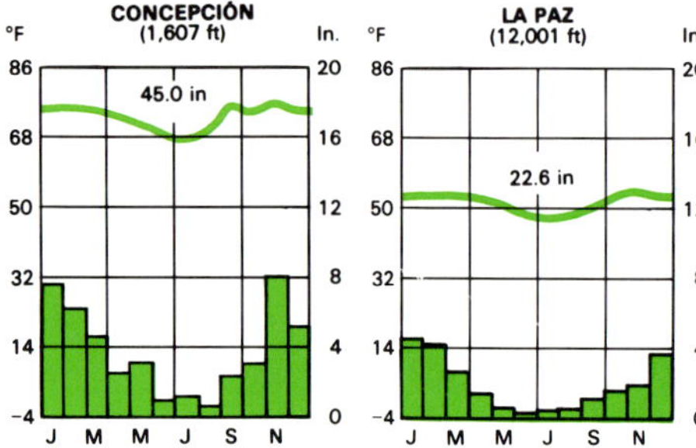

POPULATION

Bolivia's population was estimated at 7 million in 1989 (5.9 million at the 1982 census) and has been increasing over the last decade by an average annual rate of 2.6 percent. It has more than doubled over the last forty years, numbering just over 3 million at the 1950 census. Approximately 55 percent of the total population is believed to be of "pure" indigenous Indian descent, 25 to 30 percent mestizo, and about 15 percent European. The Indians make up the great majority of the population in the northern parts of the Altiplano and the higher valleys and basins of the Andes. Spanish is the official language, but more than half of the population speaks native languages. About 34 percent speaks Quechua and 25 percent Aymara (mainly in the Cordillera Oriental and southern Altiplano). More than 95 percent of the people are Catholic and about 1 percent Protestant. Native religions are still predominant among Indians in isolated parts of the country.

Bolivia's population is concentrated mainly in the northern parts of the Altiplano and the basins and valleys of the Cordillera Oriental. The eastern lowlands (with the exception of Santa Cruz and its surroundings), most of the Cordillera Occidental, and the southern parts of the Altiplano are only sparsely populated. Only two of Bolivia's nine departments (17 percent of the total area) have a population density of 16–20 persons per square kilometer (40–50 per square mile), while 59 percent of the total area has a density of less than 3 persons per square kilometer (7.5 per square mile). The average population density for the country as a whole is 6.4 persons per square kilometer (16 per square mile). The portion of the urban population is 49 percent; it was 33.5 percent in 1950. The principal cities are as follows: La Paz (the administrative capital)—1.1 million (1989); Santa Cruz—470,000; Cochabamba—340,000; Oruro—190,000; Potosí—120,000; and Sucre (the legal capital)—90,000.

POPULATION BY AGE GROUP, 1988

Age group	Percent
80+	0.3%
75-79	0.5%
70-74	0.9%
65-69	1.4%
60-64	2.0%
55-59	2.5%
50-54	2.9%
45-49	3.5%
40-44	4.4%
35-39	5.2%
30-34	6.2%
25-29	7.3%
20-24	8.7%
15-19	10.3%
10-14	12.2%
5-9	14.4%
0-4	17.3%

ECONOMY

The exploitation of mineral resources, which accounts for nearly all the country's exports, and agriculture, which caters mainly to the local market, form the basis of Bolivia's economy. It is strongly influenced by fluctuations of demand and price of gas and tin on the world market. Most of the country is underdeveloped and poverty is widespread, especially among the rural and mining populations. The GNP per capita was $570 in 1988, one of the lowest in Latin America. Bolivia is a substantial contributor to the international drug trade. The inflation rate was 16 percent in 1987.

Agriculture

While 43 percent of Bolivia's population depends on agriculture (to a large extent subsistence agriculture) for its livelihood, only three percent of the country's area is under cultivation. This is concentrated mainly in the northern part of the Altiplano, the basins and valleys of the Cordillera Oriental, and the western fringes of the eastern lowlands. In 1987, the main crops were corn (maize)—813,000 acres, 543,000 tons (grown up to an altitude of approximately 3,000 meters [10,000 feet]); potatoes—309,000 acres, 598,000 tons (to an altitude of nearly 4,000 meters [13,000 feet]); wheat—272,000 acres, 80,000 tons (to 3,300 meters [11,000 feet]; barley—205,000 acres, 67,000 tons (to 3,800 meters [12,500 feet]); rice—222,000 acres, 130,000 tons (mainly in the eastern lowlands); sugarcane—173,000 acres, 186,000 tons of sugar (lowlands); coffee—25,000 tons (mainly on the eastern slopes of the Cordillera Oriental); manioc—101,000 acres, 425,000 tons; soybeans—175,000 acres, 112,000 tons; cotton—25,000 acres, 6,000 tons of fiber; bananas (305,000 tons), citrus (69,000 tons); and various vegetables and fruit. Cultivated areas have in recent years been expanding. Coca is grown in large quantities.

EMPLOYMENT BY ECONOMIC BRANCH, 1982

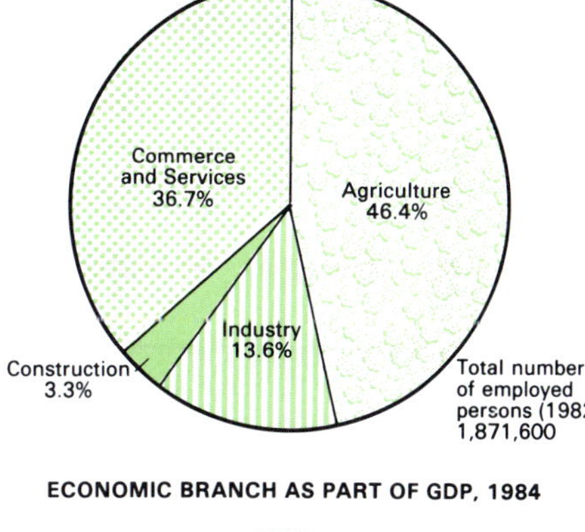

ECONOMIC BRANCH AS PART OF GDP, 1984

Agriculture 26.8%
Commerce and Services 42.4%
Industry 26.5%
Construction 4.3%

Of the total area, 24 percent is used for permanent pasture. The total number of livestock in 1987 included 5.4 million cattle, 9.5 million sheep, 2.3 million goats, 1.8 million llamas and alpacas, and 1.7 million pigs. Sheep, goats, llamas, and alpacas are raised in the Altiplano and the cordilleras; 5,200 tons of wool were produced in 1987. Of the total area, 51 percent (mainly in the eastern lowlands and northeastern flanks of the Cordillera Oriental) is covered by forests.

Mineral Resources

Oil (0.9 million tons in 1988; an average of 19,000 barrels per day in 1989) and natural gas (2,514 million cubic meters in 1985) are produced on the eastern fringes of the Cordillera Oriental (around Santa Cruz, Camiri, and Yacuiba). Pipelines carry the oil to the Pacific port of Arica (in Chile) and the gas to Argentina. Oil production, which reached its peak in the mid-1970s (1.9 million tons in 1976), has declined because of a failure to develop new sources. The production and export of natural gas has increased, however, and in 1986 provided nearly 50 percent (in value) of Bolivia's exports.

Next in importance is tin (8,100 tons in 1987), which is mined mainly in the vicinity of Oruro. Some mines are located at altitudes of over 4,000 meters (14,000 feet). Bolivia was the world's second largest producer of tin during the first half of the twentieth century. Large-scale tin mining began in 1895 and replaced silver as Bolivia's most important export, which had held this position since the sixteenth century. Other minerals produced (mainly in the Oruro and Potosí regions) are zinc—39,000 tons (in 1987), antimony—10,240 tons, sulfur—3,900 tons, copper—3,130 tons, silver—140,000 kilograms, gold—760 kilograms, lead, bismuth, and uranium. Large deposits of iron ore have been discovered but are exploited only on a small scale.

LAND USE, 1987

Arable Land 3.0%
Nonproductive Area 21.8%
Pasture Area 24.4%
Forest Area 50.8%

MAJOR AGRICULTURAL CROPS, 1987

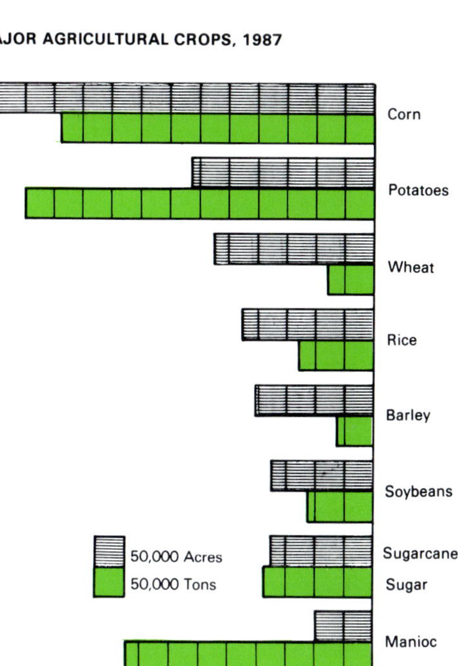

ECONOMY

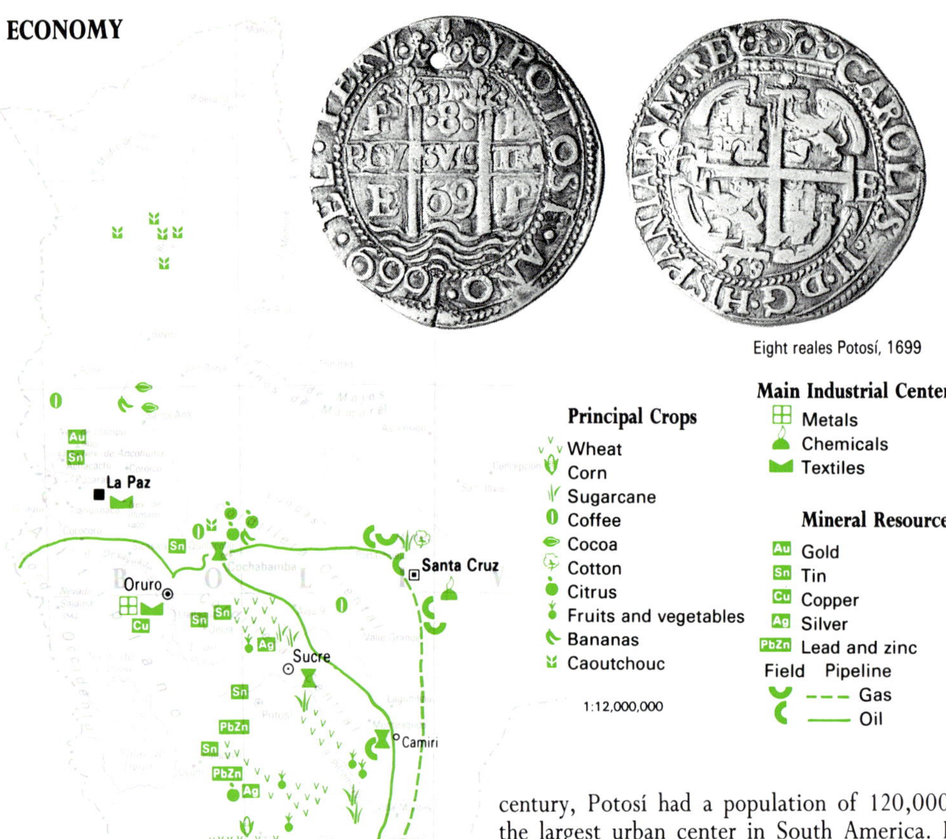

Eight reales Potosí, 1699

Industry

The few large industries are engaged mainly in processing mineral and agricultural products. Much industry is carried out by small plants concentrated in the main urban centers. Foodstuffs, tobacco products, clothing, various consumer goods, building materials (300,000 tons of cement), and agricultural tools are produced. Numerous workshops (laboratories) are engaged in processing and refining cocaine. Approximately 14 percent of the total workforce is employed in mining and industry.

Trade

Argentina is Bolivia's main trading partner, taking 56 percent of its exports in 1985 (mainly natural gas) and providing 11 percent of its imports. Trade with the United States accounted for 13.5 percent of exports and 16 percent of imports; Germany—5 and 5.2 percent; Japan—3.2 and 5 percent; and Britain—9 and 1.5 percent, respectively.

HISTORY

The western parts (Andean region) of what is today Bolivia formed part of the Inca empire when the first Spaniards reached this part of South America. Most of the indigenous Indian population lived in the highlands, mainly in clusters of comparatively dense habitation in the Altiplano (especially around and south of Lake Titicaca) and in the valleys of the Cordillera Oriental. The Spaniards, whose main interest was precious metals, discovered in 1544 rich silver deposits in a mountain at the foot of which they founded the settlement of Potosí at an altitude of 4,200 meters (13,800 feet) above sea level. By the end of the sixteenth century, Potosí had a population of 120,000, the largest urban center in South America. It held this position throughout the seventeenth and early eighteenth centuries, when its population exceeded 160,000. Potosí was preceded by Chuquisaca, later renamed Sucre, which was founded in 1538 and later became the administrative capital of the Spanish colonial rule. Other Spanish settlements followed, including La Paz (1548), Cochabamba (1574), and Oruro (1604). Alto Peru (Upper Peru), as Bolivia was known during the period of Spanish rule, was at first a dependency of the Viceroyalty of Peru. In 1776 it was transferred to the newly formed Viceroyalty of La Plata.

Spanish settlers, officials, and military commanders took possession of large areas of fertile land, forming rural estates on which the indigenous population was forced into slavery or serfdom. But the exhaustion of the main silver mines deprived Bolivia of its attractiveness to European immigrants. Potosí became virtually a ghost town inhabited by a few hundred families and remained this way for nearly two centuries, until tin became a much valued metal at the end of the nineteenth century.

Independence was declared in 1825 by an assembly which met in Chuquisaca (Sucre). General Antonio José de Sucre, who, in command of Colombian troops, played a leading role in the defeat of the Spanish garrison, was elected as the first president. The following year a constitution was drawn up by Simón Bolívar and adopted. It was then that the country received the name Bolivia. A long period of internal struggle and instability followed, with dictators, mainly military, ruling the country. Some of these dictators involved themselves in the internal struggles of Peru (in which Chile also intervened), while others struggled to prevent the annexation of Bolivia by Peru. The position of Bolivia's boundaries was uncertain and subject to conflict. However, Bolivian territory extended to the Pacific and included most of the coast of the Atacama Desert and the ports of Antafagasta and Arica. The discovery of rich nitrate deposits in the Atacama Desert and rising border tensions led to the outbreak of war between Chile and Bolivia (1879–1883), in which Peru participated on the side of Bolivia. Chile's victory in this war resulted in Bolivia's loss of its outlet to the Pacific. Efforts, mainly political, to regain some outlet to the sea failed. The railway which linked Bolivia with the Pacific coast (Oruro–Antofagasta) was inaugurated in 1892.

The number of inhabitants was estimated at nearly 1.5 million in the early 1850s and grew only to 1,696,400 by 1900. It increased to 3,019,000 over the next fifty years. The frequent changes in the regime were often accompanied by changes in the constitution. Thus, from the declaration of independence to the end of the nineteenth century, ten different constitutions were enacted. In 1904 Bolivia lost a substantial part of its possessions in the eastern lowlands to Brazil. Defeated in a war with Paraguay (1932–1935), Bolivia lost most of its territory in the Gran Chaco. At present, Bolivia extends over less than half the territory over which it claimed sovereignty when it declared independence. The expansion of mining from the end of the nineteenth to the first quarter of the twentieth century attracted foreign investment. This led to the development of three large foreign mining corporations that became dominant in Bolivia's economic and political life. These, together with large landowners and the military, actually controlled the country.

In 1952 a revolutionary party (Movimiento Nacionalista Revolucionario [MNR]) seized control of the government. This led to the expropriation of the mines by the state and to agrarian reform, by which the large estates were divided among former tenants and peasants. Before it was deposed by the army in 1964, the MNR introduced far-reaching economic and social changes. Over the next 25 years (1964–1989) Bolivia had 18 presidents (13 were generals), with only two completing a full term in office.

Explorer 1962

GOVERNMENT AND POLITICS

Bolivia is divided into nine departments, at the head of each of which is a governor (prefect) appointed by the president. Each department is divided into provinces that in turn are subdivided into cantons. Altogether there are 98 provinces and 1,272 cantons.

Under the present constitution, which came into force in 1967, the country is governed by an executive president who (together with a vice president) is elected by popular vote for a four-year term. The government is appointed by the president. The legislature includes the Senate and the Chamber of Deputies, whose members are also elected for four years. In the Senate each department is represented by three senators, for a total of 27. There are 117 seats in the Chamber of Deputies. Following elections held in May 1989, the composition of the Chamber of Deputies and Senate is as follows: MNR (today considered a central party)—40 and 9; Alianza Democrática Nacionalista (ADN, right-wing)—38 and 8; Movimiento de la Izquierda Revolucionaria (MIR, moderate left-wing)—33 and 8; Conciencia de la Patria (left)—9 and 2; and the United Left—10 and 0. Following the failure of any candidate to attain the required outright majority in these elections, the Congress in August 1989 elected Jaime Paz Zamora of the MIR as president.

La Paz is the seat of government and administrative capital. Sucre, which preceded La Paz as capital, is the seat of the Supreme Court and the legal capital.

LA PAZ

Bolivia's administrative capital (seat of government) since 1898, La Paz is also the capital of its most populated province (department). It is the world's highest capital and highest large city (3,580 meters [11,740 feet]). Its population, which was estimated at nearly 1.2 million in 1990, has doubled over the last twenty years (562,000 in 1970) and has nearly quadrupled since the 1950 census, when it was 321,000. Sixteen percent of Bolivia's population resides in La Paz. It is situated in the broad deep troughlike valley of the river that bears the same name well below (about 400 meters [1,400 feet]) the surface of the Altiplano. The surface of Lake Titicaca, about 60 kilometers (40 miles) to the northwest is higher by 235 meters (770 feet). The high snow-capped mountains, especially Mount Illimani (6,460 meters [21,200 feet]), which rise east of La Paz, provide a magnificent background to the city.

The city was founded as Nuestra Señora de La Paz (Our Lady of Peace) in 1548 by a Spanish expedition headed by Alonso de Mendoza. The site, which was inhabited by Inca peasants, has favorable climatic conditions, sheltered as it is from the cold winds that blow over the Altiplano. The city developed only after it became Bolivia's capital; it had a population of 79,000 in 1900. There is little left of the old colonial and nineteenth-century town with the exception of some steep narrow streets and the layout of some squares. The Plaza Murillo, with the city's cathedral, legislative buildings, and government institutions, is the focal area of the central part of the city, which has many modern buildings, including skyscrapers. Bolivia's most important university, Mayor de San Andrés (founded in 1830), several other institutions of higher learning, and museums give La Paz its dominant position in the country's cultural life. There are many industries, mainly producing consumer goods, in the city and its surroundings. La Paz is connected by railway and highway to Chilean ports and Peru.

Administrative Division

Departments	Capitals	area sq mi	area sq km	population (1986 estimate)
Beni	Trinidad	82,458	213,564	248,000
Chuquisaca	Sucre	19,893	51,524	471,000
Cochabamba	Cochabamba	21,479	55,631	1,005,000
La Paz	La Paz	51,732	133,985	2,156,000
Oruro	Oruro	20,690	53,588	422,000
Pando	Cobija	24,644	63,827	48,000
Potosí	Potosí	45,644	118,218	897,000
Santa Cruz	Santa Cruz	143,098	370,621	1,086,000
Tarija	Tarija	14,526	37,623	278,000
Total		**424,164**	**1,098,581**	**6,611,000**

Overall view of La Paz, with Mt. Illimani in the background

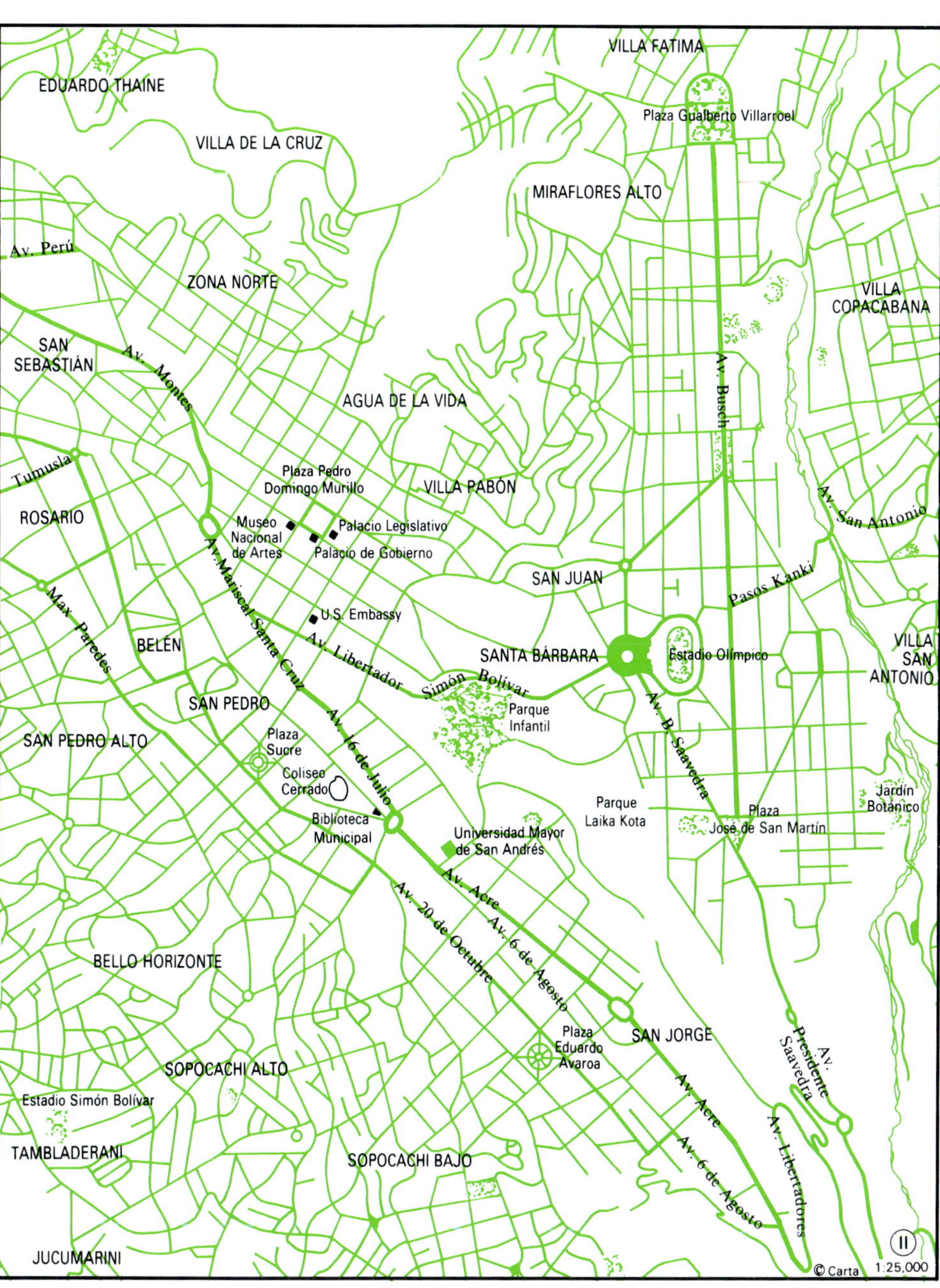

CHILE

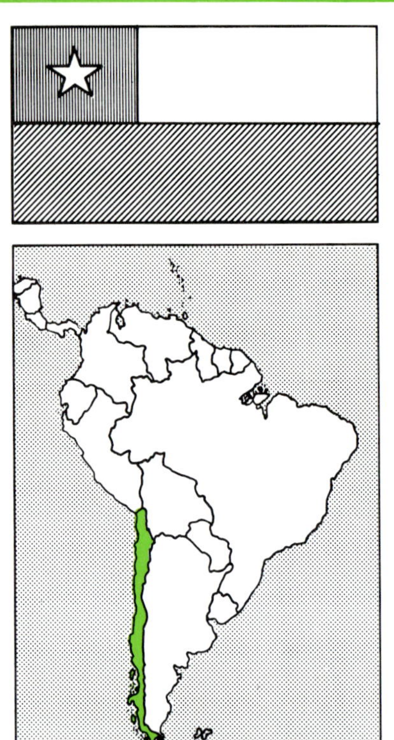

Area
736,905 sq. km.
284,520 sq. mi.

Population
13,173,000 (1990 estimate)

Capital City
Santiago

Gross National Product (GNP) Per Capita
$1,510 (1988)

Population in Main Cities
(1986 estimates)
Greater Santiago 4,913,062 (1987)
Concepción 294,375
Viña del Mar 297,294
Valparaíso 278,762
Talcahuano 231,356

Highest Point
6,880 m. 22,572 ft. (Ojos del Salado)

Currency Unit
1 new peso = 100 centavos

Density
16.7 persons per sq. km.
43.1 persons per sq. mi. (1986)

Urban-Rural
urban 83.6% rural 16.4% (1985)

Natural Increase
1.6% (1985-1990)

Life Expectancy
71.5 (1985-1990)

Doctors
2,045 inhabitants per doctor (1985)

Hospital Beds
2.7 per thousand inhabitants (1986)

Infant Mortality
18.1 per thousand live births (1985-1990)

High School Pupils
74.9% of age group 13-18 (1986)

University Students
16.6% of age group 20-24 (1986)

Illiteracy Rate
5.6% (1985)

National Holiday
Independence Day, 18 September

National Anthem
Canción Nacional
(National Song)

Chile is unique for its very long (4,270 kilometers [2,650 miles]) and comparatively narrow (maximum width approximately 400 kilometers [250 miles]) shape and for its great variety of natural features. It extends from latitudes 18° to 56° south and contains one of the driest regions in the world and one of the wettest areas in South America. It is bound on the north by Peru, on the northeast by Bolivia, on its long eastern border (5,150 kilometer [3,200 miles]) by Argentina, and on the west by the Pacific Ocean.

In its economy and public services, Chile is one of the most developed countries in South America.

NATURAL REGIONS

Chile consists of three distinct longitudinal structural regions—the Andes, the coastal range and the central valley— and a series of latitudinal and altitudinal climatic regions.

The Andes

The Andes (Cordillera) run along the entire length of the eastern part of the country. The watershed between the Pacific and Atlantic oceans, which follows the central and often highest ridges of the Andes, was adopted (by agreement with Argentina) as Chile's eastern boundary. In the north, approximately to latitude 27°, the Andes consist of two or more almost parallel ranges. Chile is included in the westernmost range and in some areas extends east beyond it. From the vicinity of Santiago southward, the Andes are made up of a single range, only the western part of which is included in Chile. The Chilean Andes are highest and most rugged and precipitous in the northern and central parts of the country, with peaks above 6,000 meters (20,000 feet). South America's highest peak, Aconcagua (6,960 meters [22,834 feet]), rises just east of Chile's border. Mountain passes in this part of the Andes are few and difficult, rising above 3,000 meters (10,000 feet). South of Santiago, the Andes become gradually lower, with peaks of approximately 3,700 meters (12,000 feet) and in the extreme south, peaks reach approximately 2,500 meters (8,000 feet) and are generally less rugged. Passes are much lower and easier to negotiate. In the extreme south, the Andes are fragmented by deep, latitudinal valleys (of glacial origin) deep ocean inlets and channels. The mountains extend through the island of Tierra del Fuego to the southern end of the continent.

Near the Chilean Andes and along their western flank is one of the world's densest concentrations of volcanoes, both extinct and active. There are over 2,000, including 48 that have erupted at least once within the last 100 years (17 in the north, 24 in central Chile, and 7 in the south). The abundance of volcanic features in Chile and its vicinity is also reflected in the frequent seismic events and the conspicuous evidence of recent tectonic movements.

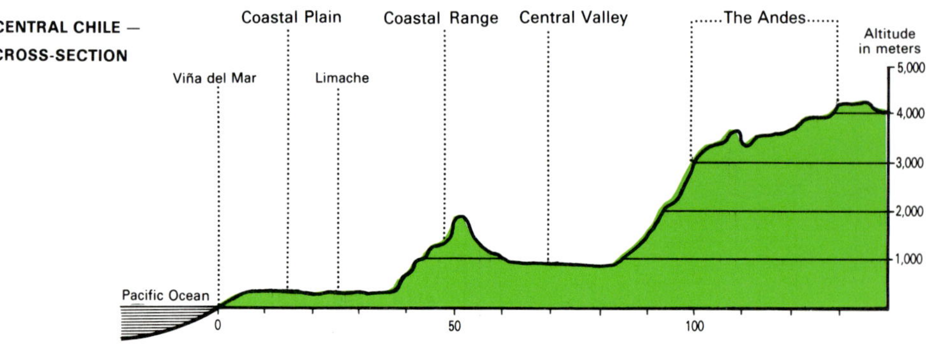

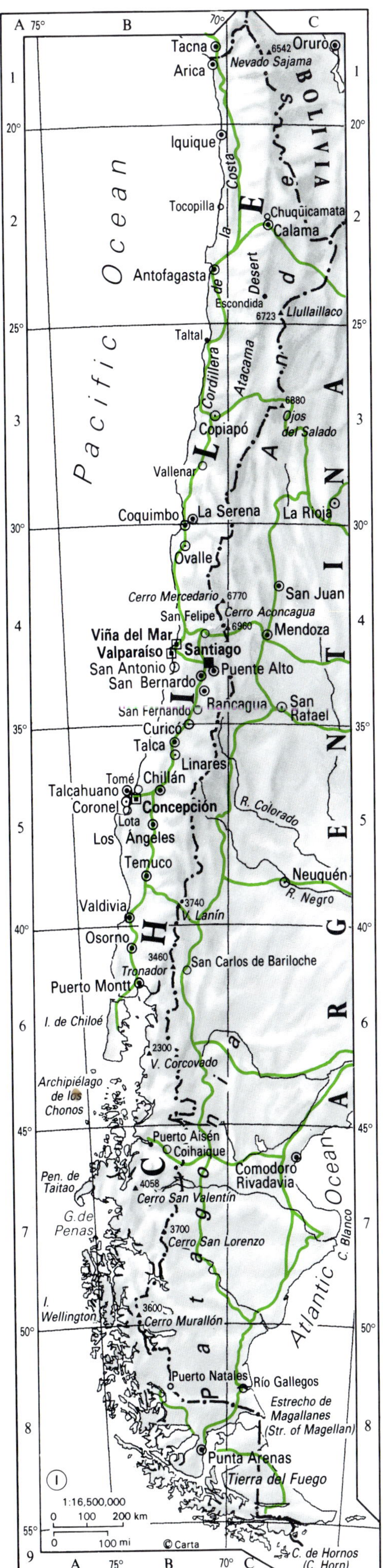

The Coastal Range

The second structural region is the coastal range (Cordillera de la Costa), which follows the coastline closely throughout northern and central Chile, from Arica to Puerto Montt. It rises abruptly from the shoreline in high cliffs that for hundreds of miles form an unbroken wall, creating a coastline devoid of natural harbors and a formidable obstacle to access inland. Large parts of the coastal range are actually an eroded plateau descending west to the sea by cliff-bound terraces. The coastal range rises to an altitude of approximately 2,700 meters (8,800 feet). It is highest in the north and in the center and gradually becomes much lower and broken south of Santiago. The few rivers that penetrate the coastal range and empty into the Pacific do so through narrow, deeply incised canyons.

The southward extension of the coastal range beyond Puerto Montt forms a chain of approximately 3,000 hilly islands, extending along a fjord-lined coast to Cape Horn at the southern extremity of the South American continent. The largest of these islands is Chiloé, just south of Puerto Montt. This chain of islands is interrupted by the Taitao Peninsula, which is a southern relic of the triple-longitudinal-belt structure that predominates farther north.

The Central Valley

The third structural region, and the most important one, insofar as human settlement is concerned, is the depression between the Andes and the coastal range known as the Central Valley. It is a long and narrow basin of varying width, reaching approximately 80 kilometers (50 miles) at its widest section. The Central Valley is not continuous; it is interrupted by spurs from the Andes and is divided by a wide mountainous intrusion into two main basins, each of which includes a number of smaller basins.

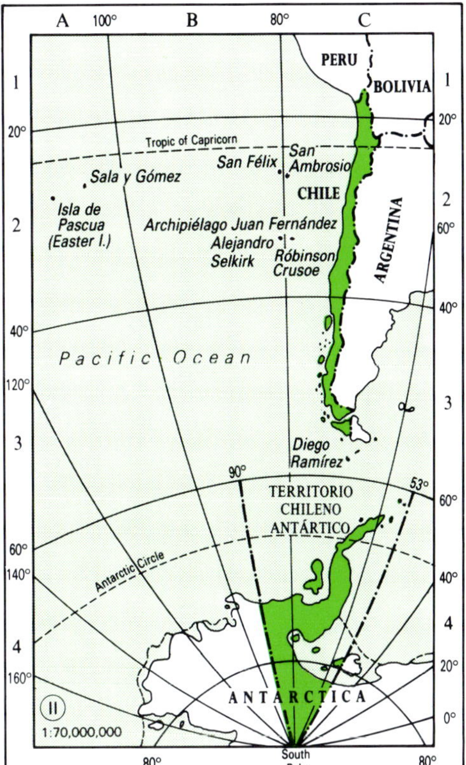

The northern basin, extending from Arica to Copiapó, is the Atacama Desert, one of the driest areas on earth. The bottom of the basin is about 600 meters (2,000 feet) in elevation; along its eastern margin stands a line of large alluvial fans. Most of this part of the Central Valley is a closed basin into which drain numerous small seasonal streams with sources in the Andes. The northern part of the Central Valley and the adjoining slopes are rich in mineral resources, especially sodium nitrate, which was mined on a large scale during the second half of the nineteenth and first quarter of the twentieth century.

The second major basin of the Central Valley is that of central Chile. It extends from Santiago southward to Puerto Montt and is Chile's main agricultural area and its most densely inhabited region. It is climatically the most attractive part of the country. Its base elevation is highest near Santiago (about 700 meters [2,300 feet]), sloping southward to about 100 meters (300 feet). The depression between the Andes and the coastal range continues south of Puerto Montt, where it becomes submerged and takes the form of straits, inlets, and bays on the fjorded coast of southern Chile, separating the extremely indented coastline from the thousands of islands and islets strewn parallel to it. The triple-longitudinal-belt structure fades away in the far south, beyond the Gulf of Penas, where only the much eroded and fragmented Andes remain. Chile includes the western, most of the northern, and the southern parts of Tierra del Fuego and the adjoining islands. The entire length of the Strait of Magellan is bordered by Chilean territory, which includes a short stretch on the Atlantic coast.

The Island Territories

Chile owns several groups of small and mostly uninhabited volcanic islands opposite its shores in the eastern Pacific: 1. The Juan Fernández Islands (179 square kilometers [70 square miles]; about 516 inhabitants), which include the island of Robinson Crusoe, 700 kilometers (430 miles) west of central Chile. 2. Easter Island (Isla de Pascua, 162 square kilometers [63 square miles]; 1,870 inhabitants), located 3,760 kilometers (2,340 miles) west of central Chile. 3. Sala y Gómez (3 square kilometers [1.2 square miles]; uninhabited), located about 3,400 kilometers [2,120 miles] west of central Chile. 4. San Félix and San Ambrosio (Islas de los Desventurados, 3.3 square kilometers [1.3 square miles]; uninhabited), 930 kilometers (580 miles) west of central Chile. 5. Diego Ramírez Islands (3 small uninhabited islets), approximately 100 kilometers (60 miles) southwest of Cape Horn. Chile claims a section of Antarctica between longtitudes 53° and 90° west and the neighboring islands.

CLIMATE

Extending over 38 degrees of latitude, from the tropics to the vicinity of Antarctica, and from sea level to altitudes of over 6,000 meters (20,000 feet), Chile has a wide variety of climatic conditions. Extreme aridity prevails over the northern part of the country; up to about latitude 30° is the Atacama Desert, which includes some of the driest areas on

EASTER ISLAND

Isla de Pascua, or Rapa Nui, is a small Pacific island 3,760 kilometers (2,340 miles) west of the Chilean coast, famous for its archaeological remains and stone-carved statues of human likenesses. The island, covering an area of 162 square kilometers (63 square miles), is volcanic in origin, with several extinct volcanoes, one of which rises to an altitude of 537 meters (1,760 feet). The island was discovered on Easter Day in 1722 by the Dutch sailor Roggeveen. It was populated at the time by Polynesian tribes, whose number was estimated at 4,000. They subsisted on agriculture and fishing. Within a century, the population was reduced to 175, as a result of slave traders carrying off to America many of the young inhabitants and diseases introduced by the Europeans. The present population, concentrated in one village, numbers approximately 1,900, some of whom are descendants of the aboriginal inhabitants. They engage mainly in subsistence agriculture.

Archaeological remains include pyramid-like structures, stone masonry, towers, cisterns, statues, and various stone and fish-bone utensils. Unique to this island are numerous statues cut from soft volcanic rock, depicting the upper part of the human body. Wooden tablets with engraved signs and images resembling a form of pictograph are another unique feature. The origins of these relics and the culture that they represent have been the subject of many studies and much speculation.

A row of seven *moai* reerected in 1960

earth. For years, there is no rainfall at all. During the first half of the twentieth century, fourteen years passed at Iquique without a single drop of rain. The average annual rainfall for Arica is 0.9 millimeters (0.04 inches). In the extreme southern part of the desert the average annual precipitation is 100–120 millimeters (4–5 inches). Extreme aridity also prevails over the mountains of this region. The average annual rainfall at Chuquicamata is only 46 millimeters (less than 2 inches) at an altitude of 2,710 meters (8,880 feet) and 106 millimeters (approximately 4 inches) at 4,820 meters (15,800 feet). Temperatures are moderate along the coast throughout the year and more extreme inland, especially in the central basin. The average temperatures for the hottest (February) and coldest (July) months at Arica (the extreme north) are 22.4°C (72°F) and 15.7°C (60°F), and at La Serena (the southern part of the arid region), 18.4°C (66°F) and 11.7°C (53°F), respectively. Rain in the southern part of this region falls during the winter, mainly from May to August.

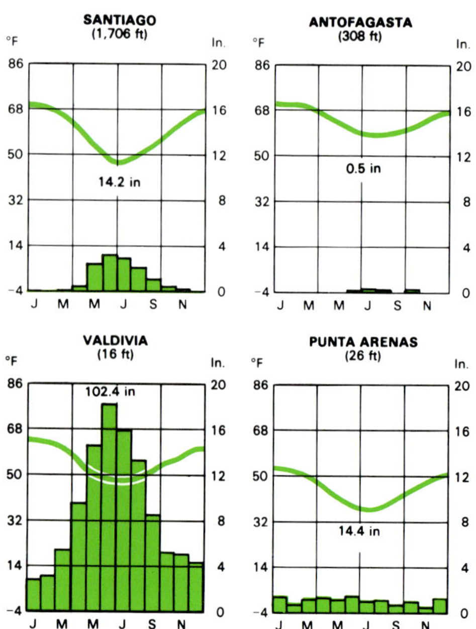

Central Chile (30°–42° latitude) has a Mediterranean type of climate, with cool and rainy winters (April to September) but without a completely dry season. Average annual precipitation increases substantially and temperatures decrease toward the south. The average temperatures for the hottest (January) and coldest (July) months at Santiago (at an altitude of 500 meters [1,600 feet] in the Central Valley) are 20°C (68°F) and 8.1°C (46.6°F), respectively, and in Puerto Montt (in the extreme south of the region), 14.9°C (59°F) and 7.8°C (46°F). The average annual precipitation at Santiago is 370 millimeters (approximately 15 inches) and at Puerto Montt, 1,840 millimeters (approximately 74 inches). Rainfall occurs throughout the year in Puerto Montt.

The climate of the southern region is cool and rainy the year round. It is characterized by abundant low clouds. The average temperature for the warmest (January) and coldest (July) months at Puerto Aisén (at 47°33′ latitude) and Punta Arenas (on the Strait of Magellan) are, respectively, 14°C (57°F) and 4.6°C (40°F), and 11.7°C (53°F) and 2.5°C (36.5°F). The average annual precipitation at Puerto Aisén is 2,973 millimeters (119 inches) and at Punta Arenas, 440 millimeters (17.6 inches). The changes in the position of the snow line on the westward-facing slopes of the Andes can serve as an indication of the variation in climatic conditions with latitude and altitude. The line of permanent snow is approximately 5,500 meters (18,000 feet) in Chile's extreme north. It descends to approximately 4,300 meters (14,000 feet) opposite Santiago, to 3,400 meters (11,000 feet) near Concepción, 2,100 meters (7,000 feet) near Valdivia, 1,500 meters (5,000 feet) opposite Puerto Montt, and to approximately 700 meters (2,200 feet) at Tierra del Fuego.

POPULATION

The population of Chile was estimated at 13 million at the beginning of 1990. It was 11,275,000 in the 1982 census and has increased at an average annual rate of 1.7 percent. It was 4.3 million in 1930 and 7.4 million in 1960. Immigration from Europe contributed much to the comparatively rapid growth of the population in the first two decades after World War II. The great majority of the population is mestizo, that is, of mixed European and American Indian descent. Estimates of the portion of the population of "pure" European descent vary between 2 and 30 percent. Only about 5 percent are "pure" descendants of the native Indian population. These are mainly concentrated in the Andes in northern Chile, in some valleys of south central Chile, and along the southern coast. The tribes of the extreme south have until recently been among the most primitive and poor inhabitants of the South American continent. The comparatively high percentage of people of mixed races is explained by the fact that over the first three centuries (sixteenth to eighteenth) of European settlement, males formed the great majority of immigrants, and many took Indian wives. Since the mid-nineteenth century, with the growth of European immigration, many of the mestizos have for several successive generations married only "pure" Europeans, which accounts for the considerable difference in the estimates of racial composition of the population. Up to the beginning of the nineteenth century, the great majority of the European settlers came from Spain, first from the south (Andalucia), but then also from the north. Beginning in the mid-nineteenth century, large numbers of immigrants came from Germany, Italy, Croatia (and other parts of what is today Yugoslavia), as well as from England, France, and other European countries. There has also been, since the beginning of the twentieth century, a large influx of Arabs (Lebanese, Syrians, and Palestinians). The German immigrants settled mainly in the southern part of central Chile, where there are a number of townships and rural areas in which they are conspicuous.

The official language is Spanish. The indigenous Indian population still uses native languages, mainly Araucanian. Approximately 89.5 percent of the population is Catholic, and 8 percent Protestant. There are still pagans among the Indian tribes in the south.

Nearly 90 percent of the population is concentrated in central Chile, in the area between Coquimbo in the north and Puerto Montt in the south, mainly in the region's Central Valley. Even in this part of the country, with the exception of the Santiago metropolitan area, the average population density does not exceed 50 inhabitants per square kilometer (130 per square mile). The population density in other parts of the country is much lower: 2.5-5.5 per square kilometer in the northern region and less than 1 per square kilometer in the southern part. The average population density for the country is 17 per square kilometer. Chile is one of the most urbanized countries in Latin America, with 86 percent of the population residing in urban areas. The urban population is greatest in the arid north, where it exceeds 90 percent of the total. Five million people, or 39 percent of Chile's population, live in the Santiago metropolitan area. Other important cities are (estimated population, 1988): Concepción—300,000; Viña del Mar—300,000; Valparaíso (main port)—280,000; Talcahuano (port and industrial center near Concepción)—235,000; Temuco—222,000; Antofagasta (main center of the arid north)—205,000; Rancagua—175,000; Arica (northern frontier center)—170,000; San Bernardo—170,000; Puente Alto—168,000; Chillán—150,000; Los Ángeles—128,000; Osorno—125,000; and Valdivia—118,000. The proportion of the urban population, especially that of Santiago, has increased considerably since the 1950s, to a large extent by migration from rural areas. This produced large slum areas in Santiago and some of the other main urban centers.

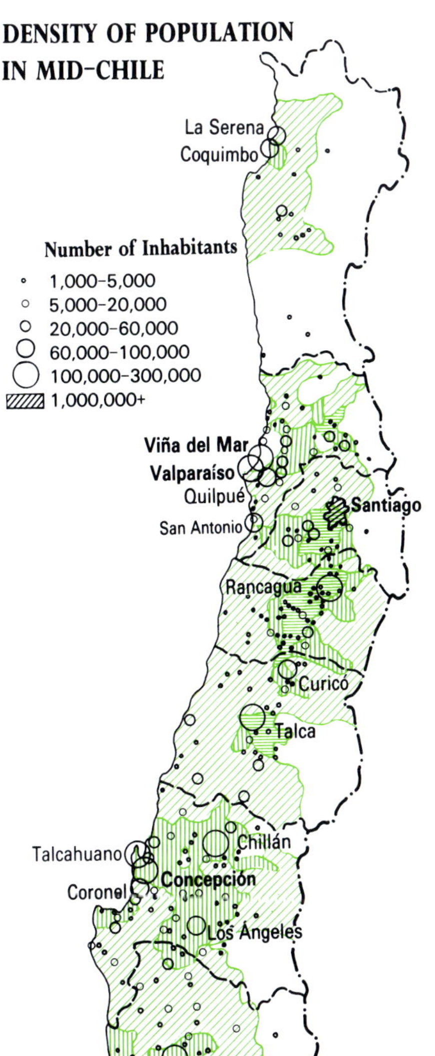

ECONOMY

Chile's economy is based on its rich mineral resources, on agriculture, which takes advantage of the wide variety of climatic conditions, on its rich fishing grounds, and on industry. There has been, however, much instability in the value of the most important minerals (copper, iron, nitrate) mined in Chile and in their contribution to the GNP and to the country's exports. These depend largely on demand and prices in the world market and on Chile's ability to compete with other mineral-producing countries. The exploitation of Chile's mineral resources is to a large extent in the hands of foreign, mainly U.S., companies. Mining plays a dominant role in the economy of the northern region, while agriculture, industry, and services play an important role in central Chile. Forestry, fishing, and mining are important in the south. The fluctuation in the extent and value of the production of minerals has prompted the development of industry and agriculture, especially for export.

The annual GNP per capita was $1,510 in 1988. It has only risen by $100 since 1978. Economic growth over recent years has been, on the average, 4 to 5 percent annually. Inflation has been one of the lowest in Latin America.

Agriculture

Only 7.3 percent of the area is agriculturally productive. Arable land is concentrated mostly in the Central Valley in central Chile. Agriculture in the northern region is largely dependent on irrigation in areas that are, in fact, oases. Agriculture is mainly engaged in the production of cereals, fodder, sugar beets, potatoes, vegetables, and fruit. The following were the main products in 1988: wheat—1.4 million acres, 1.87 million tons; corn—222,000

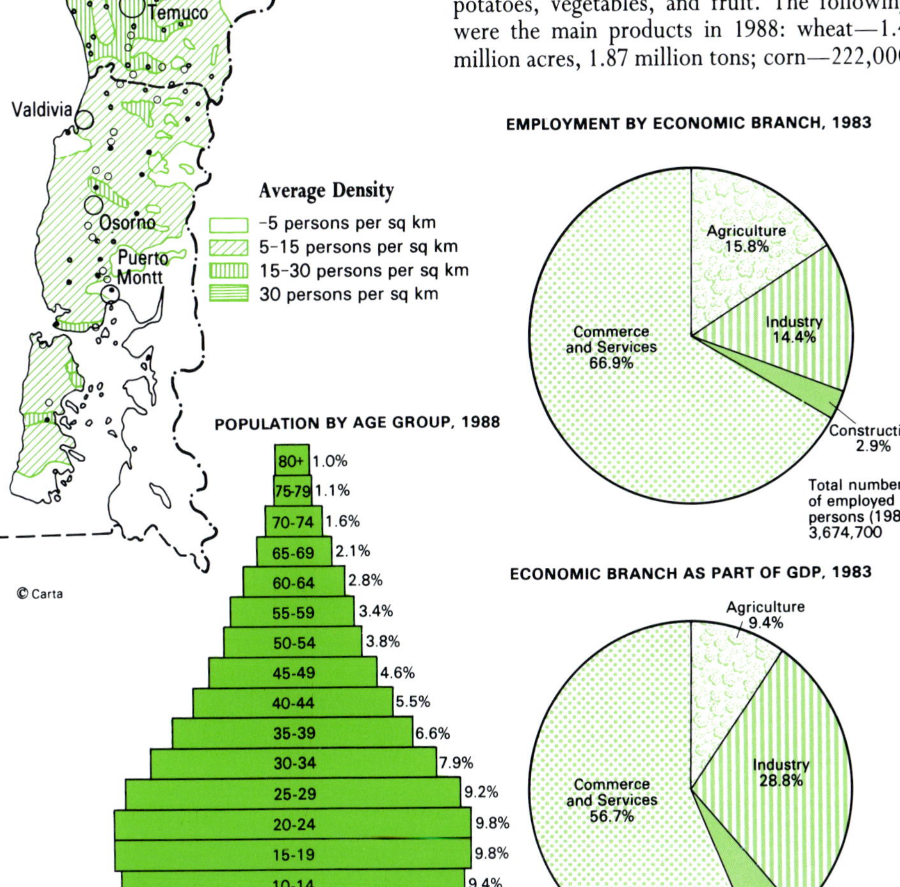

AGRICULTURE

acres, 617,000 tons; oats—150,000 acres, 127,000 tons; rice—96,000 acres, 147,000 tons; potatoes—153,000 acres, 727,000 tons; sugar beets—116,000 acres, 443,000 tons sugar; grapes—310,000 acres, 1.2 million tons; apples—590,000 tons; pears—80,000 tons; peaches—147,000 tons; prunes—72,000 tons; and citrus—145,000 tons. Much of the fruit is exported during the northern winter to the United States, Canada, and Europe. Chile also produces and exports a large quantity of wine.

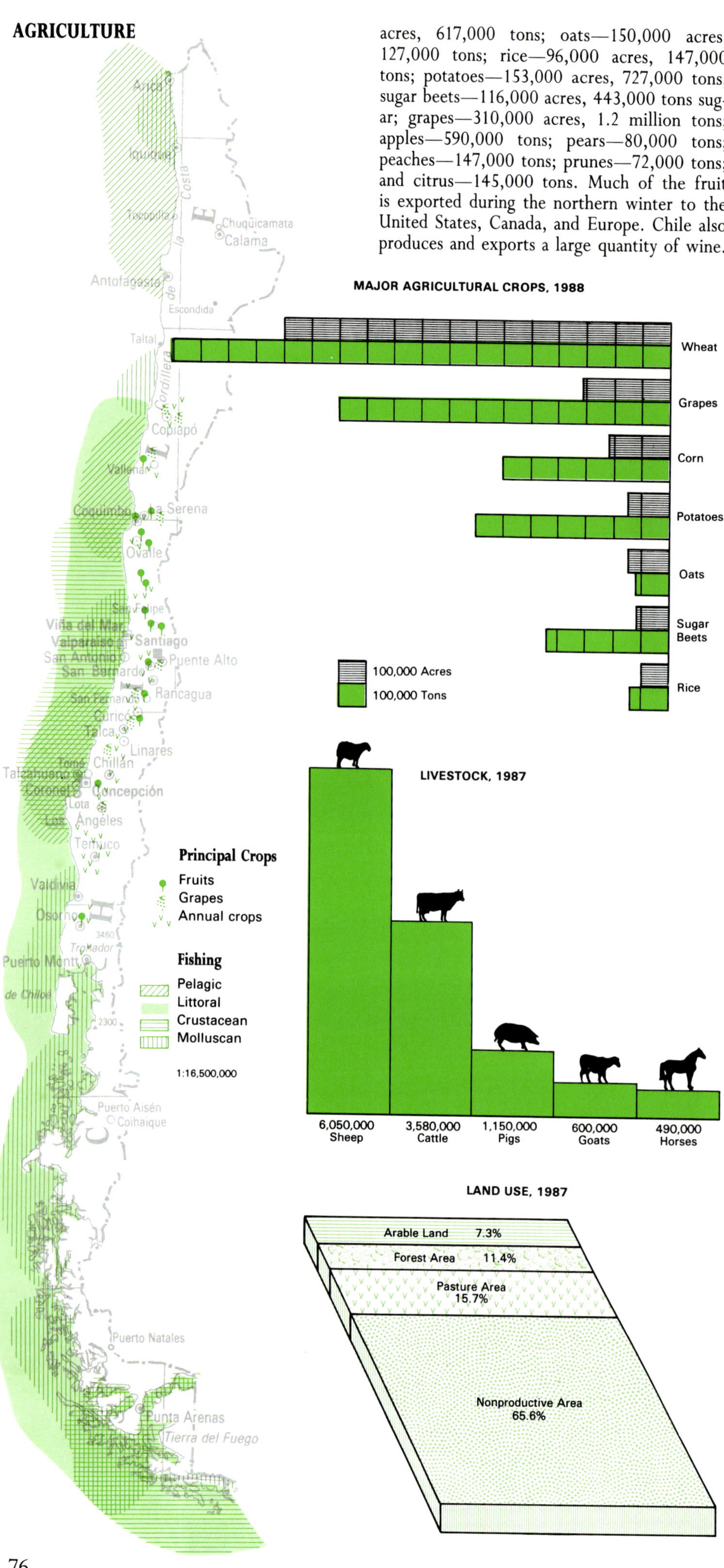

Livestock (3.6 million cattle, 6 million sheep, 600,000 goats, 1.15 million pigs, 490,000 horses) are raised, mainly in central Chile and the northern part of the southern region. Approximately 16 percent of Chile's area is classed as permanent grazing ground. Forests cover 11.4 percent of the area, mainly in the southern region, from which 18.5 million cubic meters of timber and pulp were produced in 1987.

Large estates (haciendas) occupy a substantial part of Chile's agricultural lands. These are remnants of the Spanish colonial period, when extensive land grants were made to army officers and colonial officials. In the early 1920s, nearly 90 percent of the farmland in central Chile was in large estates. Although no official land reform has taken place, many of these estates were broken up and sold as small farms. This process is still going on. However, much of the agricultural land is still cultivated by tenants or by hired labor; 13.6 percent of the workforce is employed in agriculture.

Fisheries

Chile's long coast, with its 200-nautical-mile-wide exclusive fishing zone, yields a large and varied catch of fish (220 edible species) and other seafood. Production was 5.2 million tons in 1987 (5.6 million tons in 1986). The fishing industry employs 1.5 percent of the workforce. A large part of the catch is processed and exported.

Mineral Resources

Chile is the world's largest producer of copper. It has the world's most productive mine at Chuquicamamta (in the northern region). Production reached 1.4 million tons in 1987. It is expected to rise considerably by 1991, when a rich, new mine, at Escondida, will begin production. Northern Chile also has rich, high-grade iron-ore deposits, mainly in the Coquimbo area; 6.7 million tons were mined in 1987 (7 million tons in 1986). Most of the ore is exported, and the rest is used by the local iron and steel industry. Chile has the world's richest deposits of nitrate, in the Atacama Desert in the north. The mining and exporting of nitrate (used for fertilizers and for the production of high explosives) flourished during the last quarter of the nineteenth and first quarter of the twentieth centuries. It reached its peak during World War I, when more than 3 million tons were exported annually. Production was 870,000 tons in 1985, and of a by-product, iodine, 2,760 tons.

Other minerals produced include: gold—19,200 kilograms (1987); silver—500 tons (1987); molybdenum—16,600 tons (1986); manganese—31,000 tons (1986); zinc—19,600 tons (1987); lead—800 tons (1987); bauxite—54,000 tons (1986); sulfur—109,000 tons (1985); and potash—20,000 tons (1986). Uranium, cobalt, antimony, and tungsten are also mined.

Oil and natural gas fields, near the eastern outlet of the Strait of Magellan and the northern coast of Tierra del Fuego, produced 1,940,000 tons of oil and 4,358 million cubic meters of gas in 1986. In 1989 chile's oil fields produced an average of 24,000 barrels per day. Coal production was 1.3 million tons in 1986.

INDUSTRY & MINERALS

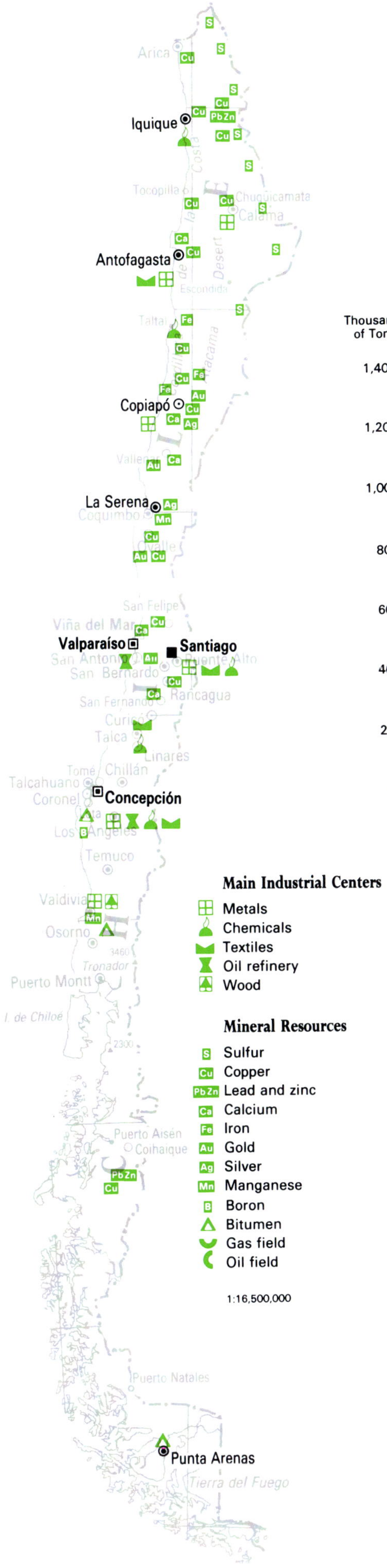

Industry

Chile's industry is largely based on local mineral resources, agricultural raw materials, and forestry. Industries include copper refining, nitrate products, iron smelting and steel production (in a large government-owned plant near Concepción), oil refining, cement and various building materials, various chemicals, timber and pulp, furniture and various wood products, a wide variety of food products, meat packing, fish packing and fish products, sugar, wine, and beer. There is also a large textile, clothing, and leather industry. Industry is mainly concentrated in and around four main urban centers: Santiago (the largest industrial center, in which 20 percent of the local labor force is employed in industry), Valparaíso, Concepción, and Valdivia. Government policy encourages the establishment of new industries in sparsely inhabited regions, especially in the south. Fifteen percent of the workforce is employed in industry.

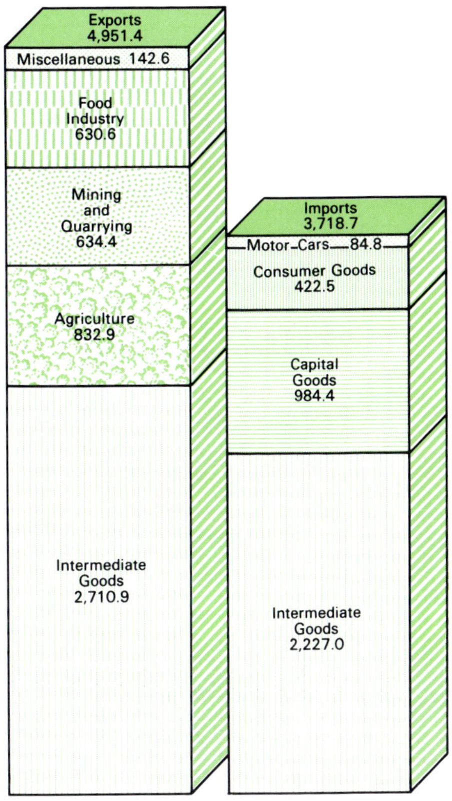

Trade

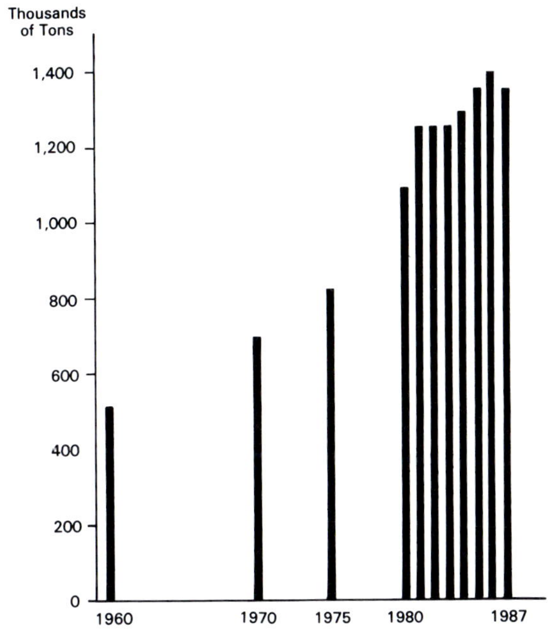

The main trading partners are the United States, which takes 22 percent of the exports and provides 20 percent of the imports; Japan—9 percent and 10 percent; West Germany—10 percent and 8 percent; and Brazil—7 percent and 8 percent. Copper accounts for 42 percent of the exports, other minerals (gold, iron, nitrate, titanium, and others) approximately 20 percent, fresh fruit—10 percent, fish and fish products—7 percent, and pulp and paper—6 percent.

HISTORY

When the first Spaniards arrived, Quechua tribes inhabited the northern region, and Araucanian tribes inhabited the central region and the northern part of the southern region. Small primitive tribes roamed the south. The Incas were in control of the northern area and part of central Chile. Warlike Araucanian tribes, who held the Incas back, dominated much of the rest of the country. The Indian population of central Chile at the time the Spaniards arrived from Peru was estimated at half a million. The first Spanish settlements were established in the mid-sixteenth century: Santiago in 1541 and Concepción in 1550. Spanish settlers, mainly from Andalucia, were attracted to central Chile because of the pleasant climate and fertile soil. The settlers had to face repeated assaults from the Araucanians. The on-and-off war with the Indian aborigines continued into the second half of the nineteenth century. The settlers, the majority of whom were men, and the Spanish soldiers stationed to protect the settlers took local wives, and thus grew a population of mixed race (mestizo). By the mid-seventeenth century, the population of the Spanish settlements and their surroundings numbered approximately 100,000, most of whom were mestizos. This population grew to about 500,000 (over two-thirds of whom were mestizos) by the mid-eighteenth century and to one million by 1830. Those with European blood were concentrated in central Chile, between Santiago and Concepción; few settled in the northern and southern regions. This pattern of dispersion began to change only in the second half of the nineteenth century, with the rapid growth of mining activities and the immigration of non-Iberian Europeans. The population increased to 1.8 million by 1865 and to approximately 3 million by 1900.

Under Spanish colonial rule, northern and central Chile were part of the Viceroyalty of Peru. The south remained under the control of the Araucanians almost until the nineteenth century. Independence was first declared in 1810. At that time, central Chile was to a large extent controlled by a small, upper class of Creoles (locally born Europeans), most of whom owned large estates. A period of internal instability and strife followed, which resulted in the restoration of Spanish rule in 1814. Combined Argentinian and Chilean forces under José de San Martín (Argentinian) and Bernardo O'Higgins (Chilean), who crossed the Andes from Argentina, managed to defeat and drive out the Spanish army and restore Chile's independence (1818). O'Higgins became Chile's first president. He ruled the country for five years. A constitution, which came into force in 1833, after a period of instability and struggle between liberal elements and the dominant Creole aristocracy, gave the latter control of the country in what amounted to a dictatorial regime. Joaquín Pérez, who became president in 1861, established a more liberal regime, which was continued by his successors. However, the interests of the upper class, comprised mainly of owners of large estates and wealthy business people, continued to predominate.

Chile defeated Bolivia and Peru in a war (1879–1883) for the control of the Atacama Desert and its rich mineral deposits. In the course of this war, Chilean troops occupied Lima. Chile won the disputed territory. Bolivia lost its outlet to the open sea and Peru the Tarapacá district.

A multiparty, parliamentary regime came into being in 1891, following a bloody eight-month war in which the forces of the ruling president were defeated. However, even this development did not deprive the upper class of its dominant position in internal politics. After a short period of military rule (1924–1925), followed by the reinstatement of the democratically elected president Arturo Alessandri, a new, more progressive constitution came into force (1925). Alessandri was re-elected president in 1932 after another period of military dictatorship. Left-wing parties, including communist, gained much influence from the 1930s onward and played an important role in the elections of several presidents. However, the right-wing parties remained in actual control. A presidential candidate of the left-wing parties, Salvador Allende, won the elections in 1970. Upon assuming office, he nationalized the mines, industries, and public services. Allende was deposed and died in a military coup in September 1973, which was followed by 16 years of military dictatorship led by General Augusto Pinochet. Democratic elections were held in 1989. Democracy was restored in 1990 with the assumption of the presidency by Patricio Aylwin Azocar, following free elections.

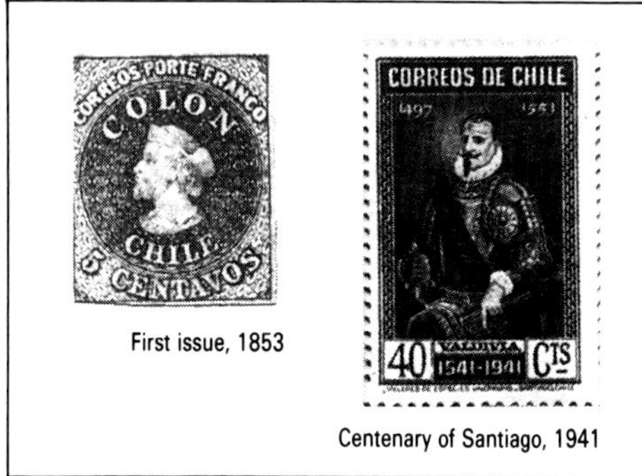

First issue, 1853

Centenary of Santiago, 1941

One peso Santiago, 1818

GOVERNMENT AND POLITICS

The country is divided into 13 administrative regions, each of which is headed by an administrator (*intendente*) appointed by the central government. The regions are divided into 40 provinces each of which is administered by a governor (*gobernador*) who is also appointed by the central government. The provinces are divided into municipalities headed by appointed mayors (*alcalde*).

In accordance with the constitution that came into force in 1981, the National Congress is composed of a Senate and a Chamber of Deputies. The Senate has 47 members (38 elected and 9 appointed) who serve an eight-year term. The Chamber of Deputies has 120 members who are directly elected for four years.

As laid down in the constitution, a plebiscite was held in October 1988 to determine whether the rule of the military dictatorship under General Pinochet should be extended. Nearly 55 percent voted against the continuation of the military regime. This led to free presidential elections in December 1989, in which Patricio Aylwin Azocar of the Christian Democratic Party (PDC) was elected, supported by a 17-party coalition. He took office on March 11, 1990. Election results to the Chamber of Deputies were as follows: Christian Democratic Party (PDC)—38 seats; National Renewal (PRN; right-wing)—29 seats; Socialist Party (PSCH)—16 seats; Independent Democratic Union (UDI; right-wing)—11 seats; Radical Socialist Democratic Party (PRSD)—6 seats; left-

Administrative Division

Regions	Capitals	area sq mi	area sq km	population (1986 estimate)
Tarapacá	Iquique	22,422	58,073	319,401
Antofagasta	Antofagasta	48,381	125,306	368,433
Atacama	Copiapó	30,219	78,268	195,221
Coquimbo	La Serena	15,308	39,647	455,916
Valparaíso	Valparaíso	6,220	16,109	1,325,141
Libertador General Bernardo O'Higgins	Rancagua	7,024	18,193	624,657
Maule	Talca	11,783	30,518	799,028
Bío-Bío	Concepción	14,218	36,824	1,617,747
Araucanía	Temuco	12,263	31,760	750,152
Los Lagos	Puerto Montt	25,904	67,090	899,807
Aisén del General Carlos Ibáñez del Campo	Coihaique	42,085	108,999	73,760
Magallanes y de la Antártica Chilena	Punta Arenas	43,363	112,310	143,606
Región Metropolitana de Santiago	Santiago	5,331	13,808	4,858,342
Total		*284,520	736,905	12,431,211

*Detail does not add to total given because of rounding.

wing independent members—12 seats; right-wing independent members—8 seats. The left-wing and central parties have a majority of 72 seats in the Chamber of Deputies. Results of the Senate elections were as follows: PDC—13; PRN—11; PSCH—6; UDI—5; PRSD—3; 22 members of the left and center; and 16 right-wing members. However, all the 9 appointed members (appointed by the National Security Council, the High Court, and the outgoing president) are supporters of the right-wing parties, thus making rightist members the majority in the Senate.

SANTIAGO

With a population that has passed the 5-million mark, or 39 percent of Chile's population, Santiago has been over the last hundred years one of the fastest growing metropolises of South America. It had nearly 50,000 inhabitants when it became the capital of independent Chile in 1818. Its population grew to 111,500 by 1865 (when it was only 6.3 percent of Chile's population), to 256,000 by 1895, to 507,000 by 1920, to 952,000 by 1940, and to 1.9 million by 1960 (26 percent of Chile's population). Despite its rapid growth, its cosmopolitan nature, and the occurrence of several highly destructive earthquakes, the city has preserved much of its original rectangular pattern, as laid down during the sixteenth and seventeenth centuries. From the time it was founded (1541) it has been the most important and active European settlement in Chile because of its favorable central location and pleasant climate.

Santiago is located at the northern end of Chile's central intermont basin, extending from the foot of the Andes toward the coastal range at an altitude of 550–610 meters (1,800–2,000 feet). The older and central part of the city was built on both sides of a small river, the Mapocho (a tributary of the Maipú, one of Chile's larger rivers), which repeatedly broke its banks, flooding and seriously damaging parts of the city; it is now to a large extent enclosed and contained. Snow-capped peaks of the Andes, reaching altitudes of over 6,100 meters (20,000 feet), rise above the city. Some of these peaks are extinct, truncated, cone-shaped volcanoes. The backdrop of high mountains gives Santiago a natural landscape of great beauty. With its rapid growth in recent years, the city began to extend over the lower slopes of the Andes. Outcrops of hard rock form small steep hills which rise above the center of the city. The old Spanish fort stood on one of these hills, Santa Lucía. The hill is now a popular playground. The city is spaciously laid out with large garden suburbs and wide avenues and streets. It has also developed crowded slums where many of the poor and destitute live.

The center of Santiago, which has preserved the original Spanish colonial pattern, is a mixture of older buildings, some dating to the eighteenth century (such as the cathedral, the churches of La Merced and Santo Domingo, and some of the main buildings of the national university), and modern skyscrapers. Facing some of the old squares (Plaza de Armas, Plaza de la Constitución) are some of the city's finest public buildings, most of which were built during the second half of the nineteenth and the early twentieth century.

Greater Santiago and its surroundings are Chile's main industrial center, with approximately 60 percent of the country's industrial plants and 56 percent of the industrial work-force.

Due to its geographical position in a closed basin and climatic conditions resulting from its proximity to the high mountains, Santiago has in recent years been suffering serious problems of air pollution, caused by industrial expansion and the great increase in automobiles.

General view of Santiago

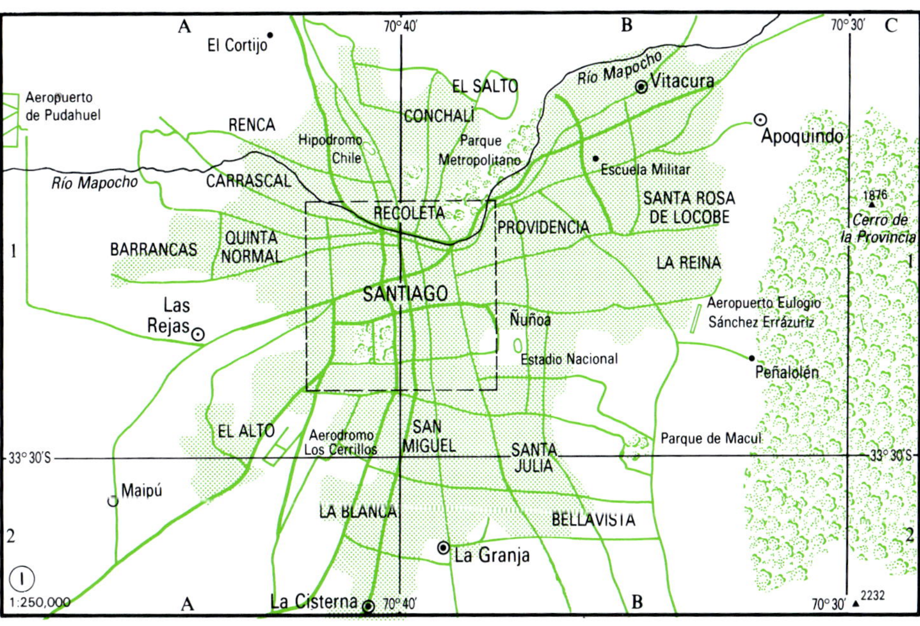

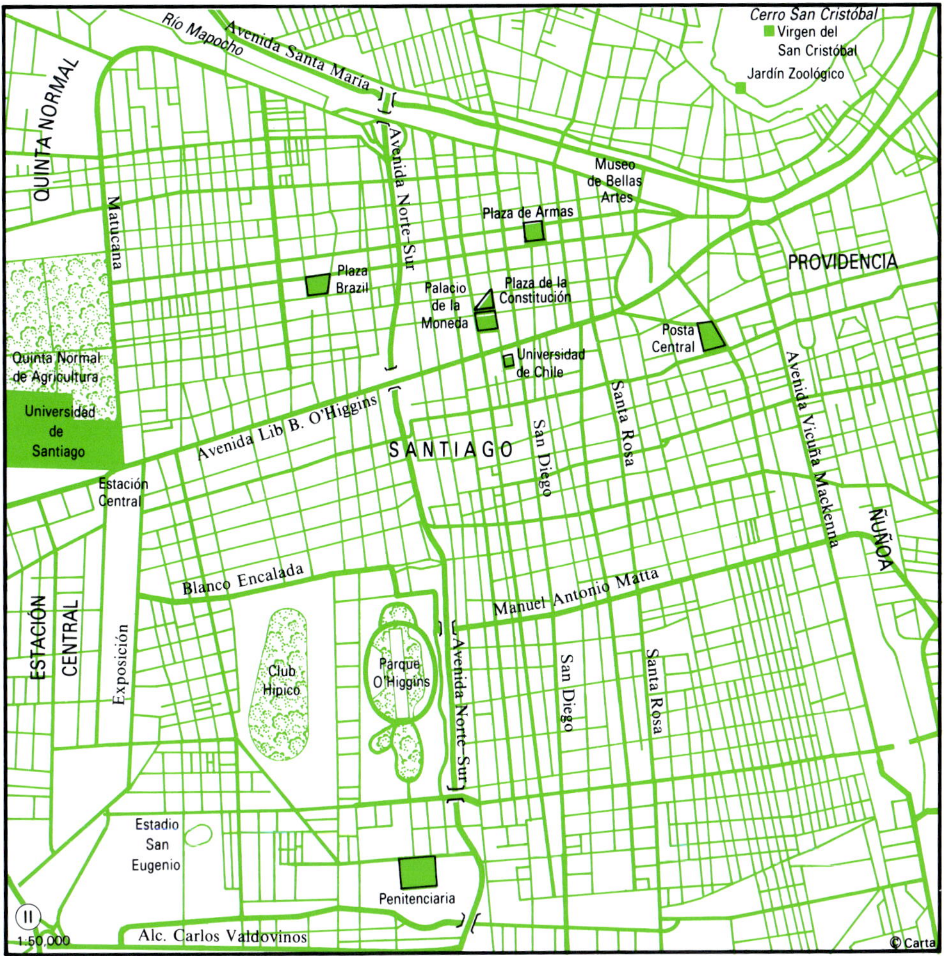

ARGENTINA

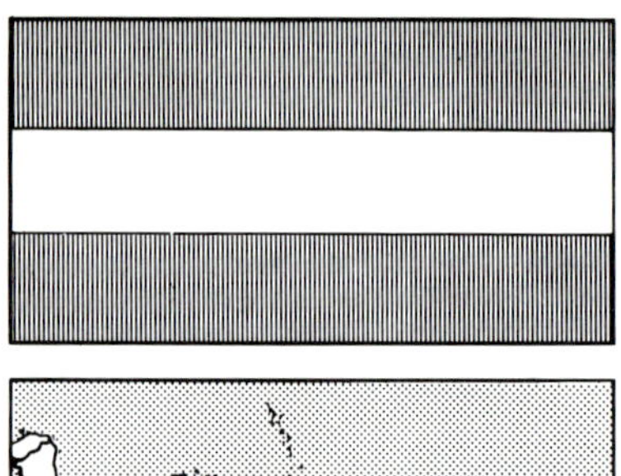

Area
2,780,092 sq. km.
1,073,399 sq. mi.

Population
32,332,000 (1990 estimate)

Capital City
Buenos Aires

Gross National Product (GNP) Per Capita
$2,640 (1988)

Population in Main Cities
(1980)
Buenos Aires 2,924,000 (1986)
Córdoba 968,700
Rosario 876,000
La Plata 454,900
San Miguel de Tucumám 392,800

Highest Point
6,960 m. 22,835 ft. (Mt. Aconcagua)

Currency Unit
1 austral = 100 centavos

Density
11.2 persons per sq. km.
28.9 persons per sq. mi. (1986)

Urban-Rural
urban 84.6% rural 15.4% (1985)

Natural Increase
1.3% (1985-1990)

Life Expectancy
70.6 (1985-1990)

Doctors
376 inhabitants per doctor (1984)

Hospital Beds
5.3 per thousand inhabitants (1985)

Infant Mortality
32.2 per thousand live births (1985-1990)

High School Pupils
74.0% of age group 13-18 (1986)

University Students
38.7% of age group 20-24 (1986)

Illiteracy Rate
4.5% (1985)

National Holiday
Independence Day, 9 July

National Anthem
beginning "Oíd, mortales, el grito sagrado Libertad" ("Hear, O mortals, the sacred cry of Liberty")

Argentina is South America's second largest country in area and population. It extends from the vicinity of Antarctica (55° south) in the south to the subtropics (21.5° south) in the north. The country has an Atlantic coastline of 4,990 kilometers (3,100 miles). Its boundary with Chile in the west, along the highest ridges of the Andes, follows the line that divides the Atlantic and Pacific watersheds. Argentina's northern neighbors are Bolivia and Paraguay. The boundary with Paraguay runs along the rivers Paraná, Paraguay, and Pilcomayo. Its border in the northeast with Brazil and Uruguay is formed mostly by the river Uruguay. The Paraná estuary, Río de la Plata, separates the most populated parts of Argentina and Uruguay. Argentina has boundary disputes with Chile and Uruguay, claims the Falkland Islands (named Islas Malvinas by Argentina), a large sector of Antarctica and adjacent islands (25°–74° west). Because of its great landmass and large number of geographical zones, Argentina has a wide variety of landscapes and climatic conditions.

NATURAL REGIONS

Argentina consists of three major natural regions, each of which is generally divided into a number of subregions. The most important, in population, economic activity, and size, is the lowlands and plains of the north, east, and center of the country. The Andes mountains and the adjoining highlands and foothills which extend along the entire western part of the country form the second region. The third region is the arid, low, deeply dissected plateau of Patagonia in the south.

The Lowlands and Plains

This is an almost featureless low ground between the Andes and the Brazilian Plateau that slopes gently southward and eastward from the watershed between the Amazon and Paraná basins toward the central part of the Argentine Atlantic coast. Most of the region consists of the plains and tributaries of the Paraguay, Pilcomayo, Bermejo, Salado, and Paraná rivers.

The northern part of these lowlands is known as the Argentinian Chaco. This is the southern part of the Gran Chaco, one of the major physical features of South America, extending from southwestern Brazil and eastern Bolivia across the western half of Paraguay into northern Argentina. The Chaco is a great plain interrupted in places by hilly areas and small depressions. Much of it is covered by deciduous, scrubby, and partly thorny woodland and grassy savanna with dense gallery forests along some of the river banks. Vast areas of the Chaco, especially along the main rivers, are inundated during the rainy season (summer) and remain swampy for much of the year. The quebracho tree, containing tannin, used in the tanning of leather, is abundant in the scrublands of the eastern Chaco, especially on the west side of the Paraguay–Paraná flood plains. The quebracho was the main incentive for the establishment of some of the European settlements in this region. The Chaco, which is the hottest part of Argentina, is sparsely populated, averaging approximately 5 persons per square kilometer (13 per square mile), with large uninhabited areas, especially in the northwest.

East and southeast of the Chaco is the region known as Entre Ríos (or Mesopotamia), which lies between the rivers Paraná and Uruguay. Much of this area has the appearance of undulating plains with rows of low hills. The higher parts are, in fact, interfluves separated by somewhat lower, gently sloping, broad valleys. Large areas of the Entre Ríos, especially the lower parts and many of the valleys, are also inundated during the rainy season and remain swampy throughout most of the year. The interfluves are covered by high grass and brush and make for good pasture, while the valleys are mostly covered by forest. Climatically, this is a more inviting region than most of the Chaco, especially since it has a more abundant rainfall. It has more than double the population density of the Chaco, averaging 11 persons per square kilometer (28 per square mile), though it is still only sparsely inhabited. Population density increases from north to south. This is primarily a pastural region with some dry farming, mainly in the south.

The most northeasterly part of Argentina, a region which forms a narrow wedge between Paraguay and southern Brazil, is the province of Misiones. Like Entre Ríos, Misiones forms part of the territory between the rivers Paraná and Uruguay. However, its physical characteristics differ. It is a southwesterly extension of the Brazilian highlands, a deeply dissected, low, flat-topped plateau in which streams have cut narrow and steep canyonlike valleys. Numerous falls and rivers run over the water-resistant rock and lava plateau, including the world-famous Iguazú Falls (4 kilometers [2.5 miles] wide and a record 82 meters [269 feet] high). Much of this territory is covered by forest. On a small part is grown yerba mate, used to brew an herbal tea popular in Argentina and other South American countries. Most of the people of this province live in villages and towns on or near the banks of the two large rivers that border on its east and west, usually on elevated sites above the normal flood level of these rivers.

The vast plain south of the Chaco and Entre Ríos and east of the Andes, is the Pampa, a grass-covered monotonous landscape that slopes gently to the east and ends in an escarpment, or barranca, along the Atlantic coast. It is generally divided into the Humid Pampa in the east and Semiarid Pampa in the west. These subregions differ not only in climate but also in some other natural attributes—mainly soil and surface features. The Humid Pampa is in fact the core area of Argentina. It is the most densely inhabited part of the country and the center of economic activity. It extends over approximately 15 percent of the total area and contains more than half of the Argentine population. The Humid Pampa includes the great conurbation of Buenos Aires, in which more than one-third of Argentina's population lives.

The Pampa is covered by a thick mantle of sediments, much of which is deposited by the rivers that flow from the Andes or is blown by strong dust winds from the semiarid west and northwest. While this mantle of sediment reaches a thickness of nearly 300 meters (1,000 feet) in the Buenos Aires area, outcrops of old resistant rocks (remnants of ancient mountains) are prominent in the eastern, southern, and northwestern parts of the Pampa, giving rise to the Sierra del Tandil (500 meters [1,600 feet]) and Sierra Ventana (1,280 meters [4,200 feet]) in the south and the Sierras de Córdoba (2,800 meters [9,150 feet]) in the northwest. There are large swampy areas in the northeast that result from the flooding or rise of the water table during the rainy season. Such marshes occur in other parts of the Pampa, especially in low-lying areas and where the natural drainage is poor. Because of the nature of the surface, rivers have changed sections of their courses and abandoned parts of their old beds.

Before European settlement, most of the Pampa was covered by tall grass with deciduous scrub trees and bushes. This type of vegetation, known locally as *monte*, still prevails in some parts of the Pampa. The Humid Pampa has taller grass and higher and more densely spaced trees. The Pampa, especially the Humid Pampa,

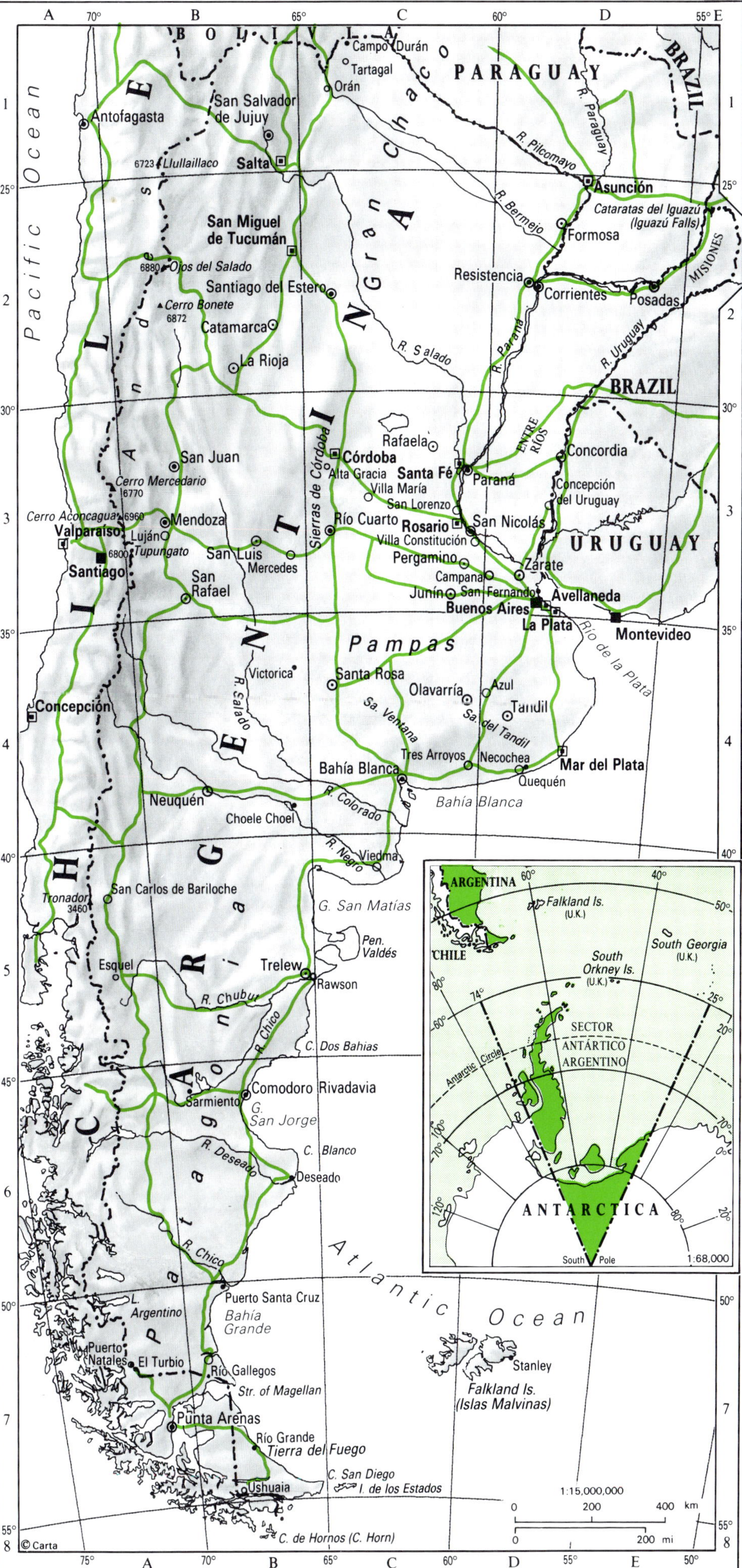

has become the heart of Argentina only since the mid-nineteenth century when most of the growing number of immigrants settled in this region; it did not attract the previous Spanish colonists. The great influx of European immigrants during the second half of the nineteenth and the first half of the twentieth century, together with natural advantages, especially the fertile soils, turned the Pampa into one of the world's important food-producing areas. Though the natural environment is more favorable to human settlement than in other parts of Argentina, it was mainly the transformation and development brought about by large-scale European immigration and settlement that turned this region into the most densely populated and important political and economic center of Argentina.

The Western Highlands (Andes)

This rugged mountainous region runs along Argentina's entire western frontier, from the complex arid high central Andes (Cordillera) in the north to the partly glaciated low mountains of the Tierra del Fuego in the south. It consists of parts of the main ranges of the Andes and their eastern foreland as well as the spurs and outlying mountainous areas. The region exhibits a wide variety of natural conditions, relative to differences in altitude and latitude, and these are reflected in the form and extent of human settlement and activity.

The northern part of the highland region extends into the widest section of the Andes. It includes the southern portion of the high intermont basins, the Altiplano, between the western and eastern ranges of the Andes, as well as the eastern part of the Andes known as Puna (this term refers to a region and not to the type of vegetation). The Altiplano here is about 3,500 meters (11,000–12,000 feet) high, while the highest peaks of the Andes reach elevations of over 6,000 meters (20,000 feet). The Andes slope gently toward the Chaco and are deeply dissected by river valleys, several of which are broad enough to attract agricultural settlement. The valleys are traversed by roads connecting the eastern lowlands with the Altiplano. The Altiplano and most of the Puna are arid to semiarid and are covered mainly by scrub that becomes scant and xerophytic toward the south. These characteristics extend to the vicinity of Tucumán, where the system of eastern ranges (Eastern Cordillera) comes to an end. From this point southward the Andes become one main system. The landscapes of the Argentine (eastern) part of the range and its foreland become conspicuously different from those of the highlands farther north. Broad river valleys and closed basins are formed by mountain spurs and outlying local ranges that run parallel to the Andes. The most extensive and desertlike of these basins is that situated between the Andes and the outlying Sierras de Córdoba. Some of the valleys and the alluvial fans at the foot of the mountains are densely populated because of their fertile soil and abundant water resources. However, agriculture in all these valleys and basins south of the Tucumán district is dependent on irrigation. The central part of the Argentine Andes, behind several of these valleys, is very high and snow-covered. Here are Mount Aconcagua (6,960 meters [22,834 feet]) and a few of South America's other highest peaks. The most densely inhabited and cultivated valleys in this part of the Andes are those of San Juan and Mendoza. The latter is also the gate to the most traveled pass across the Andes, which links the capitals of Argentina and Chile by railway and road.

In the south, facing the Patagonian plateau, the Andes are much lower. But southward the snow line gradually descends and thus snow becomes more abundant, and even glaciers appear. The cooler and wetter climate is reflected in the type and density of vegetation. Evergreen and deciduous forests cover much of the slopes, changing to scrub and grass in the lower regions that give way to the broad depression that separates the Andes from the Patagonian plateau. The Argentine side of the southern Andes is sparsely populated. Most of the inhabitants are in the foreland and in some of the valleys. There is summer grazing on some of the slopes of the central and southern Andes.

GLACIERS IN PATAGONIA

The southernmost part of the Andes, south of latitude 45° south, is characterized by peaks shaped by glaciers. The western slopes are drowned in the sea, giving the shoreline a fjordlike appearance. On the eastern slopes, large glacier-fed finger lakes (Argentino, Viedma, San Martín, Pueyrredón, Buenos Aires) form the transition to the Patagonian plateau. The Andes of Patagonia, heavily glaciated during the Ice Age, are still covered by extensive glaciers. The ice cap, which occupies about 5,000 square kilometers (1,900 square miles), sends long arms into the sea or lakes.

Lago Argentino is a large freshwater lake (1,400 square kilometers [546 square miles]) at an altitude of 187 meters (613 feet). One of its several western arms is fed by Perito Moreno, one of the largest glaciers in the area.

Perito Moreno glacier breaking into Lago Argentino

The Perito Moreno glacier is about 50 kilometers (31 miles) long and about 3 kilometers (2 miles) wide toward its end, and it is still growing. As the glacier advances eastward at a speed of about 4.5 meters (15 feet) a day, it dams the arm of Lago Argentino, causing the waters to rise as much as 30 meters (100 feet) above its normal level. The waters then burst through the glacial dam in explosive sounds of breaking ice and in a thunder of discharging falls. This remarkable phenomenon occurs during the period when snows melt in spring, every two or three years.

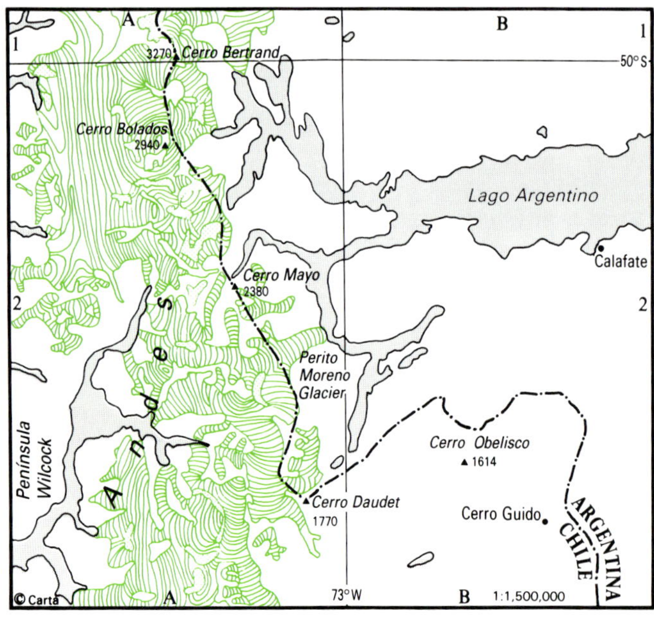

Patagonia

The Colorado River is generally considered the boundary between the lowlands of north-central Argentina and the largely arid, inhospitable plateau in the south, known as Patagonia, that covers more than a quarter of the country's area. The plateau is made up of vast areas of terracelike tableland that descends in a number of steep steps from the Andes to the Atlantic. The easternmost of these steps forms a line of high cliffs along most of the shoreline. The embayments of some of the larger river mouths are the only sites along the Patagonian coast where settlements and port facilities could be built.

The wide continental shelf extending to the Falkland Islands is structurally part of the Patagonian plateau. The flat westernmost terrace of this plateau is approximately 1,500 meters (5,000 feet) high, and that bordering the Atlantic is 60–120 meters (200–400 feet) high. The rivers flowing from the Andes to the Atlantic form deeply incised canyonlike valleys in the plateau, which can there be seen to be built up of horizontal strata of sedimentary rocks overlaid in some areas by dark volcanic rock (basalt). Outcrops of old, hard, crystalline rocks produce hilly areas that in places rise above the flat terraces. A narrow depression separates the foot of the Andes from the Patagonian plateau. This depression is largely covered by deposits carried down by glaciers from the Andes. It is well known for its numerous beautiful glacial lakes, many of which extend into the Andean valleys.

The southernmost part of this region is the southeastern, Argentine part of the Tierra del Fuego and the adjacent islands. These islands have a more rugged, hilly surface than most of Patagonia because of the intense erosive processes associated with the climatic conditions of the past.

Patagonia is sparsely populated. Most of the region is uninhabited; the settlements are mainly at points along the coast and in the river valleys at the foot of the Andes, where the climatic conditions are more favorable and irrigation is possible. Some of these settlements are in fact oases. The rural population is concentrated along sections of the Río Colorado and Río Negro in the north. The inhabitants who were attracted by mineral resources (oil, natural gas, coal, iron ore) have settled mainly in towns near these resources. The average population density of Patagonia is 1 person per square kilometer (2.5 per square mile). Most of the land is devoted to sheep ranching on large estates, some of which extend over thousands of square kilometers. There are also some large cattle ranches in the extreme northwest, where conditions are less harsh.

CLIMATE

The main factors determining the variety of climatic conditions that prevail in Argentina are the great geographical extent of the country, spanning several zones of latitude (33 degrees), and differences in altitude. Masses of cold air that move northward from Antarctica (especially in winter) over much of the country, hot and dry winds from the northwest (Gran Chaco), which blow southeast into the Pampa, and the

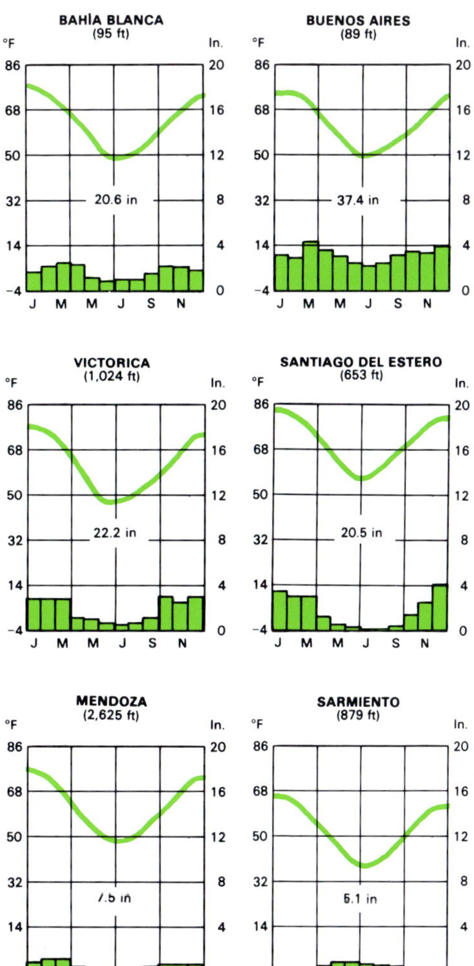

formidable mountain barrier in the west also play important roles in the prevailing climatic conditions.

The northern lowlands are the warmest area of the country and also the wettest. In the extreme north, the average temperature for the hottest month (January) is 29°C (84°F) and for the coldest month (June/July), 17°C (62.6°F). Temperatures of over 40°C (104°F) are not infrequent during the hot season. Farther south (Santiago del Estero), average temperatures range from 28.4°C (83°F) in summer to 15.3°C (60°F) in winter. Rain falls mainly during the summer months. It is abundant in the northeast (Entre Ríos, Misiones)—1,000 to 1,500 millimeters (40 to 60 inches)—and sparse in the west, where some areas receive less than 200 millimeters (8 inches). Temperatures are much lower and aridity in some basins is extreme in the corresponding latitudes west of the Andes. Thus, in the Altiplano at an altitude of approximately 3,360 meters (11,000 feet), the average temperatures for the hottest (January) and the coldest (June) months are 12.6°C (54.7°F) and 3°C (37.4°F), respectively. The average annual precipitation is 270 millimeters (11 inches).

The central lowlands (Pampa) have a more temperate climate. The average temperatures for the hottest and coldest months in the east, near the coast at Buenos Aires, are, respectively, 23.1°C (73.6°F) and 9.8°C (49.6°F); and at Bahía Blanca, 23.6°C (74.5°F) and 8°C (46.4°F). Temperatures are not much different inland and in the western margins of the Pampa and the Andes foreland. Average temperatures are 24.8°C (76.8°F) and 12°C (53.6°F), respectively, at San Miguel de Tucumán (450 meters [1,480 feet]) in the extreme northwest; 23.3°C (73.9°F) and 9.8°C (49.5°F) at Córdoba; and 24°C (75.2°F) and 8.9°C (48°F) at San Luis (710 meters [2,330 feet]). Rainfall occurs throughout the year, and is heavier in the summer months. It is abundant and sufficient for dry farming over most of the Pampa, but decreases toward the west and south. Buenos Aires receives an annual average rainfall of 950 millimeters (38 inches), Bahía Blanca—550 millimeters (22 inches), Tucumán—950 millimeters (38 inches), Córdoba—700 millimeters (28 inches), and San Luis—550 millimeters (22 inches). The valleys and basins at the foot of the parallel part of the Andes are generally much drier. Thus, the average annual rainfall at Mendoza is only 190 millimeters (7.7 inches) and at San Juan, 80 millimeters (3.3 inches).

Patagonia has generally a cool and more arid climate. It becomes cooler toward the south as precipitation increases westward and southward. In the Río Negro valley, in the north, temperatures are similar to those of the southern Pampa—24°C (75.4°F) and 7.1°C (44.8°F) for the hottest (January) and coldest (June) months, respectively, at Choele Choel. Temperatures are much lower in the south: 14.8°C (58.6°F) and 1.8°C (35.2°F) at Puerto Santa Cruz; and 9.8°C (49.6°F) and 1.3°C (33.3°F) at Ushuaia on the southern shores of the Tierra del Fuego. Average annual precipitation is 200 to 250 millimeters (8 to 10 inches) in northern Patagonia, 130 to 200 millimeters (5 to 8 inches) in the central part, and 250 to 500 millimeters (10 to 20 inches) in the southern half and the west. Ushuaia, in the extreme south, receives 480 millimeters (19 inches) of rain. Precipitation occurs throughout the year, in the south mostly in the form of snow. Strong cold winds frequently sweep across much of Patagonia, especially during the winter. This, to a large extent, forced settlement into the deeply incised and protected river valleys. On the adjoining highland to the west, temperatures are lower and precipitation higher as altitude increases. Glaciers cover mountaintops and high valleys in the south, where the line of permanent snow reaches 900 meters (3,000 feet).

POPULATION

The population of Argentina was estimated at 32.3 million in 1990. It was 27,947,000 at the 1980 census and has been increasing at an average annual rate of 1.6 percent over the last decade. It was approximately 3 million in 1890 and 3.95 million at the 1895 census. The great majority of inhabitants are of European, mainly Spanish and Italian, origin. Of the 2.2 million foreign residents at the 1970 census, 637,000 were Italians and 515,000 were Spaniards. Estimates for the mixed European-Indian (mestizo) race vary from 2 to 12 percent of the total population. Most of the people of mixed race are, in fact, descendants of families who for several generations have only married Europeans. The percentage of the mestizo population is comparatively much higher in the western and northern marginal districts and is very small among the main concentration of population in

POPULATION BY AGE GROUP, 1988

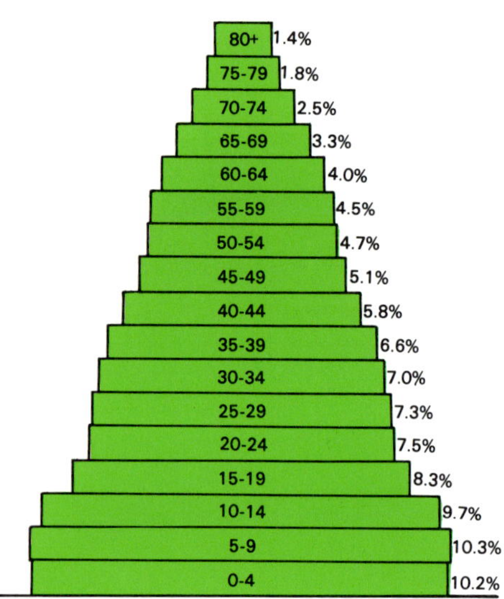

and around Buenos Aires. The few remaining native Indians live mainly in northern and northwestern Patagonia. They make up about one percent of the population. The Indians in the north are mostly of Guaraní descent and speak Guaraní. The Patagonian Indians are members of small primitive tribes, some still nomadic. They are descendants of the Tehuelche, Puelche, and Araucanian tribes. Most still practice their native religions.

In the last census (1980), 95 percent of the population gave Spanish as their primary language and 3 percent as Italian. Italian is, however, widely used by people of Italian origin. During the period of great immigration from 1857 to 1945, when over 10 million immigrants entered the country, 42 percent of the newcomers were Italians and 28 percent were Spaniards.

About 97 percent of the population is Christian (93 percent Catholic, 2 percent Protestant); nearly 2 percent is Jewish. The illiteracy rate is 4.5 percent. Over two-thirds of Argentina is sparsely populated. The average population density for the country as a whole is 11.8 persons per square kilometer (30 per square mile). More than half of the country's population is concentrated in the eastern Pampa (the provinces of Buenos Aires and southern Santa Fé), within 15 percent of the total land area. Even in these provinces the average density outside the Buenos Aires conurbation is only 42 per square kilometer (108 per square mile). There are several areas of dense population along the western fringes of the lowlands and the Andes foreland, such as the environs of Tucumán, Córdoba, San Juan, and Mendoza. The small province of Tucumán and around Buenos Aires have the densest rural population. The northern part of the country has an average population density of 8.2 persons per square kilometer (21.2 per square mile); the northern and central highlands (Andes) and their forelands have an average of 5.3 persons per square kilometer (13.7 per square mile); and Patagonia, 1.6 persons per square kilometer (4.1 per square mile), with large areas uninhabited.

The urban population is 85 percent (1988) of the whole, nearly 38 percent of whom live in Greater Buenos Aires, which has a population of over 10.6 million (within the municipal boundaries—3.1 million). The 1988 population figures for other urban centers are Córdoba—1.1 million; Rosario—1 million; Mendoza—660,000; La Plata—600,000; San Miguel de Tucumán—550,000; Mar del Plata—450,000; Santa Fé—327,000; San Juan—320,000; Bahía Blanca—250,000; and Resistencia—245,000. The Buenos Aires conurbation includes the following towns: San Justo—1 million inhabitants; Morón—670,000; Lomas de Zamora—570,000; General Sarmiento—560,000; Lanús—520,000; Quilmes—495,000; General San Martín—430,000; Caseros 380,000; Almirante Brown—372,000; Avellaneda—370,000; Vicente López—325,000; and San Isidro—320,000.

ECONOMY

Argentina is one of the major food-producing and exporting countries of the world. Its main food products are cereals, oilseed, and livestock. There is also a large and varied industry engaged mainly in the processing of agricultural and mineral products and the production of consumer goods for the local market. The country's mineral wealth is small and plays only a minor role in the economy, with the exception of its oil and natural gas resources, which supply a substantial part of the national energy requirements. There is great hydroelectric potential, but in remote frontier areas far from the main population and industrial centers. The Argentine economy experienced considerable difficulties during the 1980s, as a result primarily of internal political developments and policies of the military dictatorship between 1976 and 1983. The GNP per capita was $2,640 in 1988 ($2,350 in 1986). The economic growth rate (5.5 percent in 1989) has remained stable for a number of years. Inflation was 492.3 percent in 1989 (177 percent in 1987). Several government programs aimed at stabilizing the economy have in recent years met with little success.

EMPLOYMENT BY ECONOMIC BRANCH, 1980

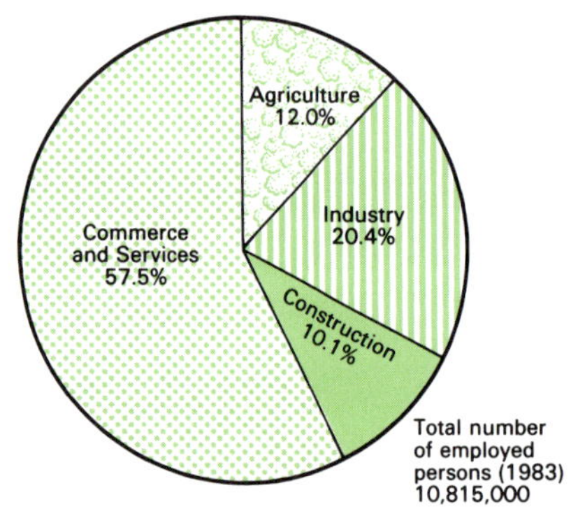

Agriculture

Despite its continuing decline in relative importance, agriculture is still a dominant segment of Argentina's economy. Cereals, oilseed, and livestock are the main products, but the diverse climatic and soil conditions make possible a wide variety of crops. In 1987, the total cultivated area was 13 percent and permanent pasture, 41 percent of the country's total area. Wheat was grown on 12.2 million acres, for a total production of 10.1 million tons; corn—7.2 million acres, 9.3 million tons; oats—1 million acres, 500,000 tons; sorghum and millet—2.7 million acres, 3.2 million tons; rice—300,000 acres, 445,000 tons; soybeans—8.6 million acres, 7 million tons; sunflowers—4.3 million acres, 2.2 million tons; flax—1.7 million acres, 590,000 tons linseed. Cereals and oilseed are grown mainly in the Pampa. Large quantities of sugarcane are grown in the Tucumán district. Cotton, tobacco, groundnuts, and subtropical fruit are grown mainly in the northeast. Grapes, olives, and Mediterranean-type fruit are grown mainly in the Andes foreland, as well as in the valleys and basins in the central west. The Mendoza is an important agricultural district.

The central lowlands are the home of most of the 55.7 million (1987) cattle raised in Argentina. Large estates account for nearly a quarter of this production. The Buenos Aires province is the center of the meat industry, where large numbers of cattle are regularly brought for fattening from the more arid parts of the Pampa and neighboring areas. Most of Argentina's 3 million horses are also raised in this province. The country's 32 million sheep and goats are raised mainly in Patagonia and the Andes foreland. Argentina has long been a major exporter of beef, mutton, meat products, hides, and wool. There has been a decline over the last 50 years in the production of cereals and of some other field crops as well as certain types of livestock (mainly sheep and goats), due to a fall in demand in Argentina's traditional markets (mainly Western Europe). Employment in agriculture and pastoralism has dropped to 11 percent of the workforce. It was over 30 percent in the mid-1950s and 25 percent in 1963.

ECONOMIC BRANCH AS PART OF GDP, 1985

LAND USE, 1987

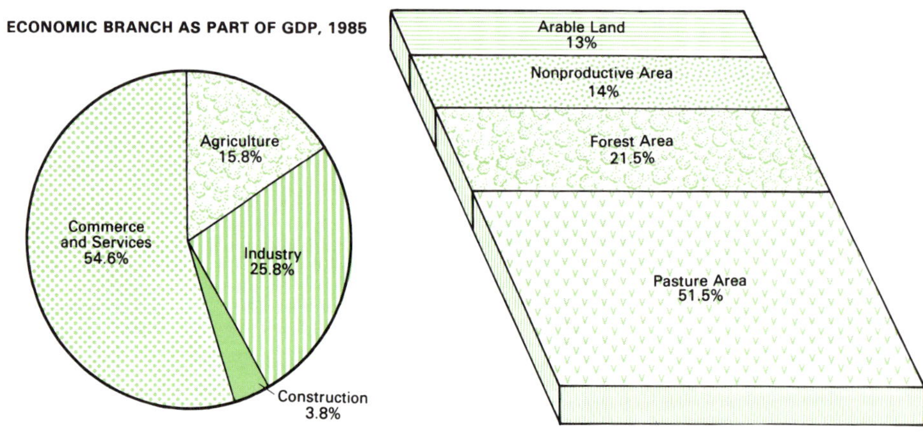

AGRICULTURE

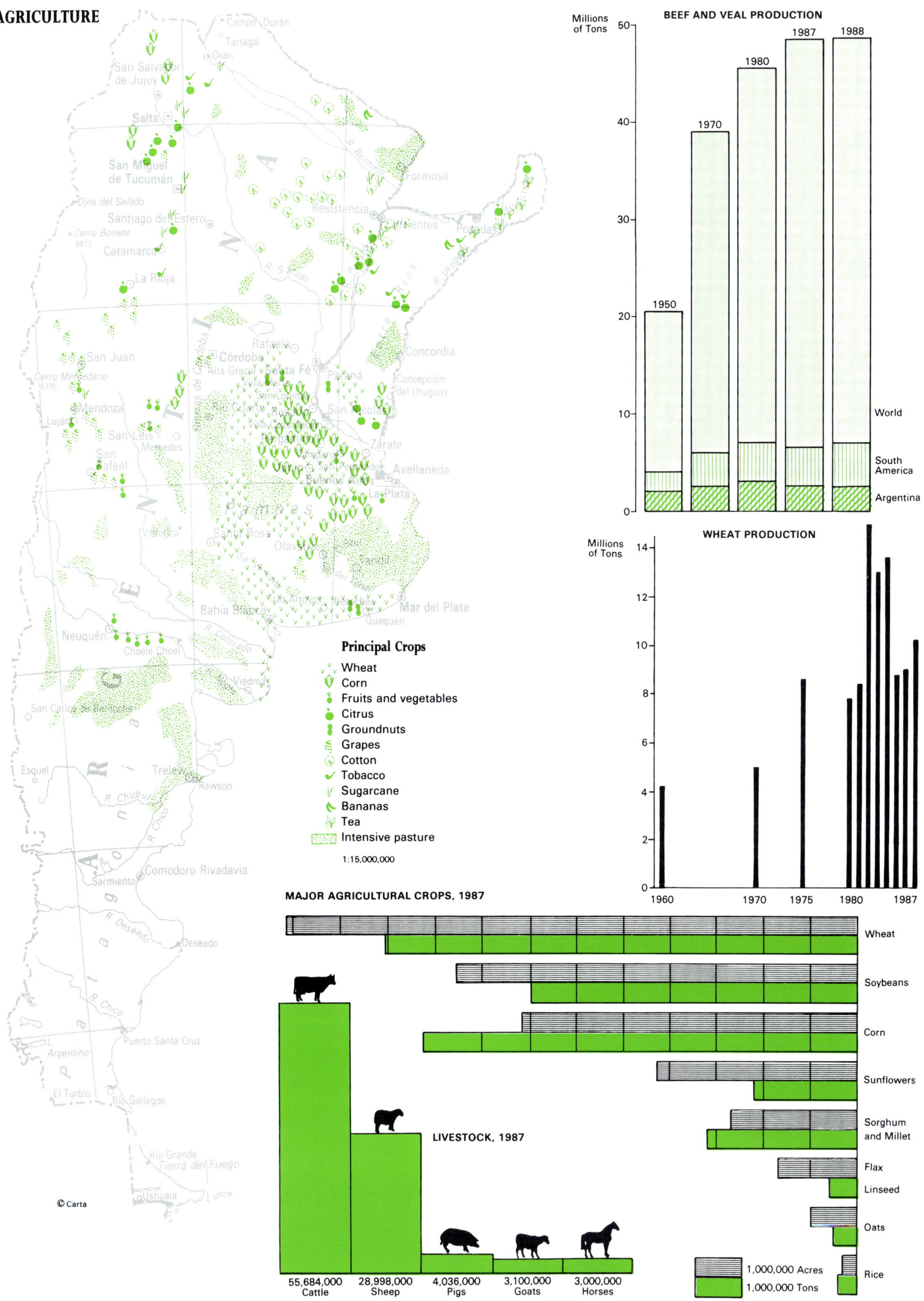

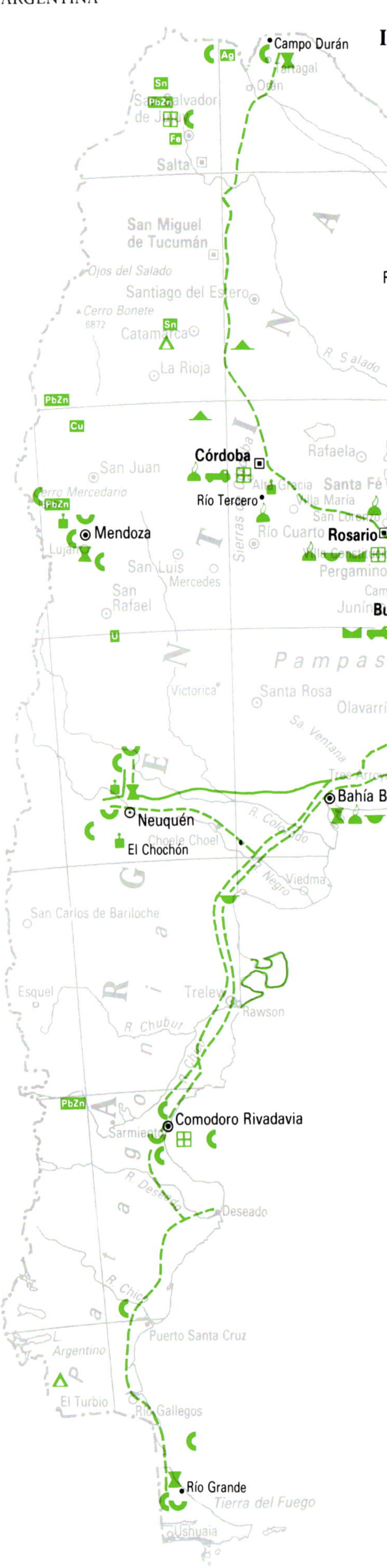

Mineral Resources

The most important mineral resources are oil (23 million tons in 1988 [an average of 449,000 barrels per day]) and natural gas (1,500 million cubic meters in 1987). These derive mainly from four oil and gas fields: in the south, in the vicinity of Comodoro Rivadavia, from where large quantities of gas are conveyed in a 1,600-kilometer (1,000-mile) pipeline to Buenos Aires; in the west, in the vicinity of Neuquén, from where the gas is conveyed by pipeline to Buenos Aires and the oil to Bahía Blanca; in the vicinity of Mendoza, from where oil is conveyed to the banks of the Paraná near Rosario; and in the north at Campo Durán, near the border with Bolivia. Pipelines running from this last field to the main population centers of Rosario–Buenos Aires are also used for oil and gas acquired from Bolivian fields across the northern border. Reportedly, new fields of oil and gas were recently discovered in the extreme south, near the Straits of Magellan and offshore in the San Jorge Gulf. Comparatively small quantities of coal (400,000 tons in 1985) are mined at Río Turbio in the south Andes foreland.

Iron ore (486,000 tons in 1985) is mined primarily near San Salvador de Jujuy. Small amounts of gold (830 kilograms in 1986), silver (59,600 kilograms in 1987), tin (200 tons), copper (300 tons), tungsten (155 tons), and manganese (2,000 tons) are mined mainly in the Andes foreland and adjacent valleys and hilly outcrops in the Patagonian plateau. The same areas are the source of lead (26,000 tons in 1987), zinc (35,000 in 1987), and uranium (115 tons in 1986). Most of the exploited and potential mineral resources are located in the Andes, their spurs and forelands, in the remote northwest, from where the minerals have to be transported over very long land routes to the industrial centers or to the coast. Many initiatives to exploit mineral resources have had to be abandoned because of the lack of profitability.

Industry

Industrial growth has taken place mainly since World War II, although international economic developments during and after World War I, which had detrimental effects on Argentina's economy (which was almost entirely agricultural) are generally thought to have encouraged the first industrial development. Argentina's large industry, in which 25 percent of the workforce is employed, is concentrated mainly in Greater Buenos Aires and its environs, the lower Paraná valley (Rosario-Paraná and vicinity), and the central part of the Córdoba province. Secondary industrial centers are located in and around the following urban areas: Jujuy and Tucumán in the north; Mendoza in the west; and Bahía Blanca in the south.

The food industry is the most dispersed, with numerous large and small plants in the rural areas of Entre Ríos, Misiones, and eastern Chaco as well as in eastern Patagonia. It is mainly engaged in slaughtering, processing, and packing various types of meat and meat products, milk processing, sugar refining (mainly in Tucumán), edible oils extraction, processing and preserving various types of vegetables and fruit, and flour and cereal milling. A large part of this production is exported. The metals industry, concentrated mainly in the Buenos Aires and Córdoba subregions, produces iron and steel (1.5 and 3.2 million tons, respectively) using both local and imported ore. Also produced are aluminium (155,000 tons in 1987) and aluminum products. Metals (mainly lead and zinc) are mined and processed. Other heavy manufacturing includes agricultural machinery, pipes, various tools, and automobiles (170,000 vehicles in 1986). The products of these industries are intended mostly for domestic use.

The textile industry is the oldest of the nonalimentary industries. It has been based largely on local cotton, wool, and flax, but at present synthetic materials are also widely used. The livestock industry provides hides for the many tanneries and a large leather and leather products industry. An electronics and electrical products industry has been developing in recent years, partly instigated by Japanese concerns that have established subsidiary plants in Argentina to supply local neighboring markets. The chemical industry produces mainly fertilizers, pesticides, various chemical and plastic materials, and pharmaceuticals. There is also a petrochemical industry. Cement and building materials, lumber and wood products, and paper are other extensive industries. Argentina is the world's largest producer of tanning material extracted from the quebracho tree.

Trade

Foreign trade is mainly with the United States (17 percent of imports; 10 percent of exports in 1986), Brazil (14 percent and 10 percent,

TRADE BALANCE, 1987
(Millions of Dollars)

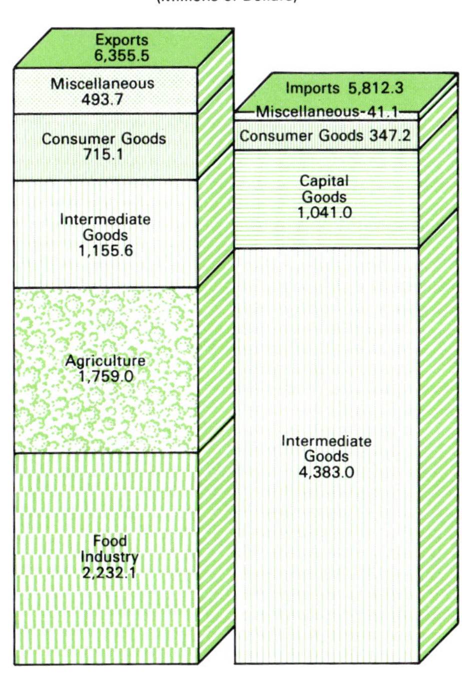

repectively), West Germany (11 percent and 5 percent), Netherlands (2 percent and 11 percent), and Japan (7 percent and 6 percent). Food products make up more than half the total exports. Imports include mainly fuel (oil), chemical products, machinery, and vehicles.

HISTORY

The first Europeans to reach the shores of what is now Argentina were Spanish sailors under Juan Diaz de Solís, who explored the coast of the La Plata estuary in 1515. In 1526 an expedition headed by Sebastian Cabot sailed up the Paraná river and established a fort near present-day Rosario. This was the first European settlement in the La Plata-Paraná region, but it lasted only a short time. In 1536 a much larger expedition headed by Pedro de Mendoza was sent to establish Spanish rule over the lands around La Plata. He founded Buenos Aires, but it had to be abandoned in 1541.

At that time the area of Argentina was very sparsely inhabited by Indian tribes, most of them nomads or seminomads and very primitive: the Guaraní in the northeast; Abipón in the northwest; Puelche in the Pampa; Tehuelche, Ona, and Yahgan in Patagonia; and the Araucanians in the Andes (southwest). Most of these tribes were hostile to the Spanish settlers and prevented European settlement in large parts of Argentina up to the second half of the nineteenth century. The first permanent Spanish settlement in the La Plata basin that became base for European expansion was Asunción (1537) in Paraguay. The violent hostility of the Indians, the inability of the Spaniards to force a substantial number of them into slavery or agricultural labor, and the lack of attractive resources were responsible for the failure of the Spaniards to establish themselves in the initial stages of colonization in the Pampa and in the lower La Plata basin. Spanish settlers from Peru and Chile established colonies during the second half of the sixteenth century in the west and north: Santiago del Estero (1551), Mendoza (1561), San Juan (1562), San Miguel de Tucumán (1565), Córdoba (1573), Salta (1582), La Rioja (1591), and San Salvador de Jujuy (1593). Spanish colonists from Asunción moved south and established themselves along the lower Paraná. Santa Fé was founded in 1573. Buenos Aires was reestablished in 1580. Expansion of Spanish settlement during the seventeenth and most of the eighteenth century was slow. Administratively, the entire region was under the Viceroyalty of Peru. Settlement on the La Plata coast was influenced by the rivalry between Spain and Portugal over the territorial control of present-day Uruguay.

The Viceroyalty of La Plata, which extended over present-day Argentina (excluding Patagonia), Uruguay, Paraguay, and Bolivia, was formed in 1776 with Buenos Aires, which became a free port, as its capital. This boosted the position of Buenos Aires and increased its population to approximately 40,000 by 1800. The period of the Napoleonic wars in Europe and especially the conquest of Spain by the French had their impact on Argentina as on other parts of the Spanish colonial empire. A British attempt to gain control of Buenos Aires in 1806 was foiled by the local population. The Spanish viceroy was deposed in 1810. This was followed by a struggle between the supporters of the independence movement and those loyal to the Spanish throne, who were supported by colonial troops, as well as between various local groups. Independence was officially declared in 1816 and a provisional constitution was adopted in 1819. A period of internal strife and civil wars followed when some of the provinces refused to submit to central rule. There was also much uncertainty about the position of the boundaries, which led to an armed struggle with Paraguay and Brazil. The dictatorship of Juan Manuel de Rosas (1829–1852) managed to extend the effective rule of the central government, but acquiesced to largely independent rule by some provincial governors and was involved in much internal and external strife.

In 1853 a new constitution was approved that turned Argentina into a federal republic similar to the United States, headed by a president with wide powers, who can serve only a single six-year term. Buenos Aires refused to join the federation. The armed struggle that ensued lasted until the leader of Buenos Aires, Bartolomé Mitre, was elected president of Argentina (1861) after his forces defeated those of the federal government.

The second half of the nineteenth century brought great changes to Argentina through the large-scale immigration of Europeans and the construction of a large railway system, mainly in the Pampa, but also between Buenos Aires and the urban centers of the west and northwest. The immigrants, 4.7 million in total, of whom 2.3 million were Italian and 1.5 million Spanish, entered the country between 1857 and 1914. The population, which numbered approximately 1 million in 1850, grew to nearly 5 million in 1900 and 7.9 million in 1914. Military operations against hostile Indian tribes (1879–1883) suppressed and drove them to remote areas. All parts of the country were now open to European settlement. The eastern Pampa and especially the Buenos Aires area became the center of population and economic activity. Strong links developed between the core area and outlying regions in the north and west.

Despite the fact that the internal political struggle continued, the presidency and the government were, to a large extent, dominated by small influential groups, mainly families with large estates. In 1860, Argentina entered a period of comparative internal stability, which was reflected in rapid economic development and extensive investment of foreign capital. Constitutional and political reforms to promote the democratic character of the regime were gradually introduced toward the end of the nineteenth and early in the twentieth century, under growing pressure from radical political organizations. The radicals won the 1916 presidential elections and controlled the government until ousted by a military coup in 1930, which returned the conservatives to power. A military junta deposed the elected president and seized power in 1943. This actually prepared the groundwork for the elections in 1946, in which Colonel Juan Domingo Perón, who held a dominant position in the military junta, was elected president. Perón organized a fascist-oriented political movement that won much support among the masses, especially the working class. Perón, who was reelected in 1951 and ruled the country in a dictatorial manner until he was ousted, introduced many economic and administrative reforms. He launched large public works, industrialization, agricultural development programs, and nationalized some vital services, including foreign railway and telephone companies. Foreign trade was subject to strict government control. Perón's policies undermined and decreased agricultural production, mainly in cereals and livestock. The suppression of civil rights caused mass emigration. Perón was deposed by a military coup in 1955. A period of military dictatorship with intervals of democratic elections and constitutional governments followed. Argentina had nine presidents (five of whom were deposed) between 1955 and 1973, when Perón returned to power. When he died in 1974, his widow, Isabel Perón, assumed

Province of Rioja, 4 reales, 1852

San Martín, 1867

1928

the presidency, but was ousted in a military coup in 1976. A brutal military dictatorship ensued, during which thousands of opponents of the regime disappeared and were executed. This regime involved Argentina in a war with Britain over the possession of the Falkland Islands (1982) which ended in Argentina's defeat. The country also drifted into serious economic difficulties. Democracy was restored in 1983 with the election of Raúl Alfonsín to the presidency.

GOVERNMENT AND POLITICS

Argentina consists of 22 provinces (each of which has a legislature), a federal district (Buenos Aires), and national territories (Tierra del Fuego, several islands in the South Atlantic, and the territory claimed in Antarctica). The country is governed by an executive president who is elected for a six-year term by a 600-member electoral college, which is elected by direct popular vote. The president must be Roman Catholic and Argentinian by birth. The government is appointed by the president.

The National Congress consists of a Senate and a House of Deputies. The legislature of each province and of the federal district nominates two members to the Senate, for a total of 46 members. The 254 members of the House of Deputies are elected by direct popular vote. Since the restoration of the constitutional government in 1983, two main parties have dominated the political arena: the Unión Cívica Radical (UCR; left-wing) and the Movimiento Justicialista Nacional (right-wing; Peronist). The 1983 elections were won by the Unión Cívica, but the Peronists had the upper hand in 1989, when their candidate, Carlos Saúl Menem, was elected president.

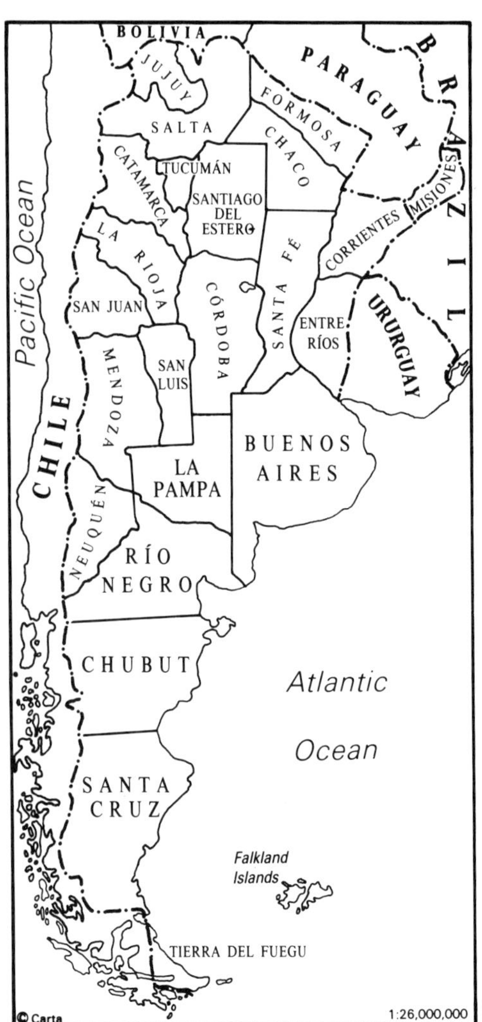

In the elections held on 14 May 1989, Carlos Saúl Menem won 47.36 percent of the vote and his opponent Eduardo César Angeloz, 32.48 percent. Menem won 310 votes (out of 600) in the electoral college, and Angeloz, 211 votes. Menem heads the Justicialist Party (FREJUPO, i.e., Peronists and their allies). Voting also took place for 127 seats in the 254-member Chamber of Deputies and for one seat in the 46-member-Senate. FREJUPO won 66 seats (44.6 percent of the vote); Radical Civil Union (UCR) 41 seats (28.9 percent of the vote); Democratic Center (UCD) 9 seats (9.5 percent of the vote); Federalist Confederation (CFI) 3 seats (3.7 percent of the vote); and smaller parties, 8 seats. This assured the Peronists of domination in the Chamber but short of an overall majority.

Argentina claims sovereignty over the Falkland Islands (officially the Islas Malvinas) and part of the Antarctic continent between longitudes 25° and 74° West.

BUENOS AIRES

Buenos Aires is one of the world's great metropolises and commercial and industrial centers, and it is the cultural core of Spanish South America. With a population that reached almost 11 million in 1990, the dominant role played by Greater Buenos Aires in the life of the nation is unmatched by any other capital in South America. Buenos Aires' rise to the forefront of the world's great cities is comparatively recent. It was a small coastal town that served a sparsely populated, poor, agricultural hinterland. It turned into a smuggling center when in 1778, shortly after becoming the capital of the newly formed La Plata Viceroyalty, its port was authorized to handle international trade. At that time its population numbered 24,000. By 1855, when it was the capital of independent Argentina, it grew to 90,000 inhabitants. Its rapid growth and expansion came with the large-scale European immigration of the late nineteenth and early twentieth century, and with the development of a railway network extending over much of central and northern Argentina. In 1890 it had 668,000 inhabitants; in 1909 it passed the 1-million mark; by 1914 it had nearly 1.5 million inhabitants; by 1932, 2.2 million; by 1960, 6.7 million; and by 1980, 9.7 million.

Administrative Division

Provinces	Capitals	area sq mi	area sq km	population (1986 estimate)
Buenos Aires	La Plata	118,754	307,571	12,226,000
Catamarca	San Fernando del Valle de Catmarca	38,984	100,967	230,000
Chaco	Resistencia	38,469	99,633	791,000
Chubut	Rawson	86,752	224,686	316,000
Córdoba	Córdoba	65,161	168,766	2,629,000
Corrientes	Corrientes	34,054	88,199	724,000
Entre Ríos	Paraná	30,418	78,781	968,000
Formosa	Formosa	27,825	72,066	338,000
Jujuy	San Salvador de Jujuy	20,548	53,219	487,000
La Pampa	Santa Rosa	55,382	143,440	231,000
La Rioja	La Rioja	34,626	89,680	183,000
Mendoza	Mendoza	57,462	148,827	1,344,000
Misiones	Posadas	11,506	29,801	690,000
Neuquén	Neuquén	36,324	94,078	315,000
Río Negro	Viedma	78,384	203,013	477,000
Salta	Salta	59,759	154,775	768,000
San Juan	San Juan	34,614	89,651	520,000
San Luis	San Luis	29,633	76,748	234,000
Santa Cruz	Río Gallegos	94,187	243,943	138,000
Santa Fé	Santa Fé	51,354	133,007	2,675,000
Santiago del Estero	Santiago del Estero	52,222	135,254	660,000
Tucumán	San Miguel de Tucumán	8,697	22,524	1,112,000
Other Federal Entities				
Distrito Federal	Buenos Aires	77	200	2,924,000
Tierra del Fuego	Ushuaia	8,210	21,263	50,000
Total		***1,073,399**	**2,780,092**	**31,030,000**

*Detail does not add to total given because of rounding.

Buenos Aires was founded near the mouth of a small tributary, Riachuelo, which for miles was the only site along the southern coast of La Plata estuary where the sea was deep enough for ships of the sixteenth century to approach the shoreline. Also, the escarpment (barranca) facing the coast on the eastern edge of the Pampa was lower and less of a barrier for access inland. The southern part of La Plata is very shallow and its coast swampy. The dredging of an access channel and the deepening of the port area had to be undertaken to accommodate steamships. This man-made harbor has been extended and deepened on several occasions since the beginning of the twentieth century. The nucleus of the present large harbor is this same site. An outport at La Plata (40 kilometers [25 miles] to the southeast) was developed to relieve the pressure on Buenos Aires.

The rapid growth of the city in the last quarter of the nineteenth and the early twentieth century was strongly influenced by European, mainly French, architecture and urban planning. This resulted in the appearance of boulevards, squares, parks, and building styles resembling those of Paris. Buenos Aires was often described as "the Paris of South America." Typical examples of this development are the Plaza de Mayo and the Avenida de Mayo leading westward to the capital building, or the Avenida Rivadavia. At a later stage, especially after World War II, the North American style gained prominence, as skyscrapers and massive business buildings began to dominate the skyline of the central business district. To overcome serious traffic congestion, new wide avenues were built through the older part of the city. A modern system of urban underground trains helped to relieve the growing pressure on public transportation. Many new suburbs and satellite towns created a continuous urban area that was expanded far beyond the limits of the federal district. Buenos Aires is now surrounded by a conurbation of eighteen municipalities, six of which have a population of over half a million. Buenos Aires, like most other metropolises of South America, is characterized by great extremes: garden suburbs with the beautiful villas of the upper-classes and large slums with masses of destitute people; wide spacious avenues lined by impressive architecture and apparently hastily built, crowded, ugly tenements. Urban development and modernization have in recent decades lagged behind the requirements of a growing population; technical and administrative capabilities have also fallen short.

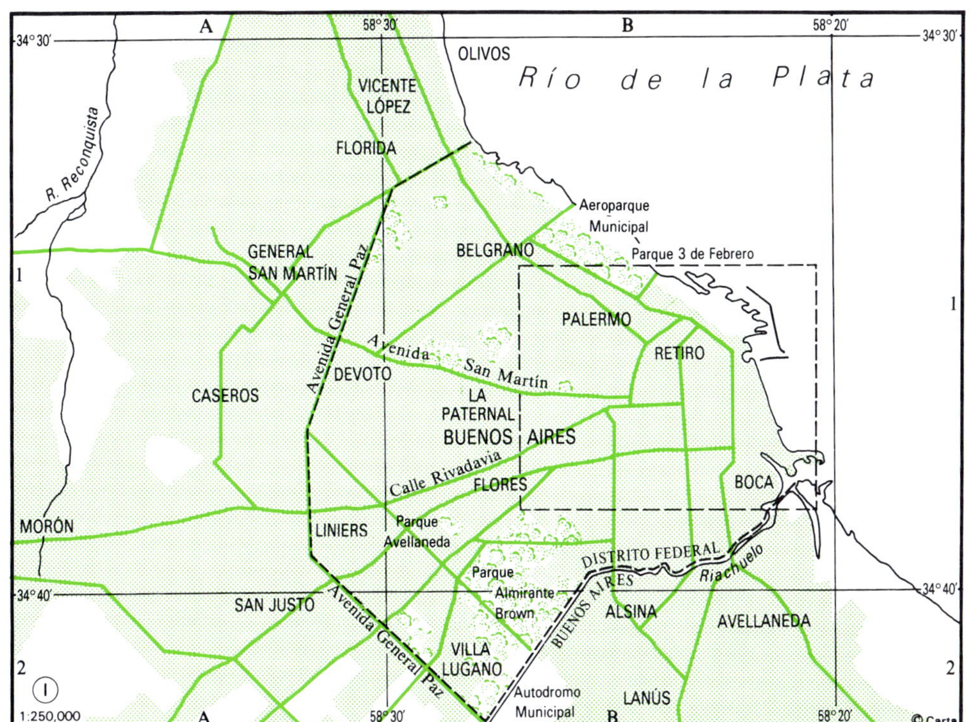

Museo Histórico del Cabildo, scene of town council meeting (Cabildo abierto) which prompted the 1810 May Revolution

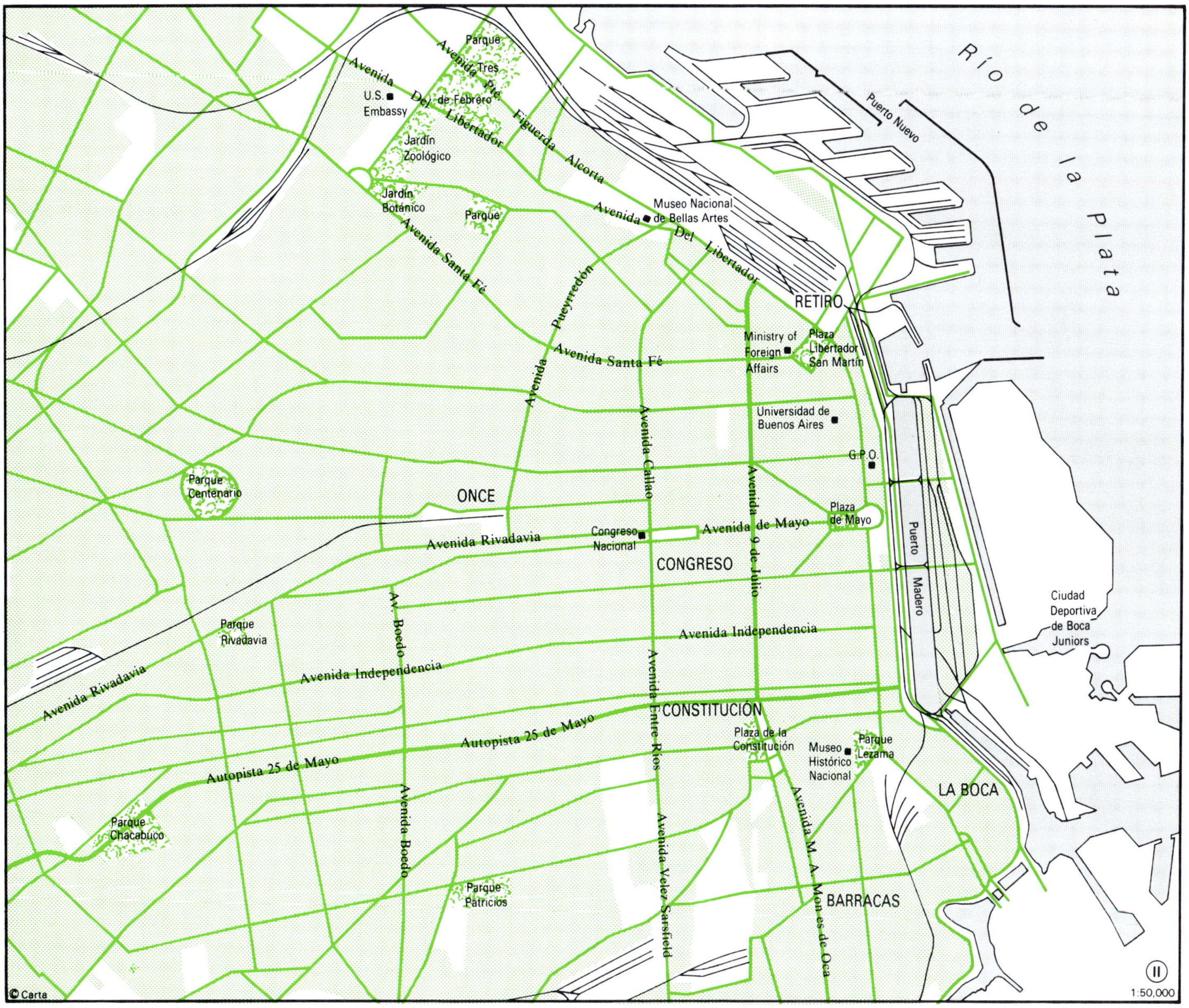

PARAGUAY

Area
406,752 sq. km.
157,048 sq. mi.

Population
4,277,000 (1990 estimate)

Capital City
Asunción

Gross National Product (GNP) Per Capita
$1,180 (1988)

Population in Main Cities
(1985 estimates)
Asunción 477,100
Fernando de la Mora 80,000
Puerto Presidente Stroessner 64,000
Lambasé 84,000
San Lorenzo 75,000

Highest Point
700 m. 2,296 ft. (Cerro Villa Rica)

Currency Unit
1 guaraní = 100 céntimos

Density
8.3 persons per sq. km.
21.5 persons per sq. mi. (1986)

Urban-Rural
urban 43.9% rural 56.1% (1985)

Natural Increase
2.9% (1985-1990)

Life Expectancy
68.9 (1985-1990)

Doctors
1,459 inhabitants per doctor (1984)

Hospital Beds
1.2 per thousand inhabitants (1985)

Infant Mortality
48.9 per thousand live births (1985-1990)

High School Pupils
31.0% of age group 13-18 (1985)

University Students
9.7% of age group 20-24 (1984)

Illiteracy Rate
11.8% (1985)

National Holiday
Independence Days, 14-15 May

National Anthem
beginning "Paraguayos, república o muerte"
("Paraguayans, Republic or death")

Paraguay is one of two landlocked countries in South America (the other is Bolivia), though it is accessible to small ocean-going vessels through the Paraná and Paraguay rivers. It is bound on the east by Brazil, where much of the boundary runs along the rivers Paraguay (in the northeast) and Paraná (in the southeast), by Bolivia on the north, and by Argentina on the west and south, where the rivers Pilcomayo (northwest), Paraguay (southwest), and Paraná (south) make up the entire length of the border. The country has very long (nearly 8,000 kilometers [5,000 miles]) and tortuous boundaries, most of which cross very sparsely inhabited areas.

NATURAL REGIONS

Paraguay is generally divided into three geographical-geological regions. The Eastern Region, comprising a third of the country, is actually the western fringe of the Paraná Plateau that extends over a large part of southwest Brazil. Much of this region is a 300-600-meter-high (1,000-2,000-foot) tabular plateau, capped to a great extent by lava flows (basalt) overlying thick beds of sandstone and deeply incised by narrow river valleys. The largest and deepest river valley is that of the Paraná along the southwestern border, site of the great Guaíra Falls. The plateau comes to an abrupt end in the west with a high scarp, which is the most conspicuous dividing line in the natural landscape of Paraguay. Most of the plateau and especially its valleys are covered by dense forests of mixed deciduous and evergreen trees, and in some parts by dense undergrowth.

The second region is a low-lying flat plain situated between the precipitous western edge of the plateau and the Paraguay River. The plain is often subjected to extensive flooding, with parts covered by seasonal swamps. Two belts of low hills, which are in fact spurs of the plateau made of resistant crystalline rock, rise above this plain. Much of this region is also covered by forests.

A wide, largely featureless plain, extending from the Paraguay River westward to the Andean foothills, is Paraguay's third region, which covers about half of the country. It is part of the Gran Chaco, a plain that extends into much of northern Argentina and eastern Bolivia. This partly swampy plain slopes gently eastward and has typical savanna features.

Most of it is scrubland, with gallery forests along the rivers. The economically valuable quebracho tree is abundant in the eastern part of this region. The plain becomes semiarid in its westernmost parts, with a much thinner scrub and more xerophytic vegetation.

CLIMATE

The temperate climate is subject to rapid variations over much of the year, due to cold winds from the south or hot air from the north. The average temperature in Asunción for the coldest month (June) is 17°C (63°F); it is slightly higher in the northern parts of the country. Temperatures may fall to near freezing as a result of cold fronts. The average temperature for the hottest month (January) is 27°C (80.5°F) in Asunción but exceeds 30°C (90°F) in the north, where temperatures of over 40°C (105°F) are not uncommon. Here the hottest part of South America extends into Paraguay. Rainfall prevails throughout the year but is heaviest during the summer (October to March). Precipitation, which is abundant in the south and east (Asunción gets an average annual amount of 1,300 millimeters [52 inches]), diminishes toward the northwest, where semiarid conditions prevail (less than 500 millimeters [20 inches]).

CLIMATE
Rainfall and Temperature

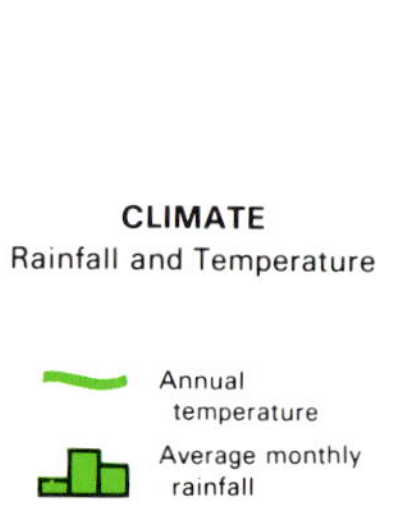

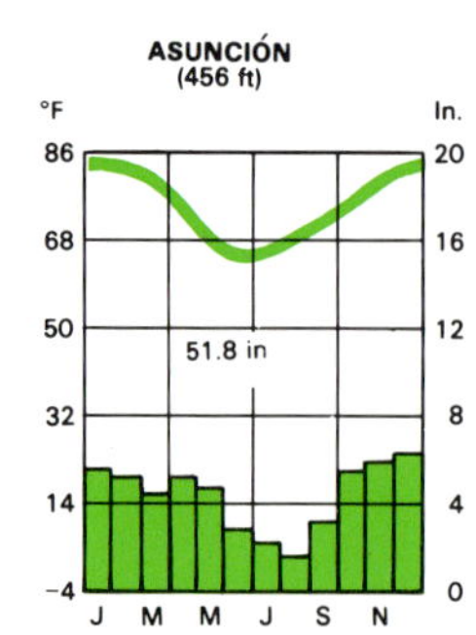

POPULATION

In 1989, the population was estimated at 4.2 million, and it has been growing in recent years at an average annual rate of 3.2 percent. It has increased more than fourfold over the last 50 years (970,000 in 1939). It was 3,035,000 at an average annual rate of 2.9 percent. It of inhabitants are mestizo, mostly descendants of the Guaraní tribes who inhabited this part of South America when the first Europeans arrived. American Indians, most of whom live in the Chaco in the northwest, comprise only about 2 percent of the population. Nearly 3 percent are European immigrants or descendants of Europeans who arrived over the last 100 years. They are mainly of German, Italian, and Spanish origin. These include about 20,000 Mennonites, who have established numerous agricultural settlements. There are also large groups of Koreans (about 8,000 families) and Japanese (7,000) who have settled in Paraguay over the last 50 years, and a small number of blacks. The official language is Spanish, but the actual language of nearly 90 percent of the population is Guaraní; about half of this segment speaks only Guaraní.

Roman Catholicism is the official religion of the country, to which approximately 97 percent of the population belongs. There are small communities of other Christian denominations, the largest of which is the Mennonites. Twelve percent of the population is illiterate. The population is mainly concentrated in the southern part of the central lowlands. Only the capital, Asunción, has a densely inhabited environment (240 inhabitants per square kilometer [615 per square mile] in the Central Department). The rest of the country is only sparsely populated, with large areas almost uninhabited. The Chaco region, which extends over 60 percent of Paraguay's total area, has an average density of 0.2 persons per square kilometer

(0.5 per square mile). The average density for the whole country is approximately 10 persons per square kilometer (25 per square mile). The urban population has grown from approximately 30 percent of the whole in 1960 to 45 percent in 1990. The capital, Asunción, with a population of 500,000 (800,000 in the metropolitan area [1988]), is the only large city. The other main towns are: Fernando de la Mora (85,000); Puerto Presidente Stroessner (80,000); Pedro Juan Caballero (70,000); Encarnación (30,000); Concepción (25,000); and Pilar (23,000).

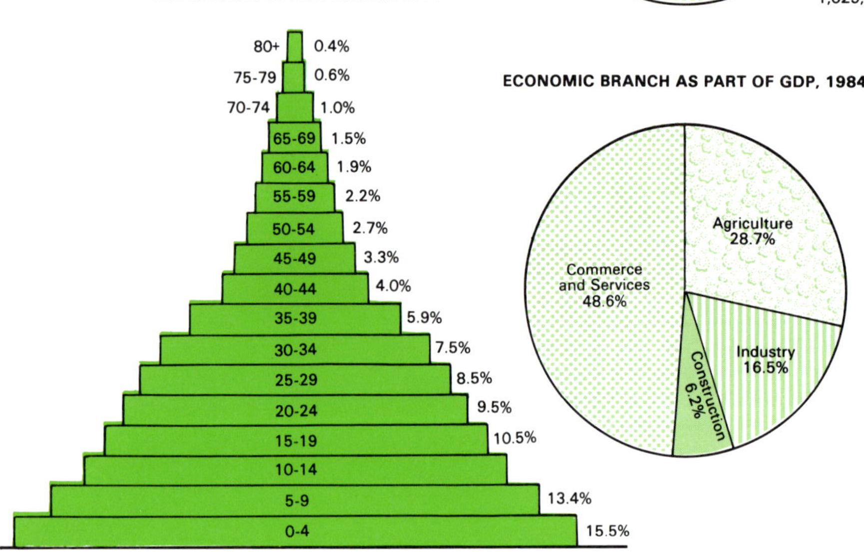

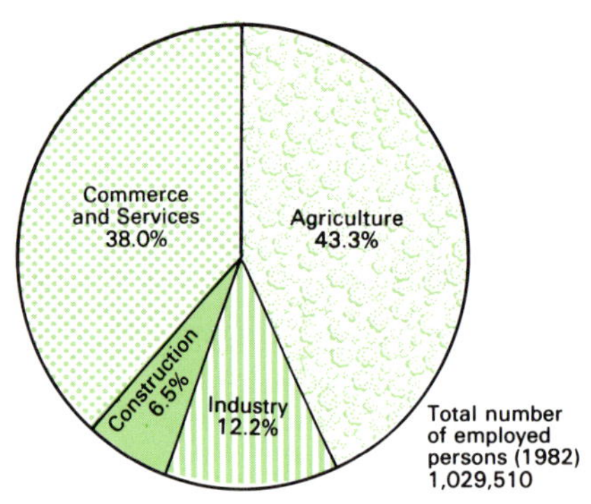

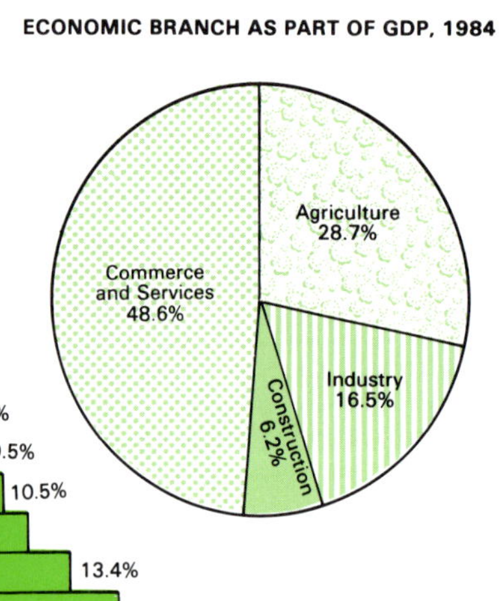

in 1987, 7.3 million cattle, 500,000 sheep and goats, 1.7 million pigs, and 317,000 horses. Meat products and hides form a substantial part of Paraguay's exports. In 1986, the forests produced 8.2 million cubic meters of timber (including hardwoods), quebracho extracts (tannin), and tung oil.

Mineral Resources

Extensive prospecting for oil and natural gas, mainly in the Chaco, has so far brought no positive results. Iron ore, manganese, copper, and some other minerals are known to exist in the eastern part of the country but have so far not been exploited.

Industry

Industry is mainly engaged in processing the country's agricultural and natural products and the production of consumer goods and building materials. Most important are meat processing, packing and freezing, processing hides; production of cotton yarn and textiles; and production of sugar, tung oil, and cement.

The country is amply supplied with electricity by two hydroelectric plants: the Itaipu Dam on the Paraná River, the largest hydroelectric project, which is a common enterprise with Brazil; and the Acaray Dam on the Acaray River. A third large plant, in partnership with Argentina, at Isla Yaciretá (on the Paraguay River) should come into operation soon.

ECONOMY

Paraguay is one of the poorest countries in South America. Largely underdeveloped, its economy is based on agriculture and pastoralism, the exploitation of forest resources, and processing for these industries. The average annual economic growth rate in recent years has been 4.5 percent. GNP per capita was $1,180 in 1988. Of the total workforce, 47 percent is engaged in agriculture and livestock raising and 19 percent in industry.

Agriculture

Only 5.3 percent of the area is under cultivation, mostly in the southern part of the central lowlands. Of the total area, 38 percent is used as permanent pasture. About 50 percent is covered by forests and scrub. Agriculture, much of which is still primitive, utilizes only part of the potentially arable land. Subsistence farming is largely practiced, the chief crops being corn (1.35 million acres, 917,000 tons in 1987), manioc (548,000 acres, 3.4 million tons), rice (104,000 acres, 24,000 tons), wheat (445,000 acres, 270,000 tons), sweet potatoes, and beans. Commercial products are mainly cotton (1.1 million acres, 114,000 tons fiber), sugarcane (160,000 acres, 72,000 tons sugar), soybeans (1.7 million acres, 1 million tons), tobacco (40,000 acres, 25,000 tons), peanuts (104,000 acres, 44,000 tons), and small quantities of coffee. Yerba maté (local tea) which was an important product, is no longer so widely grown. Large quantities of tropical fruit and citrus are also produced, as is cannabis for the international drug trade. Livestock production, mainly in the central lowlands included

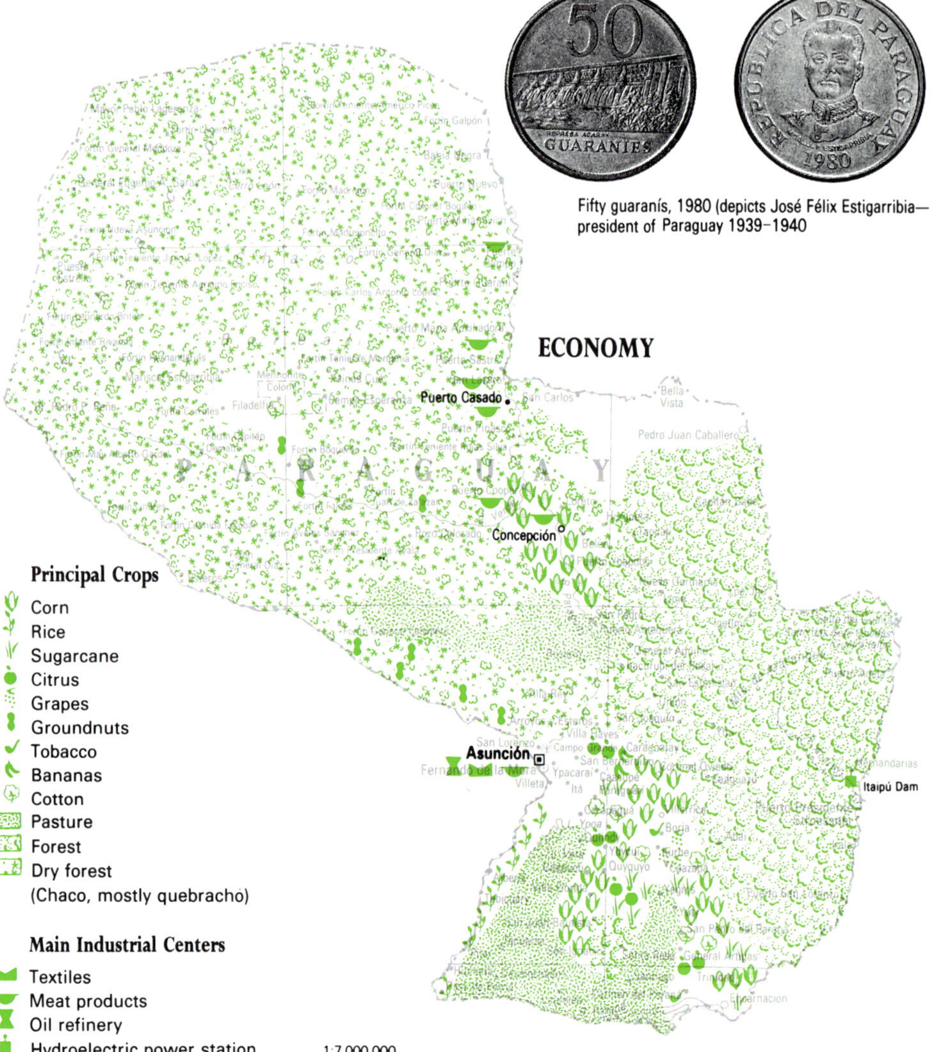

Fifty guaranís, 1980 (depicts José Félix Estigarribia—president of Paraguay 1939–1940

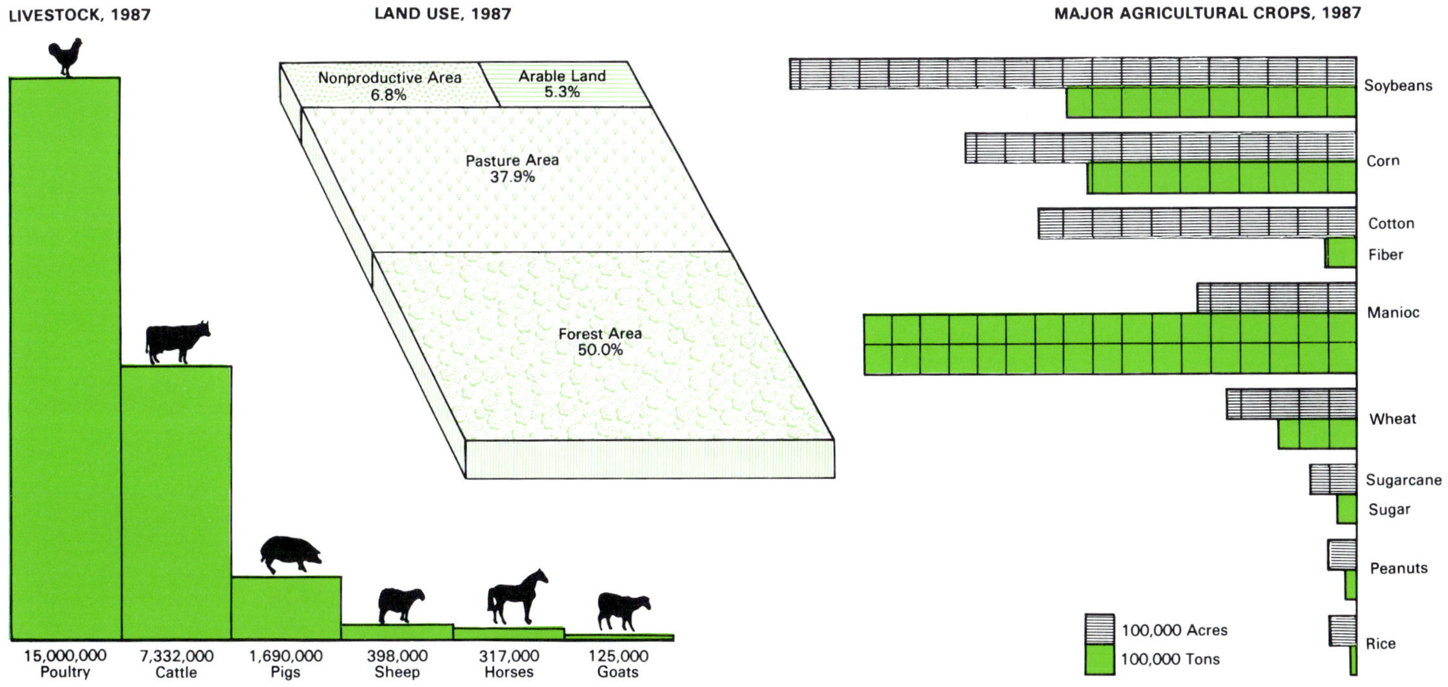

ITAIPU DAM

By the early 1990s the Itaipu Dam will have the world's largest hydroelectric power station with a total capacity of 12,600 megawatts, and powered by eighteen turbines operated by falls of over 100 meters (300 feet). The dam, containing 12 million cubic meters of concrete, is the most ambitious construction project undertaken so far in South America. It is a common venture undertaken by Brazil and Paraguay to exploit a part of the enormous hydroelectric potential of the river Paraná, the second longest river in South America and the third largest in volume. There will be further cooperation between Argentina, Brazil, and Paraguay for other projects farther down the Paraná.

The site of the dam is a short distance north of the Paraná's confluence with the Acaray where the river forms the boundary between Brazil and Paraguay. Here the Paraná descends from the Brazilian highlands and then flows along the highlands' faulted, often scarplike margins. The project, begun in 1978, poured much life and activity into an area that was only sparsely populated. It employed 40,000 workers and attracted many others employed in related industries and services. Three cement plants were established to supply the huge requirements of the dam and power station. The main beneficiary of the project has been Paraguay, whose economy has received a significant boost, especially its construction industry. Unable to use its entire share of the dam's output, Paraguay will sell electricity to Brazil and perhaps also to Argentina. Once the Itaipu power station becomes fully operative, electricity will be Paraguay's biggest export. Many of the workers who came to the site for construction work have already found permanent employment in that part of the station inaugurated in 1982 and put into operation the following year (with a capacity of 1,400 megawatts). The enormous amounts of inexpensive and clean energy that will be produced is likely to revolutionize the economy of the region.

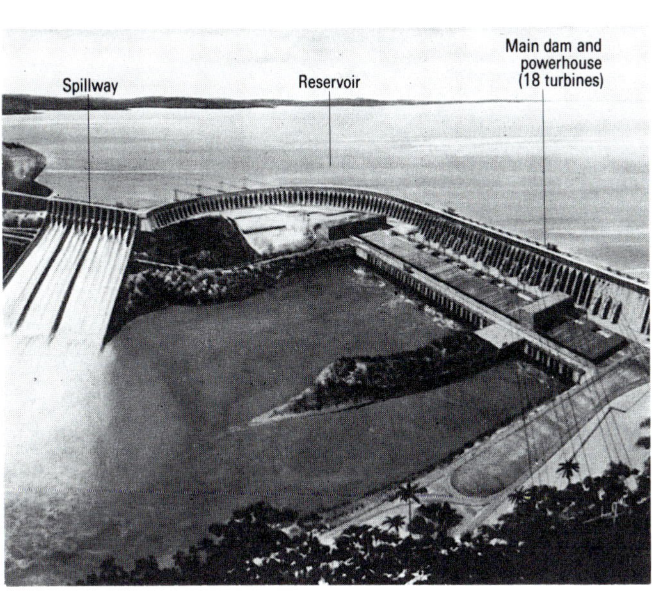

HISTORY

When the first Europeans explored the area that is now Paraguay, most of it was sparsely inhabited by numerous small Tupi-Guaraní tribes. These tribes were seminomads who practiced shifting cultivation of corn and manioc. Then, as at present, a large part of the population lived in the central lowlands. Sebastian Cabot and his crew, who in 1526 and 1529 sailed up the Paraná and Paraguay rivers, were apparently the first Europeans to reach this region. In 1537, the Spaniards founded Asunción as a base for exploring the interior of South America and seeking a land route to Peru. It became the nucleus of European settlement in this region. The Jesuits, who established 32 missions in southern and eastern Paraguay, dominated the country from 1608 until their expulsion in 1767. In addition to the introduction of Christianity, they brought about fundamental changes in the economic and social life of the aboriginal Guaraní population by turning them into sedentary peasants in mission communities. When these fell apart, many of them became serfs on large Spanish estates. Paraguay was part of the viceroyalty of Peru until 1776, from which time until its independence in 1811 it came under the viceroyalty of La Plata. It rejected the aspirations of the first independent Argentinian government to gain control over the entire area of the La Plata viceroyalty. However, the question of its boundaries with its neighbors remained unsettled. Throughout almost all its history as an independent state, Paraguay has been subjected to dictatorial rule, with periodic efforts to introduce a somewhat democratic regime. It has undergone several periods of internal strife and instability. In 1864, Paraguay became involved in a five-year-long war with its large neighbors, Brazil and Argentina, in which it suffered a disastrous defeat. The population was reduced from over 600,000 to approximately 250,000. A great majority of the adult male population was killed. It was nearly 50 years before the country recovered demographically and economically from this war. In 1932 Paraguay went to war with Bolivia for control of the Chaco. The war lasted for over three years, at the end of which Paraguay won about three-quarters of the disputed area. There were hopes of discovering oil in this area, and this was one of the main causes of the conflict, but these prospects have not materialized.

From 1954 to 1989, a military junta headed by General Alfredo Stroessner ruled the country. He was deposed in February 1989 and replaced by General Andrés Rodrígues.

GOVERNMENT AND POLITICS

The country is divided into two provinces: Oriental (14 departments) and Occidental (5 departments). The present constitution was enacted in 1967. Under it, the country is ruled by a president with wide executive powers, elected by popular vote for a five-year term with unlimited re-election periods. There is a bicameral legislature, also elected for five years: the Chamber of Deputies, with 72 seats, and the Senate, with 36 seats. There is also a Council of State whose members are nominated by the president. In elections held in May 1989, General Andrés Rodrígues (who seized power three months earlier) was elected president with the support of the Colorado Party, which has dominated Paraguayan politics since 1954. Following these elections (which were the first comparatively fair elections in 35 years), the composition of the Chamber of Deputies and the Senate was as follows: Colorado Party (right)—51 and 25, respectively; Authentic Liberal Radical Party (Partido Liberal Radical Auténtico [PLRA], central)—19 and 10; Revolutionary Februarist Party (Partido Revolucionario Febrerista [PRF], left)—1 and 1; Radical Party (left)—1. There are a number of additional small parties. Despite some land reforms introduced by President Stroessner and the relaxation in recent years of restrictions on internal political freedoms, comparatively small groups of landowners, wealthy businessmen, and senior army officers hold very influential positions in the political life of the country.

1879

Reelection of president, 1958

Administrative Division

Regions Departments	Capitals	area sq mi	area sq km	population (1985 estimate)
Occidental		95,338	246,925	50,400
Alto Paraguay	Fuerte Olimpio	17,754	45,982	10,100
Boquerón	Dr. Pedro P. Peña	18,034	46,708	12,000
Chaco	Mayor Pablo Lagerenza	14,041	36,367	300
Nueva Asunción	General Eugenio A. Garay	17,359	44,961	200
Presidente Hayes	Pozo Colorado	28,150	72,907	27,800
Oriental		61,710	159,827	3,228,600
Alto Paraná	Puerto Presidente Stroessner	5,751	14,895	255,000
Amambay	Pedro Juan Caballero	4,994	12,933	69,400
Asunción	Asunción	45	117	477,100
Caaguazú	Coronel Oviedo	4,430	11,474	333,000
Caazapá	Caazapá	3,666	9,496	111,400
Canendiyú	Salto del Guairá	5,663	14,667	77,100
Central	Asunción	952	2,465	572,500
Concepción	Concepción	6,970	18,051	143,000
Cordillera	Caacupé	1,910	4,948	194,000
Guairá	Villarrica	1,485	3,846	149,600
Itapúa	Encarnación	6,380	16,525	284,500
Misiones	San Juan Bautista	3,690	9,556	80,100
Ñeembucú	Pilar	4,690	12,147	69,500
Paraguarí	Paraguarí	3,361	8,705	201,900
San Pedro	San Pedro	7,723	20,002	210,500
Total		**157,048**	**406,752**	**3,279,000**

ASUNCIÓN

Asunción, Paraguay's capital and (main) river port, is the country's only large urban center with well over half of its total urban population. Greater Asunción, which in the mid-1980s numbered more than 800,000 persons, is one of South America's oldest continuously inhabited European (Spanish) settlements. It played a leading role as a base for Spanish exploration, for the penetration and settlement of the Paraná-Paraguay basin, and as a link in the landroute between the initial Spanish colonization of the Pacific coast (Lima) and that of the La Plata region.

Asunción's location has conspicuous physiogeographical advantages. It was founded on a promontory descending to the Paraguay River, near its confluence with the large tributary of Pilcomayo. It stands above neighboring areas that are liable to be flooded by the Paraguay.

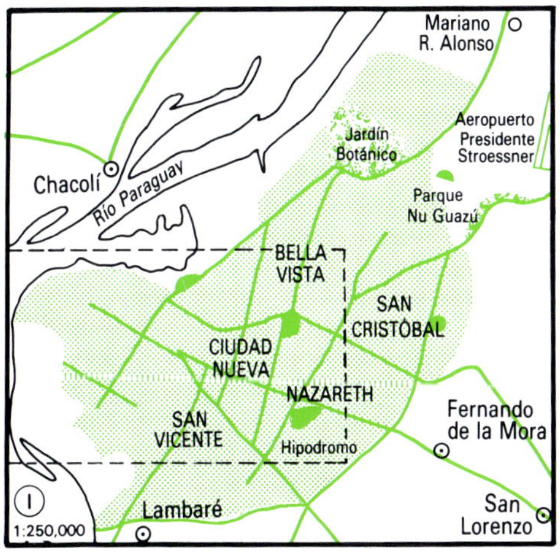

Asunción, founded in 1537, was at that time the Spanish settlement farthest inland in South America, and until the end of the sixteenth century it was the main Spanish base in what is today Argentina, Uruguay, Paraguay, and Bolivia. Toward the end of the sixteenth and throughout the seventeenth century it was the center of extensive Jesuit activities that led to the conversion of Guaraní tribes to Christianity and their settlement on permanent sites. Asunción became the capital of independent Paraguay in 1811 but remained a small town well into the twentieth century. It was held and administered by Brazil from 1868 to 1876 following a war between the two countries. In 1900, its population was estimated at approximately 50,000, and in the late 1930s, it reached 100,000. Its main growth came only after World War II, when it attracted many immigrants from Europe. From its beginnings, the great majority of the city's population has been mestizo. From the sixteenth to the eighteenth century most Spanish settlers were males who took local Indian (Guaraní) wives. The population had increased to 206,000 by 1950 and, in Greater Asunción, to over 400,000 by 1970.

Much of the city consists of small one-story buildings, many in Spanish colonial style. It has a modern administrative and business center with many large buildings. These include the presidential palace, some government buildings, and a French-style pantheon built in the nineteenth century. Prominent among the modern structures is the Guaraní Hotel, designed by Oscar Niemeyer. Asunción is Paraguay's main industrial center and the terminus of the railway lines to Buenos Aires. It is also home to the country's two universities.

Statue of Marshal López, Avenida Costanera

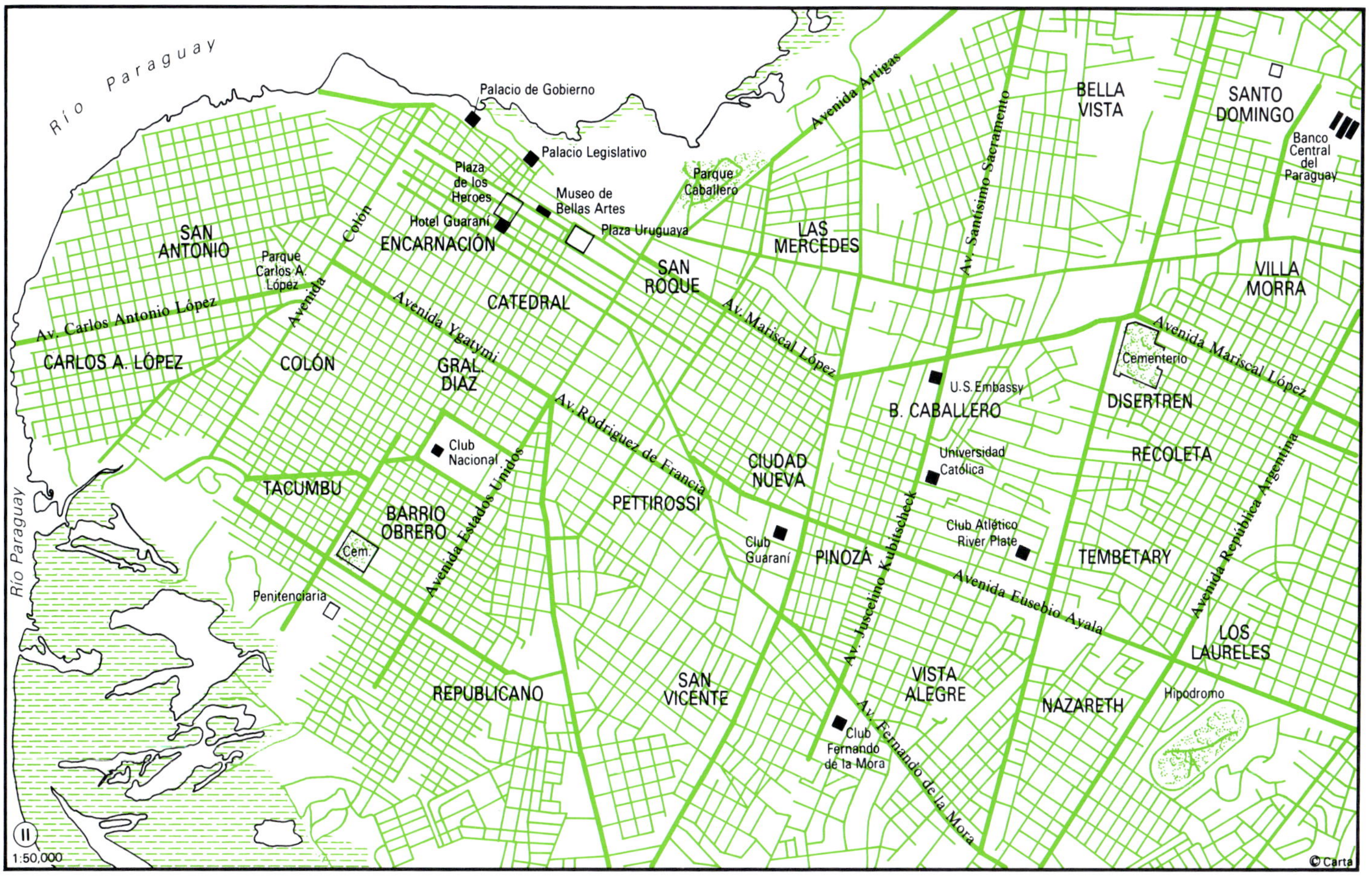

URUGUAY

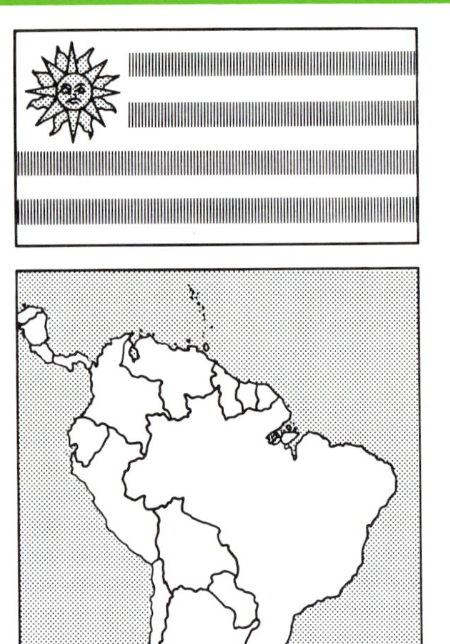

Area
176,215 sq. km.
68,037 sq. mi.

Population
3,128,000 (1990 estimate)

Capital City
Montevideo

Gross National Product (GNP) Per Capita
$2,470 (1988)

Population in Main Cities (1985)
Montevideo 1,247,920
Salto 80,787
Paysandú 75,081
Las Piedras 58,221
Rivera 56,335

Highest Point
501 m. 1,643 ft. (Cerro de las Ánimas)

Currency Unit
1 new peso = 100 centésimos

Density
17.3 persons per sq. km.
44.9 persons per sq. mi. (1986)

Urban-Rural
urban 85.0% rural 15.0% (1985)

Natural Increase
0.8% (1985-1990)

Life Expectancy
71.0 (1985-1990)

Doctors
465 inhabitants per doctor (1986)

Hospital Beds
5 per thousand inhabitants (1985)

Infant Mortality
34 per thousand live births (1985-1990)

High School Pupils
73.6% of age group 13-18 (1986)

University Students
37.4% of age group 20-24 (1986)

Illiteracy Rate
4.6% (1985)

National Holiday
Independence Day, 25 August

National Anthem
beginning "Orientales, la patria o la tumba" ("Easterners [Uruguayans] our country or death")

Wedged between Argentina and Brazil, Uruguay is bounded by the river Uruguay along its entire western length, by the La Plata estuary to the south, and by the Atlantic Ocean to the east. Its northern boundary, with Brazil, runs through a hilly region.

NATURAL REGIONS

Low undulating plains extend along the southern and eastern coast. The eastern coast is followed by extensive stretches of sand dunes and numerous lagoons. Much of the rest of the country consists of low hills, rising to an altitude of approximately 500 meters (1,500 feet). The hills are built of hard crystalline rock, mainly granite, partly overlain by old sedimentary formations or sheets of lava. Two belts stand out in this hilly landscape. The first is the Cuchilla Grande ("great hills"), which extends in a north-south direction along almost the entire length of the country. The watershed between the rivers that flow eastward directly into the Atlantic and those flowing into the rivers Uruguay and La Plata runs along this range. The second belt, the Cuchilla de Haedo, in the northwest, is a southward extension of the Paraná Plateau of southern Brazil. Broad wooded valleys with a dense network of small rivers and streams are common in most of the hilly parts of the country. The only comparatively large and partly navigable of these rivers is the Río Negro, the upper part of which has been dammed and turned into the large Rincón de Bonete water reservoir. The river Uruguay (along the boundary with Argentina) is navigable (to ocean-going steamers) only up to Paysandú, above which it is interrupted by falls.

CLIMATE

Uruguay has a temperate climate with rainfall distributed evenly throughout the year. Seasonal differences, due to altitude and distance from the sea, are small. The average temperature of the coldest month (July) in Montevideo is 12°C (54°F) and of the hottest month (January), 22°C (72°F). Great variablility in temperature, especially in winter, is common due to changes in wind direction. Frost is very rare. The average annual rainfall at Montevideo is 950 millimeters (38 inches). For the wettest parts of the country, the average annual rainfall is 1,250 millimeters (50 inches) and for the driest areas it is 700 millimeters (28 inches). Droughts are rare, although there are considerable differences between years of high and low rainfall. The maximum annual rainfall recorded in Montevideo was 2,350 millimeters (94 inches) and the minimum was 550 millimeters (22 inches).

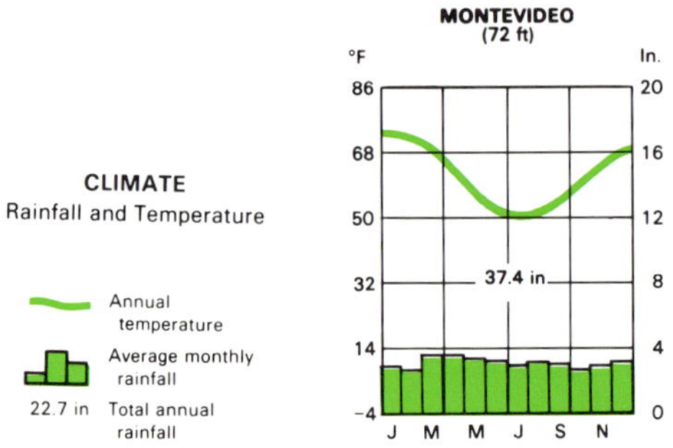

CLIMATE
Rainfall and Temperature

Annual temperature
Average monthly rainfall
22.7 in Total annual rainfall

MONTEVIDEO
(72 ft)

°F: 86, 68, 50, 32, 14, -4
In.: 20, 16, 12, 8, 4, 0
37.4 in.
J M M J S N

POPULATION BY AGE GROUP, 1988

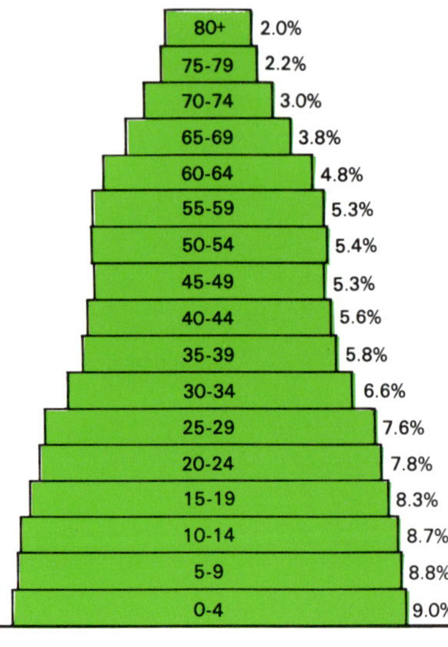

POPULATION

The official population estimate for the end of 1989 was 3,085,000. In the last census (October 1985), it was 2,931,000. The average annual growth rate in population over the last five years has been 0.8 percent. The population growth rate in Uruguay has been one of the slowest in Latin America, only 36 percent over the last 50 years. Nearly 88 percent of the population is of European descent, mainly of Spanish and Italian origin, about 8 percent are of mixed Indian-European race (mestizo), and 2 percent are blacks. There are almost no pure Indians. Approximately 94 percent of the population is Catholic, 3 percent is Protestant, and nearly 2 percent is Jewish.

The population is concentrated mainly in the south and southwestern parts of the country, while the northern and eastern parts are only sparsely populated. The population density in some of the latter regions is less than 5 persons per square kilometer (12.5 per square mile). The average population density for the country as a whole is 17.6 persons per square kilometer (45 per square mile). The most densely inhabited district outside that of the metropolitan area of the capital is 81 persons per square kilometer (202 per square mile). Eighty-five percent of the population is concentrated in urban areas, half in the capital Montevideo (with a population of 1,270,000 in 1989). Other towns are much smaller, numbering less than 100,000 inhabitants, such as Salto (82,000), Paysandú (76,000), Las Piedras (59,000), Rivera (57,000), and Melo (43,000). Four percent of the population is illiterate.

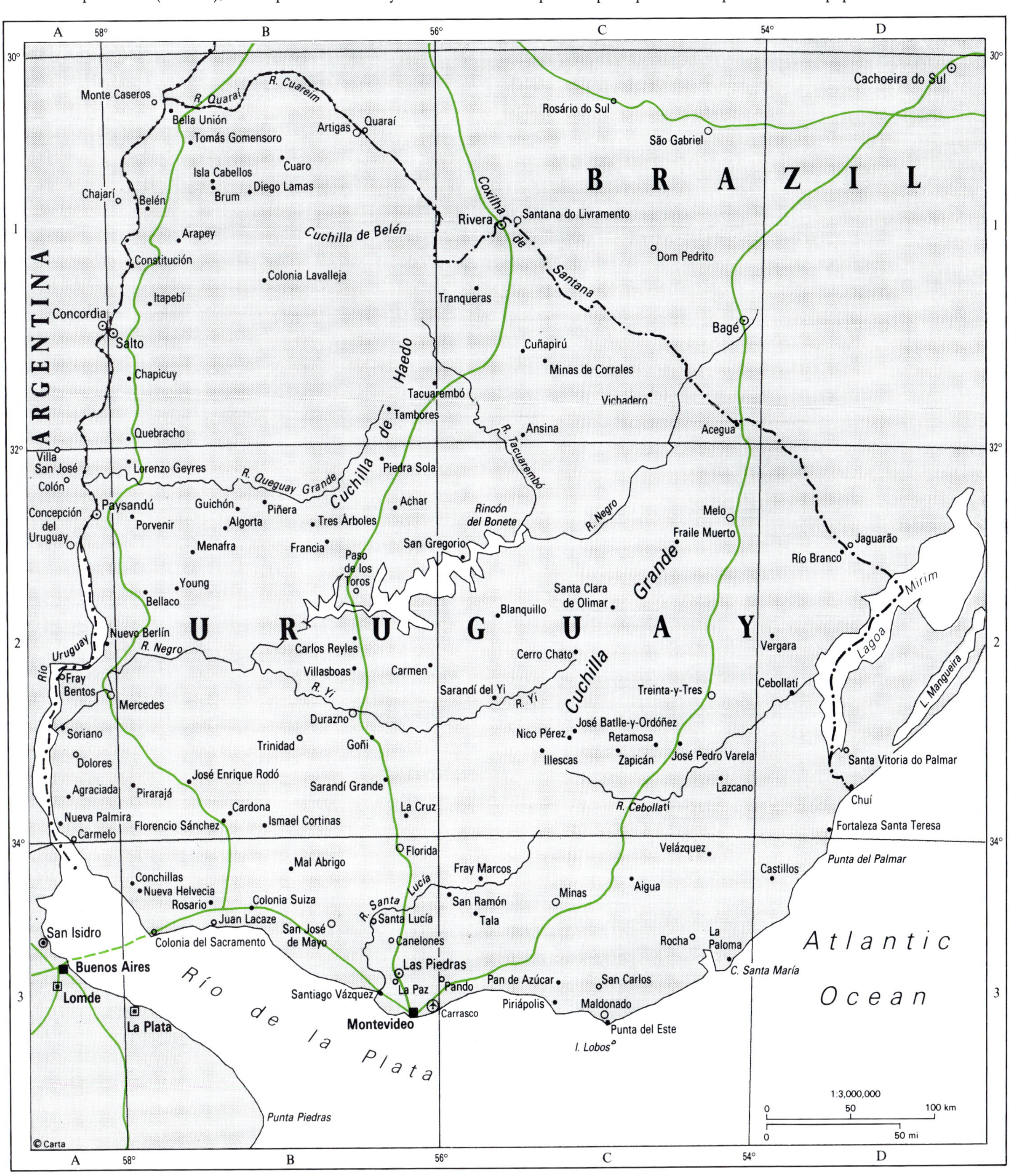

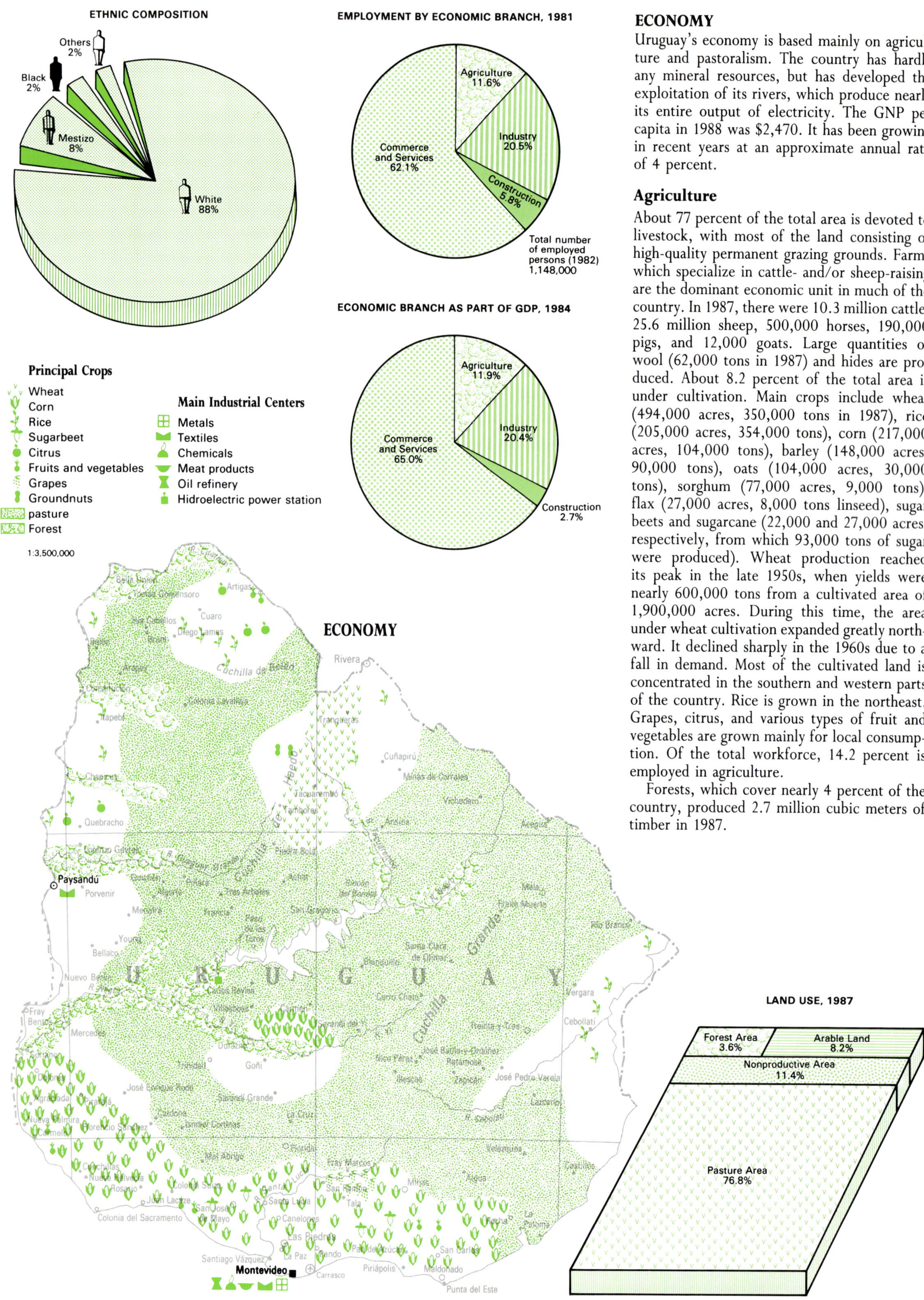

ECONOMY

Uruguay's economy is based mainly on agriculture and pastoralism. The country has hardly any mineral resources, but has developed the exploitation of its rivers, which produce nearly its entire output of electricity. The GNP per capita in 1988 was $2,470. It has been growing in recent years at an approximate annual rate of 4 percent.

Agriculture

About 77 percent of the total area is devoted to livestock, with most of the land consisting of high-quality permanent grazing grounds. Farms which specialize in cattle- and/or sheep-raising are the dominant economic unit in much of the country. In 1987, there were 10.3 million cattle, 25.6 million sheep, 500,000 horses, 190,000 pigs, and 12,000 goats. Large quantities of wool (62,000 tons in 1987) and hides are produced. About 8.2 percent of the total area is under cultivation. Main crops include wheat (494,000 acres, 350,000 tons in 1987), rice (205,000 acres, 354,000 tons), corn (217,000 acres, 104,000 tons), barley (148,000 acres, 90,000 tons), oats (104,000 acres, 30,000 tons), sorghum (77,000 acres, 9,000 tons), flax (27,000 acres, 8,000 tons linseed), sugar beets and sugarcane (22,000 and 27,000 acres, respectively, from which 93,000 tons of sugar were produced). Wheat production reached its peak in the late 1950s, when yields were nearly 600,000 tons from a cultivated area of 1,900,000 acres. During this time, the area under wheat cultivation expanded greatly northward. It declined sharply in the 1960s due to a fall in demand. Most of the cultivated land is concentrated in the southern and western parts of the country. Rice is grown in the northeast. Grapes, citrus, and various types of fruit and vegetables are grown mainly for local consumption. Of the total workforce, 14.2 percent is employed in agriculture.

Forests, which cover nearly 4 percent of the country, produced 2.7 million cubic meters of timber in 1987.

GAUCHOS

The gaucho was a type of nomadic or seminomadic cowhand who roamed the pampas (prairies) of Uruguay and Argentina, mostly in small groups, from the mid-eighteenth to the late nineteenth century. The great majority were of mixed European and Indian race, but some were European or black. The gauchos were skilled and brave horsemen whose main occupations were ranching, protecting cattle herds, rounding up stray cattle and horses, and leather making. They were a conspicuous part of the human landscape of the prairies, especially during the first half of the nineteenth century. The gauchos developed their own way of life: they had a special type of dress (an important part of which was leather), a special kind of dwelling (a low hut), their own eating and drinking habits, social behavior, and religious beliefs (based on Catholicism and superstition), as well as their own moral standards and family life. Arrogance, reliance on the use of force, a form of chivalry, defense of "natural justice," and dignity were among their traits. They had their own songs and music, folklore, legends, and ballads, which were integrated into popular and classical music and were even glorified in some of the best-known Argentine and Uruguayan literature of the nineteenth and twentieth centuries.

The gauchos flourished from the late eighteenth and early nineteenth century, when they dominated large areas of the sparsely inhabited pampas, which were rich in half-wild (escaped) cattle and horses. With the expansion of settlement and the development of better organized and fenced estates and farms beginning in the mid-nineteenth century, the gauchos gradually gave up their traditional life-style and began working as hired labor on large farms. Many workers on large cattle-raising estates still wear gaucho costumes and preserve some of the gaucho traditions, but the old-time, wandering, independent gaucho has disappeared.

MAJOR AGRICULTURAL CROPS, 1987

Wheat
Corn
Rice
Barley
Oats
Sorghum
Linseed
Sugar

50,000 Acres
50,000 Tons

LIVESTOCK, 1987

25,560,000 Sheep
10,323,000 Cattle
500,000 Horses
190,000 Pigs

Ten centésimos, 1960 (depicts Artigas)

TRADE BALANCE, 1987
(Millions of Dollars)

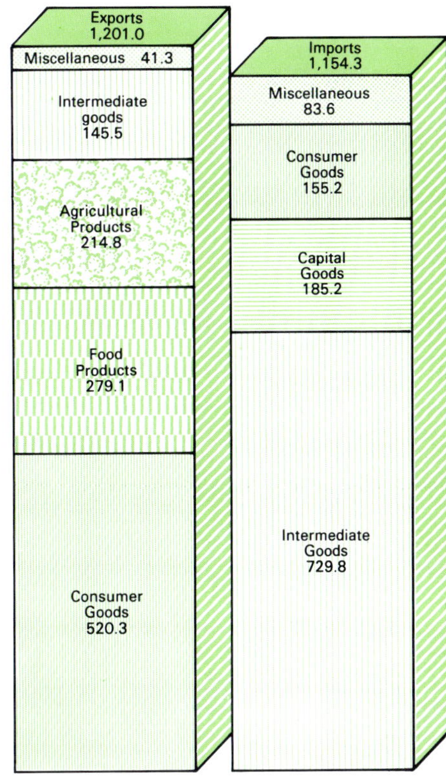

Mineral Resources

Small quantities of talc, quartz, marble, granite, and limestone are produced for local consumption.

Industry

The most important industries are the processing of agricultural products, meat packing and various meat products, foodstuffs, tanning, textiles, building materials (mainly cement), chemicals, and a wide variety of consumer goods. Industrial development has been slow. Much industrial activity is carried out in small plants. Approximately 12 percent of the total workforce are engaged in manufacturing industries.

HISTORY

The area that is now Uruguay was sparsely inhabited by small seminomadic groups of the Charrúa tribes. The first Spaniards to reach the La Plata estuary early in the sixteenth century sailed along the Uruguayan coast and probably landed at some points along the way. However, the area must have been uninviting, for throughout the sixteenth and most of the seventeenth century, long after permanent Spanish settlements were established on the southern shores of La Plata (Argentina), Uruguay, which at the time became known as the "Banda Oriental del Uruguay" (eastern shore of Uruguay), remained unsettled. The rivalry over the possession of the area between the Portuguese, who held southern Brazil, and Spain, who controlled what became Argentina, led to the establishment of the first European settlement in Uruguay, Colonia del Sacramento (150 kilometers [90 miles] west of Montevideo), by the Portuguese in 1680. This was followed in 1726 by the building of a fortress by the Spaniards at Montevideo, at a strategically advantageous site where the hills, the Cuchilla Grande, reach the shores of the La Plata estuary. Small bands of herdsmen, or gauchos, of European or mixed descent, began roaming parts of Uruguay already in the second half of the seventeenth century. These gauchos later took possession of land and founded the first ranches, "estancias," as they were locally known. A growing number of ranches, villages, and towns were established during the eighteenth century, mainly in the south, but gradually appeared further inland and even in the north. Following the withdrawal of Spanish and Portuguese colonialism, the contention over the area of Uruguay developed into an armed conflict between Brazil and Argentina. The country was first occupied by Brazil in 1820 and then by Argentina in 1825. British intervention led to a peace agreement under which Uruguayan independence was recognized, creating a buffer state between Argentina and Brazil (1828). Disputes with each of these neighbors over sections of the boundaries remain still unsolved.

The populating of Uruguay took place primarily during the second half of the nineteenth and the first quarter of the twentieth century, when many European immigrants arrived. The population, which was nearly one million at the turn of the century, had more than doubled by 1930. Population growth has since been slow.

Two political bodies, the Colorados and the Blancos, have dominated the political arena since the first stages of Uruguayan independence. These parties have been based more on personalities and influential social and economic groups than on ideologies and policies. Since independence, the Colorados have been in actual control of the government, interrupted by a number of attempts on the part of the Blancos to seize power. Throughout the nineteenth century Uruguay was practically a dictatorship. It was only from 1900, and especially under the administration of President José Batlle y Ordóñez (1911–1915), whose family played a leading role in government since 1880, that changes in the constitution and the form of government were instated. These changes, coupled with social reforms, established real democracy and gave Uruguay the most progressive rule in South America. The reforms introduced by President Batlle encouraged immigration and economic growth, imposed control on monopolies and vital services, and developed the educational system. After a short period (1933–1938) of dictatorial rule, democracy was restored. The Colorados were defeated in the 1958 presidential elections after 94 years of continuous rule, returning to power in 1966. The country was subjected for 12 years to a military dictatorship following a coup in 1973. Democratic rule was restored in 1985 with the election of a civilian president and legislature.

GOVERNMENT AND POLITICS

Uruguay is divided into 19 departments; 58 percent of the population resides in Montevideo and the adjacent Canelones departments.

Uruguay has a bicameral legislature—a Senate with 31 members and a Chamber of Representatives with 99 members, both elected for a four-year period. The president, who has wide executive powers, is elected for a single five-year term. The present constitution was enacted in 1966, abolished by the military junta in 1973, and reinstated in 1985. A new constitution produced during the military rule was rejected by a referendum in 1980. At present, three main parties dominate the local political scene: the Colorado (center left, which won the presidency and 41 percent of the votes in the 1984 elections); the National or Blanco (center right—35 percent of the votes); and the Broad Front (left—22 percent). These parties hold 40, 36, and 21 seats, respectively, in the Chamber of Representatives. Senate seats are divided as follows (1989): Colorado—13; Blanco—12; and Broad Front—6. An extreme left-wing terrorist organization (the National Liberation Movement, known as Tupamaros) was very active during the 1960s and early 1970s, but was suppressed during the military rule and was granted amnesty following the restoration of democracy in 1985. Serious economic recession developed during the military rule, leading to an unemployment rate of almost 30 percent, inflation of 66 percent and a fall in the annual average income per capita of $1,000. Gradual recovery since the restoration of democracy has decreased unemployment to 9 percent (1988), but inflation has remained high—57 percent (1988). Uruguay has a large foreign debt.

Administrative Division

Departments	Capitals	area sq mi	area sq km	population (1985)
Artigas	Artigas	4,605	11,928	68,994
Canelones	Canelones	1,751	4,536	359,913
Cerro Largo	Melo	5,270	13,648	77,985
Colonia	Colonia del Sacramento	2,358	6,106	112,348
Durazno	Durazno	4,495	11,643	53,864
Flores	Trinidad	1,986	5,144	24,381
Florida	Florida	4,022	10,417	65,873
Lavalleja	Minas	3,867	10,016	61,241
Maldonado	Maldonado	1,851	4,793	92,618
Montevideo	Montevideo	205	530	1,303,942
Paysandú	Paysandú	5,375	13,922	103,487
Río Negro	Fray Bentos	3,584	9,282	48,590
Rivera	Rivera	3,618	9,370	88,801
Rocha	Rocha	4,074	10,551	66,440
Salto	Salto	5,468	14,163	105,617
San José	San José de Mayo	1,927	4,992	88,020
Soriano	Mercedes	3,478	9,008	79,042
Tacuarembó	Tacuarembó	5,961	15,438	82,809
Treinta-y-Tres	Treinta-y-Tres	3,679	9,529	46,599
Total		***68,037**	***176,215**	**2,930,564**

*Includes 463 sq mi (1,199 sq km) of water area not shown separately.

MONTEVIDEO

Montevideo is not only Uruguay's largest city (with nearly 16 times more inhabitants than in the second largest city), but it is, in many respects, the main part of the country as a whole. Over 42 percent of Uruguay's population live in Montevideo, more than in all the other urban areas combined. It is the country's only major port, handling by far more trade than Uruguay's seven minor ports combined, and is also one

Square in downtown Montevideo

of the main fishing and bunkering ports in the South Atlantic. Most of Uruguay's industrial production is concentrated in Montevideo, as are nearly all its major business and financial enterprises and institutions. All the country's major railways, roads, shipping, and other forms of communications originate from Montevideo. The city is Uruguay's only center of higher education, scientific research, and, for the most part, culture.

The old part of the city, around which the modern business center has grown, stands on a rocky promontory 148 meters (486 feet) high that projects into the La Plata estuary, forming the eastern flank of a natural harbor. Spanish immigrants from the Canary Islands established a settlement here in 1726, following the erection on this site of a walled fort by the Spanish governor of Buenos Aires. Despite its advantageous position and pleasant climate, the town grew very slowly. In 1828 it became the capital of independent Uruguay. It developed rapidly with the large influx of European immigrants during the second half of the nineteenth and the first half of the twentieth century. By 1900 the population was approximately 300,000, and by 1935, it had grown to 660,000. Since then, it has nearly doubled. The city has expanded northward and eastward over rolling country around the hill (Cerra) on which the old city stands. The city has many beautiful parks, wide boulevards and streets, and several attractive squares (plazas), of which the Plaza de la Constitución, Plaza de la Independencia, and Plaza Libertad are the most prominent. The cathedral, with a 40-meter high (133-foot) tower, the colonial municipal palace, and the government palace are the most impressive buildings of the older part of the city. The modern city has many tall business buildings, public institutions, and some attractive garden suburbs.

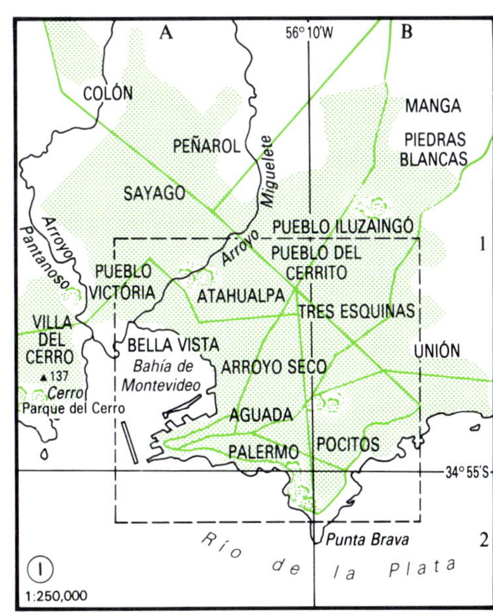

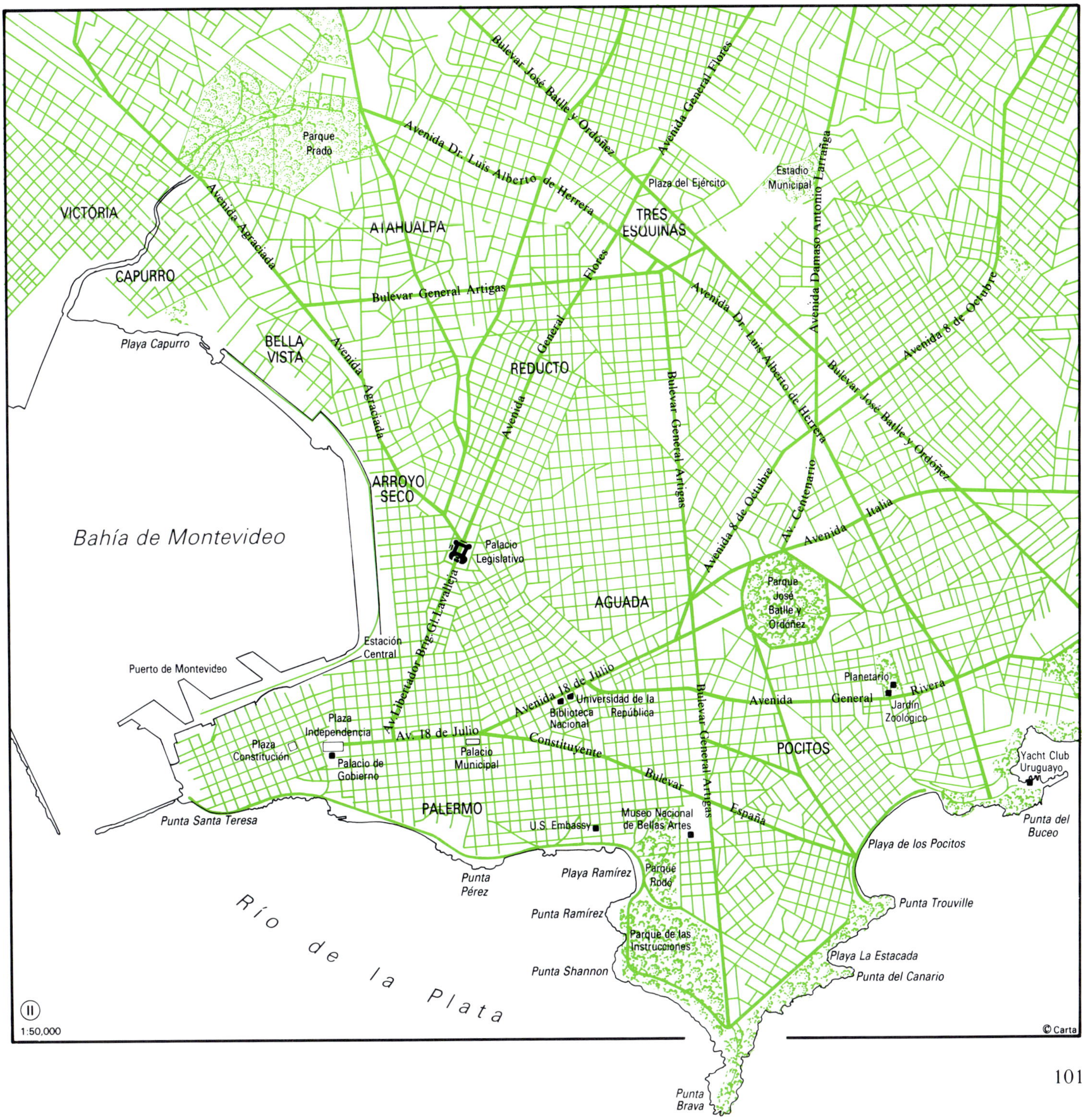

A
B
56° 10'W
34° 55'S
1
2
COLÓN
MANGA
PEÑAROL
PIEDRAS BLANCAS
SAYAGO
Miguelete
Arroyo Pantanoso
PUEBLO ILUZAINGÓ
Arroyo
PUEBLO DEL CERRITO
PUEBLO VICTÓRIA
ATAHUALPA
TRES ESQUINAS
VILLA DEL CERRO
137
Cerro
Parque del Cerro
BELLA VISTA
Bahía de Montevideo
ARROYO SECO
UNIÓN
AGUADA
PALERMO
POCITOS
Punta Brava
Río de la Plata
1:250,000

Parque Prado
Bulevar José Batlle y Ordóñez
Avenida General Flores
Avenida Dr. Luis Alberto de Herrera
Plaza del Ejército
Estadio Municipal
Avenida Dámaso Antonio Larrañaga
VICTÓRIA
Avenida Agraciada
ATAHUALPA
TRES ESQUINAS
CAPURRO
Bulevar General Artigas
Flores
Avenida 8 de Octubre
Playa Capurro
BELLA VISTA
REDUCTO
Avenida General
Bulevar General Artigas
ARROYO SECO
Avenida 8 de Octubre
Av. Centenario
Avenida Italia
Bahía de Montevideo
Palacio Legislativo
AGUADA
Parque José Batlle y Ordóñez
Estación Central
Puerto de Montevideo
Av. Libertador Brig. Gl. Lavalleja
Avenida 18 de Julio
Universidad de la República
Biblioteca Nacional
Planetario
Avenida General Rivera
Jardín Zoológico
Plaza Independencia
Av. 18 de Julio
Plaza Constitución
Palacio Municipal
Constituyente
Palacio de Gobierno
POCITOS
Yacht Club Uruguayo
Bulevar España
PALERMO
Punta Santa Teresa
U.S. Embassy
Museo Nacional de Bellas Artes
Punta del Buceo
Playa de los Pocitos
Punta Pérez
Playa Ramírez
Parque Rodó
Punta Trouville
Punta Ramírez
Parque de las Instrucciones
Río de la Plata
Playa La Estacada
Punta Shannon
Punta del Canario
1:50,000
© Carta
Punta Brava

BRAZIL

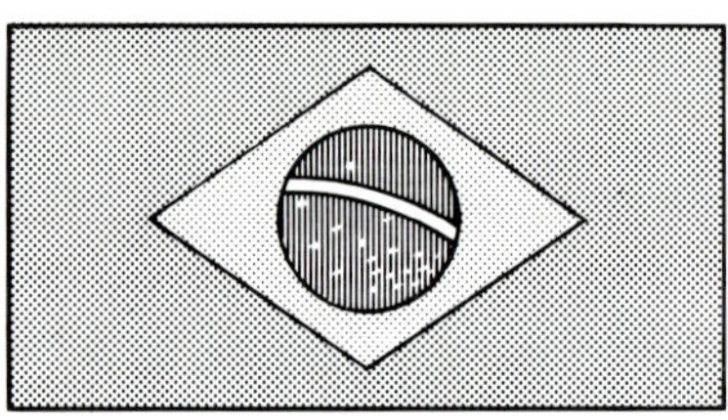

Area
8,511,965 sq. km.
3,286,487 sq. mi.

Population
150,368,000 (1990 estimate)

Capital City
Brasília

Gross National Product (GNP) Per Capita
$2,280 (1988)

Population in Main Cities
(1985)
São Paulo 10,099,086
Rio de Janeiro 5,615,149
Belo Horizonte 2,122,073
Salvador 1,811,367
Fortaleza 1,588,709

Highest Point
3,014 m. 9,888 ft. (Pico da Neblina)

Currency Unit
1 cruzado=100 centavos

Density
16.3 persons per sq. km.
42.1 persons per sq. mi. (1986)

Urban-Rural
urban 72.7% rural 27.3% (1985)

Natural Increase
2.1% (1985-1990)

Life Expectancy
64.9 (1985-1990)

Doctors
683 inhabitants per doctor (1984)

Hospital Beds
4.1 per thousand inhabitants (1984)

Infant Mortality
63.2 per thousand live births (1985-1990)

High School Pupils
35.9% of age group 15-17 (1985)

University Students
10.0% of age group 20-24 (1985)

Illiteracy Rate
22.3% (1985)

National Holiday
Independence Day, 7 September

National Anthem
beginning "Ouviram do Ipiranga"
("Listen to the cry of Ipiranga")

Brazil is the largest country in South America in area and population. It occupies nearly half the continent and has slightly more than half its inhabitants. It is the fifth largest state in the world and a country of great diversity and natural wealth, with vast, virtually unsettled spaces and untapped resources. With land boundaries that extend for 14,700 kilometers (9,100 miles) and a coastline of 7,500 kilometers (4,700 miles), Brazil borders all the South American countries except Ecuador and Chile. Brazil has boundary disputes with Uruguay and Paraguay. The preservation of its vast expanses of natural tropical rain forest, by far the most extensive in the world, is considered vital for the maintenance of global environmental quality.

Brazil possesses a number of small islands in the Atlantic in addition to those close to its coast. The largest and most important of these is Fernando de Noronha, with an area of 26 square kilometers (10 square miles). The other islands are much smaller, and most are not permanently inhabited.

NATURAL REGIONS

Brazil consists of three major geographical regions: the lowlands (the plains of the Amazon Basin) in the north and northwest; the Brazilian Highlands in the center, east, and south; and the southern part of the Guiana Highlands in the extreme north. However, taking climatic and population factors into consideration, Brazil is generally divided into five main geographical regions: the north; the northeast; the central west; the southeast; and the south.

The Lowlands

The lowlands, which are part of the Amazon Basin, are mostly an undulating plain whose main surface features are river terraces and occasional lines of low hills. The lowlands extend west to the foothills of the Andes (beyond the western boundaries of Brazil) and slope very gently eastward toward the Atlantic coast. The Amazon plain is widest in the northwest and becomes narrower downstream toward the east. It is most narrow in the neighborhood of Santarém, where the Guiana and Brazilian highlands come closest to one another, then widens again east of the confluence with the river Xingu as the Amazon approaches its mouth. Brazil's lowlands include a small portion of the floodplain of the river Paraguay and some of its tributaries. It also includes small, discontinous bits of lowland along the Atlantic coast. Brazil has no extensive coastal plain except in the extreme north.

The Highlands

The highlands, which make up by far the greater part of Brazil, are to a large extent extremely faulted, dissected, and eroded plateaus. Both the Brazilian Highlands and the Guiana Highlands are constructed of a basement of ancient, resistant, crystalline rocks, largely overlaid with thick beds of sandstone, in some areas by limestone, and in the south by volcanic rock. Where the ancient crystalline rocks have been exposed to long processes of erosion, the landscape is characterized by rounded hills with gentle slopes and broad valleys. Only extremely resistant rocks that protrude well above the surface form areas with a distinct mountainous nature, especially in the southeast and central west. East and northeast of Rio de Janeiro, for example, peaks such as Pico da Bandeira, at 2,890 meters (9,480 feet), and Agulhas Negras, at 2,787 meters (9,140 feet), rise well above the surface of the highlands. Much of the highlands, however, consist of nearly flat surfaces often cut by deep precipitous valleys. This type of landscape generally appears wherever rocks exposed at the surface are volcanic or of hard sandstone. Seen from the Atlantic coast, the Brazilian Highlands resemble a mountain range. Along much of the narrow coastal strip, particularly between the vicinity of Salvador in the north and Pôrto Alegre in the south, the highlands drop sharply, forming a high escarpment of over 600 meters (2,000 feet) or, in some sections, as high as 2,100–2,400 meters (7,000–8,000 feet). The rivers that flow down from the highlands into the Atlantic generally cut deep narrow valleys through this escarpment. Most of the Brazilian and Guiana highlands are not drained directly eastward to the Atlantic. Except for a comparatively small area in the extreme east, the Brazilian share of the Guiana Highlands is drained southward by tributaries of the Amazon. The Brazilian Highlands are drained mainly northward by tributaries of the Amazon and a number of rivers flowing directly into the Atlantic, and westward by the Paraná River and its tributaries. Several tributaries of the Paraná rise within a short distance of the Atlantic but flow westward over a long and tortuous route into the Paraná. Nearly all the rivers which drain the highlands flow down their steep, often abrupt, edge in deep, narrow valleys. These rivers form falls and rapids that make navigation along their courses into the highlands impossible. The São Francisco, the longest river which flows almost along the entire length of the Brazilian Highlands, descends to the coast through the famous Paulo Afonso falls (84 meters [275 feet]). The main rivers that drain large parts of the highlands into the Amazon—the Tocantins, Araguaia, Xingu, and Tapajós—form falls and rapids before entering the lowlands.

The North

This is Brazil's largest region, extending over 42 percent of the total area (but inhabited by only 5.5 percent of the population). It includes the entire Brazilian part of the Amazon plain and Guiana Highlands as well as the northern fringes of the Brazilian Highlands. Most of the Amazon plain consists of flat low ground that forms the floodplains of the Amazon and its tributaries, separated by much larger areas of undulating higher ground situated well above even the highest floods. Some of these floodplains are bordered by bluffs 45–60 meters (150–200 feet) high. About 90 percent of the Amazon plain is above the level of the highest floods; 10 percent is regularly or occasionally flooded and swampy. The widest area flooded by the Amazon is in its lower course (below Manaus), where the flood area may reach a width of about 100 kilometers (60 miles). Along the middle course of the Amazon, the flooded area hardly ever exceeds 32 kilometers (20 miles). The rivers that meander across the floodplains occasionally shift their channels, leaving small lakes and marshes. The most fertile areas in the vast lowlands are the floodplains of the Amazon and its tributaries, which are often covered by new deposits of silt. Much of the higher ground is covered by poor leached soils. Nearly the entire land area of the lowlands of this region is covered by dense tropical rain forest filled with lush undergrowth. The sparse population is concentrated mainly along the banks of the Amazon and its main tributaries, where navigation is the main means of transport. In the highland areas on the northern and southern fringes of this region the forests are less dense, with many areas covered with scrub and grasses.

The Central West

This is Brazil's second largest region, occupying 22 percent of the total area (but inhabited by only 6.8 percent of the population). It is the heart of the Brazilian Highlands and has many of the most distinct structural and landscape features of a plateau nature. Vast, almost level or slightly inclined surfaces at an altitude of about 1,100–1,600 meters (3,600–5,200 feet) comprise much of the central part of this region. A few peaks rise to approximately 1,800 meters (6,000 feet). This tabular landscape is interrupted by river valleys that become steeper and more deeply incised toward the margins of the region. The plateau is least dissected by such valleys along the divides of the headwaters of the Paraná and its tributaries and those of the Amazon and São Francisco tributaries. It is in this part of the plateau that the new capital, Brasília, was sited, a step that has given great impetus to populating this part of the region. The plateau ends in the southwest in a scarp that faces the swampy plain of the river Paraguay and the southern Mato Grosso (Mato Grosso do Sul). Much of the region is covered with a mantle of coarse soils of low fertility. There are also areas of barren rock. The small percentage of arable land is concentrated in valleys and low parts of the plateau on which better-quality soils have accumulated. The cover of natural

TRANS-AMAZON (TRANSAMAZÔNICA) HIGHWAY

At the end of the 1960s, the Brazilian government announced its plan for an ambitious road network project in the Amazon region focused on the Transamazônica, the road designed to cross the widest part of the South American continent and the largest continuous rain forest on earth. The highway should facilitate settlement and the exploitation of the vast underpopulated Amazon Basin. It is planned to settle about one million families (mainly from the poor areas in the northeast) in the Amazon region.

The project will include three arteries which will run from north to south and two from east to west across the Amazon Basin. The most important of these will be the Transamazônica, with a total length of about 5,000 kilometers (3,100 miles). Land within a 100-kilometer- (60-mile-) wide strip on both sides of the road will be distributed among the new settlers, each family receiving about 250 acres. The project has so far failed to achieve a substantial part of its goals. Problems have arisen related to low soil fetility, distance from main population centers, administrative shortcomings, and insufficient financial support. Some of the settlers have already left the region.

Some of the ecological consequences of the project, such as the extensive destruction of virgin forests and land erosion, were overlooked by the planners. The interests of the aboriginal Indian tribes were ignored. Sections of the road have meanwhile been made unusable by heavy rains or overgrowth of the natural vegetation.

Transamazônica under construction

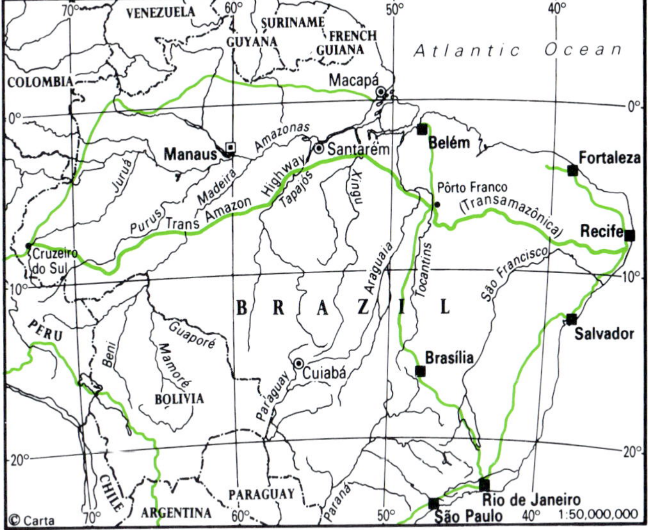

vegetation is often a reliable indication of land quality. The natural vegetation cover varies with soil, climate, and relief conditions. Most of the region is covered by dense scrub woodlands (*cerradão*) and savanna, with wide transitional areas (*campo cerrado*) between these two dominant types of vegetation.

The Northeast

This region, which was the focus of European settlement and economic activity during most of the colonial period of Brazil, had been relegated to second place (after the southeast) in the nineteenth century with regard to population and economic importance. The region occupies 18 percent of Brazil's area and is inhabited by nearly 29 percent of its population. It has a variety of structural features and landscapes. In the north, where the coastline has a northwest to southeast direction, the land rises gradually from the coast southward to an altitude of about 450 meters (1,500 feet) in what resembles a slightly inclined plain over which several isolated low hillocks and sharply pointed rocks are prominent. This is followed farther south and southeast by an upland with summits reaching 750–900 meters (2,500–3,000 feet) of low rounded mountains with gentle slopes and broad valleys. This is, in fact, typical of those parts of the Brazilian Highlands where ancient crystalline rocks have been exposed to long processes of erosion. Those parts of the region where the crystalline rocks are overlaid with sandstone are generally flat-topped, with an altitude of about 600 meters (2,000 feet), but extensively dissected by river valleys. Much of the interior, locally known as the "Caatingas," suffers from recurring droughts and floods. The natural vegetation of scrub and brush reflects the comparative aridity of the Caatingas. An economically important structural feature of the southern part of this region is an elongated basin, known as the basin of Bahia. It is covered with a thick mantle of comparatively recent sediment that provides fertile agricultural land. A dominant feature here is the river São Francisco, which flows northward through its eastern part and turns eastward in a wide bend to reach the Atlantic coast. It is the region's most important potential source of water and energy, but so far has been only partially utilized. Only the central section of the river (from Pirapora to Juazeiro) is navigable to small steamers. It flows for most of its course through a narrow valley that contains only small irrigable areas. In its lower part, below the tremendous Paulo Afonso falls, the São Francisco flows through a deep gorge, with small areas of flatland near its mouth.

The Southeast

The Southeast is the heart of present-day Brazil. Occupying only about 11 percent of the country's area, it is the home of nearly 44 percent of its population. The region includes two of the world's largest conurbations. Except for small and narrow lowland areas along the Atlantic coast, it forms part of the Brazilian Highlands, with the typical combination of dissected tablelands, hilly uplands and low mountains, escarpments, and some structural basins. The surface features are more complex and diverse in the northern part; they are less so in the south (the São Paulo state) and therefore this area has been more conductive to settlement. Most of the region has a rugged relief. Remnants of what had been a plateau during a previous period in the geological history of the region are deeply dissected. Much of the eastern part is mountainous, with areas that stand well above the general surface of the highlands. These include Brazil's highest peak, Pico da Bandeira, and the ranges Serra dos Orgãos (2,318 meters [7,600 feet]) northeast of Rio de Janeiro, Serra da Mantiqueira (2,820 meters [9,250 feet]), and Serra do Espinhaço (1,876 meters [6,150 feet]). The eastern edge of the highlands, which reaches almost to the Atlantic coast, forms over much of this region a great escarpment whose highest section rises to 885 meters (2,900 feet). It is a serious obstacle to access from the narrow coastal strip to inland, except where it is broken through by rivers and by a few other gaps and passes.

In contrast, the descent inland from the crest of the escarpment into the adjoining valleys is gentle. In the southern part of this region (between Rio de Janeiro and São Paulo) the escarpment is known as the Serra do Mar, an unbroken precipitous slope from the edge of the highlands to the Atlantic coast. Inland beyond this escarpment, within the more gentle parts of the highlands, are broad valleys and basins, some of which are densely inhabited. Conspicuous among these is the São Paulo basin. The long valley of the river Paraíba, which flows almost parallel to the coast north of the escarpment, is also densely populated. The southwestern part of this region, largely covered by volcanic rocks, slopes gently westward toward the Paraná valley.

The South

The northern part of the southern region, roughly up to the Jacuí river valley and near Pôrto Alegre, is structurally part of the Brazilian Highlands, with surface features similar to those of the neighboring areas farther north. The great escarpment, which faces most of Brazil's eastern coast, continues southward almost to Pôrto Alegre. Southward, too, run the highland landscape of rounded hills and broad valleys in the eastern part of this region and the tablelands of the western part that slope toward the Paraná valley. The southern half of the region is quite different in its structure and surface features. Not only is the escarpment absent but also the coast is lined by extensive sandbars and areas covered by dunes, with an almost continuous chain of lagoons that extends into Uruguay. The largest of these, the Lagoa (lagoon) dos Patos, covers most of the coastal area in this part of the region. There is a gentle gradual rise inland into a rolling hill country, reaching altitudes of 300–450 meters (1,000–1,500 feet), much lower than the highlands of the northern part of the region. This rolling hill country extends southward over most of Uruguay. The western part of the southern region is covered with lava, forming a low plateau deeply dissected by canyon-like narrow valleys. The river Paraná and its tributaries flow through this plateau, forming spectacular waterfalls, the most famous of which is the Iguaçu Falls on the border with Argentina.

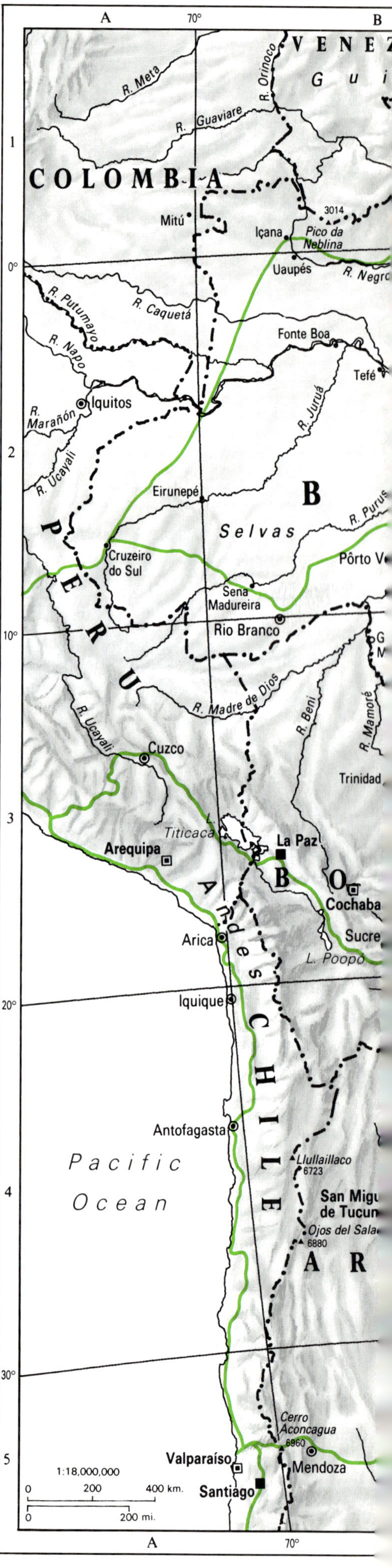

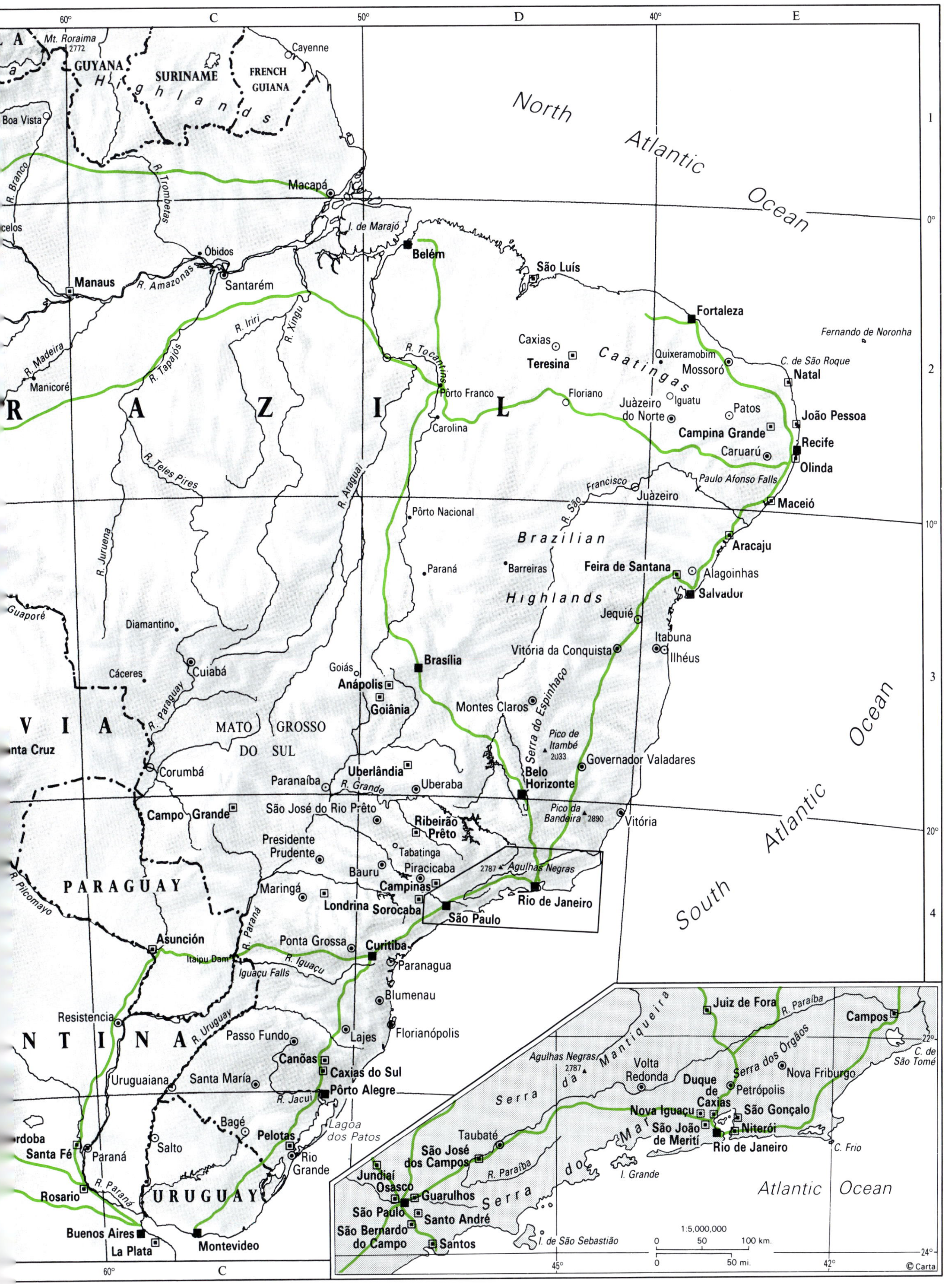

North Atlantic Ocean
South Atlantic Ocean
GUYANA
SURINAME
FRENCH GUIANA
Highlands
Mt. Roraima 2772
Cayenne
Boa Vista
Macapá
R. Branco
R. Trombetas
I. de Marajó
Belém
São Luís
Óbidos
Santarém
Manaus
R. Amazonas
Fortaleza
Fernando de Noronha
C. de São Roque
Natal
Caxias
Teresina
Caatingas
Quixeramobim
Mossoró
R. Iriri
R. Xingu
R. Tocantins
R. Madeira
R. Tapajós
Manicoré
Pôrto Franco
Floriano
Juàzeiro do Norte
Iguatu
Patos
João Pessoa
Campina Grande
Recife
Caruarú
Olinda
BRAZIL
Carolina
R. Teles Pires
R. Araguai
Francisco
R. São
Paulo Afonso Falls
Juàzeiro
Maceió
Pôrto Nacional
Brazilian Highlands
Aracaju
R. Juruena
Paraná
Barreiras
Feira de Santana
Alagoinhas
Salvador
Guaporé
Diamantino
Jequié
Itabuna
Ilhéus
Vitória da Conquista
Cáceres
Cuiabá
Goiás
Anápolis
Brasília
Goiânia
Montes Claros
Serra do Espinhaço
R. Paraguay
MATO GROSSO DO SUL
Pico de Itambé 2033
Governador Valadares
BOLIVIA
Santa Cruz
Corumbá
Uberlândia
Paranaíba
R. Grande
Uberaba
Belo Horizonte
Campo Grande
São José do Rio Prêto
Ribeirão Prêto
Pico da Bandeira 2890
Vitória
Presidente Prudente
Tabatinga
PARAGUAY
R. Pilcomayo
Bauru
Piracicaba
2787 Agulhas Negras
Maringá
Campinas
Londrina
Sorocaba
Rio de Janeiro
São Paulo
R. Paraná
Asunción
Ponta Grossa
Curitiba
Itaipu Dam
R. Iguaçu
Iguaçu Falls
Paranagua
Blumenau
Resistencia
ARGENTINA
R. Uruguay
Passo Fundo
Lajes
Florianópolis
Canõas
Caxias do Sul
Uruguaiana
Santa María
Pôrto Alegre
R. Jacuí
Lagoa dos Patos
Córdoba
Santa Fé
Paraná
Bagé
Pelotas
Salto
Rio Grande
Rosario
R. Paraná
URUGUAY
Buenos Aires
La Plata
Montevideo
60°
50°
40°
C
D
E
1
2
3
4
0°
10°
20°
Juiz de Fora
R. Paraíba
Campos
Serra da Mantiqueira
Serra dos Órgãos
Agulhas Negras 2787
Volta Redonda
Duque de Caxias
Nova Friburgo
C. de São Tomé
Petrópolis
Nova Iguaçu
São Gonçalo
São João de Meriti
Niterói
Rio de Janeiro
C. Frio
Taubaté
São José dos Campos
Serra do Mar
I. Grande
Jundiaí
Osasco
Guarulhos
São Paulo
Santo André
São Bernardo do Campo
Santos
I. de São Sebastião
Atlantic Ocean
1:5,000,000
0 50 100 km.
0 50 mi.
45°
42°
22°
24°
© Carta

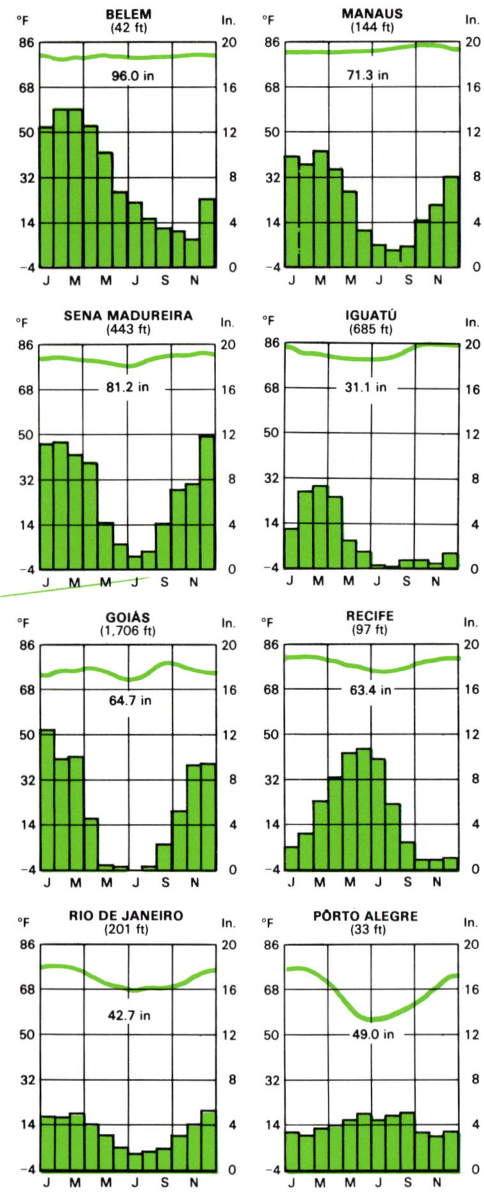

CLIMATE

Extending over nearly 40 degrees of latitude, from the equatorial to the subtropical zones, and for more than 2,250 kilometers (1,400 miles) inland from the open sea, Brazil has a large variety of climates in which, in addition to geographical position, surface features play an important role. Generally, temperature ranges between the warmest and coolest months, which are very small in the equatorial zone, increase as one goes south. The diurnal ranges, which are small near the coast, increase inland, especially in parts of the highlands. Frost occurs as far north as the neighborhood of São Paulo. The summer months are the main, or only, rainy season. Most of the country has no completely dry season. In the southern region rainfall is distributed almost evenly throughout the year. With the exception of the Caatingas zone in the northeastern region, which is semiarid (with frequent drought), with some small areas receiving on the average less than 250 millimeters (10 inches) of rain annually, and some sheltered valleys in the highlands, Brazil is adequately provided with rainfall, with annual averages ranging from 750 to 4,750 millimeters (30 to 190 inches). The following are average temperatures for the warmest and coolest months and average annual rainfall for the main natural regions of Brazil:

The north: Belém 26.6°C (79.9°F, November), 25.2°C (77.4°F, February), 2,150 millimeters (86 inches); Manaus 28.2°C (82.8°F, September), 26.5°C (79.7°F, March), 1,750 millimeters (70 inches); Santarém 26.9°C (80.4°F, September), 24.7°C (76.5°F, February), 1,760 millimeters (70.4 inches).

The central west: Brasília (at altitude 915 meters [3,000 feet]) 23.3°C (73.9°F, September), 19°C (66.2°F, June), 1,720 millimeters (68.8 inches); Goiás (altitude 520 meters [1,700 feet]), 25.6°C (78.1°F, September), 22.4°C (72.3°F, June), 1,670 millimeters (66.8 inches); Corumbá (altitude 120 meters [390 feet]) 26.8°C (80.2°F, January), 20.8°C (69.4°F June), 1,230 millimeters (49.2 inches).

The northeast: Natal 27.2°C (81°F, January), 24.4°C (75.9°F, July), 1,440 millimeters (57.6 inches); Quixeramobim (altitude 207 meters [680 feet]), 28.6°C (83.5°F, December), 26.2°C (79.2°F, June), 840 millimeters (33.6 inches); Aracaju 27.2°C (81°F January), 24.9°C (76.8°F, July),1850 millimeters (74 inches).

The southeast: Rio de Janeiro 26.1°C (79°F, February), 20.4°C (68.7°F, July), 1,140 millimeters (45.6 inches); São Paulo (altitude 820 meters [2,690 feet]) 22°C (71.6°F, February), 15.2°C (59.3°F, July), 1,430 millimeters (57.2 inches); Curitiba (altitude 910 meters [2,980 feet]) 20.6°C (69°F, February), 12.2°C (54°F, June), 1,470 millimeters (58.8 inches); Blumenau 24.4°C (75.9°F, January), 14.6°C (58.3°F, July), 1,480 millimeters (59.2 inches).

The south: Pôrto Alegre 24.7°C (76.5°F, February), 13.5°C (56.3°F, June), 1,250 millimeters (50 inches).

POPULATION

Brazil's population was estimated at 151 million in 1990, having nearly tripled over the last 40 years. It was 51.9 million at the 1950 census, nearly 71 million in 1960, 94.5 million in 1970, and 119 million at the 1980 census. The growth in population is mainly from natural increase, the annual rate of which has been 2.2 percent over the last decade. Natural increase was highest in the late 1950s and early 1960s, when it exceeded 3 percent annually. Since World War II immigration has accounted for only a small part of the population growth. The most rapid growth (natural and by internal migration) over the last decade has been in the northern region, where population increased by over 60 percent (over 100 percent in the state of Acre), and in the Federal District, where it increased by over 50 percent.

The racial composition is as follows: 52–55 percent white, mainly of Portuguese, Spanish, and Italian descent; 34–38 percent mestizo; 6–11 percent black and mulatto; about 0.5 percent Asian (mainly Japanese); and only 0.1 percent American Indian. The percentage of whites is on the decrease (it was 62 percent in the 1950s) while that of mixed race persons is on the increase (from about 27 percent in the 1950s to about 40 percent in the 1980s). There are substantial differences in racial composition of the population between the various regions. There are comparatively few blacks, mulattos, and mestizos in the southern region or in the southern part of the southeastern region, where the great majority of the inhabitants are white. The blacks and mulattos are concentrated mainly in the northeast and north (to which most of the African slaves were brought during the colonial period) and in parts of the central west. Most of the mestizos reside in the same states and in the northern part of the southeast. The remaining indigenous Indians live in the north, with some tribes in isolated areas of the equatorial rain forest to which access is difficult. During the height of European immigration to Brazil, from the 1870s to World War II, more than 75 percent, on the average, came from Portugal, Spain, and Italy. They settled mainly in the southeast and south. Of the total population, 89 percent is Roman Catholic, 6.6 percent is Protestant, 1.7 percent declared no religion, and the remainder either belong to various Orthodox and Eastern Christian churches or are Muslim (0.25 percent), Jewish (0.1 percent), or practice native religions.

Nearly 60 percent of Brazil's population lives in the southern and southeastern regions that cover only 17.6 percent of the country's area. Here are the most densely inhabited states and the largest conurbations. The average population density for the states of Rio de

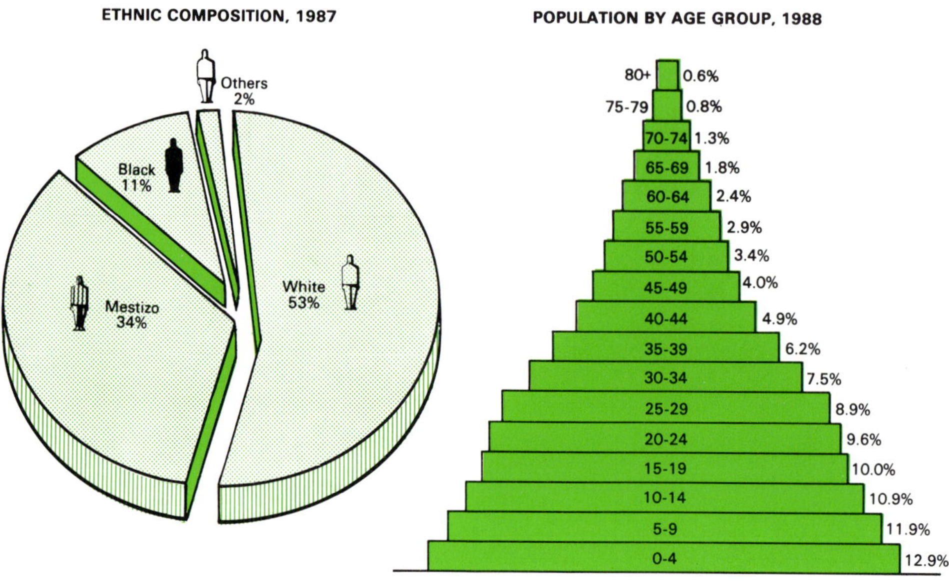

Janeiro and São Paulo in 1990 was 310 and 134 persons per square kilometer, respectively. Some states in the northeastern region also have a comparatively dense population with large urban centers. The average density for the states of Alagoas and Pernambuco is 89 and 76 persons per square kilometer. Most areas of the northern region are very sparsely populated. The average density for the region is 2.4 persons per square kilometer, but the state of Amazonas, which is Brazil's largest, occupying 18.4 percent of the country's area, has an average density of only 1.2 persons per square kilometer, while that of the neighboring territory (Roraima) has only 0.4 persons per square kilometer. The central western region is also sparsely populated; nearly half its area has an average density of 2 persons per square kilometer, the only exception being the tiny Federal District (5,814 square kilometers [2,270 square miles]) with the capital Brasília and its surroundings, where the population is 312 persons per square kilometer. The average population for Brazil as a whole is 17.7 persons per square kilometer.

The urban share in the population is 74.5 percent, having more than doubled over the last 40 years. It was 36.2 percent in 1950. The main conurbations and large urban centers have attracted migration from rural areas at a higher rate than the average growth of the urban population. The main urban centers (with 1989 population estimates) are Brasília (capital)—500,000 (conurbation 1.8 million); Rio de Janeiro (former capital)—6.3 million (conurbation 11.4 million); São Paulo—11 million (conurbation 16.5 million); Belo Horizonte—2.4 million (conurbation 3.4 million); Recife—1.4 million (conurbation 2.6 million); Pôrto Alegre—1.4 million (conurbation 2.5 million); Salvador—1.9 million (conurbation 2.3 million); Fortaleza—1.1 million (conurbation 1.6 million); Curitiba—1.4 million; Belém—1.3 million; Nova Iguaçu—1.1 million; Goiânia—1 million; Manaus—950,000; Campinas—939,000; São Gonçalo—820,000; Guarulhos—800,000; Duque de Caxias—740,000; Santo André—720,000; Osasco—650,000; São Luís—630,000; São Bernardo do Campo—630,000; Natal—580,000; Maceió—540,000; Teresina—530,000; Santos—520,000; São João de Meriti—520,000; and Niterói—500,000. Nineteen other cities have a population of 250,000-500,000. The illiteracy rate is 22 percent.

ECONOMY

Brazil is one of the world's wealthiest countries in terms of natural resources. Despite the considerable progress that has been made in recent decades in the utilization of these resources, much remains undeveloped. The economy is based on agriculture (in which coffee holds a dominant position), industry, and the exploitation of mineral and forest resources. The GNP per capita was $2,280 in 1988 (it was $1,740 in 1986) and has in recent years been growing at an annual rate of approximately 8 percent. For many years Brazil has suffered from high inflation (it was 360 percent in 1986). A new monetary unit, worth 1,000 of the old currency, was introduced at the beginning of 1989 as part of the measures to curb inflation. Brazil has one of the world's largest foreign debts. Tourism has in recent years been playing a growing role in Brazil's economy (there were about 2 million tourists in 1988).

EMPLOYMENT BY ECONOMIC BRANCH, 1984

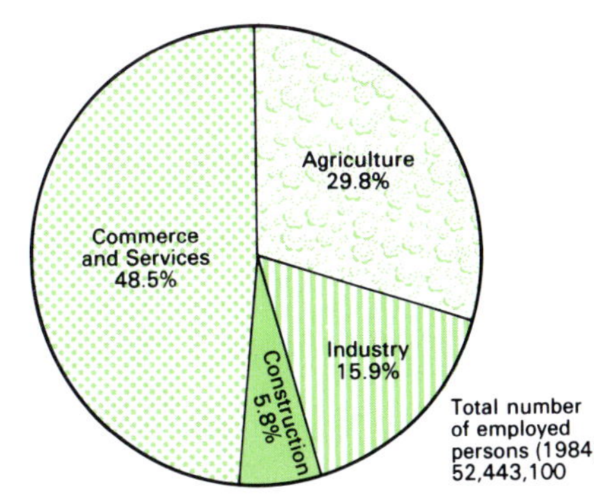

ECONOMIC BRANCH AS PART OF GDP, 1985

LAND USE, 1987

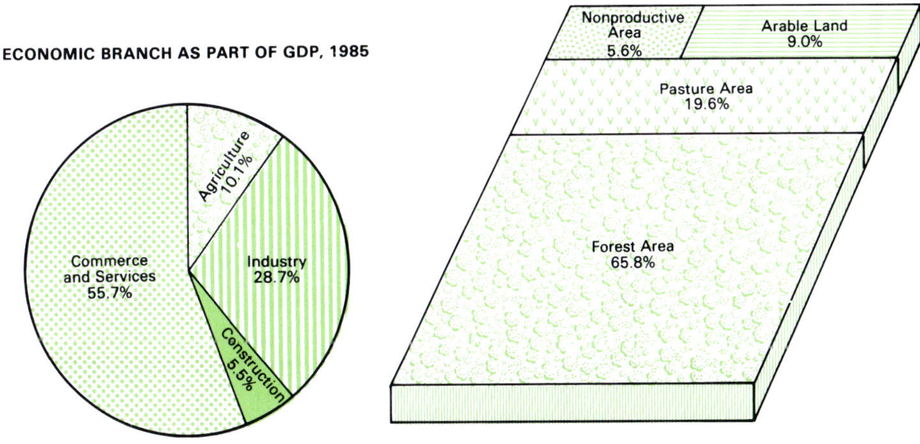

MAJOR AGRICULTURAL CROPS, 1987

LIVESTOCK, 1987

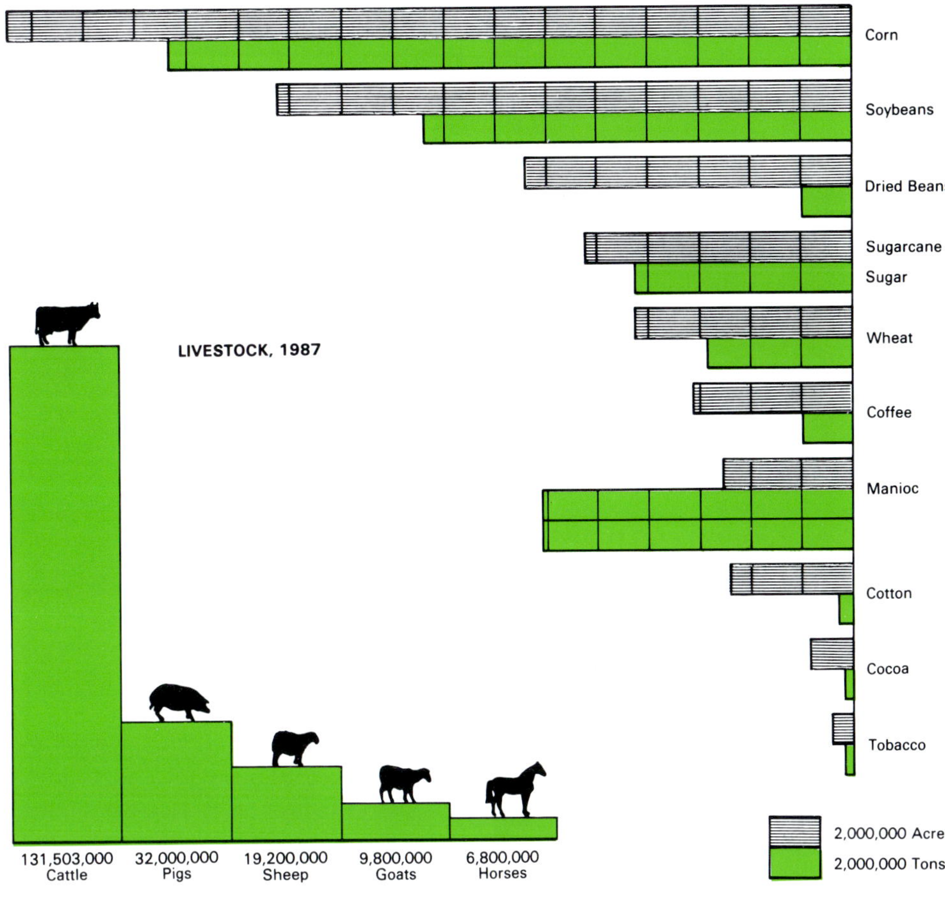

Agriculture

Despite the fact that over the last decades agriculture has lost its relative importance in Brazil's economy, it remains the largest employer and provides a high percentage of the exports. During the last 25 years, the share of agriculture in the total workforce has decreased from 44 to 23 percent, but the actual number of those employed in agriculture has risen from 12.6 to 14.4 million. The area under cultivation has also increased considerably during this period. Most of the agricultural activity and production is concentrated in the southeastern and southern regions and to a lesser extent in the northeast. Two-thirds of Brazil, the northern region and to a great extent the central western region, contribute only a small, though

AGRICULTURE

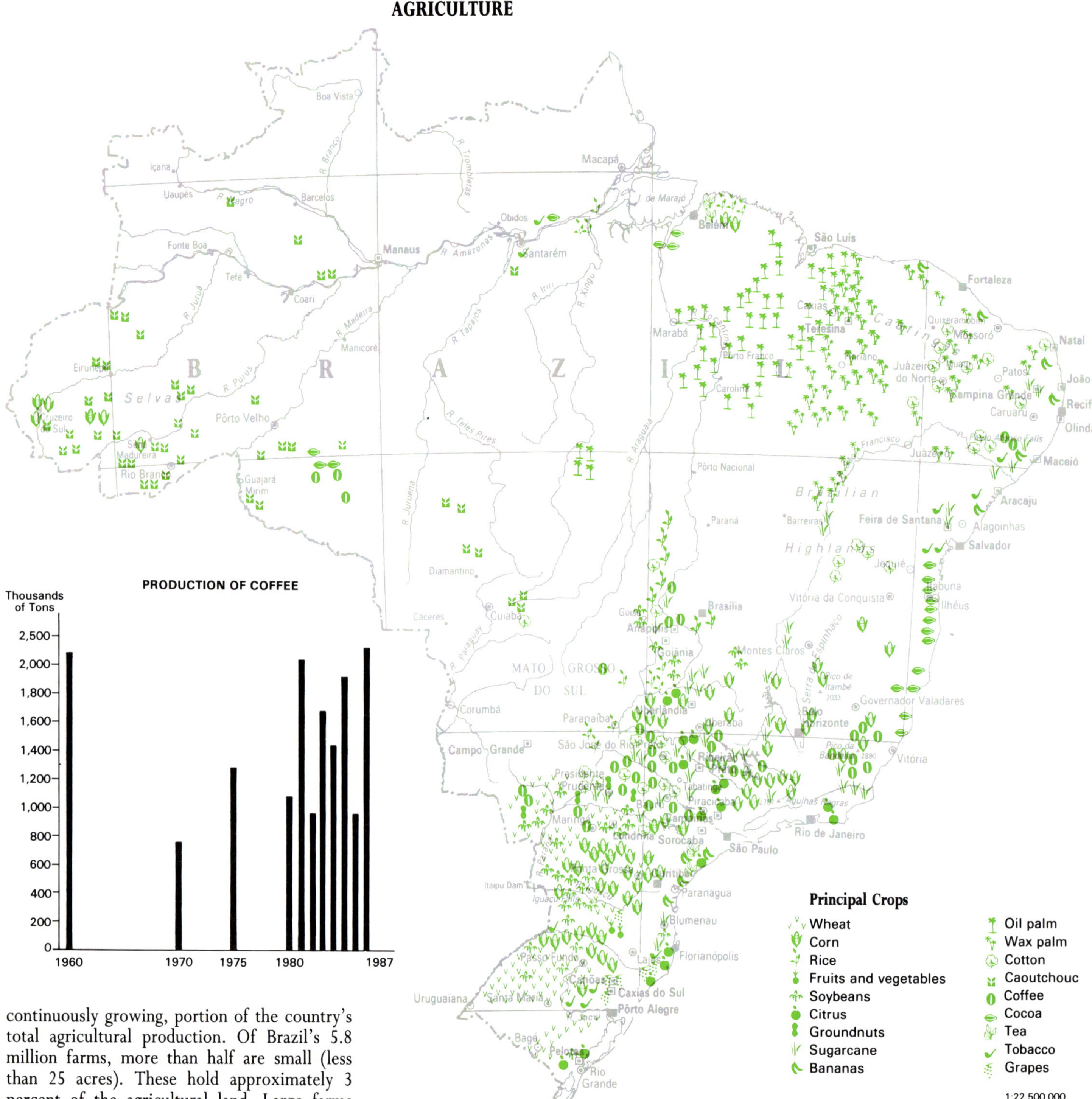

continuously growing, portion of the country's total agricultural production. Of Brazil's 5.8 million farms, more than half are small (less than 25 acres). These hold approximately 3 percent of the agricultural land. Large farms and estates (with over 2,500 acres), which form only 1 percent of the total number of farms, hold about 40 percent of the farmland. Most of the small farms are too small and inefficient to provide an adequate standard of living. Large estates are most common in the northeastern region, where they control over 60 percent of the agricultural area. A large proportion of farmers in this region are tenants. Shifting cultivation is still practiced, mainly in the north, northeast, and central west. Subsistence agriculture is widespread, mostly in the latter regions.

Of Brazil's total area, 9 percent is officially listed as utilized agricultural land. This includes the area of the large estates, which in many cases is only partly cultivated. Nearly 20 percent of the land area is classed as permanent pasture, while 66 percent is covered by forests, scrub, and bush. The proportion of cultivated land is high in the south and southeast but very small (less than 1 percent) in the north.

Brazil has long been the largest producer of coffee, the country's main commercial crop. In the 1960s, Brazil produced nearly half the world's coffee crop, and coffee comprised nearly half the country's exports. Brazil's share in world coffee production and its export crop have since decreased substantially. The state of São Paulo is the heart of the coffee-growing area; important also are the three neighboring states of Paraná, Espírito Santo, and Minas Gerais. The area under coffee cultivation was 7.2 million acres, producing 2.7 million tons of beans in 1988. Sugarcane, of which Brazil had been the world's largest producer (overtaken by India in 1988), is also grown mainly in the state of São Paulo. From the early colonial period to the early 1970s, the northeast had dominated Brazilian sugar production. Sugarcane, which was grown over an area of 10.7 million acres in 1987, yielded 8.65 million tons of sugar. Brazil is the world's second largest producer of cocoa, grown mainly in the northeast in the state of Bahia (over 80 percent). The area under cocoa cultivation was 1.6 million acres in 1987, producing 405,000 tons of cocoa beans. Other commercial crops include cotton (4.9 million acres, 529,000 tons of fiber) mainly in the states of Bahia, Paraná, and São Paulo; soybeans (22.6 million acres, 17 million tons); castor beans; tobacco (740,000 acres, 401,000 tons); citrus (15 million tons); pineapples (958,000 tons); bananas (519,000 tons); and various other tropical and subtropical fruit, including sisal (190,000 tons), coconuts (375,000 tons), oil palms (250,000 tons of oil), Brazil nuts, and tung (4,500 tons of oil). The main crops for local consumption, partly grown by peasants who practice subsistence agriculture, are (1987) corn (maize; 33.4 million acres, 26.8 million tons); wheat (8.5 million acres, 5.7 million tons); beans (12.9 million acres, 2 million tons); and manioc (5 million acres, 24.7 million tons).

Livestock is raised in all the regions and forms a substantial part of the agricultural activity of many of the large estates. Brazil is one of the world's largest cattle-raising countries (135.7 million head in 1988). There are also 20 million sheep, 10.8 million goats, 32.5 million pigs, and 5.9 million horses. Nearly 12 million cattle were slaughtered in 1988.

The forests in 1986 yielded 237.8 million cubic meters of timber and various types of wood. Rubber production is small, meeting only 6 percent of Brazil's own needs in 1987.

Mineral Resources

Brazil is one of the largest mineral-producing countries in the world and among the richest in mineral resources. The discovery of gold was what drew the first big waves of European immigrants (mainly Portuguese) to Brazil in the seventeenth and eighteenth centuries. Production in 1987 was 35,000 kilograms (mined mainly in the states of Pará, Mato Grosso, and Minas Gerais). About 522,440 carats of diamonds and 2,064 kilograms of silver were mined in Minas Gerais and Mato Grosso. Brazil has some of the world's largest high-grade iron ore deposits (in Pará and Minas Gerais) with an output in 1987 of 183 million tons, most of which is exported. The local iron and steel industry has been growing in importance. Other important minerals (with 1987 production figures) are manganese (mined in Amapá, Bahia, and Mato Grosso do Sul) 3 million tons; chrome (in Bahia, Goiás, and Minas Gerais) 185,000 tons; bauxite (in Minas Gerais) 10.3 million tons; copper (in Rio Grande do Sul) 39,300 tons; tin (in Rondônia) 40,300 tons; nickel (in Goiás) 13,400 tons; lead (in Paraná, Bahia, and São Paulo) 13,000 tons, zinc (as lead) 93,000 tons; magnesite (in Bahia and Ceará) 5,500 tons; mica (in Minas Gerais and Goiás) 3,500 tons; uranium (in Pernambuco) 26 tons; tungsten (in Rio Grande do Norte) 1,900 tons; beryllium (in

INDUSTRY & MINERALS

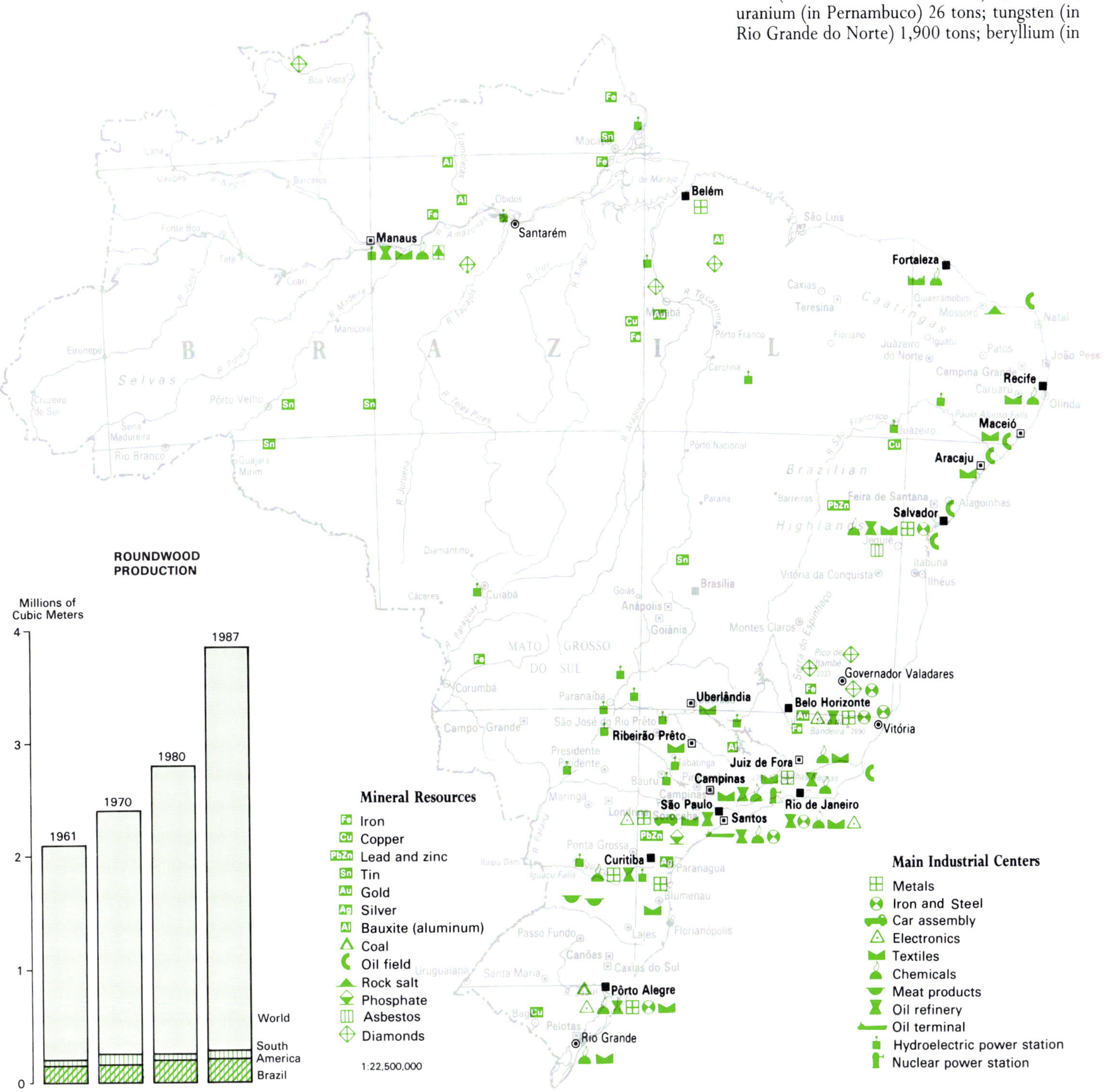

Mineral Resources

- Iron
- Copper
- Lead and zinc
- Tin
- Gold
- Silver
- Bauxite (aluminum)
- Coal
- Oil field
- Rock salt
- Phosphate
- Asbestos
- Diamonds

1:22,500,000

Main Industrial Centers

- Metals
- Iron and Steel
- Car assembly
- Electronics
- Textiles
- Chemicals
- Meat products
- Oil refinery
- Oil terminal
- Hydroelectric power station
- Nuclear power station

ROUNDWOOD PRODUCTION

Millions of Cubic Meters

1961, 1970, 1980, 1987

World, South America, Brazil

Minas Gerais) 207 tons; columbite and apatite (in São Paulo) 582 tons; asbestos (in Alagoas and Goiás) 3.2 million tons; and phosphate (in São Paulo and Pernambuco) 28 million tons. Other minerals include titanium, zircon, barite, high-grade quartz, and a variety of semiprecious stones (gems), of some of which Brazil is the world's main producer.

Oil production (most of which comes from offshore wells) was 8 million tons in 1970 and reached 30 million tons in 1989 (an average of 617,000 barrels per day). It meets about half the domestic requirements. Natural gas production (in Bahia) was 5,686 million cubic meters in 1986. Coal output (7.7 million tons in 1985), from deposits in the states of Paraná, Minas Gerais, Santa Catarina, and Rio Grande do Sul, provides only a minor part of the country's energy requirements. Brazil's potential hydroelectric capacity, one of the largest in the world, is only partly (about half) utilized, providing about 90 percent of the country's electricity needs.

Industry

Brazil has by far the largest industrial output of any Latin American country. Manufactured goods account for a continuously growing share in the value of Brazil's exports. Small industries, such as manufacturing of iron products (from local ore), cotton and wool textiles, foodstuffs, and processing some agricultural and forest products, had already existed in the latter half of the nineteenth century. Brazil's modern industrial boom came during and shortly after World War I, when the number of factories doubled and many new products, mainly consumer goods, were locally manufactured. Industrial expansion was primarily aimed at import substitution. From World War II industrial development has been proceeding at a rapid rate. A large integrated iron and steel industry was established, supporting a wide range of machinery, vehicle, and tool production, shipbuilding, and other industries. Production in the iron and steel industry had increased from 60,000 tons in 1930, to 1.7 million tons of pig-iron and 1.8 million tons of steel in 1960, and to 21 million tons of pig-iron and 22 million tons of steel in 1987. Assembly and production of motor vehicles, initiated in 1955, was 31,000 units in 1957 and 1.1 million units (including tractors) in 1987. There is a large chemical industry, which manufactures fertilizers, pharmaceutical products, various synthetic materials, petrochemical products, and a wide range of consumer goods. Other major industries are textiles and clothing, food products (including 8.6 million tons of sugar and processing, freezing, packing and conserving large quantities of meat), wood products, paper (4.7 million tons in 1988), building materials (25.3 million tons of cement), processing of various minerals (including production of 844,000 tons of aluminum), electronics, arms and military equipment.

More than 5 million workers are employed in Brazil's industries. Most of the industry is concentrated in the southern and southeastern states. São Paulo and its surroundings is the largest industrial center, followed second by Rio de Janeiro and its environs, and third by Belo Horizonte. These three dominate the manufacture of machinery, vehicles, metal products, textiles, and consumer goods. Volta Redonda, in the vicinity of Rio de Janeiro, is Brazil's main iron and steel town. Numerous smaller industrial centers, some specializing in the manufacture of certain products, have developed mostly in the eastern parts of the southeastern and southern regions. The Salvador and Recife conurbations are the only centers in the northeastern region with substantial industrial output. Government policy to foster the development of industries in the northeast and north have met with only partial success. Manaus is developing into an industrial center in the heart of the Amazon plain.

Trade

The United States is Brazil's main trading partner, which in 1986 took 28 percent of the exports and provided 23 percent of the imports. There are also important trading relations with Japan (7 percent of exports and 4 percent of imports); the Netherlands (6 and 2 percent); Germany (5 and 7 percent); Italy (4 and 2 percent); France (3 and 3 percent); Argentina (2 and 3 percent); Saudi Arabia (1 and 6 percent [oil imports]); and Iraq (1 and 7 percent [oil]).

Four-thousand reis, 1824 (depicts Emperor Peter I)

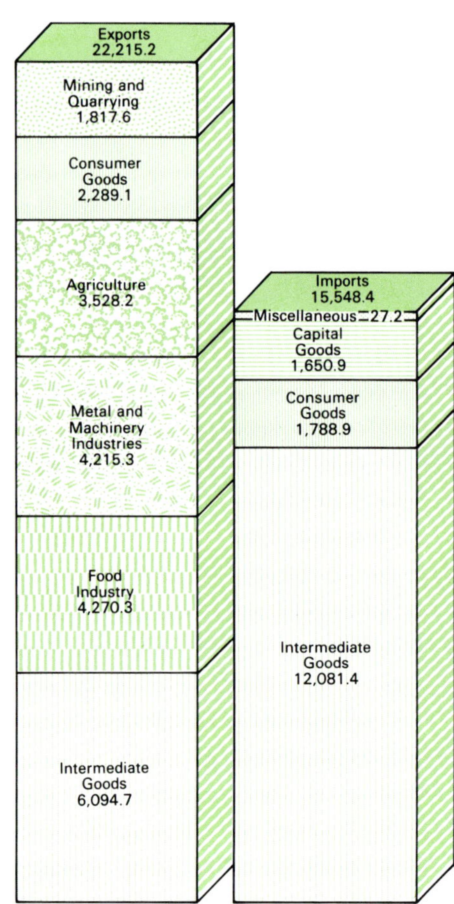

HISTORY

When the first Europeans arrived, the eastern and southern parts of Brazil were inhabited by numerous small tribes of the Tupí-Guaraní group. They subsisted mainly on hunting and fishing. Some practiced to a small extent shifting cultivation of manioc and corn (maize). Small Carib and Arawak tribes lived in areas north of the Amazon (bordering on present-day Venezuela and the Guianas). Small, more primitive and isolated tribes were scattered throughout the central and western parts of the Amazon plain. The estimated total aboriginal population of the area that became Brazil was about 800,000 in 1500. The Portuguese under Pedro Álvares Cabral discovered the coast of Brazil in the spring of 1500. The Treaty of Tordesillas (1494) between Spain and Portugal gave the Portuguese the right to take possession and colonize Brazil (up to around longitude 50° west). The initial exploration of the discovered lands was disappointing since no gold or other commercially valuable resources were found. Settlement, therefore, began only in the 1530s after the Brazilian coast was divided administratively into fifteen sections (*capitanias*), each of which was granted as hereditary property to one of Portugal's prominent aristocratic families. The first permanent settlement was established in 1532 at São Vicente (near present-day Santos). This was followed by other settlements along the coast. The first settlement inland, on the site of São Paulo, was established in 1554. Rio de Janeiro was founded in 1567. Beginning in 1538, slaves from Africa were brought to work on plantations in the northeast. The indigenous Indians proved inadequate as a source of labor. Sugarcane plantations introduced by the Portuguese from their island possessions in the Atlantic (Madeira) proved successful and developed into a highly profitable activity that expanded rapidly. Northeastern Brazil became in the seventeenth century the world's chief source of sugar. The Dutch, who dominated the sugar trade in Europe, seized the sugar-producing region of northeastern Brazil in 1630 and held it for 24 years before it returned to Portuguese control. Sugar attracted many Portuguese immigrants and large shipments of African slaves to the northeast. It brought much wealth to the Portuguese plantation owners.

The discovery of gold in 1698 in Minas Gerais and later in Mato Grosso and Goiás brought a rush of immigrants to the southeastern and central western regions. The gold rush period, which lasted throughout the eighteenth century, reached its peak in the 1780s and began to decline early in the nineteenth century. By that time the prosperity of the sugar plantations had also passed. As in other South American countries, European settlers during the sixteenth and seventeenth centuries were mostly males who took indigenous Indian wives (or, in the northeast, black women), resulting in the high proportion of inhabitants of mixed racial origin.

Rio de Janeiro became the capital of the Portuguese colonial administration in 1763. Bahia (Salvador) in the northeast had been the former capital and a center of colonization since 1549. Following the conquest of Portugal by Napoleon in 1807, the Portuguese government under the prince regent Dom John (João) VI moved to Brazil. The seat of government in Rio de Janeiro brought about a series of reforms that radically changed the status of the colony. Ports were opened to free trade and the running and control of vital services (such as justice and finance) were entrusted to newly formed local bodies. Steps were taken to encourage the development of the economy, education, and other public services. In 1815 Brazil's status was changed from a colony to a member of the United Kingdom of Portugal, Brazil and the Algarve (formerly the southern part of Portugal). Following the restoration of Portugal's sovereignty (after the final defeat of Napoleon) an antagonism gradually developed between the Brazilians and the Portuguese government. The latter favored restoring Brazil to the status of a colony, a move that was supported by the majority in parliament (Cortés). This and other acts taken by the Portuguese government, which enraged the Brazilians, led to a break with Portugal and Brazil's declaration of independence in 1822. A few weeks later the former regent Dom Pedro was crowned emperor of independent Brazil. In 1825 Brazil lost the area of Uruguay (annexed by the Portuguese in 1817) after its defeat in a war with Argentina. Dom Pedro, whose popularity among the Brazilians declined seriously, abdicated in 1831 in favor of his five-year-old son Dom Pedro II. A regency was set up to rule the country. A period of instability and much internal lawlessness followed. Dom Pedro II was crowned in 1840 and remained head of state until 1889, when he was forced to abdicate and Brazil was made a republic. The slave trade was actually stopped in 1853 and slaves were released gradually from 1871 until 1888, when slavery was banned and about 700,000 slaves were freed. The abolition of slavery was opposed by owners of estates, plantations, and mines, who supported an uprising, which led to the collapse of the monarchy. This was succeeded by a military dictatorship and the enactment of a new constitution.

During the nineteenth century, coffee became Brazil's main commercial product. It brought rapid development and much wealth, especially to the state of São Paulo, which was the focus of the coffee boom. The number of European immigrants, which was 230,000 over the period 1850–1875, grew to over 2 million during the last quarter of the century. The great majority settled in the southeast region, which also attracted much internal migration. The military dictatorship of the late nineteenth century was followed by a succession of elected presidents who, with the exception of one (Marshall Hermes da Fonseca), were all civilians. Brazil, which was neutral in the first years of World War I, declared war on Germany in 1917 after Brazilian ships were sunk by German U-boats. Getúlio Dornelles Vargas, who was governor of the state of Rio Grande do Sul, seized the presidency in 1930 after he was defeated in presidential elections held earlier that year. He ruled Brazil until 1945. Vargas changed the constitution several times and, although nominally elected as president, his rule had been dictatorial. Vargas was succeeded in 1945 by a democratically elected president (who enacted a new constitution in 1946) but was reelected to the presidency in 1950, this time in free democratic elections. He committed suicide in 1954 after he was accused of involvement in acts of violence. Juscelino Kubitschek de Oliveira, who was elected to the presidency in 1955 (he served previously as governor of the state of Minas Gerais), decided on the transfer of the capital from Rio de Janeiro to a newly planned and built capital, Brasília, in the heart of the Brazilian Highlands. Between 1961 and 1990 Brazil had eight presidents, five of whom were generals. The country was under an actual military dictatorship from 1964 to 1985. A new constitution, which came into force in 1969, was replaced in 1988 (the eighth since independence) following the restoration of democratic rule.

1983

Administrative Division

States	Capitals	area sq mi	area sq km	population (1987 estimate)
Acre	Rio Branco	58,915	152,589	374,000
Alagoas	Maceió	10,707	27,731	2,335,000
Amazonas	Manaus	604,035	1,564,445	1,833,000
Bahia	Salvador	216,613	561,026	11,170,000
Ceará	Fortaleza	58,159	150,630	6,100,000
Espírito Santo	Vitória	17,605	45,597	2,381,000
Goiás	Goiânia	247,913	642,092	4,659,000
Maranhão	São Luis	126,897	328,663	4,863,000
Mato Grosso	Cuiabá	340,156	881,001	1,599,000
Mato Grosso do Sul	Campo Grande	135,347	350,548	1,687,000
Minas Gerais	Belo Horizonte	226,708	587,172	15,021,000
Pará	Belém	482,906	1,250,722	4,476,000
Paraíba	João Pessoa	21,765	56,372	3,102,000
Paraná	Curitiba	77,048	199,554	8,228,,000
Pernambuco	Recife	37,946	98,281	6,992,000
Piauí	Teresina	96,886	250,934	2,532,000
Rio Grande do Norte	Natal	20,469	53,015	2,204,000
Rio Grande do Sul	Pôrto Alegre	108,952	282,184	8,732,000
Rio de Janeiro	Rio de Janeiro	17,092	44,268	13,278,000
Rondônia	Pôrto Velho	93,840	243,044	818,000
Santa Catarina	Florianópolis	37,060	95,985	4,256,000
São Paulo	São Paulo	95,714	247,898	31,263,000
Sergipe	Aracaju	8,492	21,994	1,339,000
Other Federal Entities				
Distrito Federal	Brasilia	2,245	5,814	1,720,000
Amapá	Macapá	54,161	140,276	227,000
Fernanado de Noronha	Fernando de Noronha	10	26	1,000
Roraima	Boa Vista	88,844	230,104	112,000
Total		***3,286,487**	**8,511,965**	**141,302,000**

*Detail does not add to total given because of rounding.

GOVERNMENT AND POLITICS

Brazil is a federal republic that consists of 23 states, 3 territories controlled by the federal government and a Federal District. Each state has its own governor, legislature (whose members are elected for a four-year term), and judiciary. Under the present constitution the country is governed by an executive president who is elected (together with a vice president) by popular vote for a five-year term. The president must obtain 51 percent of the vote; otherwise, a second ballot is held between the two candidates who win the largest number of votes. Fernando Collor de Mello, elected president in 1989, assumed office in March 1990. The bicameral legislature consists of a 72-member Senate and a 487-member Chamber of Deputies. In the Senate each state is represented by three members and each of the territories by one member. Two-thirds are elected by direct vote and one-third indirectly. One-third of the Senate members are elected for an eight-year term, the others for four years. The Chamber of Deputies is elected for a four-year term by universal franchise. The composition of the Chamber of Deputies after the 1986 general elections was as follows: Partido de Movimento Democrático Brasileiro (PMDB, or Brazilian Democratic Movement Party, which won 55 percent of the votes)—259 members; Partido da Frente Liberale (PFL, or Liberal Front Party)—115; Partido Democrático Social (PDS, or Social Democratic Party)—36; Partido Democrático Trabalhista (PDT, or Democratic Workers' Party)—24; Partido Trabalhista Brasileiro (PTB, or Brazilian Workers' Party)—19; Partido Liberal (PL, or Liberal Party)—7; and other small parties—8. The states of the southern and southeastern regions (with nearly 60 percent of Brazil's population), especially the states of São Paulo (22 percent of the population), Rio de Janeiro (nearly 10 percent), and Minas Gerais (nearly 11 percent) have a dominant position in the internal political arena. Patriotism toward one's state has developed in most of the Brazilian states, especially in the south and southeast. This and the wide gaps in wealth and standards of living between the regions are important factors in internal politics.

BRASÍLIA

Brazil's modern planned capital, Brasília, inaugurated in 1960, is at the heart of a conurbation with eight satellite towns and a population of 1.8 million (1990). It is built in the center of the Brazilian Highlands on a plateau at an elevation of 1,100 meters (3,500 feet), nearly 950 kilometers (600 miles) from the Atlantic coast. When the decision was taken (in 1956) to build a new capital in Brazil, the site chosen was well inside the highlands, in the Federal District of 5,814 square kilometers (2,270 square miles) carved out of the Goiás state. The choice of this site in an area only sparsely populated was meant to open up Brazil's vast interior in order to develop and utilize its untapped resources. A suggestion to move the capital to the interior was proposed toward the end of Brazil's colonial period (1789) and reiterated shortly after the country declared its independence (1822). It was only after Juscelino Kubitschek de Oliveira assumed the presidency (1956) that the necessary measures were taken to plan and build the new capital named Brasília. The process of building the city and its surroundings, with the environmental development work that it involved, attracted tens of thousands of workers to the site who came mainly from the poor urban population of Rio de Janeiro and the northeast. The city's master plan was designed by Lúcio Costa, while the main public buildings were designed by Oscar Niemeyer, whose impact on the center of the city is conspicuous.

The layout of the central city resembles a large, eastward-facing aircraft with backward-bent wings. It has two main thoroughfares: the east-west axis, lined by the federal buildings and civic institutions; and the north-south axis, Brasília's main transportation artery. The city faces in the east a large, arc-shaped artificial lake. The presidential palace, the National Congress building, and the Supreme Court stand on a peninsula that protrudes into this lake. The city is connected by highways and rail to the main urban centers in the southeastern region and to other parts of the country. It has a large modern airport. With its official inauguration (1960), the federal government began to move to Brasília, a process that took several years. The University of Brasília began academic activites and scientific operations in 1962. The foreign embassies moved to Brasília in the early 1970s.

Brasília's population has grown rapidly since 1960. The population of the entire Federal District was 142,000 in 1960, 538,000 in 1970, and 1.18 million in 1980, while that of Brasília (within its municipal confines) was 277,000 in 1970 and 411,000 in 1980. It was estimated at well over half a million in 1990, with a conurbation of about 1.8 million. Many industries have developed in Brasília's environs. Agricultural activity has also greatly expanded, much of it for the supply of the newly created local urban markets.

RIO DE JANEIRO

Described as one of the world's most strikingly beautiful cities, Rio de Janeiro, one of South America's largest conurbations, with a population of nearly 12 million in 1990, is Brazil's most important economic, communicatons, and cultural center. It has maintained this position even though it ceased in 1960 to be Brazil's official capital, a position it held for nearly 200 years. The bay (Baía de Guanabara), on the western shores of which the city is built, was first reached by the Europeans (Portuguese) on January 1, 1502. They assumed it to be the mouth of a river and named it Rio de Janeiro (River of January). The settlement which grew into the metropolis of Rio de Janeiro (or "Rio" for short) was established in 1565 and named in

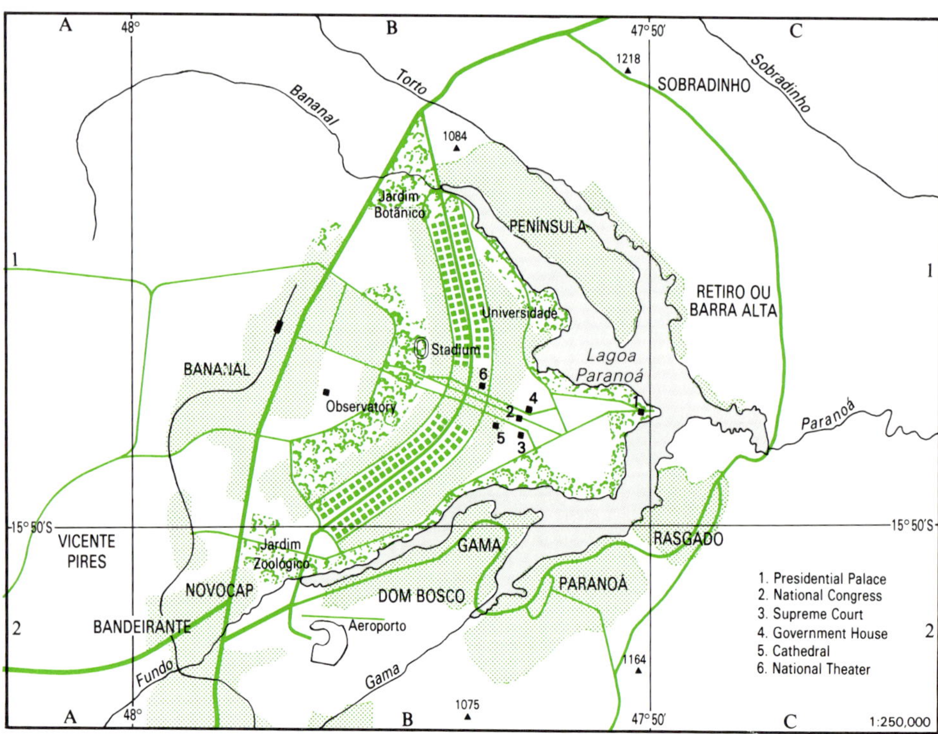

Rio de Janeiro's slums

honor of the king of Portugal, São Sebastião do Rio de Janeiro, and was preceded by a French settlement on a small island nearby. It grew into an urban center and busy port only in the second half of the seventeenth century with the discovery of gold in Minas Gerais, at which time it became the outlet for the wealth of the southeastern region and the regional capital of southern Brazil. In 1762 Brazil's capital was moved to Rio, which for a few years during the Napoleonic conquest of Portugal functioned as the capital of the Portuguese empire and the seat of its royal court. In 1822 it became the capital of independent Brazil. Large-scale immigration from Europe in the last half of the nineteenth and the first half of the twentieth century, together with internal migration from the northeast, greatly enhanced Rio's growth. Its population rose to 800,000 by the turn of the century, crossed the 1-million mark in 1914, was nearly 1.8 million in 1940, 3.2 million in 1960, and 5.1 million in 1980. From the 1930s much of this growing population, due to migration and natural increase, spilled over into satellite towns, resulting in a more rapid growth rate of the conurbation than the city itself, that is, from about 3 million in 1950 to 9 million in 1980, and to nearly 12 million in 1990.

Rio stands partly on a narrow, flat, coastal plain, originally swampy and malarial, formed by the accumulation of sediments brought by a number of rivers flowing into the Guanabara Bay. Mountainous spurs of the Brazilian Highlands rise behind this plain and at some points project into it. With its growth the city expanded up the slopes, into the valley, and around these spurs, one of which closes onto the entrance of the bay from the south and terminates in the famous 390-meter- (1,290-feet-) high rock known as the Sugar Loaf (Pão de Açúcar), overlooking the city. Another landmark farther inland from this spur is the 700-meter- (2,300-feet-) high Corcovado (Hunchback), on which a huge statue of Christ was placed in 1931. The city is well known for its broad avenues, beaches (some artificically widened), its architecturally impressive modern buildings, high-class suburbs and many skyscrapers, and for its parks and gardens. It is, however, also known for its large slums (*pavelas*) in which millions of inhabitants (mainly black, mestizo, and mulatto) live in extreme poverty and squalor. The University of Rio (founded in 1920) is one of the largest in South America. There are also several other universities, scientific institutions, various schools of higher vocational training, academies of art and music, many museums, botanical gardens, and an astronomical observatory. The city is South America's largest and most popular entertainment center.

Rio de Janeiro, with the Baía de Guanabara and Sugar Loaf in the background

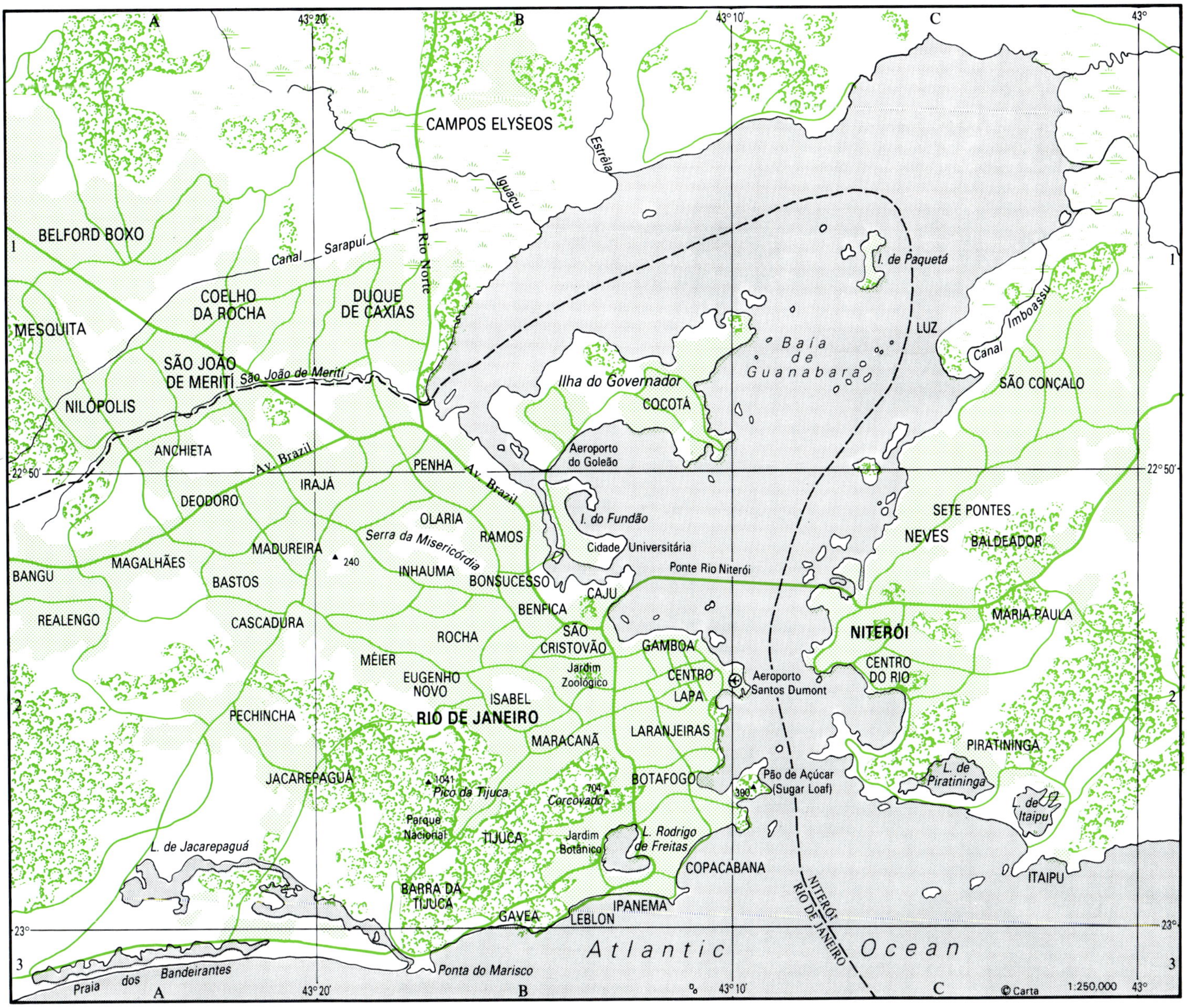

GUYANA

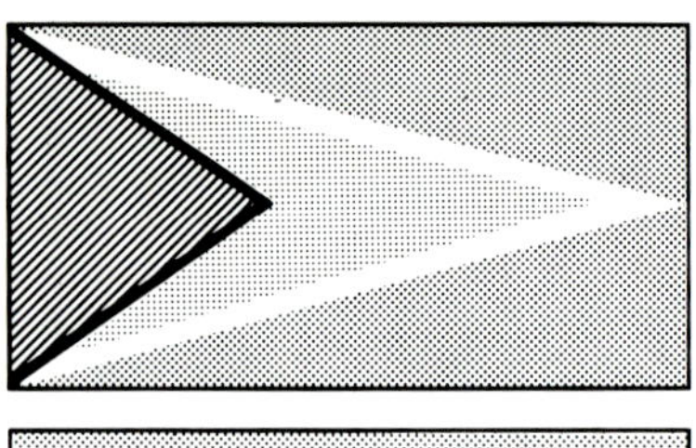

Area
215,000 sq. km.
83,000 sq. mi.

Population
1,040,000 (1990 estimate)

Capital City
Georgetown

Gross National Product (GNP) Per Capita
$410 (1988)

Population in Main Cities
(1980 estimates)
Georgetown 195,000 (1985)
Linden 30,000
New Amsterdam 26,000
Corriverton 13,700
Rose Hall 5,300

Highest Point
2,810 m. 9,219 ft. (Mt. Roraima)

Currency Unit
1 Guyanese dollar = 100 cents

Density
3.7 persons per sq. km.
9.6 persons per sq. mi. (1986)

Urban-Rural
urban 31.2% rural 68.8% (1985)

Natural Increase
2.0% (1985-1990)

Life Expectancy
69.7 (1985-1990)

Doctors
7,480 inhabitants per doctor (1984)

Hospital Beds
212 inhabitants per bed (1979)

Infant Mortality
30.0 per thousand live births (1985-1990)

High School Pupils
56.0% of age group 13-18 (1984)

University Students
2.2% of age group 20-24 (1985)

Illiteracy Rate
4.1% (1985)

National Holiday
Republic Day, 23 February

National Anthem
beginning "Dear land of Guyana, of rivers and plains"

The former British colony British Guiana borders Suriname in the east, Brazil in the south and southwest, Venezuela in the northeast, and the Atlantic Ocean in the north. The boundaries with Venezuela and with Suriname are in dispute. Guyana is one of the most underdeveloped and sparsely populated countries in South America.

NATURAL REGIONS

Three types of landscapes with different structural features make up the natural regions of Guyana. A low-lying, swampy coastal plain, with numerous lagoons partly covered by mangrove and dense wet savanna vegetation, forms the northern region along the Atlantic coast. Parts of this plain are frequently inundated by high tides and by the rivers that cross it. The coast is lined with sand bars. The plain rises very gently southward toward the country's second natural region—the hilly region—which takes up more than two-thirds of the total land area. This is a very deeply eroded northeastern fringe of the extensive plateau known as the Guiana Highlands, which covers large parts of Venezuela, northeast Brazil, and Suriname. The hills, which rise to 600 meters (2,000 feet), are built of crystalline rocks (mainly granite), with slopes and valleys overlain with heavy clay soils. Most of this region is covered by dense tropical rain forest. Some areas in the southwest are covered by scrublands and savanna vegetation that extends into Brazil. The third region, the westernmost part of the country, known as the Pakaraima Mountains or the Western Uplands, is a much higher part of the Guiana Plateau, where the crystalline rock formations of the hilly region are overlain with thick beds of very resistant sandstone. Although generally flat, the plateau reaches a maximum altitude of 2,810 meters (9,220 feet) at Mount Roraima, where the boundaries of Guyana, Brazil, and Venezuela meet. These uplands are greatly dissected by numerous abrupt, narrow, and deep river valleys; the rivers empty into the Atlantic after draining nearly the entire area of Guyana. The flow of these rivers through the uplands and hilly regions is interrupted by falls and rapids, making the rivers navigable only in the coastal plain. The most famous of the waterfalls is the Kaieteur Falls (226 meters, [740 feet]), one of the highest in the world, situated on a tributary of the Essequibo, the main river of Guyana. The uplands are also covered by dense tropical rain forest, except in some of the drier frontier areas in the south, which have a more savanna type of vegetation.

CLIMATE

The climate is equatorial—hot and humid throughout the year except for in the more elevated parts of the plateau in the west. Seasonal and diurnal temperature variations are small. The average temperature of the hottest month (September) in the capital Georgetown is 28°C (82.3°F) and of the coolest month (January), 26.3°C (79.3°F). The average diurnal range is 5.5°C (10°F) on the coastal plain and a few degrees higher in the uplands to the west. The average annual rainfall in Georgetown is 2,200 millimeters (87.8 inches). Precipitation varies from region to region and is lowest in the southwest—approximately 1,500 millimeters (60 inches). Rainfall mostly occurs from December to July, with maximum precipitation in December and June.

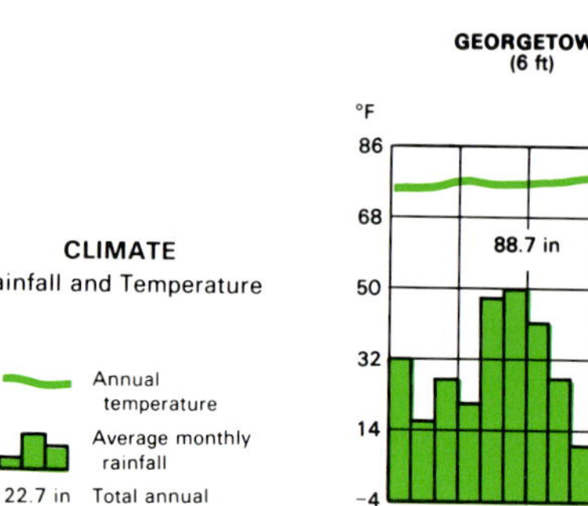

Atlantic
Ocean
VENEZUELA
GUYANA
SURINAME
BRAZIL
R. Orinoco
Waini Pt.
Morawhanna
Mabaruma
Hossororo
Port Kaituma
Baramanni
Arakaka
Koriabo
Matthews Ridge
Marlborough
Charity
Damelstown
Anna Regina
Pickersgill
Suddie
El Callao
Towakaima
Spring Garden
Wakenaam I.
Leguan I.
Enterprise
Kanaima Falls
Vreed en Hoop
Georgetown
R. Cuyuni
Schoon Ord
Buxton
Enmore
Helena
Kartuni
Mahaicony
Timehri
Isseneru
Kamaria Falls
Arimu Mine
Fort Wellington
Bartica
New Amsterdam
Rosignol
Rose Hall
Peaima Falls
R. Mazaruni
Tumereng
Peters Mine
Everton
Mara
Kamakusa
Rockstone
Linden
Keweigek
Issano
Corriverton
Nieuw Nickerie
King George VI Falls
Great Fall
Luepa
Imbaimadai
Tiboku Falls
R. Essequibo
R. Demerara
Malali Rapids
Paradise
Ayanganna
2040
Kalkuni
Amaila Falls
Omai
Ituni
Pakaraima Mountains
Tumatumari
2772
Mt. Roraima
R. Potaro
Kaieteur Falls
(226 m.)
Kangaruma
Mahdia
R. Berbice
Kwakwani
Orealla
Epira
Saveretik
Holmia
Itabru Falls
R. Arabopó
Canister Falls
Kurupukari
Santa Elena
Orinduik
Guiana
Maipuri Landing
R. Courantyne
R. Corantijn
Pan American Highway
Makarapan Mt.
Apoteri
Annai
Kumaka
Karanambo
Yapukarri
Highlands
R. Essequibo
Pirara
Lethem
St. Ignatius
Dome Hill
Boa Vista
Dadanawa
Shea
Oronoque
Aishalton
Karaudanawa
Isherton
Johi
Amuku Mts.
Caracaraí
Biloku
Kamoa Mts.
R. Branco
1:3,500,000
0 50 100 km
0 50 mi
© Carta
A B C
60° 58°
8° 6° 4° 2°
1 2 3 4 5

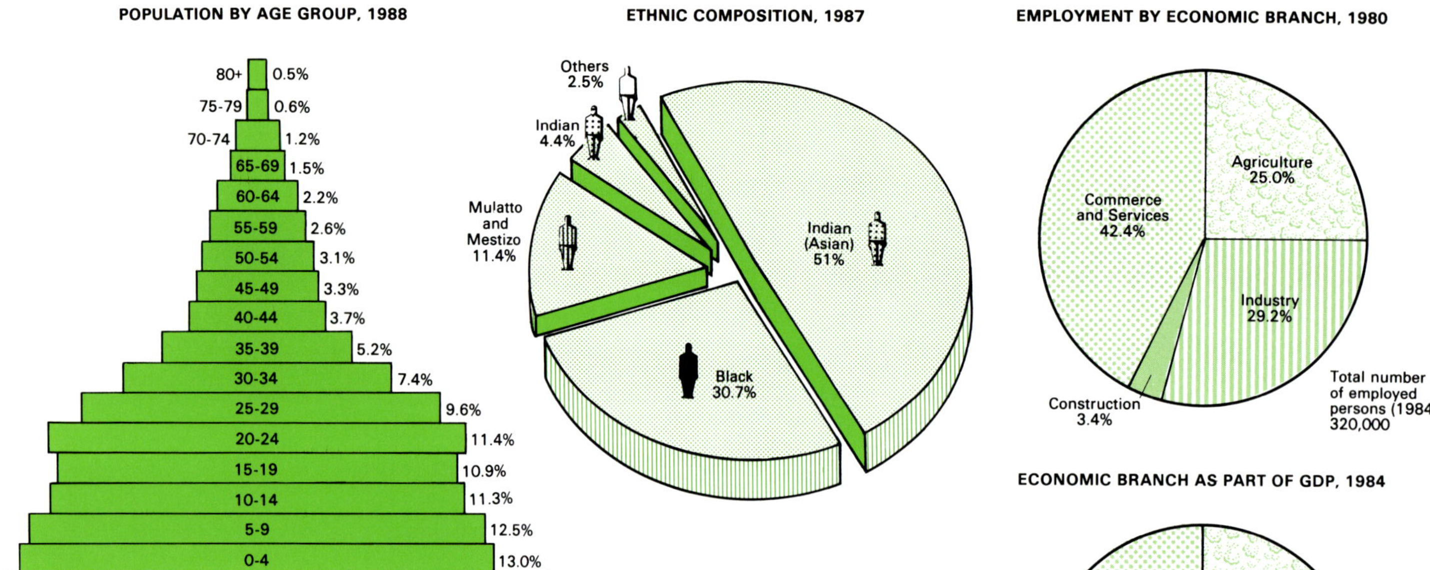

POPULATION

A few small Arawak and Carib tribes lived in Guyana, mainly on the coastal plain, when the first European (Dutch) settlements were established. Most of the country was then and remains to this day uninhabited. The present population, estimated at 1,000,000 (1989), consists mainly of descendants of immigrants from India (51 percent), most of whom were brought to the country during the second half of the nineteenth and the early twentieth century to work on European plantations, and blacks (31 percent), descendants of slaves brought from Africa during the seventeenth and eighteenth centuries. Approximately 11 percent are of mixed race (mulatto and mestizo), 4 percent are American Indians, who live mainly in the interior, some still in primitive tribal societies, nearly 2 percent are Europeans (mainly of Portuguese origin), and there are a few thousand Chinese. Fifty-six percent of the population is Christian (about two-thirds Protestant and one-third Catholic), 33 percent Hindu, and 9 percent Muslim. About two-thirds of the people of Indian (Asian) origin are Hindu and the remainder mostly Muslim. However, part of the black population still adheres to some pagan religious beliefs and practices. The average annual natural increase of the population in recent years has been 1.9 percent. The population has more than doubled over the last 40 years. It was 365,000 in 1943 and 865,000 in 1980. More than 90 percent of the population lives on the coastal plain, concentrated mainly in the central part. The average population density is 4 persons per square kilometer (10 per square mile) and for the coastal plain, 24 per square kilometer (60 per square mile). The urban population is 35 percent of the whole, 70 percent of whom live in the metropolitan area of the capital, Georgetown (210,000 inhabitants). All the other towns are small: New Amsterdam (26,000), Linden (30,000).

The official language is English. Other widely spoken languages are Hindi, Urdu (by the Asian Indians), and a Creole English (a local, largely distorted English dialect spoken by blacks). About 5 percent of the population is illiterate.

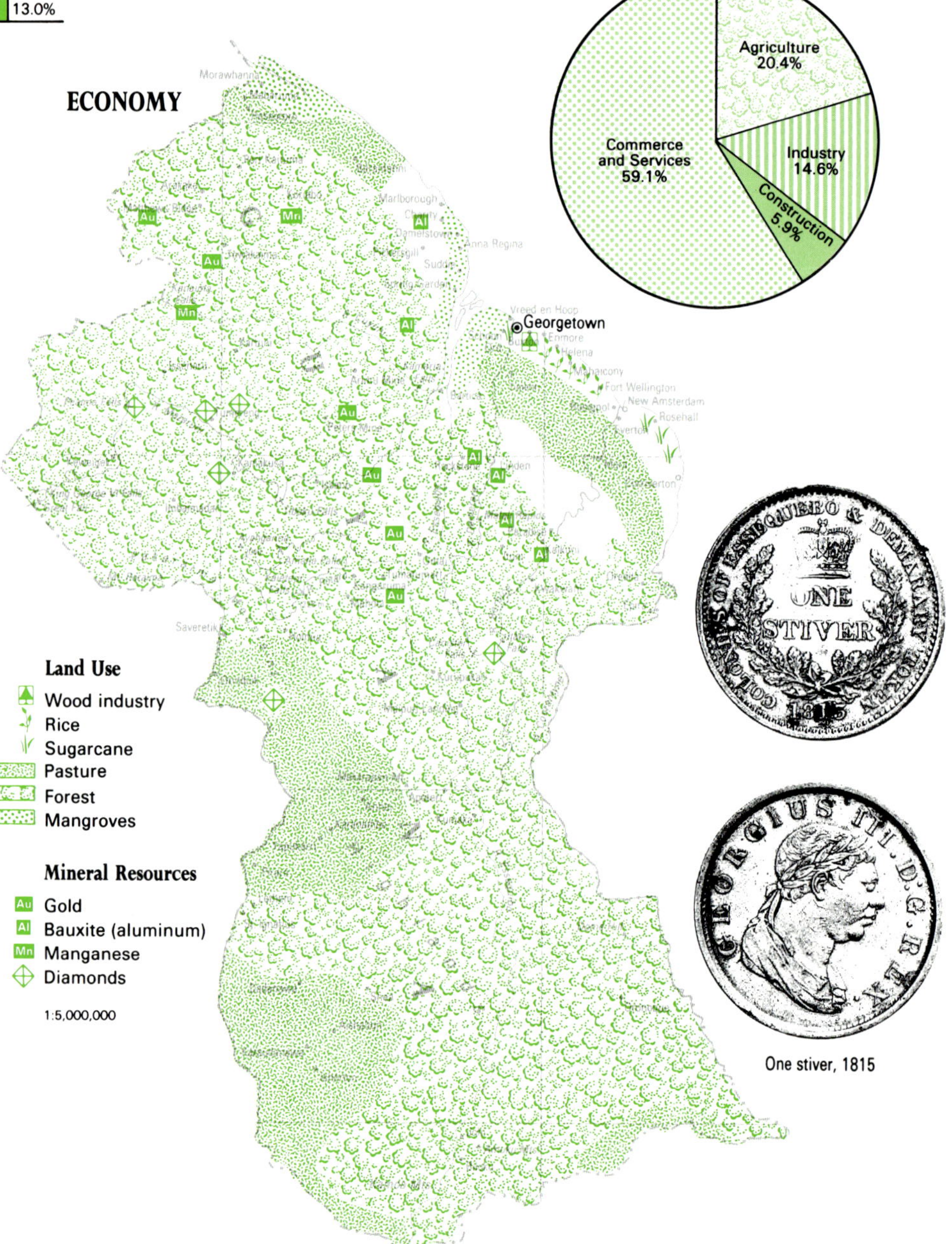

One stiver, 1815

ECONOMY

The economy is based mainly on agriculture, mineral resources, and forestry. Guyana is one of the most underdeveloped countries in South America and has one of the poorest populations. The annual GNP per capita in recent years has been approximately $400. The average annual economic growth is 4 percent. Unemployment and underemployment are high, estimated at over 20 percent. The country is rich in mineral and forest resources that are only partly exploited. Of the total area, 76 percent is covered by forests.

Agriculture

Agriculture is almost entirely concentrated on the coastal plain. Only 2.3 percent of the country's area is under cultivation. The potentially arable land is estimated at over 15 percent. Nearly 6 percent is used for permanent pasture. The main crops in 1987 were rice (227,000 acres, 350,000 tons); sugarcane (116,000 acres, 230,000 tons sugar), coconuts (40,000 tons), and bananas, citrus, and other tropical fruits. Some subsistence agriculture is still practiced, mainly by the descendants of black slaves who when freed settled in squatter settlements in areas of the coastal plain.

Livestock is raised almost entirely in the coastal region; 210,000 cattle, 200,000 sheep and goats, and 185,000 pigs were raised in 1987. The forests produced 209,000 cubic meters of timber and small quantities of various extracts. Of the workforce, 24.1 percent is engaged in agriculture and pastoralism.

RICE PRODUCTION

Thousands of Tons

0, 50, 100, 150, 200, 250, 300, 350, 400

1960, 1970, 1975, 1980, 1987

LIVESTOCK, 1987

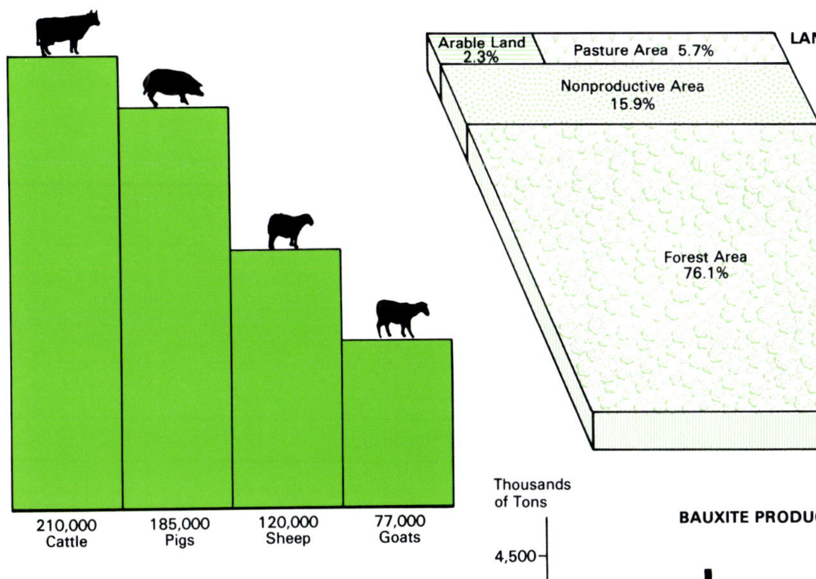

LAND USE, 1987

Arable Land 2.3%

Pasture Area 5.7%

Nonproductive Area 15.9%

Forest Area 76.1%

Mineral Resources

The hilly region west of the coastal plain is rich in mineral resources. Placer mining for gold has been going on since 1884. In 1986, 14,400 ounces were mined. In 1987, diamond mining yielded 11,000 carats. Guyana is one of the world's largest producers of bauxite—2.8 million tons in 1987—which is mainly shipped to Canada and the United States. Other minerals mined include manganese, copper, molybdenum, and uranium.

Industry

Industry, in which 22 percent of the workforce is employed, is engaged mainly in processing agricultural (sugar, rum) and mineral (bauxite) products and in the manufacture of foodstuffs and some consumer goods. The potentially extensive hydroelectric resources are unexploited.

Exports include mainly sugar and its by-products (rum and mollasses), and bauxite ore and processed bauxite.

BAUXITE PRODUCTION

Thousands of Tons

0, 500, 1,000, 1,500, 2,000, 2,500, 3,000, 3,500, 4,000, 4,500

1960, 1970, 1975, 1980, 1987

HISTORY

Christopher Columbus (1498), Amerigo Vespucci (1499), and Vicente Yáñez Pinzón (1500) were the first Europeans to sail along the Guyana coast. The Spaniards, some of whom probably sailed short distances inland along some of the rivers that cross Guyana, did not establish any settlements, due to the land's inhospitable nature and lack of economic resources. The Dutch sailed along the Essequibo river up to the hilly region, where they established the first European station in 1596. Along the coast they founded the settlement of Stabroek, which under British rule became Georgetown. By 1613 the Dutch had four small settlements. By draining some areas near the coast, they made land available to plantations, on which were grown mainly sugar and tobacco. During the seventeenth and eighteenth centuries Dutch settlement expanded slowly on the coastal plain, mainly southward. Small settlements based on subsistence agriculture (mainly manioc) were established further inland by runaway Negro slaves. These Negro settlements grew substantially in both number and size after the abolition of slavery in 1834, when large numbers left the sugar plantations and moved inland. The area of Guyana came under British rule in 1796 and was officially ceded to Britain in 1814. The population grew during the nineteenth century, mainly when immigrants from India came to work in the plantations and mines. The population was estimated at 300,000 at the turn of the twentieth century. The population has since grown by natural increase. The country gained autonomy in 1952 and its independence in 1966 and became a member of the British Commonwealth. It declared itself a cooperative republic in 1970.

GOVERNMENT AND POLITICS

The country is divided into ten administrative regions. Under the constitution adopted in 1980, the government is headed by an executive president with wide powers, elected by popular vote for a five-year term. The unicameral legislature consists of the National Assembly, with 65 members also elected for five years, 53 by proportional votes. In the elections of December 1985, Desmond Hoyte, candidate of the People's National Congress (PNC), was elected president. The PNC won 42 seats (78 percent of the votes) in the National Assembly, the People's Progressive Party (PPP) 8 seats (16 percent of the votes), the United Force (UF) 2 seats, and the Working People's Alliance (WPA) 1 seat. Twelve members are elected by various organizations. The PPP, an extreme leftist party headed by Dr. Cheddi Jagan (a dentist of East Indian origin), held a dominant position in local politics from the inception of self-government to 1964. It derived its strength mainly from the Asian Indian population. This government was deposed by the British authorities. Since 1964 the PNC, a moderate socialist party initially supported in large by the black population, has been in control. The party was headed by Forbes Burnham (a black) until his death in 1985, and since then by Desmond Hoyte.

Administrative Division

Regions	Capitals
East Berbice	New Amsterdam
East Demerara	Enmore
Essequibo	Suddie
Essequibo Islands	Enterprise
Georgetown	Georgetown
Mazaruni-Potaro	Bartica
North West	Mabaruma
Rupununi	Lethem
West Berbice	Fort Wellington
West Demerara	Vreed en Hoop

GEORGETOWN

Georgetown is the largest and most important urban center on the South Atlantic coast between the estuaries of the Amazonas and Orinoco rivers, with a population estimated at greater than 200,000 (1988). It is situated near the mouth of the Demerara, one of Guyana's larger rivers and its main arteries for access inland. Georgetown has been the administrative center and chief settlement and port of Guyana since 1812. Occupied in 1781 by British settlers and named after King George III, the town fell into French and Dutch hands before it was finally restored to British rule in 1812. The population growth during the nineteenth century was slow despite the importation of large numbers of Asians (from India) to work on plantations in the vicinity. The area was malarial until the 1940s, and the disease claimed many lives. Georgetown's population was approximately 40,000 in 1900, 65,000 in 1935, and nearly 90,000 in 1955. The population has nearly doubled since it became the capital of independent Guyana in 1970.

A large part of the city consists of one-story wooden houses, many of them on stilts. During the colonial period, wood had been the most widely used material for the construction of public and commercial buildings in the center of the city. Large fires (especially one in 1951) burned down many of these buildings. Today, the modern center is built mainly of concrete and brick. Georgetown is Guyana's chief commercial and industrial center. It has large botanical gardens and a university, which opened in 1963.

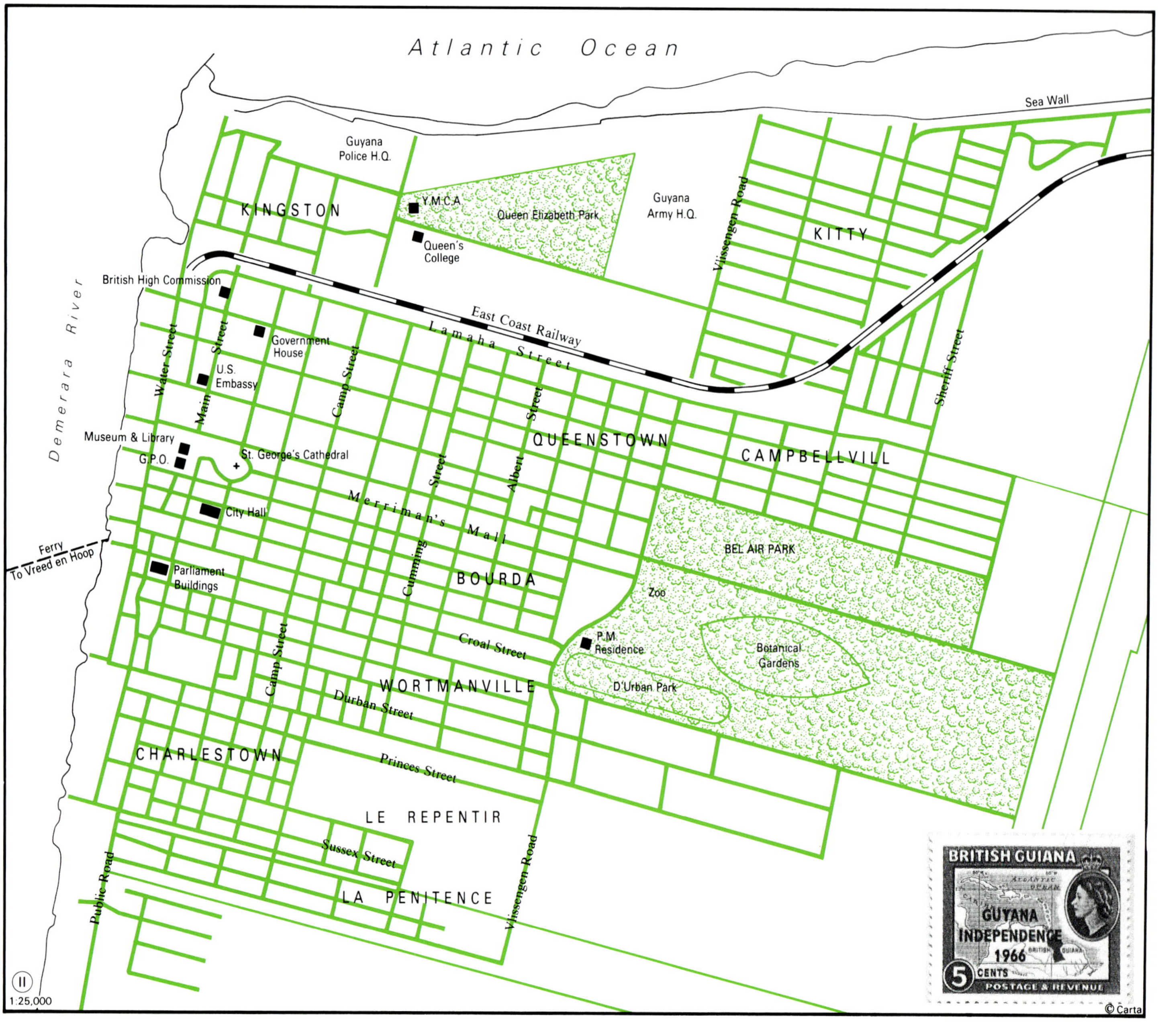

THE GUIANAS

The Spaniards and Portuguese had little interest in the untamed forests of the Guiana region. This region, situated between the colonies of Spain and Portugal, was settled by merchants and farmers from Holland, England, and France in the sixteenth and seventeenth centuries. The scattered settlements were joined under a series of exchanges and the colonies grew larger, their ownership rights ensured through treaties.

The Treaty of Breda, signed on July 31, 1667, following the second Anglo-Dutch War, arranged, among other things, the exchange of territories held by the powers in Africa and America. Within this framework, Suriname was placed under Dutch rule and French Guiana under French rule.

During the Napoleonic wars, 1799–1802 and 1804–1816, Suriname was again placed under British rule, and by 1816 the final partition of the Guianas was established.

17TH TO 18TH CENTURIES

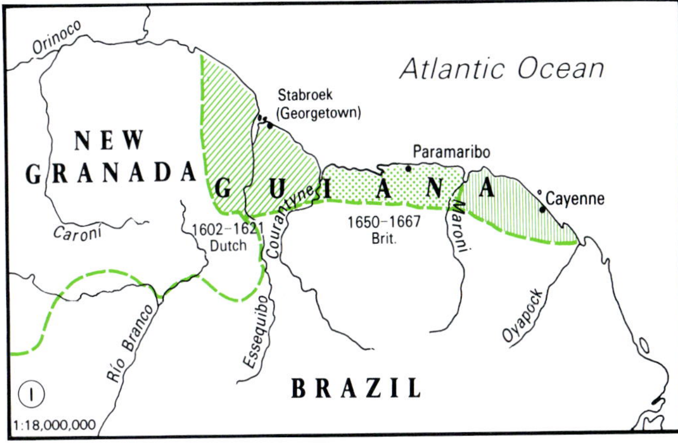

EARLY 19TH CENTURY

LATE 19TH CENTURY

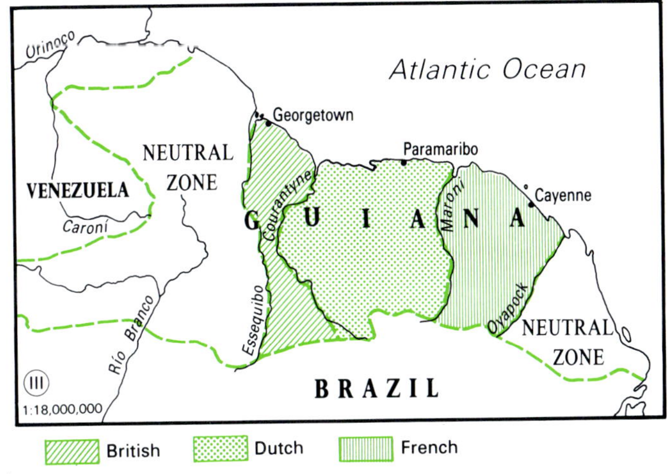

20TH CENTURY

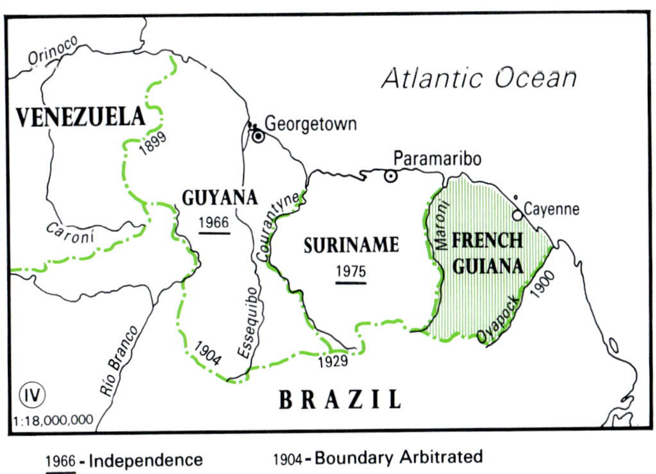

British Dutch French

1966 - Independence 1904 - Boundary Arbitrated

SURINAME TOAD

Frogs are more prevalent in South America than in any other part of the world. Among the various species found here is the Suriname toad. The Suriname toad is a native of Suriname and other parts of tropical South America. It is a tongueless, tailless amphibian that is unusual in several respects, and is one of several species of the family Pipidae. It has a flat body and an extremely flattened, triangular head. It is from 6 to 8 inches long and 4 or 5 inches wide. The Suriname toad is remarkable for the development of the young in pouches on the back of the female. The eggs may number about 100 and measure 5-7 millimeters in diameter. The eggs are deposited by the female in the ordinary way and are placed by the male on the soft skin of the female's back and then impregnated, forming by their pressure little pits over which the skin closes. They develop entirely within these pouches for about 80 days, after which the young hop out as miniatures of the adults.

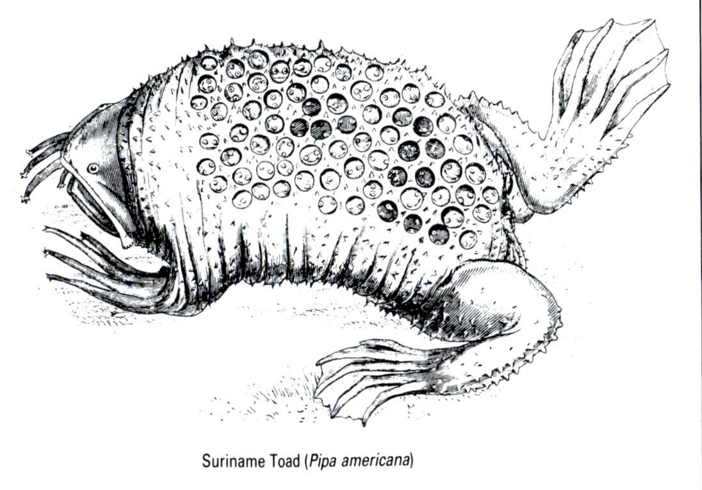

Suriname Toad (*Pipa americana*)

SURINAME

Area
163,820 sq. km.
63,251 sq. mi.

Population
403,000 (1990 estimate)

Capital City
Paramaribo

Gross National Product (GNP) Per Capita
$2,450 (1988)

Population in Main Cities
(1980)
Paramaribo 67,905
Nieuw Nickerie 6,078
Meerzorg 5,355
Marienburg 3,633

Highest Point
1,230 m. 4,035 ft. (Juliana Top)

Currency Unit
Suriname guilder = 100 cents

Density
2.4 persons per sq. km.
6.2 persons per sq. mi. (1986)

Urban-Rural
urban 45.2% rural 54.8% (1985)

Natural Increase
1.5% (1985-1990)

Life Expectancy
69.5 (1985-1990)

Doctors
1,612 inhabitants per doctor (1979)

Hospital Beds
160 inhabitants per bed (1979)

Infant Mortality
32.5 per thousand live births (1984)

High School Pupils
51.0% of age group 13-18 (1984)

University Students
6.5% of age group 20-24 (1985)

Illiteracy Rate
10.0% (1985)

National Holiday
Independence Day, 25 November

National Anthem
beginning "God zij met ons Suriname"
("God be with our Suriname")

Suriname, formerly Dutch Guiana, is one of the most underdeveloped and sparsely inhabited countries in South America. It borders Brazil in the south and the Atlantic Ocean in the north. The river Corantijn runs along its western boundary with Guyana and the river Marowijne forms its eastern boundary with French Guiana. There are border disputes with both these neighbors in the southwest and southeast frontier areas. Large areas in the southern half of the country are almost inaccessible.

NATURAL REGIONS

The country is generally divided into three main landscape and structural regions. The first is a low-lying coastal plain in the north, with extensive swamps and wide areas subject to tidal and river flooding. A belt of mangroves several miles wide forms a barrier between the coastline and the interior. The plain, which is 30–60 kilometers (20–40 miles) wide, rises only slightly toward the south. Most of it is covered with dense, wet savanna vegetation. This is followed southward by a region of low, gently sloping hills rising to 180–245 meters (600–800 feet), with a few isolated, resistant rock outcrops forming somewhat more elevated peaks. Wide forest-covered river valleys and sandy areas with savanna vegetation are dominant in this region. The southern two-thirds of the country is part of an extremely eroded and broken ancient plateau, the Guiana Highlands, built mainly of crystalline rock overlain with hard resistant sandstone. Generally flat-topped with deeply incised precipitous river valleys, the plateau in Suriname reaches an altitude of 1,280 meters (4,200 feet), although most of its upper level is 460–610 meters (1,500–2,000 feet). Most of the plateau is covered by dense tropical rain forest. Because many rivers that drain this region are repeatedly interrupted by rapids and falls, it is impossible to use the watercourses for access into this part of the country. The rivers are navigable to small steamers only in the coastal plain and in parts of the hilly region.

CLIMATE

The country has a typical equatorial climate, with high temperatures and humidity throughout the year and minor seasonal variations. There is no dry season. Diurnal and seasonal variations are somewhat greater in the higher parts of the plateau in the south. The average temperature for the hottest month (July) in the capital Paramaribo is 27.2°C (81°F) and for the coolest month (January), 26.7°C (80°F). The average daily range is 6°C (10.8°F). The average annual rainfall is 2,230 millimeters (89 inches). The driest months are from September to October, with an average monthly precipitation of 70–80 millimeters (2.8–3.2 inches).

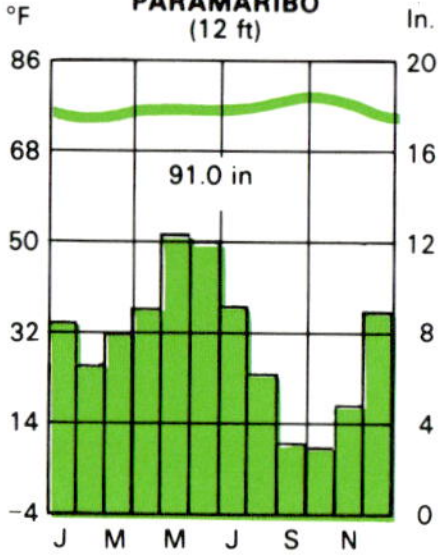

POPULATION BY AGE GROUP, 1988

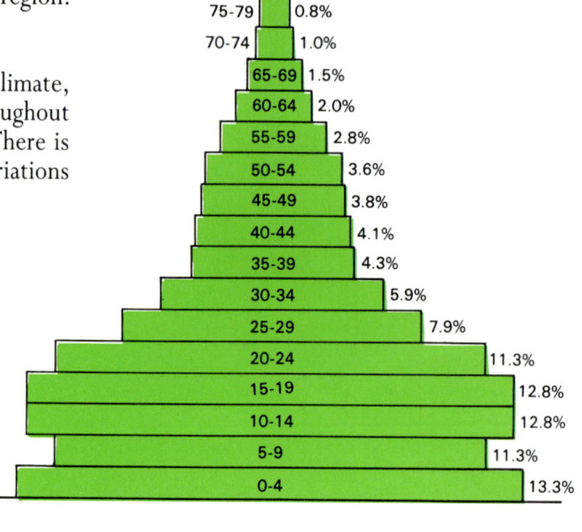

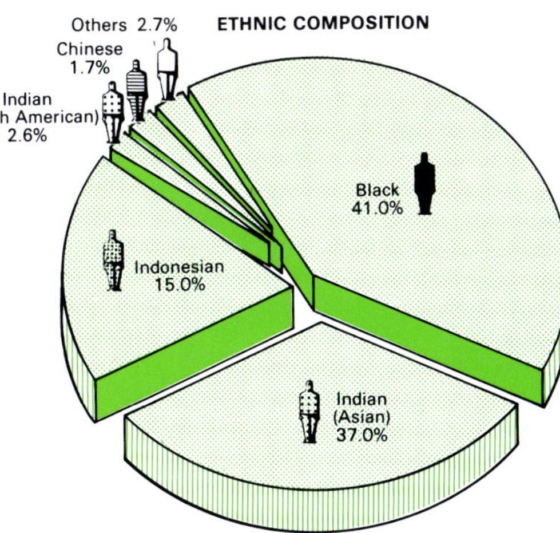

POPULATION

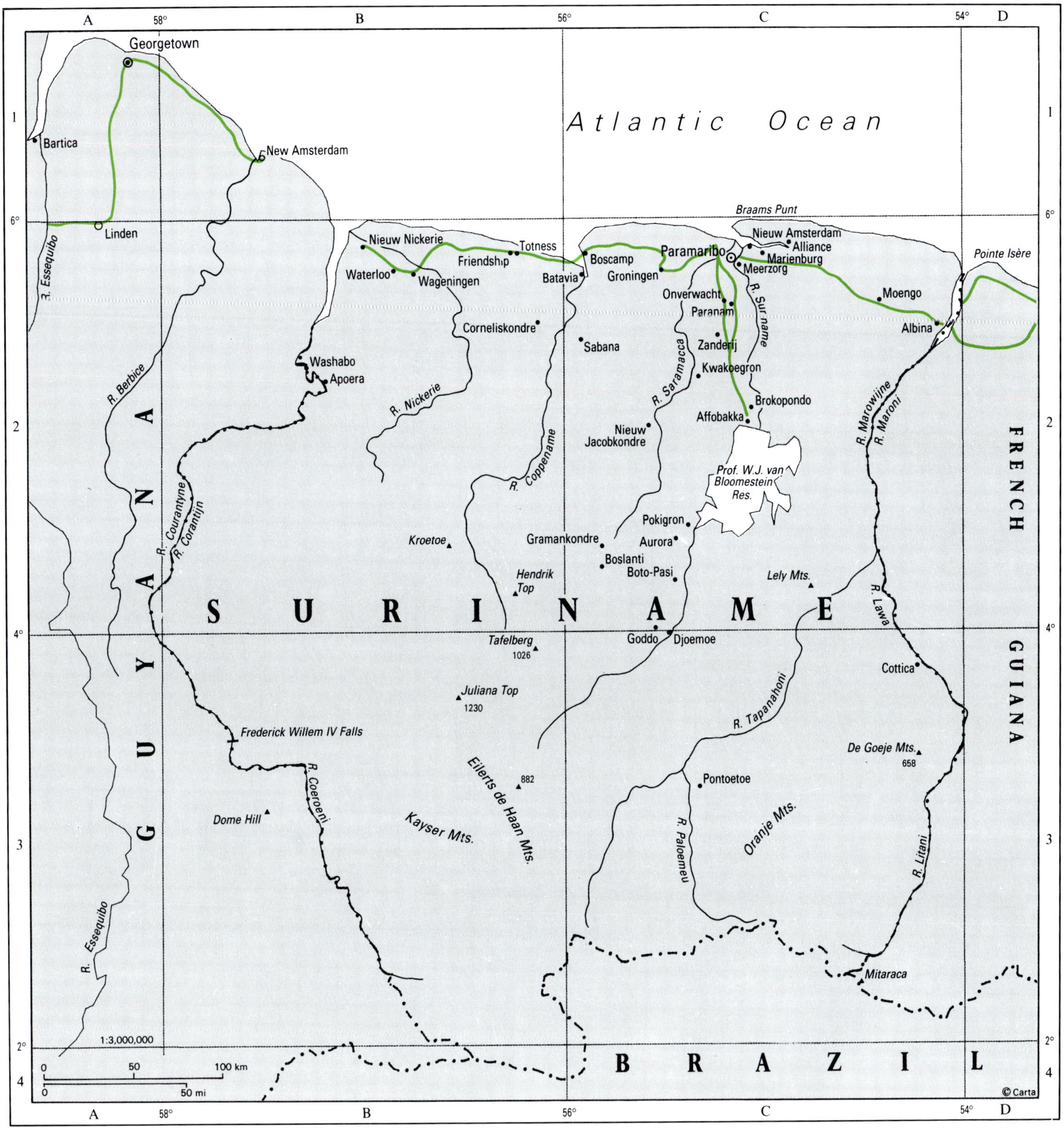

The population was estimated at 395,000 in 1989. It was 355,000 in 1980, and has been increasing at an average annual rate of 2 percent. The population consists mainly of descendants of Negro slaves (41 percent), who were brought from Africa during the eighteenth and early nineteenth century and descendents of laborers brought from India (37 percent) and Java (15 percent) during the second half of the nineteenth and the early twentieth century following the abolition of slavery. About one-quarter of the Negro population are Bush Blacks or Djukas, descendants of slaves who absconded into the jungle and have since lived there in small isolated settlements in which they practice subsistence agriculture. There are also small communities of American Indians (2.6 percent), of Chinese (1.7 percent), and of Europeans (1 percent). The religious division corresponds largely to the ethnic origin of the population: 27.4 percent are Hindu (the great majority originating from India); 19.6 percent Muslim (nearly all of Javanese origin and some from India); nearly 50 percent are Christian (25.2 percent of whom are Protestant, mainly Moravian Brethren, and 22.8 percent Catholic). The Negro, American Indian, and mulatto population is almost entirely Christian. Some of the Bush Blacks practice a locally developed religion. The official language is Dutch. English is widely spoken, especially in the capital and in other urban centers. A mixed local language, Surinamese or Taki-Taki, is also widely used, as are Hindi and Javanese within the respective communities. The illiteracy rate is 10 percent. Nearly the entire population is concentrated on the coastal plain, which is sparsely populated except in its central part and around the capital district. The population density for the country is 2.2 persons per square kilometer (5.5 per square mile). Only the district around the capital has a population density of more than 20 per square kilometer (50 per square mile). Over 95 percent of the area has a population density of less than 1 person per square kilometer (2.5 per square mile). Approximately half of the population is urban. The metropolitan area of the capital Paramaribo numbers 120,000 (the city proper—72,000). All the other towns have less than 20,000 inhabitants.

ECONOMY

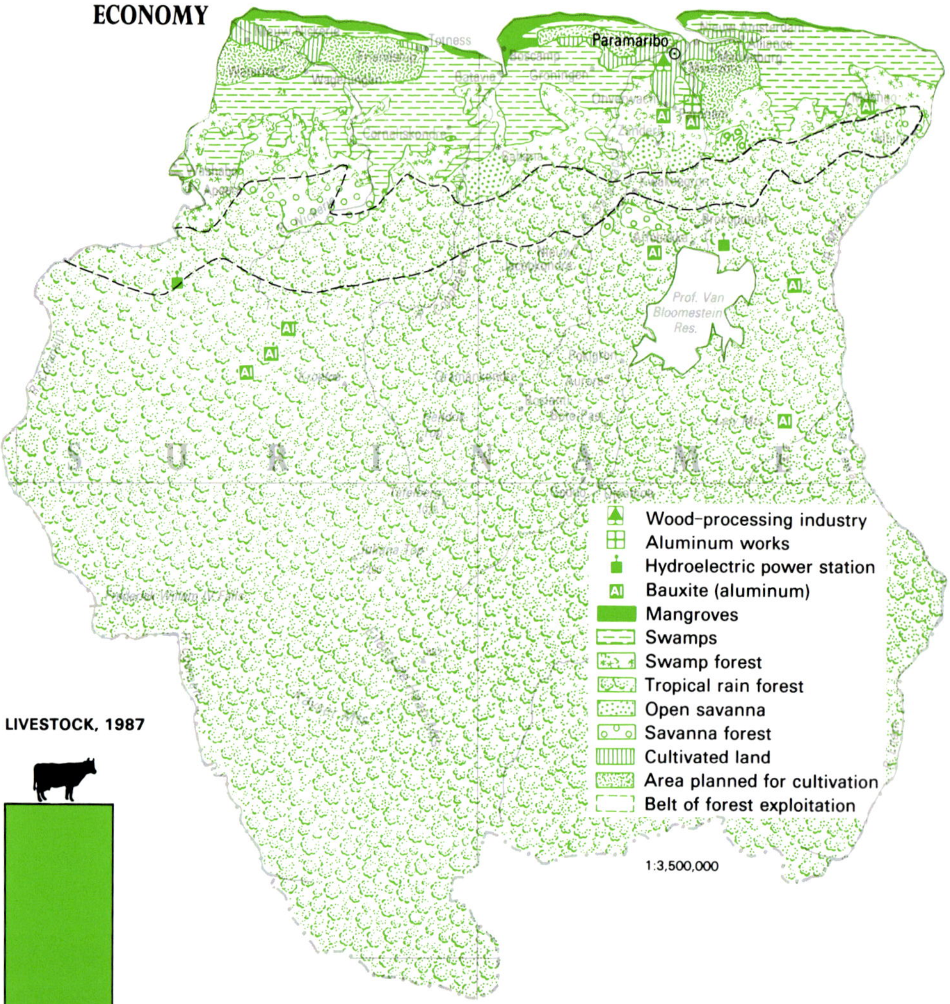

Paramaribo

Prof. Van Blommestein Res.

Wood-processing industry
Aluminum works
Hydroelectric power station
Bauxite (aluminum)
Mangroves
Swamps
Swamp forest
Tropical rain forest
Open savanna
Savanna forest
Cultivated land
Area planned for cultivation
Belt of forest exploitation

1:3,500,000

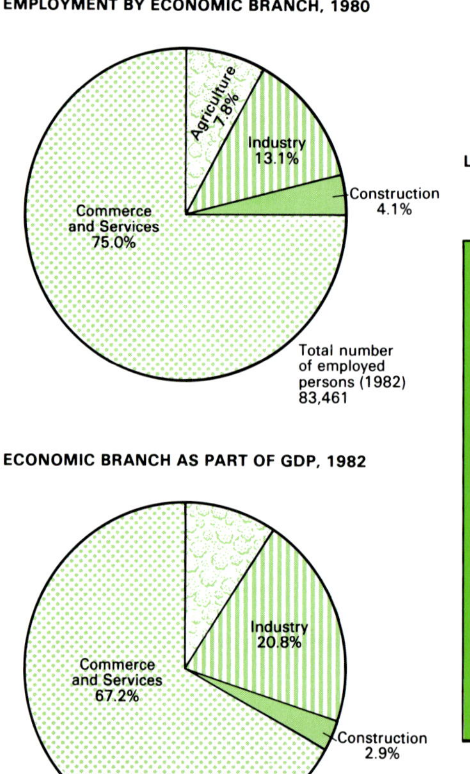

LIVESTOCK, 1987

66,000 Cattle	23,000 Pigs	5,000 Goats	3,000 Sheep

voor het kind
75+35c
suriname

Independence, 1981

Five cents, 1962

ECONOMY

The economy is based on agriculture and the exploitation of mineral and forest resources. Economic activities are confined to small areas in the northern plain and the northern fringes of the hilly region. The GNP per capita in 1988 was $2,450. Economic growth has been at an average annual rate of 2 percent. Unemployment has been high for many years; it reached 25–30 percent in 1987.

Agriculture

Only 0.3 percent of Suriname's area is under cultivation; rice (175,000 acres, 279,000 tons in 1987) and sugarcane (7,400 acres, 11,000 tons) are the main crops. Other products are citrus, bananas, coconuts, and other tropical fruit. The Bush Black population practices subsistence agriculture. Of the total area, 0.1 percent serves as permanent pasture. The country's livestock includes 66,000 heads of cattle, 8,000 sheep and goats, and 23,000 pigs. The agricultural sector employs 17.3 percent of the workforce.

Forests cover 95 percent of the total area. They yield small quantities of timber and various types of wood (total 196,000 cubic meters in 1987).

Mineral Resources

Bauxite, mined in the hilly region, is the only mineral exploited on a large scale (3.7 million tons in 1986). Part of the ore is processed locally into alumina. Small quantities of placer gold are also produced.

Industry

Industry is engaged mainly in the processing of bauxite ore, agricultural products (sugar and rice mills), forest products, and a small range of consumer goods. Fifteen percent of the workforce is employed in industry.

Hydroelectric power plants supply 70 percent of the country's electricity.

HISTORY

The Suriname coast was apparently sighted by Christopher Columbus on his fourth voyage in 1498, by Amerigo Vespucci in 1499, and by Vicente Yáñez Pinzón in 1500. The inhospitable natural conditions and lack of economic interest made the coast unattractive to Spanish and Portuguese explorers and settlers. A few small indigenous Indian tribes, Arawaks and Caribs, were roaming the Guiana coastal plain when the first Dutch and English settlers took interest in the area toward the end of the sixteenth and early seventeenth centuries. In 1652 the English actually took possesion of the coastal area of what is now Suriname and established the first sugar plantations. Under the Treaty of Breda (1667), the English ceded this territory to the Dutch in exchange for the colony of New Amsterdam (present-day New York City and its surroundings). This was followed by the establishment of Dutch plantations operated by large groups of black slaves brought from Africa. Suriname again came under British rule for two short periods, 1799–1802 and 1804–1816 (the Napoleonic wars), before it was finally handed back to the Dutch.

Slavery was abolished in 1863. Asian labor, from India and Java, was imported to replace some of the freed slaves and later to expand plantations and to work in the mines and other industries. These Asian immigrants doubled the population of the Dutch colony. The population was estimated at 86,000 in 1900. It grew to 178,000 by 1940 and to 240,000 by 1956. The colony was integrated into the Kingdom of The Netherlands in 1948 and was granted home rule in 1950. Suriname gained full independence in 1975.The army took again control of the government at the end of 1990.

GOVERNMENT AND POLITICS

The country is divided into nine districts. It is governed by an executive president, elected for a five-year term, and a unicameral legislature with 51 members. The initial democratic government established after independence was ousted by a military coup in 1980. A military council ruled the country until 1988, when a democratically elected government was restored. Political parties are largely based on ethnic divisions. A coalition of three parties—the National Party of Suriname (NPS; Negro); the Progressive Reform Party (VHP; Asian Indian); and the Indonesian Peasant Party (KTPI; Javanese)—controls 40 of the 51 seats in the National Assembly. Other parties include two small extreme leftist organizations: the Revolutionary People's Party (RVP) and the Progressive Workers and Farmers (PALU).

Administrative Division

Districts	Capitals	area sq mi	area sq km	population (1982)
Brokopondo	Brokopondo	8,278	21,440	20,249
Commewijne	Nieuw Amsterdam	1,587	4,110	14,351
Coronie	Totness	626	1,620	2,777
Marowijne	Albina	17,753	45,980	23,402
Nickerie	Nieuw Nickerie	24,946	64,610	34,480
Para	Onverwacht	378	980	14,867
Saramacca	Groningen	9,042	23,420	10,335
Suriname	Paramaribo	629	1,628	166,494
Town District				
Paramaribo	Paramaribo	12	32	67,905
Total		**63,251**	**163,820**	**354,860**

PARAMARIBO

Greater Paramaribo, with its 180,000 inhabitants (1988), is in fact Suriname's only city. All the country's other urban settlements are small towns or townships. The city has typical Dutch colonial features both in its layout and architecture. The canals that cross it give the city some semblance to a Dutch urban landscape. Paramaribo stands on the left (west) bank of a bend in the Suriname river, 15 kilometers (9 miles) from the Atlantic coast, at about the limit of the river's accessibility to ocean-going steamers. The older and main part of the city is built on an elevated reef that stands a few meters above the river level at maximum high tide.

Paramaribo was established by French settlers in 1640 near a small village of local Indians. The site was taken over by English settlers in 1651. It was ceded to the Dutch with the rest of the Suriname coast in 1674, but was twice occupied by the British (1799–1802; 1804–1816) before finally being returned to Dutch control in 1816. It became the capital of independent Suriname in 1975. Paramaribo had a population of 30,000 in 1910, 52,000 in the mid-1930s, and 86,000 in 1952. Most of the inhabitants are of African origin (black or mulatto), and a high percentage are of Asian origin (Indian or Javanese).

Paramaribo consists largely of one-story wooden houses. It has a modern city center with large concrete public and commercial buildings. Paramaribo is the commercial and industrial center of the country. Its port cannot handle large ships due to the shallowness of the Suriname river estuary. Paramaribo has a university, as well as botanic gardens with rich collections of tropical plants.

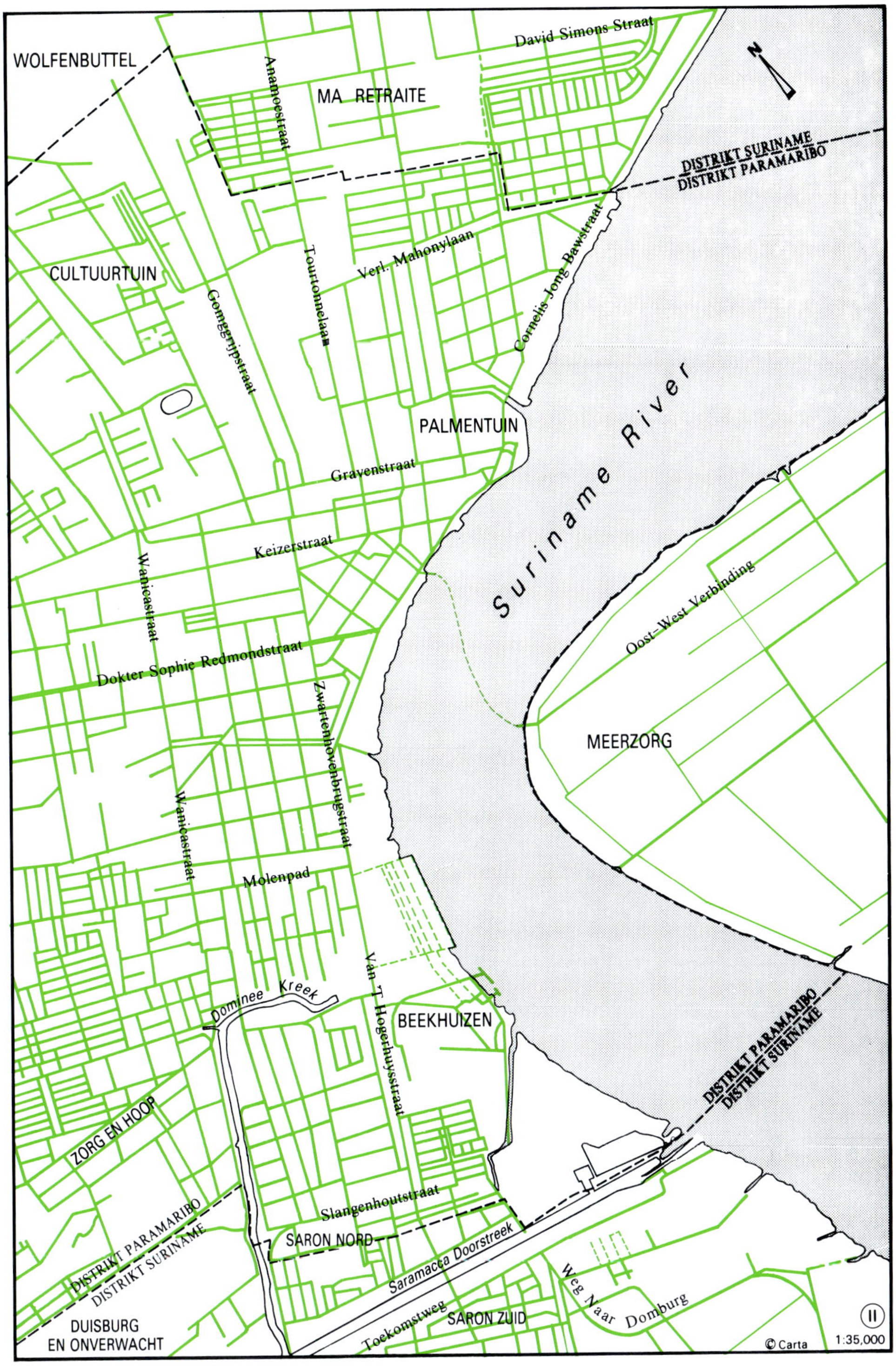

FRENCH GUIANA

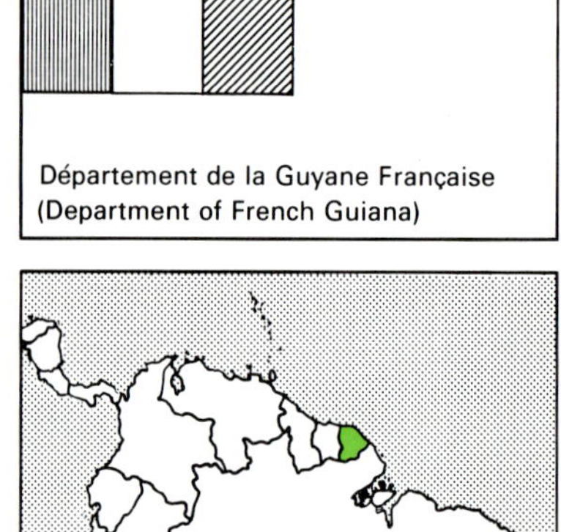

Département de la Guyane Française
(Department of French Guiana)

Area
93,000 sq. km.
35,900 sq. mi.

Population
98,000 (1990 estimate)

Capital City
Cayenne

Gross National Product (GNP) Per Capita
$3,230 (1982)

Population in Main Cities
(1982 estimates)
Cayenne 38,091 (1985)
Kourou 6,465
Rémire-Montjoly 5,921
St. Laurent du Maroni 5,042

Highest Point
690 m. 2,264 ft. (Mitaraca)

Currency Unit
1 franc = 100 centimes

Density
1.0 persons per sq. km.
2.5 persons per sq. mi. (1986)

Urban-Rural
urban 73.4% rural 26.6% (1982)

Natural Increase
2.9% (1984)

Life Expectancy
male 63.4 female 69.7
(1975-1979)

Doctors
194 inhabitants per doctor (1982)

Hospital Beds
78 inhabitants per bed (1981)

Infant Mortality
22.6 per thousand live births (1984)

High School Pupils
5,529 (1984-5)

University Students
239 (1984-5)

Illiteracy Rate
18.0% (1985)

The last European colonial territory on the American continent, French Guiana is an overseas *département* (administrative district) of France. The river Maroni runs along its western boundary with Suriname and the river Oyapock forms the eastern boundary with Brazil. It is bordered on the north by the Atlantic Ocean. Its southern boundary with Brazil runs through a rugged, densely forested, mountainous region, the Tumuc Humac Highlands. Part of the boundary with Suriname is in dispute. Most of the territory is uninhabited and almost inaccessible.

NATURAL REGIONS

A low-lying, flat, ill-drained, swampy plain forms the northern region along the Atlantic coast. It is widest in the west (approximately 50 kilometers [30 miles]) and becomes narrower toward the east (to about 16 kilometers [10 miles]). A belt of mangroves lines much of the coast. Most of the plain is covered by dense, wet savanna vegetation. This is followed farther inland to the south by a region of low hills (90–180 meters [300–600 feet]) with gentle slopes and wide valleys. The hills are built mainly of old crystalline rocks that have been greatly eroded. This region rises gradually southward to the plateau that forms the third region, which covers more than two-thirds of the total area. The generally flat-topped plateau, deeply dissected by a dense network of narrow river valleys, is built of old crystalline rocks (mainly granite and gneiss) overlain with resistant sandstone. Its most elevated part is in the extreme south, in the Tumuc Humac Highlands, where it reaches an altitude of 690 meters (2,260 feet). Rivers in this region are interrupted by falls and rapids; they are navigable only through the coastal plain and part of the hilly region. Both the plateau and hilly regions are covered by dense rain forest.

There are a number of small islands along the coast. One group of these, the Îles du Salut, which includes the infamous Île du Diable (Devil's Island), was used as a penal colony.

CLIMATE

The climate is equatorial—hot and humid the year round. Diurnal and seasonal variations are small, with a somewhat greater range on the plateau in the southern region. In Cayenne, the capital, the average temperature for the hottest months, July and August, is 27.5°C (81.5°F) and for the coolest month, January, 26.4°C (79.5°F). The average annual rainfall is 2,350 millimeters (94 inches). There is no dry season, but rainfall is lightest from September to November. Rainfall is plentiful over all parts of the territory.

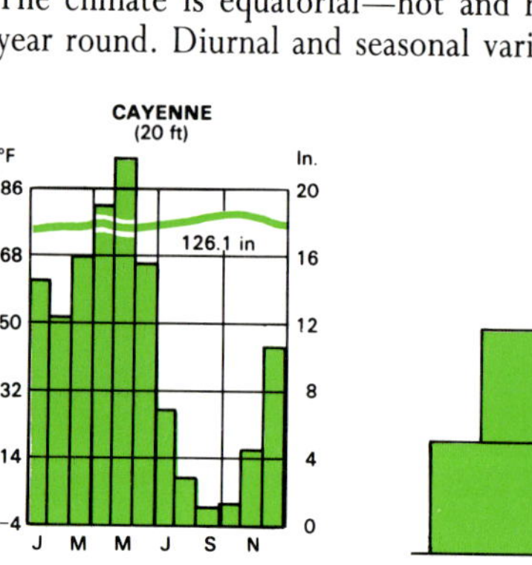

POPULATION BY AGE GROUP, 1982

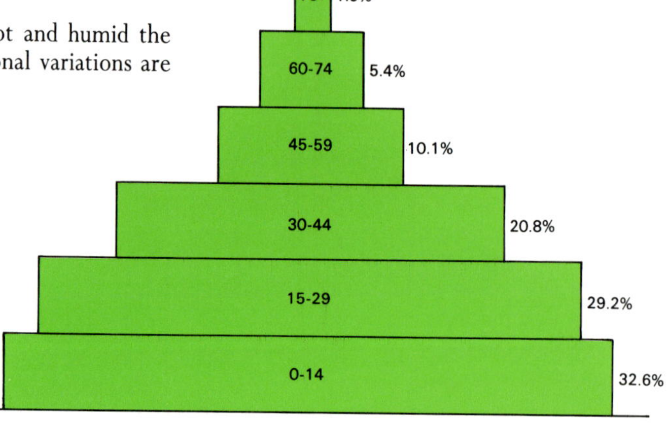

POPULATION

The population was estimated at 98,000 in 1990. It was 73,000 at the 1982 census and has been increasing at an average annual rate of 3.2 percent. Blacks and mulattos, descendants of slaves brought from Africa during the eighteenth and nineteenth centuries, make up approximately two-thirds of the population; Asians (mainly Chinese), 12 percent; and Europeans, 10 percent. Small groups of American Indians still live in isolation in the hilly region. Nearly 90 percent of the population is Catholic, and 4 percent is Protestant. Some Bush Negroes have their own religion. The official language is French. The great majority of the population speaks a local Creole French. The illiteracy rate is 18 percent. Almost the entire population is concentrated in a small area in the northern part of the coastal plain. The average density for the country as a whole is 1 inhabitant per square kilometer (2.5 per square mile), but over 90 percent of the territory has less than 0.2 persons per square kilometer (0.5 per square mile). About 70 percent of the population is urban, with half residing in the capital, Cayenne, (with a population of approximately 40,000) and in its vicinity.

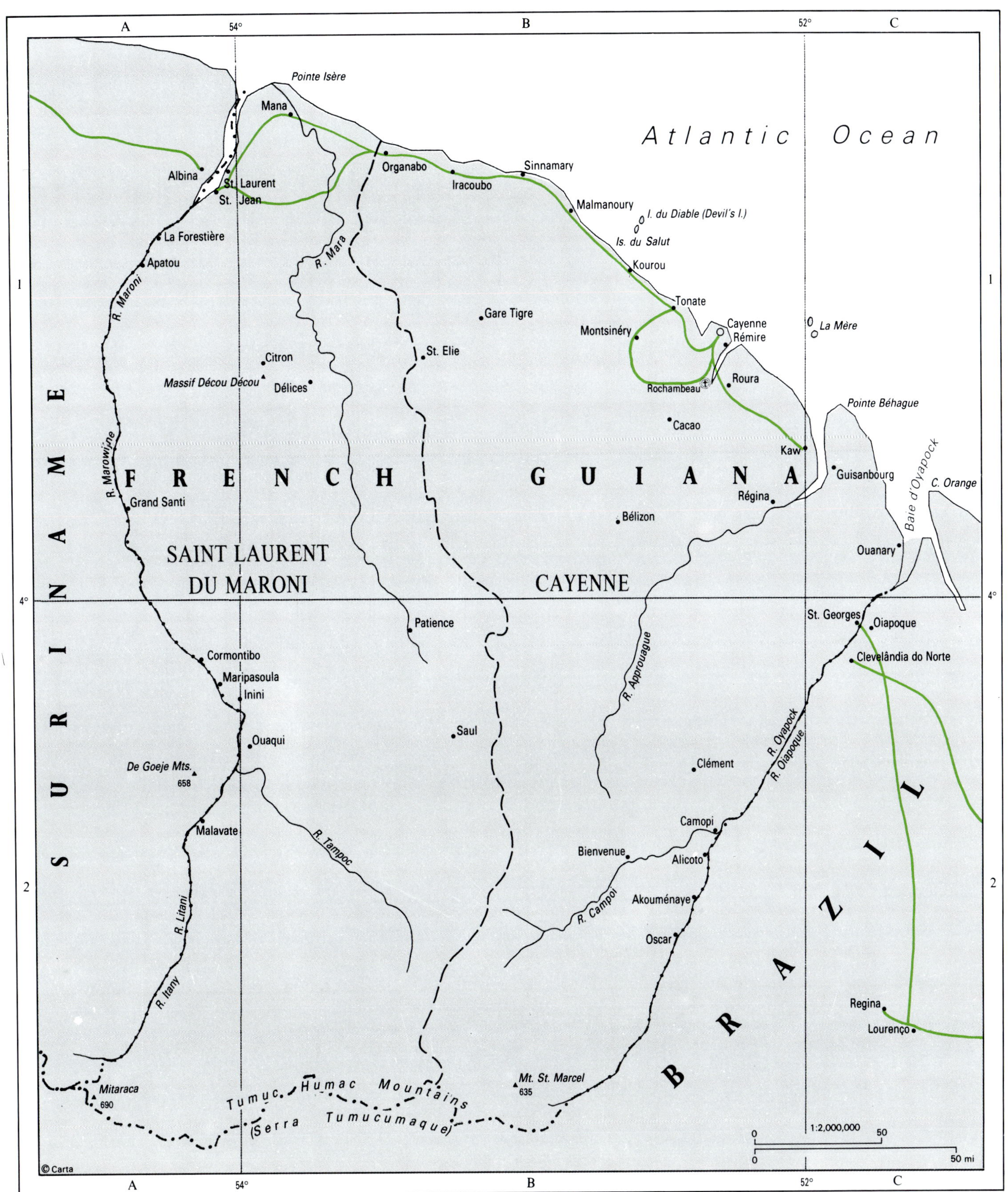

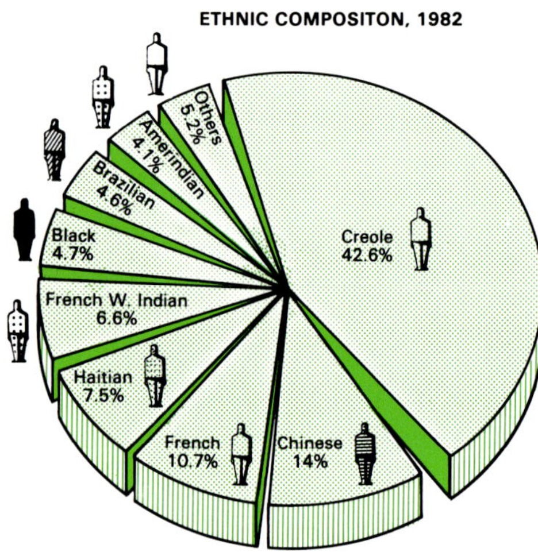

ECONOMY

The economy is based on agriculture, fishing, and the exploitation of mineral and forest resources. It is an extremely underdeveloped territory, with only a small portion of its potential resources being tapped. The annual GNP per capita in recent years has been approximately $3,200. It has been growing at an average annual rate of 0.4 percent. Unemployment has remained static for a number of years at a rate of about 10 percent.

Agriculture

Agriculture is confined to small areas of the coastal region, mainly in the vicinity of Cayenne. The total area under cultivation is 13,500 acres (1987). The main crops are rice, sugarcane, vegetables, manioc, and tropical fruit. Most of the products are used for local consumption. Fourteen percent of the workforce is engaged in agriculture.

There is much fishing along the coast and in river estuaries, with shrimp being the principal catch for export.

Over 80 percent of the territory is covered by dense rain forest, from which timber (254,000 cubic meters in 1986), various types of wood (mainly rosewood—84,000 cubic meters), and some extracts are produced.

Mineral Resources

Small quantities of gold (326 kilograms in 1986) are mined at a number of mines in the hilly and plateau regions. Deposits of bauxite, iron ore, and cinnabar are known.

Industry

Industry is engaged mainly in processing agricultural, fishing (shrimp), and forest products. Twelve percent of the workforce is employed in industry.

EMPLOYMENT BY ECONOMIC BRANCH, 1982

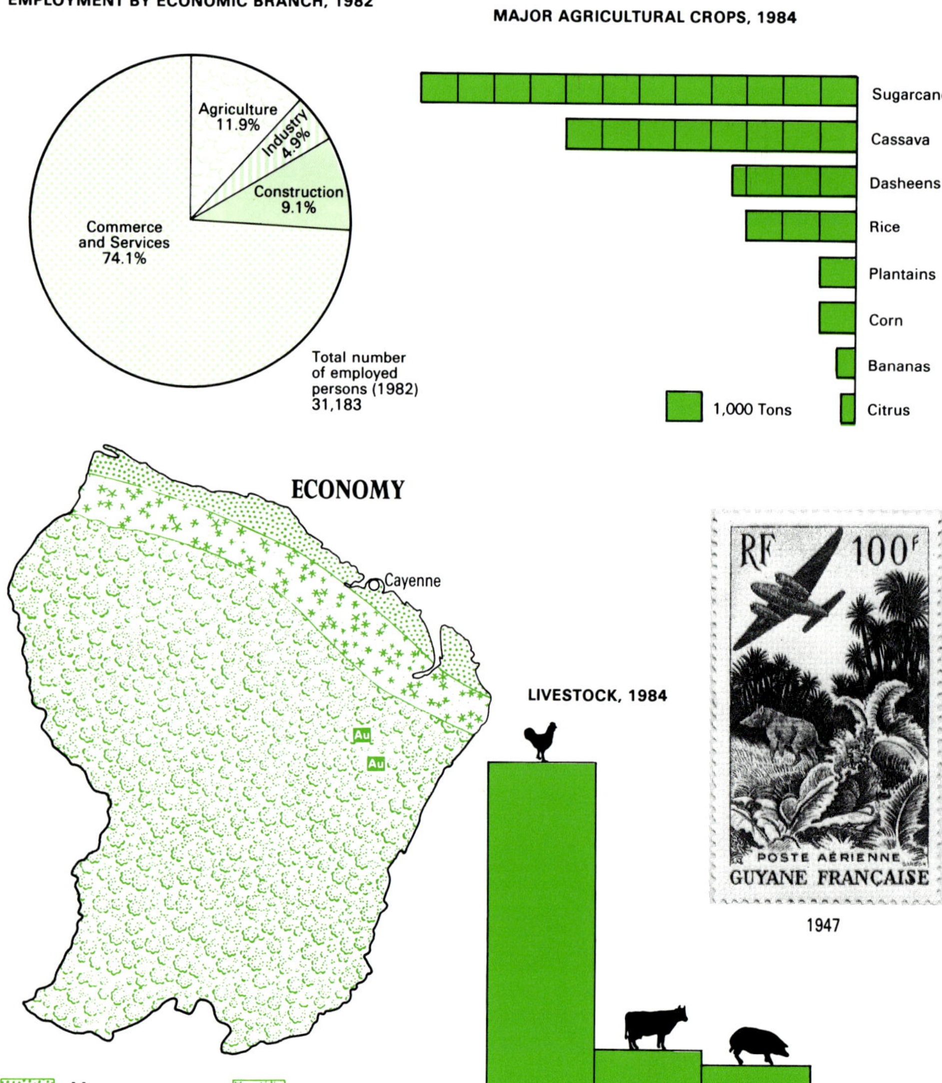

1947

Ten centimes, 1887

HISTORY

The first Spanish and Portuguese explorers of the South American coast, such as Alonso de Ojeda (1499) and Vicente Yáñez Pinzón (1500), apparently sailed along what was to become French Guiana, but due to the unattractive nature of the region they did not establish a station on its coast. The French first explored the coastal area in 1604 and established their first settlement in 1626. Cayenne was founded in 1635. Several additional attempts during the seventeenth and eighteenth centuries to colonize the territory failed; some ended in the death of most settlers. During the French Revolution many royalists were exiled to Cayenne, where most of them perished. Britain and Portugal took control of the colony during the Napoleonic wars, but it was restored to France in 1817. The colonization process was then resumed, with an economy based mainly on sugar plantations operated by Negro slaves. This system received a serious setback with the abolition of slavery in 1848. In 1852 it became a penal colony to which many thousands convicted of serious crimes were exiled. Those sentenced to long terms of hard labor were held at the notorious Devil's Island jail. Prisoners and released convicts who were obliged to remain a few years in the colony formed a substantial part of its population (17 percent in 1936). The penal settlements were abolished in 1945. In 1946 French Guiana became an overseas *département* of France and in 1974 an administrative region.

GOVERNMENT AND POLITICS

The colony is administratively divided into two subdistricts (*arrondissements*). A commissioner appointed by the French government heads the administration. The colony is represented in the French National Assembly by two deputies and in the Senate by one senator. The local legislature consists of two bodies: a General Council, with 19 members, and the Regional Council, with 31 members; members of both bodies are directly elected for six years.

Local politics are dominated by three parties: the Guianese Socialist Party (PSG), which absorbed the small leftist Union of Guianese People (UPG); the Rally for the Republic (RPG; rightist); and the National Anti-Colonial Guianese Party (PANGA). There is also the Popular and National Party and a Communist party. The colony is subject to the French legal system.

Administrative Division

Arrondissements	Capitals	area sq mi	area sq km	population (1980)
Cayenne	Cayenne	20,100	52,000	61,587
Saint-Laurent-du-Maroni	Saint-Laurent-du-Maroni	15,800	41,000	11,435
Total		**35,900**	**93,000**	**73,022**

DEVIL'S ISLAND

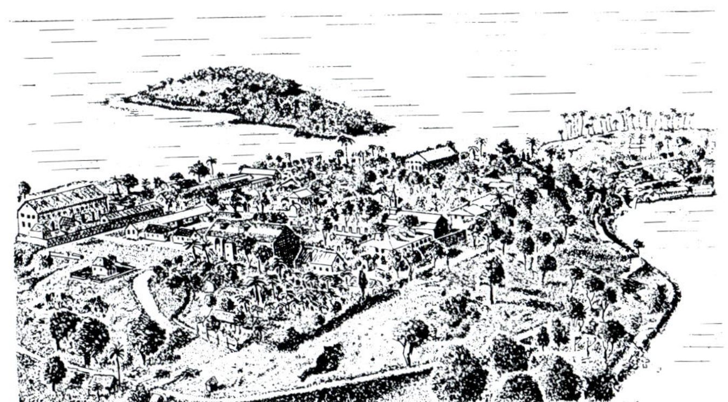

Îles du Salut: I. du Diable (Devil's I.) in the left background, I. Royale on the right, and I. St. Joseph in the foreground

For nearly 140 years, Île du Diable served as France's most severe and isolated prison, to which dangerous criminals who were sentenced to long terms of imprisonment were exiled. Many prisoners did not survive the torrid climate, tropical diseases, and harsh prison conditions. Most famous of these prisoners was Alfred Dreyfus, a Jewish officer in the French army who spent four years there (1895–1899); he was framed and convicted, through anti-Semitic motives, of spying, based on false evidence. He wrote in his diaries a vivid, detailed account of conditions and life in this prison.

Devil's Island is one of a group of three small islands, the Îles du Salut, situated about 10 kilometers (6 miles) off the coast of French Guiana. The island is an elongated rocky hill partly covered by palms. Its total area is approximately 120 acres (0.5 square kilometer). It was uninhabited when assigned in 1789 to become France's most dreaded prison. It was closed down in 1938. Devil's Island has recently become a popular winter resort for tourists.

CAYENNE

Nearly half of the population of French Guiana lives in the capital Cayenne and its vicinity. Cayenne is a small, typical, colonial-style urban center; it attracted much literary interest in the past, and at present some tourism. The city is situated at the northwestern end of the island Cayenne (Île de Cayenne), between the mouths of the Cayenne and Mahury rivers in an area which was at one time malaria infested. It has a population of nearly 40,000 (1989). Founded by French settlers in 1643, it was overrun and destroyed by a local Indian tribe. Cayenne was rebuilt in 1777 as a plantation settlement based on slave labor. Following the abolition of slavery in 1848, it soon became France's main overseas penal settlement, to which convicts sentenced to more than 7 years' imprisonment were exiled. Under the terms of their imprisonment, many of the convicted were compelled to remain in exile in Cayenne for several years after having served their term. From the end of the nineteenth to the early twentieth century, a substantial part of Cayenne's population was made up of convicts or exconvicts. The population numbered approximately 10,000 in 1955. The penal settlement was closed in 1944.

In addition to its administrative role, Cayenne is the commercial and industial center of French Guiana. Its industries are engaged mainly in processing of agricultural, fishing, and forest products. Due to its shallow waters, the port can handle only small ocean-going steamers; much of French Guiana's exports are handled by other ports. The French Institute of Tropical America is located in Cayenne.

FALKLAND ISLANDS

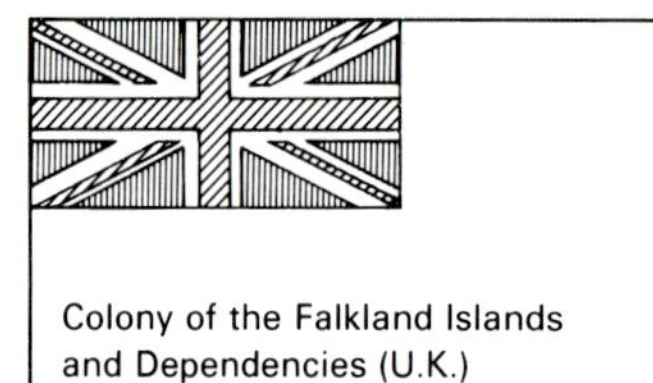

Colony of the Falkland Islands and Dependencies (U.K.)

Area
12,173 sq. km.
4,700 sq. mi.

Population
1,916 (1986 census)

Capital City
Stanley 1,231 inhabitants (1986)

Highest Point
705 m. 2,315 ft. (Mt. Adam)

Currency Unit
1 pound=100 new pence

Density
0.2 persons per sq. km.
0.4 persons per sq. mi. (1972)

Urban-Rural
urban 55.1% rural 44.9% (1972)

Natural Increase
1.5% (1972)

Doctors
511 inhabitants per doctor (1970)

Hospital Beds
76 inhabitants per bed (1970)

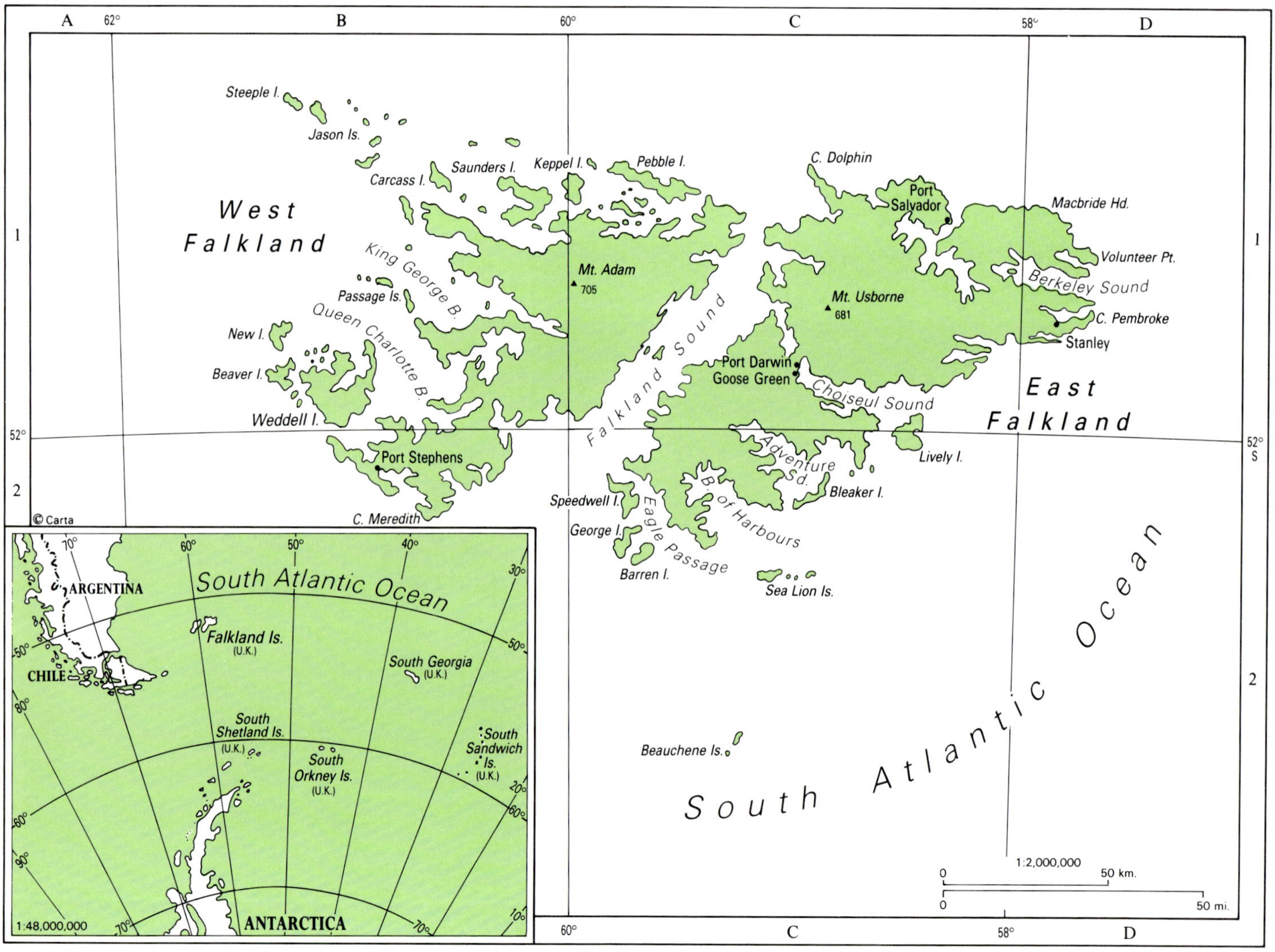

The object of the only direct war in this century between a European power (Great Britain) and a South American state (Argentina) was the Falkland Islands (Islas Malvinas to the Argentinians), a small group of islands northeast of the southern tip of South America, about 480 kilometers (300 miles) off the mainland. The group consists of some 200 islands and islets with a total area of 12,030 square kilometers (4,700 square miles).

NATURAL REGIONS

The two main islands, East Falkland (5,760 square kilometers [2,250 square miles]) and West Falkland (4,480 square kilometers [1,750 square miles]), are inhabited. These two are separated by a narrow strait, the Falkland Sound, running in a southwest-northeast direction. The coastline of the main islands is deeply indented and provides many natural harbors. A belt of partly rugged low mountains, reaching altitudes of about 700 meters (2,300 feet), crosses the northern part of the main islands in an east-west direction. The remainder of the islands consists mainly of undulating ground with some shallow, peat-covered valleys and small streams.

Pasture and morass covers much of the islands, but there are large areas of barren rock, especially in the hilly areas. Valleys in which large masses of white glistening quartzite have accumulated are a distinctive feature. The islands are treeless, with some parts carrying a dense vegetation of low shrubs. The Falkland Islands are surrounded by a comparatively shallow sea and are believed to rest on the continental shelf (or a submarine plateau) that extends from the adjacent coast of South America (Patagonia).

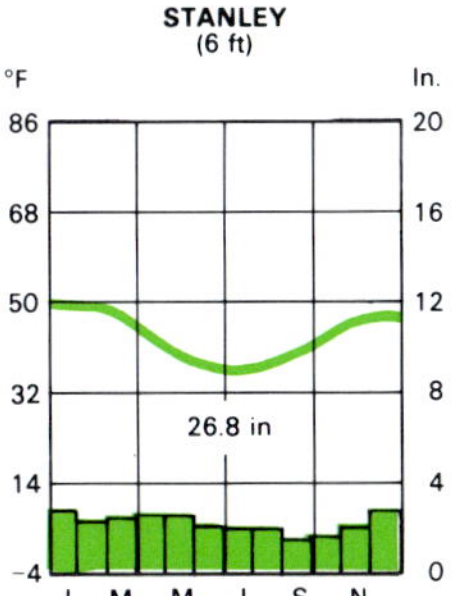

CLIMATE

The Falkland Islands have a cool, wet climate with only moderate seasonal and diurnal variations in temperature. The average temperatures for the warmest (January) and coolest (July) months are 8.9°C (48°F) and 2.2°C (36°F), respectively. Temperatures above 20°C (68°F) and below -6.7°C (20°F) are rare. The lowest temperature recorded was -11°C (12°F). The average annual precipitation is 680 millimeters (27 inches). Rainfall, spread throughout the year, is heaviest in December and January and lightest in September and October. There are occasional, generally light, snowfalls during the winter months. The climate is dominated by strong westerly winds that blow on the average several times each month, but only rarely reach storm force. These winds are chiefly responsible for the treeless landscape. Cloudy skies are usual.

POPULATION

The number of local inhabitants is slightly more than 2,000 (1990). The population was 1,916 at the 1986 census. In East Falkland, there are about 1,700 inhabitants, of whom 1,200 reside in the capital Stanley, the only township on the islands. The rural population lives in small, scattered, isolated communities of sheep-raising farms. The population was highest in the early 1930s, when it reached about 2,400. There has been a large garrison stationed on the islands (East Falkland) since the war with Argentina in the early 1980s. About 98 percent of the inhabitants are of British descent, with 67 percent born on the islands. The religious makeup is as follows: Church of England—66 percent; other Protestant churches—22 percent; and Catholic—11 percent. English is the official language.

POPULATION BY AGE GROUP, 1972

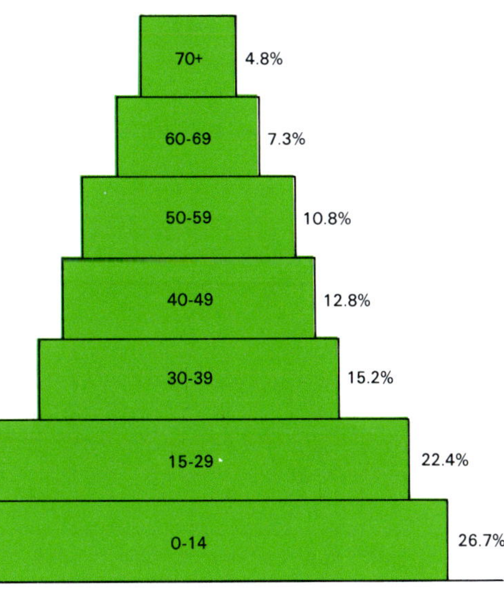

TRADE BALANCE, 1969
(Falkland Island Pounds)

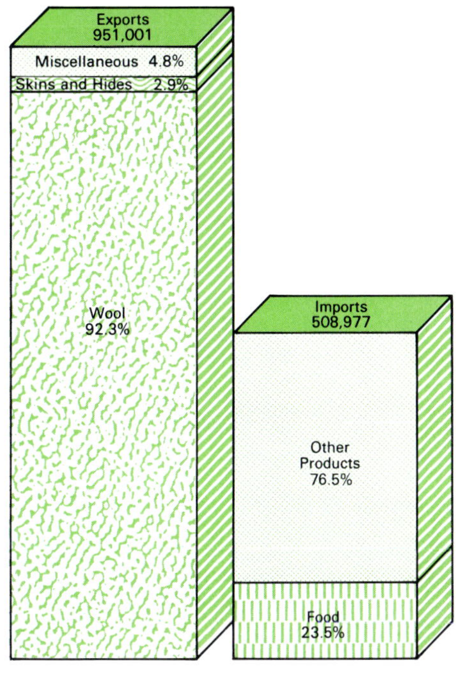

ECONOMY

Sheep farming and the production of wool and hides are the basis of the islands' economy. In recent years fishing has been assuming an important role as well. Most of the area of the main islands is taken up by farms or pasture, and the majority of the male population is employed in the sheep industry. There are about 700,000 sheep (1988), producing 2,600 tons of wool, and 6,000 cattle. The area under cultivation is small, dedicated to fodder and some vegetables. No mineral resources have been discovered on the islands.

Wildlife

The islands have a rich variety of birds, including several species of penguins. Seals of various types are in abundance along the coast.

Jackass Penguin (*Spheniscus demersus*)

HISTORY

There are no indications that the islands were ever inhabited before the arrival of the first Europeans late in the sixteenth century. It is believed that they were discovered in 1592 by the English sailor John Davis. They were named the Sebald Islands a few years later (1598) when visited by a Dutch expedition under Sebald van Weerdt. The strait between the main islands was named Falkland Sound (after Lord Falkland) by British sailors under Captain John Strong, who sailed it in 1690. The British name later came to refer to the whole group. During the second half of the eighteenth century, the islands were visited and claimed by the French, British, and Spaniards. The French were the first to establish a settlement on the islands (1764), Port Louis (on East Falkland), which was bought by the Spaniards in 1766 and renamed Soledad. Britain regained the islands in 1771, but a few years later they were abandoned by both Britain and Spain. The Argentinians made their first claim to the islands in 1829, when they established a settlement at Port Louis. In 1833 they were driven out by the British, who have since held the islands. The British established the settlement at Stanley (Port Stanley), which was first called Port William, and made it the center of their administration in 1844. The Argentinians repeatedly claimed the islands, which they named Malvinas. Talks between Britain and Argentina on the future of the islands were held intermittently during the 1960s and 1970s. In April 1982 the Argentinians invaded and captured the islands. Argentina was defeated in the two month war that ensued, and the islands were restored to British sovereignty.

THE FALKLANDS WAR APRIL–JUNE 1982

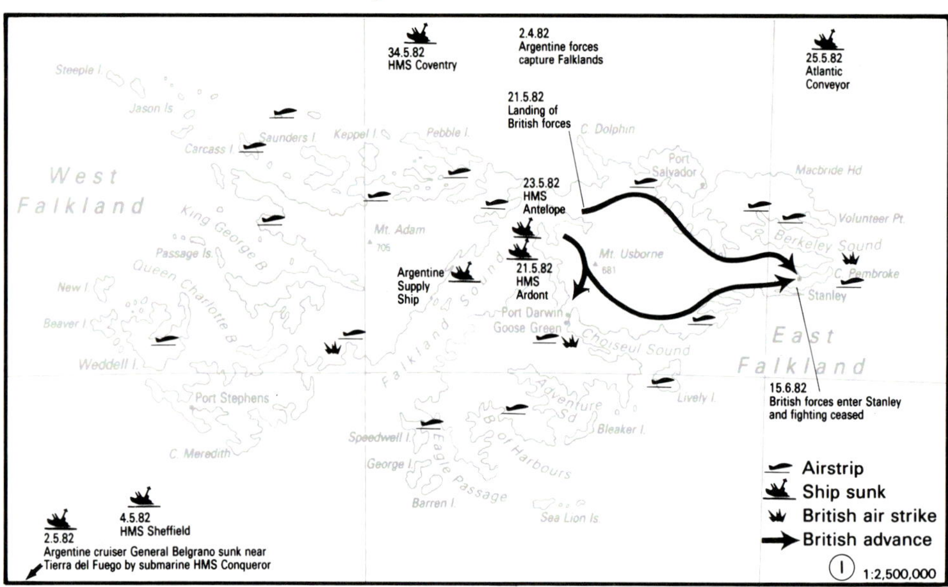

St. Mary's Church, Stanley

1982

1933

Argentinian claim, 1964

GOVERNMENT AND POLITICS

The Falkland Islands are a British crown colony, ruled by a governor appointed by Britain. Under a new constitution, which came into force in 1985, the governor chairs a local legislative council consisting of ten members (eight elected and two ex officio) with whom he must consult. Only the elected members of the council have the vote. There is also an executive council of five members (three elected and two ex officio) under the chairmanship of the governor. The commander of the local British garrison is in control of defense matters. Stanley, the islands' capital, is the center from which the uninhabited South Georgia and South Sandwich islands (south and southeast of the Falklands) as well as the British Antarctic Territory are administered and defended. Stanley was until 1989 the official seat of the governor of these territories.

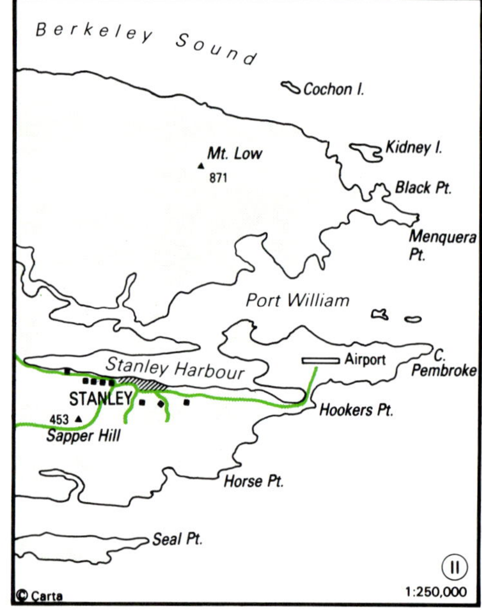

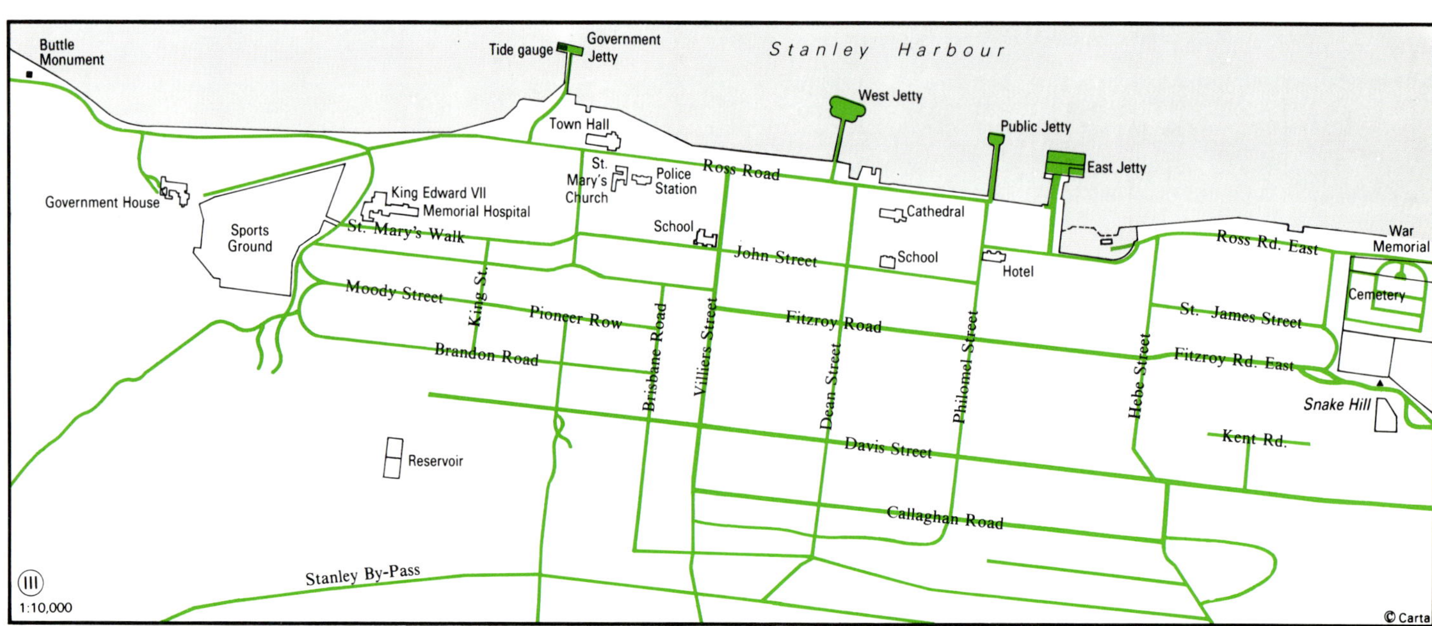

List of Sources

General

Altmir, O., *The Extent of Poverty in Latin America.* Bird Working Paper 522, Washington, 1982.
Blackmore, H. & Smith, C.T. *Latin America.* London, Methuen, 1983.
Bulterworth, D., *Latin American Urbanization.* Cambridge, Cambridge University Press, 1981.
Butland, G.J., *Latin America.* John Witey & Son. N.Y., 1966.
Central Intelligence Agency, *The World Factbook 1990.* Washington D.C.
Encyclopaedia Britannica, Inc., *1987 Britannica World Data.* Chicago, 1987.
Gleich, A., *The Political and Economic Relations between Europe and Latin America.* I.E.I. Hamburg, 1983.
Heinemann Educational, *Geographical Digest 1990-91.* Oxford, 1990.
Instituto Geografico de Agostini, *Calendario Atlante De Agostini 1990.* Novara, 1989.
Jones, Preston E., *Latin America.* 3rd Ed. London, Cassel, 1969.
Lambert, D.C., *Ameriques Latines.* Declins et Decollages, Ed. Economica, Paris, 1984.
Morris, A.S., *Latin America Economic Development and Regional Differentiation.* Totowa, N.J., Barnes and Noble, 1981.
Morris, A., *South America.* Totowa, N.J., Barnes and Noble, 1987.
Pearce, E. A., and C. G. Smith, *The World Weather Guide.* London, 1990.
United Nations Publications, *Statistical Yearbook for Latin America and the Caribbean.* 1988.
Unité et diversité de l'Amérique Latine, CNRS, Bordeaux, 1983.
Worldmark Encyclopedia of the Nations, Americas. New York, 1988.

Atlases and Maps

Aguilar, *Gran Atlas Aguilar.* Madrid, 1969.
Beradt Publication (England). "Kevin Healey's Contemporary Reference Map of South America" (1981), Scale = 1:5,000,000.
Der Grosse Welt Atlas. R.V. Verlag, 1989
Encyclopaedia Britannica, *Britannica Atlas.* Chicago, 1989.
Times Books, *The Times Atlas of the World.* London, 1985.
Westermann, *Diercke Weltatlas.* Braunschweig, 1988.

Regional

Venezuela

Anuario Estadistico de Venezuela. Caracas, 1989
Area Handbook Series: *Venezuela — A Country Study.* The American University. Washington D.C.
Ewell, J., *Venezuela, A Country of Changes.* London, 1989
Ministerio de obras publicas, *Atlas de Venezuela.* Venezuela, 1969.

Colombia

Anuario General de Estadistica de Colombia. Bogota, 1988.
Area Handbook Series: *Colombia — A Country Study.* The American University, Washington D.C.
Atlas de Colombia. Bogotá, 1969.
Cartur (Bogotá). "Plano de Bogotá" (1988), Scale = 1:25,000.
Hartlyn, J. *The Politics of Coalition Rule in Colombia.* California University Press, 1988.

Ecuador

Area Handbook Series: *Ecuador — A Country Study.* The American University, Washington D.C.
Bradt Publications (England). "The Galápagos Islands" (1988), Scale = 1:500,000.
Martz, Y. D., *Politics and Petroleum in Ecuador.* New Brunswick, 1987.

Peru

Anuaro Estadistico del Peru. Lima, 1988.
Area Handbook Series: *Peru — A Country Study.* The American University, Washington D.C., 1981.
Thorpe, R. & Bertran, G. *Peru — 1890-1977: Growth and Policy in an Open Economhy.* London, 1978.
Times Books, *Past Worlds, The Times Atlas of Archaeology.* London, 1988.

Bolivia

Anuario Geográfico. Estadistico de La Republica de Bolivia. La Paz, 1988.
Area Handbook Series: *Bolivia — A Country Study.* The American University, Washington D.C.
Dummerley, J., *Rebellion in the Veins, Political Struggle in Bolivia 1951-1982.* Verso, 1984.
Fifer, J.V., *Bolivia: Land, Location and Politics Since 1825.* California University Press, 1972.

Chile

Anuario Estadistico. Instituto Nacional de Estadistica. Santiago, 1988.
Area Handbook Series: *Chile — A Country Study.* The American Universtiy. Washington D.C.
Instituto Geográfico Militar, *Atlas Geográfico de Chile, para la Educación.* Santiago, 1985.
Olivares, T.X., & Alvarado, E.Z., *Geografia de Chile,* Editoria Universitaria, 1984.

Argentina

Area Handbook Series: *Argentina — A Country Study.* The American University, Washington D.C.
Bridges, E. L., *Uttermost Part of the Earth: Tierra del Fuego.* Hodden & Stoughton, London, 1948.
Ediciones Nauta, S. A., *Geografia y Atlas de Argentina y el Mundo.* Barcelona, 1985.
Grand Enciclopedia Argentina. Santillan. D.A. (Edit.), Buenos Aires, 1956-64.
Rock, D., *Argentina 1516-1982.* London, 1986.
Wynia, G.A., *Argentina,* Hoddesdon, 1986.

Paraguay

Anuario Estadistico de la Repulica del Paraguay. Asuncion, 1987.
Area Handbook Series: *Paraguay — A Country Study.* The American University, Washington D.C.
Maybury, L. D., and Howe, J., *The Indian Peoples of Paraguay.* Harvard University Press, Cambridge, Massachusetts, 1980.

Uruguay

Area Handbook Series: *Uruguay — A Cι untry Study.* The American University, Washington D.C.
Finch, M.H.J., *A Political Economy of Uruguay since 1870.* London, 1981.
Government of Uruguay, *Annual Statistical Report.* 1988

Brazil

Anuario Estatistico do Brazil. Fundacão Instituto Brasileiro de Geografie e Estatistico, Rio de Janeiro, 1989.
Aroldo de Azevedo, *Brasil a terra e o homen.* São Paulo, 1964.
Baer, W., *Industrialization and Economic Development in Brazil.* Irwin, 1965.
Morvan de Melo Moreira, *Brazil a Country Profile.* Population Council N.Y., 1978.
Pauwels, P. G. J., *Atlas Geográfico Melhoramentos.* São Paulo, 1968.

Guyana

Area Handbook Series: *Guyana — A Country Study.* The American University, Washington D.C., 1969.
Baber, C. and H. B. Jeffrey, *Guyana: Politics, Economics and Society.* London, 1986.

Suriname

The General Bureau of Statistics, *Suriname in Figures.* Paramaribo, 1987.

French Guiana

Papy, L., *La Guyane Française: Les Cahiers d'Outre Mer.* Vol. 8. Paris, 1955.

Falkland Islands

Phipps, C., *What Future for the Falklands?* London, 1977.
Shackleton, E., *Falkland Islands: Economic Study 1982.* HMSO, London, 1982.

Annotated Bibliography

prepared by Linda S. Vertrees

THE REGION. The book that first popularized interest in South America is John Gunther's *Inside South America* (Harper & Row Publishers, 1966). It is an aging but still excellent introduction to the people, geography, and politics of the region. The best and most comprehensive history of South America is the *Cambridge History of Latin America*, 8 volumes (Cambridge University Press, 1985–). *Handbook of South American Indians*, 7 volumes, edited by Julian H. Steward (Smithsonian Institution Press, 1944–1957), is the definitive work on South American Indians. It explores all aspects of Indian tribal life and presents the information in an understandable manner. J. H. Parry's *The Discovery of South America* (Taplinger Publishing Co., 1979) is an excellent overview of the discovery and exploration of South America. It contains many black-and-white illustrations and maps and uses original documents whenever possible. See also John A. Crow's one-volume history *The Epic of Latin America* (University of California Press, 1980). It covers pre-Columbian history and culture through the modern-day relationships of the South American countries. Sakai Sariola's *Power and Resistance* (Cornell University Press, 1972) studies the patterns of social and political life in Latin America from the conquest to independence. Alexander von Humboldt's *Personal Narrative of Travels to the Equinoctial Regions of America*, 3 volumes (George Bell & Sons, 1900), is the personal story of the exploration of the waters around South America. While the style is somewhat difficult, it provides a fascinating account of his voyages between 1799 and 1804, especially of the scientific instruments used. James Colnett's *A Voyage to the South Atlantic and Round Cape Horn into the Pacific Ocean* (N. Israel & DaCapo Press, 1968) is the story of the voyage of the Royal Navy ship *Rattler* in 1798. Included are excellent foldout reproductions of the charts used by Captain Colnett.

Indian Art in South America by Frederick J. Dockstader (New York Graphic Society Publishers Ltd., 1967) covers pre-Columbian art throughout South America. It includes many excellent color and black-and-white photographs and brief descriptions of the archaeological areas and their histories. *The Copper and Bronze Ages in South America* (AMS Press, 1979) is a highly technical analysis of weapons and farm implements made of copper and bronze in South America, including many photographs and line drawings. Edward J. Goodman's *The Explorers of South America* (Macmillan, 1972) is an excellent summary of 450 years of exploration. It supplements the personal accounts of the explorers with writings by noted historians. David Hatcher Childress's *Lost Cities & Ancient Mysteries of South America* (Adventures Unlimited Press, 1986) is a personal travelogue of the ancient cities and regions of South America. The photographs and maps supplement an enjoyable narrative.

Peoples and Cultures of Native South America, edited by Daniel R. Gross (Doubleday, 1973), is a collection of short articles discussing the social and economic development of the local Indian tribes. The importance of natural geologic features and climate and their relationship to the evolution of the tribes is presented. Three classic works by Claude Lévi-Strauss are *The Raw and the Cooked* (Harper Colophon Books, 1975), which provides a careful analysis of myths as well as showing the interaction between different tribes; *From Honey to Ashes* (Harper & Row, 1973), which discusses the roles of honey and tobacco in local customs; and *The Origins of Table Manners* (Harper & Row, 1978), which extends the study of myths and the importance of food to North American tribes. *Native South American Ethnology of the Least Known Continent*, edited by Patricia J. Lyon (Little, Brown, 1974), is a collection of articles on the Indians' relationships to natural resources, the supernatural, outside influences, and their own tribe. *The Mythology of South America* by John Bierhorst (Morrow, 1988) is a scholarly study of mythology as it relates to various tribes. There are many illustrations and maps locating the tribes that have preserved this aspect of their culture. *South American Mythology* by Harold Osborne (Hamlyn Publishing Group Ltd., 1968) emphasizes pre-Columbian beliefs. It is a coffee-table book with many color and black-and-white photographs and line drawings. After the Spanish conquest, Indian mythology blended with Christian motifs. The only comprehensive history of South American religions is Lawrence E. Sullivan's *Icanchu's Drum: An Orientation to Meaning in South American Religions* (Macmillan, 1987).

New Iberian World, 5 volumes (Time Books, 1984), presents a documentary history of the discovery and settlement of Latin America. This interesting set covers the Caribbean, Mexico, and Central America as well as South America to the early 1600's. Earl Parker Hanson's *South from the Spanish Main* (Delacorte Press, 1967) is a general history of the exploration of South America. Included are interesting biographies of Alexander von Humboldt, Charles Darwin, and Henry W. Bates. Clarence Haring's *The Spanish Empire in America* (Harcourt Brace Jovanovich, 1947) covers the period from 1492 to the wars of independence. It discusses the transfer of old-world ideas, government, and society to the new world and their eventual decay leading to the independence movement. *Early Latin America* by James Lockhard and Stuart B. Schwartz (Cambridge University Press, 1983) is an excellent single-volume history of colonial Spanish America and Portuguese Brazil. To understand the importance of the Catholic Church in South America, read *A History of the Church in Latin America* by Enrique Dussel (Eerdmans Publishing Co., 1981). This is a comprehensive history of the formation, growth, and change of the Catholic tradition in South America from 1492 to 1979.

David Bushnell and Neill MacAulay's *The Emergence of Latin America in the Nineteenth Century* (Oxford University Press, 1988) is a history of the political changes of the 1800's. John Lynch's *The Spanish American Revolutions 1808*–1826, 2d edition (Norton & Co., 1986), is an excellent survey of the subject. Lawrence A. Clayton's *The Bolívarian Nations of Latin America* (The Forum Press, 1984) presents a collective history from independence to the 1980's for Bolivia, Peru, Ecuador, Colombia, and Venezuela. They are called the Bolívarian nations because the great liberator, Simon Bolívar, declared their independence. Two very good biographies of Bolívar are Donald E. Worchester's *Bolívar* (Little, Brown, 1977), and *Bolívar the Liberator* by Lauran Paine (Roy Publishers Inc., 1970). Bolívar was a *criollo* born in 1783 in Caracas, Venezuela. His dream of uniting Ecuador, Colombia, and Venezuela into Gran Colombia did not succeed, once each country's regionalism became apparent. *Selected Writings of Bolívar*, 2 volumes, compiled by Vicente Lecuna (Colonial Press, 1951), presents another interesting aspect of Simón Bolívar. His letters, proclamations, and speeches provide insight into this very turbulent time in South American history. *Admirable Warrior: Marshal Sucre, Fighter for South American Independence* by John P. Hoover (Blaine Ethridge Books, 1977) is a fine biography of Antonio José de Sucre, a contemporary of Bolívar and San Martín.

Struggle for a Continent by Glen Barclay (New York University Press, 1972) is a diplomatic, economic, and military history of the South American countries after World War I. The roles played during World War II are an intriguing aspect of their independence. For an excellent general history, read *Modern Latin America* by Thomas Skidmore (Oxford University Press, 1984). It puts the events of the 1980's into the context of preceding years and includes separate chapters for Argentina, Chile, Brazil, and Peru. Robert L. Scheina's *Latin America: A Naval History 1810–1987* (Naval Institute Press, 1987) discusses the navies of the coastal countries and their various assignments. There is an overview of nineteenth-century activity, but the twentieth century is presented in greater detail. *Latin America: Perspectives on a Region*, edited by Jack W. Hopkins (Holmes & Meier, 1987), is a collection of essays on the background and foundations of Latin American development. Contemporary problems and relationships are examined closely. An interesting general biography is *The Legacy of Che Guevara* by Donald C. Hodges (Thames and Hudson, 1977). His impact on liberation movements in many South American countries is discussed. George Philip's *The Military in South American Politics* (Croom Helm, 1985) is a scholarly analysis of military involvement in South American politics. This analysis covers individual countries as well as South America in general. Jeffrey W. Barrett's *Impulse to Revolution in Latin America* (Praeger, 1985) discusses the reaction to economic, social, and political problems presented by the events of the twentieth century. Also discussed is how the countries evaluate themselves as they relate to other peoples. *Liberalization and Redemocratization in Latin America*, edited by George Lopez and Michael Stohl (Greenwood Press, 1987), presents a series of essays on the major changes in the "authoritarian" regimes. Some Central American countries are analyzed as well as Peru, Brazil, Uruguay, Chile, and Argentina. *Churches and Politics in Latin America*, edited by Daniel H. Levine (Sage Publications, 1980), is an interesting analysis of the relationship of the church and governments in South America. These essays discuss the changes in the church and their effects on politics. See also Levine's *Religion and Political Conflict in Latin America* (University of North Carolina Press, 1986), which examines the relationships between various countries' political and social communities and the Catholic Church.

Desperados: Latin Drug Lords, U.S. Lawmen, and the War America Can't Win by Elaine Shannon (Viking, 1988) is a very interesting account of the international drug problem. "Desperados" refers to U.S. agents in Latin America, not drug dealers. The difficulty of the U.S. role in Latin America is fully discussed. Rensselaer W. Lee's *The White Labyrinth* (Transaction, 1989) approaches the drug problem from the economic and political realities that make cocaine profitable.

Economies and Societies in Latin America by Peter R. Odell and David A. Preston (Wiley & Sons, 1973) is an interesting if somewhat dated account of the economic and social conditions of South America. *Trade, Stability, Technology, and Equity in Latin America*, edited by Moshé Syrquin and Simón Teitel (Academic Press, 1982), is a series of essays covering 1960 to the 1980's economic development in South America as it relates to, for example, international trade, technology, stability, and growth. Jonathan Kandell's *Passage Through El Dorado* (Morrow & Co., 1984) is a personal account of life at the Petroleum Exploration Zone as well as traveling through the Amazon Basin. The author provides some insights into the developing economy of the countries visited. *Latin America* by James Petras et al. (Rowman & Littlefield, 1986) is a series of essays on the global implications of economic development in South America. Included is a discussion of the relationship between the United States and Latin America in light of the reassertion of democracy in many of the countries. John Sheahan's *Patterns of Development in Latin America* (Princeton University Press, 1987) uses the topical approach to the assessment of economic conditions in the late 1980's. The possibility of a role for the United States in future economic development in South America is suggested. For a general history on the economic development in South America, see *Latin American Development: Geographical Perspectives*, edited by David Preston (Longman Scientific & Technical, 1987), which contains a series of essays covering developments from the colonial times to the present. Rural as well as urban changes are presented. Howard J. Wiarda's *Latin America at the Crossroads* (Westview, 1987) is an analysis of current social, political, and economic trends, including a discussion of relationships with the United States.

Arthur P. Whitaker's *The United States and the Southern Cone* (Harvard University Press, 1976) is a study of Argentina, Uruguay, and Chile, known collectively as the Southern Cone. The historical development of these countries both individually and as a group is analyzed. *Geopolitics of the Southern Cone and Antarctica*, edited by Philip Kelly and Jack Child (Lynne Rienner Publishers, 1988), is a collection of scholarly essays analyzing the feasibility of regional economics and politics, potentials for conflict within the Southern Cone, and Brazil's influence in the area. Philip O'Brien and Paul Commack edited *Generals in Retreat* (Manchester University Press, 1985), a contemporary analysis of this area plus Brazil. For an economic analysis, see Joseph Ramos's *Neoconservative Economics in the Southern Cone of Latin America, 1973–1983* (The Johns Hopkins University Press, 1986). A separate analysis of each country is presented as well as an analysis of the region.

Latin America and the United States, edited by Robert Bacon and James Brown Scott (Cambridge University Press, 1917), contains the collected addresses and papers of Elihu Root, Secretary of War, Secretary of State, and U.S. Senator. These documents represent U.S. policy through the turn of the century. For an excellent and thoughtful presentation of U.S. policy toward Latin America prior to the Cuban revolution, read Milton S. Eisenhower's *The Wine is Bitter* (Doubleday, 1963), which discusses how the Alliance for Progress, the Act of Bogotá, and the Charter of Punta del Este can be used as a framework for better relations between the United States and South America. *Partners in Conflict* by Abraham F. Lowenthal (The Johns Hopkins University Press, 1987) provides an analysis of U.S. policy since 1960. *Finding Our Way?*, edited by Howard J. Wiarda (American Enterprise Institute for Public Policy Research, 1987), contains essays on current U.S. economic policy and its future.

The Giant's Rival: The USSR and Latin America by Cole Blasier (University of Pittsburgh Press, 1987) is a general discussion of Soviet relations with Latin America. It provides insight into Soviet and Latin American economic ties, for example, as they relate to Argentina's and Brazil's export of grain to the USSR. See also *The USSR and Latin America: A Developing Relationship*, edited by Eusebio Mujal-León (Unwin Hyman, 1989).

Lives on the Line, edited by Doris Meyer (University of California Press, 1988), contains essays that represent the development of Latin American literature from 1960 to 1986. Since nearly all major writers are represented, this is an excellent introduction to contemporary Latin American literature. Marie-Lise Gazarian Gautier's *Interviews with Latin American Writers* (Dalkey Archive, 1989) is a series of fifteen interviews with contemporary writers. Issues discussed range from private emotions to Latin America's literary productions to politics and protest. For an understanding of contemporary art, read *Drawing the Line* by Oriana Baddeley and Valerie Fraser (Verso, 1989).

AMAZON BASIN. Thomas L. Sterling's *The Amazon* (Time-Life International, 1975) contains many beautiful color photographs of the flora and fauna and people who live in the Amazon Basin. It includes a special section on Henry Bates, the young, self-taught naturalist who spent the years 1848–1859 in the Amazon. *The Fate of the Forest: Developers, Destroyers and Defenders of the Amazon* by Susanna Hecht and Alexander Cockburn (Verso, distributed by Routledge, 1989) puts current concerns in historic and economic perspective. The settling of the area, the rubber industry, and other damaging development policies of the governments and industries have all contributed to the deterioration of the Amazon forest. Dennis Werner's *Amazon Journey* (Simon & Schuster, 1984), based on research among the Mekranoti, describes the methods a modern anthropologist uses to collect and analyze data. *Amazon Frontier* by John Hemming (Macmillan, 1987) is a scholarly work that provides an extensive chronological listing of scientists and artists and the Indian tribes they studied. *Explorers of the Amazon* by Anthony Smith (Viking, 1990) is a history of the Amazon River Basin and the people who explored it, beginning at the headwaters in Ecuador in 1541 with a Spanish expedition and ending in 1913 with the evils of the rubber industry exposed.

A Narrative of Travels on the Amazon and Rio Negro by Alfred Russel Wallace (Haskell House Publishers, Ltd., 1969) is a reprint of the 1853 classic. On a joint expedition of the Amazon with Henry Bates, Wallace continued his journey up the Rio Negro to the upper waters of the Orinoco *Jungle Paths and Inca Ruins* by William M. McGovern (The Century Co., 1927) is a personal account of the exploration of the northwest Amazon Basin. *Exploring the Amazon* by Helen and Frank Schreider (National Geographic Society, 1970) begins in Cuzco at the beginning of the Amazon. It contains many illustrations of birds, fish, plant life, and local tribes. The problems of tribal economy and development are discussed. Joe Kane's *Running the Amazon* (Knopf, 1989) is the adventure story of eleven people who began the 4,200-mile trip down the Amazon; only four finished. The author tells of the effects of development, drug traffic, and personal and team accomplishments. Redmond O'Hanlon's *In Trouble Again* (Atlantic Monthly, 1989) is the often amusing story of a four-month journey to Venezuelan Amazonia. *Who Goes Out in the Midday Sun?* by Benedict Allen (Viking, 1986) recounts an Englishman's entertaining exploits with animals, insects, Indians, and gold miners in the Amazon.

ANDES. *An Ancient World Preserved* by Frederic André Engel (Crown Publishing, Inc., 1976) is a scholarly presentation of excavating in the Andes from the Antilles to Tierra del Fuego. It portrays the social, economic, and political lives of the Andean peoples over the last 10,000 years and includes excellent maps and photographs. *Ancient Civilizations of the Andes* by Philip Ainsworth Means (Gordian Press, 1973) presents an archaeological history and geography of Ecuador, Peru, and Bolivia. John Hyslop's *The Inka Road System* (Academic Press, 1984) is an excellent archaeological and historical study of the 14,000 miles of Inca roads, which tied Inca society together through transportation, communication, and administration from the governing cities of Cuzco and Machu Picchu. Heinrich Ubbelohde-Doering's *On the Royal Highways of the Inca* (Praeger, 1966) discusses and illustrates pre-Inca culture and artifacts. *Journey along the Spine of the Andes* by Christopher Portway (The Oxford Illustrated Press, 1984) is an interesting personal adventure in Bolivia, Peru, Ecuador, and Colombia. *The Route of the Incas* (Viking Press, 1976) is a beautifully photographed coffee-table book with many illustrations of artifacts, landscapes, and people. Tony Morrison's *Land above the Clouds: Wildlife of the Andes* (Universe Books, 1972) includes many color and black-and-white photographs of wildlife and geography.

Magnus Mörner's *The Andean Past* (Columbia University Press, 1985) provides an economic history of the Andean region. It covers Peru, Ecuador, and Bolivia from the time of the Incas through the conquest and colonization by Spain to the establishment of independent countries.

VENEZUELA. A good general history is *Venezuela* by John V. Lombard (Oxford University Press, 1982). It reflects the evolutionary nature of the country's development, with sections on land resources and people as well as political history from colonialism to the 1980's. Judith Ewell's *Venezuela: A Century of Change* (Stanford University Press, 1984) covers the 1890's to the 1980's. It concentrates on politics and the effect of oil on the economy. Also provided are short biographies of the rulers during this time.

Irving Rouse's and José M. Cruxent's *Venezuelan Archaeology* (Yale University Press, 1963) is a useful overview, including a number of line drawings and black-and-white photographs. *The Headman and I* by Jean Paul Dumont (University of Texas Press, 1978) is the personal story of an anthropologist among the Panare Indians and how they came to accept one other. The same author's *Under the Rainbow* (University of Texas Press, 1976) is a scholarly analysis of the cultural and economic systems of the Panare Indians. It emphasizes daily life. A more recent anthropological study is *The Panare* by Paul Henley (Yale University Press, 1982). He found that the Panare have been able to retain their social and cultural traditions even in close proximity to civilization. *Survivors of El Dorado* by Johannes Wilbert (Praeger Publishers, 1972) discusses four Indian societies and their refuge from the Spanish conquerors in the desert, jungle, and swamps of the region.

The Conquest and Settlement of Venezuela by Don José de Oviedo y Baños (University of California Press, 1987) was first printed in 1723 and is considered a classic on early Venezuelan history. For an analysis of Spain's colonial policies, see Stephen Stoan's *Pablo Morillo and Venezuela 1815–1820* (Ohio State University Press, 1974). Morillo was the commander of the Spanish Expeditionary Army during that time. *Gunboat Diplomacy 1895–1905* by Miriam Hood (A. S. Barnes & Co., 1977) is the story of the involvement of Great Britain, Germany, and the United States in the development of Venezuela. After Cipriano Castro seized control of the government in 1899, Britain and Germany, who had many large investments there, blockaded the country. Castro demanded that the United States intercede by upholding the Monroe Doctrine.

For recent history, see Winfield J. Burggraaff's *The Venezuelan Armed Forces in Politics, 1935–1959* (University of Missouri Press, 1972). This book provides a clear understanding of the nature of military involvement in national politics from the death of General Juan Vicente Gómez in 1935 to the presidency of Rómulo Betancourt in 1959. *Democracy and Dictatorship in Venezuela, 1945–1958* by Glen L. Kolb (Connecticut College in association with Archon Books, 1974) is a concise presentation of events after the October revolution in 1945 to the fall of the dictator Pérez Jiménez in 1958. Robert J. Alexander's *Rómulo Betancourt and the Transformation of Venezuela* (Transaction Books, 1982) is an excellent biography of Betancourt (1908–1981), the first president to be elected and to be succeeded by another democratically elected president. His political career was devoted to turning Venezuela into a democratic nation. An interesting study of

Venezuelan foreign policy development is *Diplomacy and Dependency* by Sheldon B. Liss (Documentary Publications, 1978), which analyzes how power politics as practiced by North and South American countries have affected Venezuela.

Two interesting but technical books on the oil industry are *The Politics of Oil in Venezuela* by Franklin Tugwell (Stanford University Press, 1975) and *The Nationalization of the Venezuelan Oil Industry* by Gustavo Coronel (Lexington Books, 1983).

COLOMBIA. There are two excellent books on cocaine trafficking between Colombia and the United States. Paul Eddy, Hugo Sabogal, and Sara Walden's *Cocaine Wars: Murder, Money, Corruption, and the World's Most Valuable Commodity* (Norton, 1988) is an in-depth investigation of the drug cartel's activities from the jungle through the refining process and eventual shipment to the United States. *Kings of Cocaine: Inside the Medellín Cartel* by Guy Gugliotta and Jeff Leen (Simon and Schuster, 1989) is based on the authors' prize-winning series in the *Miami Herald*. It analyzes the complex hierarchy of the cartel and its terrorist methods.

An excellent history is *Colombia before Columbus* by Armand J. Labbé (an Americas Foundation Book in association with the Bowers Museum, Rizzoli, 1986). *Gold of El Dorado*, a coffee-table book, published by Abrams in 1979 provides a short history of the legend of El Dorado, including maps indicating where the artifacts were found and discussion of individual pieces.

Michael Taussig's *Shamanism, Colonialism, and the Wild Man* (University of Chicago Press, 1987) is an interesting anthropological study based on many years of personal observation. It provides insight into the role of myth and magic in colonial violence and healing practices. Another anthropological study is *The Shaman and the Jaguar* by G. Reichel-Dolmatoff (Temple University Press, 1975), describing the use of hallucinogenic plants in the practice of native religions, creation myths, and initiation rites by the many Northwest Amazon Indian tribes. LeRoy Gordon's *Human Geography and Ecology in the Sinú Country of Colombia* (Greenwood Press, 1977) describes this region and provides a history of the peoples who use it, both past and present. This work shows the influence of land on development by the inhabitants as well as the influence of the inhabitants on the land.

For an illustration of the importance of the frontier in Spanish Colombia, see *A Tropical Plains Frontier* by Jane M. Rausch (University of New Mexico, 1984). This work traces the history of the Llanos region of Colombia from 1531 to 1831. *The Darien Disaster* by John Prebble (Holt, Rinehart & Winston, 1968) is the story of a Scots colony from its establishment in 1698 to 1700 when the Spanish drove the settlers off the continent.

Gerhard Masur's *Simon Bolívar* (University of New Mexico Press, 1948) is an excellent biography of the great liberator and his plans for a Gran Colombia. *Nariño: Hero of Colombian Independence* by Thomas Blossom (University of Arizona Press, 1967) is a summary of the struggle for independence in Colombia as well as the other South American countries against the corrupt Spanish system. Antonio Nariño was a wealthy, educated, creole leader who was instrumental in the fight for independence. James William Park's *Rafael Núñez and the Politics of Colombian Regionalism, 1863–1886* (Louisiana State University Press, 1985) concentrates on the period of Colombia's history when regionalism predominated over national disintegration. Núñez presided over the establishment of the national constitution in 1886 that began a period of political stability, economic recovery, and industrial development. Charles W. Bergquist's *Coffee and Conflict in Colombia, 1886–1910* (Duke University Press, 1978) presents an excellent analysis of economy and politics after resurgence of central rather than regional control. *Gaitán of Colombia* by Richard E. Sharpless (University of Pittsburgh Press, 1978) is a biography of Jorge Eliécer Gaitán, a populist leader during the 1930's and 1940's. This is a detailed account of his political career and the frustrations of both the rural and urban working class. *The Assassination of Gaitán* by Herbert Braun (University of Wisconsin Press, 1985) deals with his assassination in 1948 and subsequent events. Hundreds of people died in a riot in Bogotá, and the political compromise between the liberals and conservatives disintegrated.

Mid-twentieth century Colombian history is marred by extensive violence. *When Colombia Bled* by James D. Henderson (University of Alabama Press, 1985) is a general history of the from the mid 1940's through the mid 1960's during which time an estimated 150,000 to 200,000 people were killed. Evelio Buitrago Salazar's *Zarpazo the Bandit* (University of Alabama Press, 1977) tells the story of this conflict fought mostly in the interior highlands. It is a thought-provoking insight into this time period from the soldiers' point of view. *Camilo Torres* by Walter J. Broderick (Doubleday and Co., Inc., 1975) is the biography of a priest-revolutionary killed in 1966. He had become a symbol of Christian commitment and resistance to oppression. Jonathan Hartlyn's *The Politics of Coalition Rule in Colombia* (Cambridge University Press, 1988) provides an interesting discussion of Colombian politics and government.

Diego and Nancy Asencio's *Our Man Is Inside* (Atlantic Monthly Press, 1982) is the suspenseful account of the U.S. ambassador to Colombia's sixty-one days of captivity in 1980 at the Dominican Republic's Embassy in Bogotá. Fifteen other ambassadors were also held by Marxist terrorists.

Structural Change in a Developing Economy by Richard R. Nelson, T. Paul Schultz, and Robert L. Slighton (Princeton University Press, 1971) is a scholarly analysis of Colombia's economy. This work attempts to show the relationship among economic development, rapid population growth, and policymaking as a government response to a changing society. Vinod Thomas's *Linking Macroeconomic and Agricultural Policies for Adjustment with Growth* (The Johns Hopkins University Press, 1985) is an excellent economic analysis of the factors that have contributed to the long-term development of the Colombian economy. *Essays on Industrialization in Colombia*, edited by Albert Barry (Arizona State University Press, 1983), provides a general introduction to the economic history of Colombia.

ECUADOR. For a beautiful coffee-table book with many color photographs, see *Ecuador: Island of the Andes* by Kevin Kling (Thames & Hudson, 1988). Betty J. Meggers's *Ecuador* (Praeger, 1966) is an archaeological study with many black-and-white photographs, maps, and line drawings of artifacts.

The Jívaro: People of the Sacred Waterfalls by Michael J. Harner (Doubleday/Natural History Press, 1972) is an account of the only tribe to revolt successfully against the Spanish and remain unconquered in the forest east of the Andes. The Jívaro were fierce warriors and kept shrunken head trophies of their enemies. *Sacha Runa* by Norman E. Whitten, Jr. (University of Illinois Press, 1976), is a scholarly ethnohistory of the area near Puyo, a town in the Quichua jungle, with photos, line drawings, and maps. The sequel, *Sicuanga Runa* (University of Illinois Press, 1985), discusses the myths present in the everyday life of these tribes. A more traditional approach to anthropological study is Whitten's *Class, Kinship, and Power in an Ecuadoran Town* (Stanford University Press, 1965). It discusses the construction of a rail line in 1957 linking the highlands with the port town San Lorenzo and how the community coped with the resulting economic changes. Mary J. Weismantel's *Food, Gender, and Poverty in the Eucadoran Andes* (University of Pennsylvania Press, 1988) is a study of the economic, social, and cultural changes affecting the Zumbagua in the early 1980's.

The Kingdom of Quinto in the Seventeenth Century by John Leddy Phelan (University of Wisconsin Press, 1967) is an informative history of the bureaucratic politics of the Spanish empire in Ecuador. Frank MacDonald Spindler's *Nineteenth-Century Ecuador: A Historical Introduction* (George Mason University Press, 1987) provides a basic history from pre-Columbian times through the beginning of the twentieth century. Each presidential term from 1830 to 1912 is analyzed, and short biographies of the influential people of each administration are presented. *The Process of Political Domination in Ecuador* by Agustín Cueva (Transaction Books, 1982) is a concise history of Ecuador since independence from Spain, emphasizing the political history of the twentieth century. For an excellent history of modern Ecuador, see David W. Schodt's *Ecuador* (Westview Press, 1987). It presents the diverse aspects of the geography, people, and economy in an informative narrative. The importance of cacao, bananas, and petroleum to the economy is analyzed. *Ecuador* by David Corkill (Oxford University Press, 1989) is another good general history and provides an excellent bibliography.

Edward Whymper's *Travels amongst the Great Andes of the Equator* with additional color photographs and a new introduction by Loren McIntyre (Gibbs M. Smith Inc., 1987), was originally published in 1879. It describes the methods of travel and mountain climbing in the late 1800's. A more recent travel book is *Two Wheels & a Taxi* by Virginia Urrutia (The Mountaineers, 1987). The author's personal experiences while on a bicycle trip through the Ecuadoran Andes with only a taxi as her "support vehicle" is very entertaining. Rhoda and Earle Brooks's *The Barrios of Manta* (New American Library, 1965) is the story of a husband-and-wife team of Peace Corps volunteers and their experiences in Ecuador.

Galápagos Islands. There are many different editions of Charles Darwin's classic works *The Voyage of H. M. S. Beagle* and *On the Origin of Species*. New York University Press has produced the complete 29-volume set titled *Works of Charles Darwin*. For the general reader, David W. Steadman and Steven Zousmer's *Galápagos: Discovery on Darwin's Islands* (Smithsonian Institution Press, 1988) is superbly illustrated. It provides a description of the natural and human history of the islands as well as presenting a theory on their formation. Also, see John Hickman's *The Enchanted Islands: The Galápagos Discovered* (Longwood Publishing Group, 1985). *Subtidal Galápagos: Exploring the Waters of Darwin's Islands* by James Cribb (Camden House Publishers, 1986) concentrates on the unusual marine life in the surrounding waters. There are many color photographs and maps of this fascinating area. *My Father's Island: A Galápagos Quest* by Johanna Angermeyer (Viking Press, 1989) is told from the perspective of the people who settled on the islands in the 1930's. It provides an interesting look at the reality of living in "paradise."

PERU. One of the most intriguing geophysical aspects of Peru is Nazca and its "lines". Evan Hadingham's *Lines to the Mountain Gods* (Random House, 1987) challenges many of the wildest theories. He presents Maria Reiche and her theory of a huge calendar pointing to the sun and stars and discusses new clues and theories. *Pathways to the Gods* by Tony Morrison (Harper & Row, 1978) discusses the lines and their relationship to astronomy and religion. Both books have many illustrations, line drawings, and photographs of the Nazca lines.

Inca Architecture by Graziano Gasparini and Luise Margolies (Indiana University Press, 1980) is a well-illustrated book with maps, many black-and-white photographs, and line drawings representing the architecture of the Incas. Susan A. Niles's *Callachaca* (University of Iowa Press, 1987) is a nicely illustrated architectural study of an Inca settlement near Cuzco. The use of natural features such as caves, springs, and rock outcrops in the site designs is discussed. *Pottery Style and Society in Ancient Peru* by Dorothy Menzel (University of California Press, 1976) presents the archaeology of the Ica Valley with many black-and-white photographs and line drawings of the artifacts. Henri Stierlin's *Art of the Incas* (Rizzoli, 1984) is a beautiful coffee-table book. It concentrates on the aesthetic creativity of the pre-Columbian artisans.

For an enjoyable history of the Inca Empire, read Loren McIntyre's *The Incredible Incas* (National Geographic Society, 1975). *History of the Inca Empire* by Bernabé Cobo (University of Texas Press, 1979) is a classic history published in the early 1600's. This is a comprehensive study of Inca culture, character, style of dress, social institutions, and legends. *Peru before Pizarro* by George Bankes (Phaidon, 1977) presents a picture of life in ancient Peru as it was shaped by elevation, terrain, and climate. This account covers environment, social system, religion, and economics. Another excellent history is *The Incas*, edited by Alain Gheerbrant (Orion Press, 1961). It presents different kings and their social, economic, legal, and architectural accomplishments. *Royal Commentaries of the Incas* by Garcilaso de la Vega (University of Texas Press, 1966) is an account of Inca history from the perspective of a contemporary Inca. Burr Cartwright Brundage's *Empire of the Inca* (University of Oklahoma Press, 1963) discusses territorial expansion as a function of religious beliefs. The empire was called Tahuantinsuyo ("the Four Quarters") by the Incas.

The classic work on Inca life is William H. Prescott's *History of the Conquest of Peru*, 2 volumes (Phillips, Sampson & Co., 1859). It narrates the social, religious, economic, and political aspects of Inca culture. *The Conquest of the Incas* by John Hemming (Harcourt, Brace Jovanovich, Inc., 1970) is an excellent study of the relationship between the Spaniards and the Indians. All levels of Inca society from royalty to peasants and miners are presented in detail. For the perspective of the conqueror, read Pedro Pizarro's *Relation of the Discovery and Conquest of the Kingdoms of Peru*, 2 volumes (The Cortes Society, 1921), a translation of Pizarro's own account of the conquest of Peru. *The Last Inca Revolt 1780–1783* by Lillian Estelle Fisher (University of Oklahoma Press, 1966) is the story of the uprising led by the Inca noble Túpac Amaru II.

Lords of Cuzco by Burr Cartwright Brundage (University of Oklahoma Press, 1967) is a chronology of the city of Cuzco from 1532 to 1572. Cuzco was the community of households in support of the sacred kings. Also by Brundage is *Empire of the Inca* (University of Oklahoma Press, 1963). Inca culture was totally engulfed by religion, and when religion began to fail, and the Spanish invaded, the empire collapsed.

Hiram Bingham's *Lost City of the Incas* (Atheneum, 1979) is an account of the discovery of the royal city of Vilcapampa in 1911. The city was lost for 300 years after the death of the last Inca ruler and is now called Machu Picchu after the nearby mountain. *Portrait of an Explorer: Hiram Bingham, Discoverer of Machu Picchu* by Alfred M. Bingham (Iowa State University Press, 1989) is mostly about the discovery and exploration of Machu Picchu and includes many of the first pictures of the city. *Machu Picchu* by John Hemming (Newsweek, 1981) is a coffee-table book with many color photographs of the city, surrounding landscape, and artifacts. It is an excellent companion for *Lost City of the Incas*.

Terrence Grieder's *The Art and Archaeology of Pashash* (University of Texas Press, 1978) is an account of the discovery and excavation of the richest pre-Columbian burial cite in Peru. The treasures discovered provide new perspectives on the meaning of Andean funerary practices. *Peasants in Transition* by Ted Lewellen (Westview Press, 1978) is a scholarly study of the Aymara Indians of the Lake Titicaca Basin and their transition from subsistence agriculture to a money economy. Changes in the social, religious, and kinship structures are also discussed. *The Flocks of the Wamani* by Kent V. Flannery and Joyce Marcus (Academic Press, Inc., 1989) is an anthropological study of the Llama herders on the Punas of Ayacucho basin. Their current lives represent the survival of an ancient way of life. Paul T. Baker's *Man in the Andes* (Dowden, Hutchinson & Ross, Inc., 1976) is a scholarly study of the effects of high-altitude living on an Andean community. Billie Jean Isbell's *To Defend Ourselves* (University of Texas Press, 1978) is an ethnographic study, similar in approach to Baker's, of a south-central Andean community. Barbara Bode's *No Bells to Toll* (Scribner, 1989) is the story of the earthquake in 1970 that claimed 75,000 lives. The author visited the area one year later and again after ten years to reassess her study.

Chronicle of Colonial Lima by Josephe de Mugaburu and Francisco de Mugaburu (University of Oklahoma Press, 1975) is the cooperative diary of Spanish soldier-brothers covering the years 1640 to 1697; it provides insights into the history, conditions, and religion of Lima. Clements R. Markham's *A History of Peru* (Greenwood Press, 1968) is a comprehensive history including discussions of sociology, natural resources, and literature as well as politics and government. *Peru* by David P. Werlich (Southern Illinois University Press, 1978) provides a brief history from the pre-Columbian period to 1914. It concentrates on twentieth-century events. Watt Stewart's *Chinese Bondage in Peru* (Duke University Press, 1951) tells the story of the use of cheap Chinese labor in Peru in the middle of the nineteenth century. *Revolution in Peru: Mariátegui and the Myth* by John M. Baines (University of Alabama Press, 1972) is a biography of José Carlos Mariátegui (1895–1930). It discusses not only his political ideas but also his ideas for social change. *The Japanese and Peru 1873–1973* by C. Harvey Gardiner (University of New Mexico Press, 1975) discusses the history of diplomatic relations between Japan and Peru. Peru was the first South American country with which Japan established diplomatic relations. Peru has a large number of Japanese immigrants.

The Politics of the Miraculous in Peru by Fredrick B. Pike (University of Nebraska Press, 1986) is a biography of Victor Raúl Haya de la Torre, the founder of the APRA political party. Steve Stein's *Populism in Peru* (University of Wisconsin Press, 1980) is a good history of twentieth-century Peru. The politics of social control and the APRA political party are presented. *The Peruvian Experiment Reconsidered*, edited by Cynthia McClintock and Abraham F. Lowenthal (Princeton University Press, 1983), contains a series of essays discussing the military government's economic and political perspectives during their regime from 1968 to 1980. For an excellent contemporary history, see Raúl P. Saba's *Political Development and Democracy in Peru* (Westview Press, 1987), which discusses politics, economics, and ideology under the military regime and the civilian government. Of current concern is *Cocaine: White Gold Rush in Peru* by Edmundo N. Morales (University of Arizona Press, 1989). Many possible options to eliminate drug trafficking are presented, from military intervention to buying crops of cocoa leaves and destroying them.

Pedro-Pablo Kuczynski's *Peruvian Democracy under Economic Stress* (Princeton University Press, 1977) analyzes the economic and political policies of the Belaúnde administration (1963–1968). Rapid economic and social expansion caused a serious economic crisis and eventual military coup in 1968. *The Political Economy of Peru 1956–78* by E.V.K. Fitzgerald (Cambridge University Press, 1979) is a scholarly analysis of the economic growth of Peru since 1956. The effect of this economic growth on different social classes is also discussed. Stephen B. Brush's *Mountain, Field, and Family* (University of Pennsylvania Press, 1977) is an interesting analysis of the resources of an Andean valley and its continued economic and cultural development. A brief history of the valley from the Spanish conquest is also presented.

BOLIVIA. Bolivia's early history is tied to Peru and the Inca empire. Simon Bolívar declared the country's independence, and was honored when it took his name on August 25, 1825. Bartolomé Arzáns de Orsúa y Vela's *Tales of Potosí* (Brown University Press, 1975) is a good description of Spanish daily life in colonial South America. Potosí has one of the richest silver deposits in the world. *Bolivia: Land, Location, and Politics since 1825* by Valerie J. Fifer (Cambridge University Press, 1972) examines the related aspects of location, accessibility, and boundary changes. Also presented are the effects of being one of two landlocked countries in South America. Charles W. Arnade's *The Emergence of the Republic of Bolivia* (Russell & Russell, 1970) is a good general history to the early 1950's that discusses the problems of the development of a new nation. Also discussed are the problems of agriculture at very high elevations. Christopher Mitchell's *The Legacy of Populism in Bolivia* (Praeger, 1977) is a general political history of the mid-twentieth century. It discusses the change from civilian populism to military rule and the influence of the Nationalist Revolutionary Movement (MNR), the most important populist party.

Beyond the Revolution: Bolivia since 1952, edited by James M. Malloy and Richard S. Thorn (University of Pittsburgh Press, 1971), is a series of essays on the revolution, economic transformation, land reform, and Bolivia's relations with the United States. A popular revolution overturned the military junta and reinstated Víctor Paz Estenssoro as president. James Dunmerley's *Rebellion in the Veins: Political Struggle in Bolivia* (Verso, 1984) is a scholarly study of Bolivian society since the 1952 revolution. It presents an analysis of the general problems of the economy, politics, and society as well as of the military dictatorships from 1964 to 1982. *Modern Day Bolivia*, edited by Jerry R. Ladman (Center for Latin American Studies, Arizona State University, 1982), is a collection of scholarly essays dealing with Bolivian history since 1952. It covers political and economic development, foreign influence and relations, and social and economic change. An interesting presentation of modern history is *Revolution and Reaction: Bolivia, 1964–1985* by James M. Malloy and Eduardo Gamarra (Transaction Books, 1988). It analyzes the politics and economy of military rule from the overthrow of President Víctor Paz Estenssoro in 1964 to his return in 1985.

For a personal and unique perspective on U.S. relations with Bolivia, see *My Missions for Revolutionary Bolivia 1944–1962* by Victor Andrade (University of Pittsburgh Press, 1976). The author was the Bolivian ambassador to the United States at various times from 1944 to 1962. See also *The Great Rebel: Che Guevara in Bolivia* by Luis J. González and Gustavo A. Sánchez Salazar (Grove Press, Inc., 1969).

Erick D. Langer's *Economic Change and Rural Resistance in Southern*

Bolivia 1880–1930 (Stanford University Press, 1989) is a scholarly history of economic development in southern Bolivia around the silver mines of Potosí. The rural economy of the other provinces that make up the southern part of Bolivia are also analyzed. *A History of the Bolivian Labor Movement 1848-1971* by Guillermo Lora (Cambridge University Press, 1977) provides an interesting history of the labor movement and the economy that centered on the silver mines of Potosí. Lawrence F. Salmen's *Listen to the People* (World Bank by Oxford University Press, 1987) is an evaluation of World-Bank-assisted urban development projects in LaPaz, Bolivia, and Guayaquil, Ecuador. The author was a participant-observer of the projects in both cities.

CHILE. Junius B. Bird's *Travels and Archaeology in South Chile* (University of Iowa Press, 1988) is a classic study of archaeological excavation in Chile in 1936 and 1937. It includes black and white photographs, graphs, and line drawings of various artifacts. The description of each site includes a diary of daily activity, climate, and finds. *Chile*, edited by Andrea T. Merrill (USGPO, 1982), provides basic information on the history, society, economy, government, and national security of Chile. Two excellent histories of Chile are Harold Blakemore's *Chile* (Oxford University Press, 1989), which has a good bibliography, and *Out of the Ashes*, by James R. Whelan (Regnery Gateway, 1989), which provides a chronology of events from 1833 to the present.

Pedro de Valdivia: Conqueror of Chile by R. B. Cunninghame Graham (Milford House, 1973) describes the early life of Valdivia in Spain and his success as a soldier in Venezuela and Peru. He marched south to Chile in 1541 where he established the settlement of Santiago and was killed in a battle with the Mapuches natives in 1554. Eugene H. Korth's *Spanish Policy in Colonial Chile* (Stanford University Press, 1968) is a study of Spanish rule from 1535 to 1700. It provides information regarding the many struggles between the Spanish colonists and the Indians and the eventual emancipation of all Indian slaves in 1674. Two good books on Bernardo O'Higgins are Jay Kinsbruner's *Bernardo O'Higgins* (Twayne Publishers, Inc., 1968) and Stephen Clissold's *Bernardo O'Higgins* and the Independence of Chile (Praeger, 1968). O'Higgins was the illegitimate son of the viceroy of Peru and a Chilean mother. In 1810 he led the revolt against Spain that lasted seven years and led to Chilean independence in 1817, when he became dictator supreme.

Simon Collier's *Ideas and Politics of Chilean Independence 1808–1833* (Cambridge University Press, 1967) describes the development of political ideas and attitudes of the revolutionary Chilean creole leaders. *The Civil Wars in Chile* by Maurice Zeitlin (Princeton University Press, 1984) analyzes the historical significance and the events leading up to each of the civil wars in Chile in 1851, 1859, and 1891. William F. Sater's *The Heroic Image in Chile: Arturo Prat, Secular Saint* (University of California Press, 1973) is a study of the naval career of Arturo Prat, killed in 1879 during the war in the Pacific with Peru. While this is basically a biography, it also provides insights into the creation of heroes by society in general. Frederick M. Nunn's *The Military in Chilean History* (University of New Mexico Press, 1976) is an analysis of the military and its relationship with the government from 1810 to 1973.

The Tragedy of Chile by Robert J. Alexander (Greenwood Press, 1978) attempts to describe and explain how the governmental crisis developed in the early 1970's. Edward Boorstein's *Allende's Chile* (International Publishers, 1977) provides general background to the election of Salvador Allende as president and his Unidad Popular (UP) government. An analysis of his term and the social and economic problems that led to the overthrow of his government is presented. *Crisis in Allende's Chile* by Edy Kaufman (Praeger, 1988) is a scholarly analysis of Allende's Unidad Popular government and offers some new and different explanations of his downfall. Also discussed are Chilean and international politics. One of the more interesting presentations concerning the period of 1971 to 1973 is *The Last Two Years of Salvador Allende* by Nathaniel Davis (Cornell University, 1985).

Disaster in Chile, edited by Les Evans (Pathfinder Press, 1974), is a series of essays on the Chilean revolution and its aftermath. Also published by Pathfinder Press in 1974 is José Yglesias' *Chile's Days of Terror: Eyewitness Accounts of the Military Coup*. Samuel Chaukin's *The Murder of Chile* (Everest House, 1982) is a collection of personal experiences after the coup. Approximately 30,000 people were killed and 100,000 jailed.

Genaro Arriagada's *Pinochet: The Politics of Power* (Unwin Hyman, 1988) is an informative political biography of General Augusto Pinochet Ugarte from 1973 to 1988. *Fear in Chile: Lives under Pinochet* by Patricia Politzer (Pantheon, 1989) discusses the accounts of continuous killings, disappearances, and police brutality under the regime of Pinochet. *Chile: Death in the South* by Jacobo Timerman (Knopf, 1987) is a vivid and interesting description of the oppression that has grown in Chile since the overthrow of Salvador Allende in 1973. Gabriel García Márquez's *Clandestine in Chile* (Henry Holt and Co., 1986) is the author's account of his impersonation of a Uruguayan businessman while shooting a film in Chile under Pinochet.

Brian H. Smith's *The Church and Politics in Chile* (Princeton University Press, 1982) provides an excellent analysis of twentieth-century Chilean politics and the Catholic church.

The Growth and Structure of the Chilean Economy by Markos J. Mamalakis (Yale University Press, 1976) is a technical study of the historic and economic developments from 1840 to 1973. Sergio Bitar's *Chile* (Institute for the Study of Human Issues, 1986) is an excellent economic and political analysis of the Allende regime from the perspective of a former minister in his cabinet. See also Barbara Stallings's *Class Conflict and Economic Development in Chile, 1958–1973* (Stanford University Press, 1978).

Easter Island. Thor Heyerdahl has written a number of books on Easter Island, the most famous and fascinating is *Aku-Aku* (Rand McNally & Co., 1958), a personal account of the archaeological exploration. Also by Heyerdahl is *Art of Easter Island* (De Boekerij Baarn, 1975), which concentrates on non-archaeological discoveries, including a brief history of Easter Island and its discovery. It is illustrated with many black-and-white and some color photographs of the artifacts found on the island. Heyerdahl's *Easter Island: The Mystery Solved* (Random House, 1989) was written after his return to the island after thirty years. *Rapa Nui Tradition and Survival* by Grant McCall (University Press of Hawaii, 1980) is an excellent anthropological study of the people of Easter Island. Information on the relationship with the other Polynesian islands is presented in an interesting narrative. Another history is *Easter Island* by Peggy Mann (Holt, Rinehart & Winston, 1976). *Island of Secrets* by Jacek Machowski (Robert Hale, 1975) provides a concise history of Easter Island and the explorations of the last 250 years. Thomas S. Barthel's *The Eighth Land* (University Press of Hawaii, 1978) is a scholarly presentation and the most detailed analysis of the myths and legends of Easter Island.

ARGENTINA. David Rock's *Argentina 1516–1982* (University of California Press, 1985) is an excellent general history from Spanish colonization to the Falklands War. It discusses the impact of the Spanish regime on the development of Argentina. *Tierra Del Fuego: The Fatal Lodestone* by Eric Shipton (Charles Knight & Co., 1973) is the story of the exploration of the area at the southernmost tip of South America and the channel islands. Throughout the early years many missionaries attempted to settle in the region only to be driven out by either the Indians or the climate. *San Martín* by Ricardo Rojas (Doubleday, Doran & Co., 1945) is a biography of General José de San Martín. Educated as an officer in the Spanish army, in 1810 he fought for the independence of Argentina, which was declared in 1816. Later, he led his army across the Andes to assist Bernardo O'Higgins in the fight for Chilean independence. Robert Weisbrot's *The Jews of Argentina* (The Jewish Publication Society of America, 1979) is the story of the development of Jewish communities in Argentina from the Inquisition to Perón. Argentina has the fifth largest Jewish population in the world after the United States, USSR, Israel, and France.

Argentine Dictator Juan Manuel de Rosas 1829–1852 by John Lynch (Clarendon Press, 1981) is a biography of the landowner, rural caudillo, and governor of Buenos Aires from 1829 to 1852. Richard W. Slatta's *Gauchos and the Vanishing Frontier* (University of Nebraska Press, 1983) is a history of the gauchos in the rural Rio de la Plata area (Pampas). *A House Divided* by Eduardo Crawley (St. Martin's Press, 1984) is a study covering the growth and change in Argentine ideology from 1880 to 1980.

Donald Hodges's *Argentina, 1943–1987* (University of New Mexico Press, 1988) is a history of Argentine politics since World War II and the country's relations with other South American countries. It also provides a study of Juan Perón and the Perónist movement. Two of the best biographies of Perón are *Perón* by Joseph A. Page (Random House, 1983) and Robert D. Crassweller's *Perón and the Enigmas of Argentina* (Norton, 1987), which puts Perón into the larger context of the instability of Argentine government, economy, social values, and politics. Two interesting biographies of Eva Perón are John Barnes's *Evita: First Lady* (Grove Press, 1978) and *Eva Perón* by Nicholas Fraser and Marysa Navarro (Norton, 1980).

For a history of modern Argentina, read Gary W. Wynia's *Argentina: Illusions and Realities* (Holmes & Meier, 1986), which covers the time from Perón's death in 1974 through the South Atlantic conflict with Great Britain in 1982. Between 1976 and 1979, the most oppressive of military rules resulted in about 30,000 disappearances. *Argentina: Political Culture and Instability* by Susan and Peter Calvert (University of Pittsburgh Press, 1989) presents historic and contemporary causes of Argentine political instability. Daniel Poneman's *Argentina* (Paragon House, 1987) examines that country's political system after military defeat in the South Atlantic and the 1983 election of the Unión Cívica Radical party candidate Dr. Raúl Alfonsín to the presidency.

Prisoner without a Name, Cell without a Number (Knopf, 1981) is the personal story of newspaper publisher Jacobo Timerman's imprisonment during the "dirty war" against dissidents. It is a fascinating account of his survival and eventual release. Another book on the same subject is Alicia Partnoy's *The Little School* (Cleis Press, 1986). It portrays the daily life of fear, terror, and torture in a military concentration camp called "The Little School".

Patagonia: Windswept Land of the South by Roger Perry (Dodd, Mead & Co., 1974) is a study of an area of extreme contrasts in climate and geological conditions. Some of the area designated as Patagonia is actually in Chile, although most is in Argentina. Bruce Chatwin's *In Patagonia* (Summit Books, 1977) is an exciting, personal account of the author's travels throughout Patagonia.

Buenos Aires, edited by Stanley R. Ross and Thomas F. McGann (University of Texas Press, 1982), is a collection of essays covering 400 years in the history of one of the most interesting and dynamic cities in the Americas. George Reid Andrews's *The Afro-Argentines of Buenos Aires, 1800-1900* (University of Wisconsin Press, 1980) is a scholarly history of blacks in Argentina, specifically Buenos Aires. Richard J. Walter's *The Province of Buenos Aires and Argentine Politics 1912-1943* (Cambridge University Press, 1985) analyzes Argentina's wealthiest, largest, and most populous province. With 25 percent to 40 percent of the votes, this province is the key to many major national elections.

The Argentine Economy by Aldo Ferrer (University of California Press, 1967) is an historical analysis of the development of the Argentine economy from the sixteenth century. Eduardo R. Conesa's *The Argentine Economy: Policy Reform for Development* (University Press of America, 1989) presents a short discussion of the economy from 1930 to the mid 1980's. William C. Smith's *Authoritarianism and the Crisis of the Argentine Political Economy* (Stanford University Press, 1989) is a scholarly analysis of the economy and the effects of the Argentine military on it.

PARAGUAY. Adalberto López's *The Revolt of the Comuñeros, 1712-1735* (Schenkman Publishing Co., 1976) studies the events that led to the independence movements in South America. This is the first book in English to present a detailed account of this revolt. *Paraguay's Autonomous Revolution 1810-1840* by Richard Alan White (University of New Mexico Press, 1978) is a scholarly analysis of the causes of the Paraguayan revolution.

Madam Lynch and Friend by Alyn Brodsky (Harper & Row, 1975) is the story of Eliza Alicia Lynch and Francisco Solano López, the oldest son of the dictator Carlos Antonio López, and their rise and fall from power. An excellent book on the War of the Triple Alliance is *Tragedy of Paraguay* by Gilbert Phelps (St. Martin's Press, 1975). It discusses the early history of Paraguay and the events that led to the war. More than half the population of Paraguay died during the war; fewer than 28,000 men and 180,000 women survived. *Paraguay and the Triple Alliance* by Harris Gaylord Warren (Institute of Latin American Studies, University of Texas Press, 1978) studies the postwar decade from 1869 to 1878. This is a detailed account of Paraguay's political, economic, and social problems after the War of the Triple Alliance and how the country survived the occupation. See also Warren's *Rebirth of the Paraguayan Republic* (University of Pittsburgh Press, 1985), an analysis of the recovery of the country from 1878 to 1904.

Paul H. Lewis' *Paraguay under Stroessner* (University of North Carolina Press, 1980) is a study of the man and his politics. General Alfredo Stroessner has governed since he seized power in 1954. *Paraguay: A Country Study*, edited by Dennis M. Hanratty and Sandra W. Meditz (USGPO, 1990), includes sections on society, environment, economy, government, politics, and national security.

URUGUAY. An interesting study of how a major Latin American reform leader gained and consolidated power is *José Batlle y Ordóñez of Uruguay: The Creator of His Times 1902-1907* by Milton I. Vanger (Harvard University Press, 1963). Batlle rise through the ranks to become leader of the Colorado Party and his election as president in 1903 are presented. Uruguay became a stable democracy during this time. See also Vanger's *The Model Country* (University Press of New England, 1980), which continues the study of Batlle. Based on his private papers, government documents, and other sources, this book focuses on his second term as president.

Major Carlos Wilson's *The Tupamaros: The Unmentionables* (Branden Press, 1974) attempts to explain the actions and reasons for this group of successful urban guerrillas who challenge capitalist government. *The Tupamaros* by Maria Ester Gilio (Secker & Warburg, 1972) tells the history of the development of the group from 1965 to 1970.

Uruguay: The Politics of Failure by Martin Weinstein (Greenwood Press, 1975) is a concise history of Uruguay in the twentieth century, analyzing the ideology and development of political institutions. Also by Weinstein is *Uruguay: Democracy at the Crossroads* (Westview Press, 1988), an excellent history of the twentieth century and how the country moved from Batllismo (welfare state) to collapse and political and economic crisis (1960's-1970's) through military rule (1973-1984) to the current redemocratization and económic stability.

The *Area Handbook for Uruguay* (USGPO, 1971) needs revising, but the introductory history and the information on the natural resources is still good. For a good economic history, see *A Political Economy of Uruguay since 1870* by M. H. J. Finch (St. Martin's Press, 1981). It provides an analysis of the population and society, land and farming, exports and imports, public utilities, and other aspects of economic and political life.

BRAZIL. Roberta C. Wigder's *Brazil Rediscovered* (Dorrance & Co., 1977) is the personal account of the author's return to Brazil. It describes in great detail the landscape, flora and fauna, and customs of the different ethnic groups in an easy, entertaining style. It includes a section on legendary historical and folk heroes as well as a review of Brazilian history. *Brazil* (Time-Life Books, 1986) is a wonderful photographic study, in color, of the varied historical, cultural, and economic regions of this country. Edited by Richard F. Nyrop, *Brazil: A Country Study* (USGPO, 1983) profiles Brazil in the early 1980's, providing introductory information on history, society, economy, government, politics, and national security.

Vital Souls by Jon Christopher Crocker (University of Arizona Press, 1985) is an ethnographic study for the general reader. It describes Bororo ideas regarding social institutions, shamans, and cosmology. The author expresses concern as to whether the Bororo will be able to adapt as their world changes or die out as a tribe. Another interesting anthropological analysis is *The Tenetehara Indians of Brazil: A Culture in Transition* by Charles Wagley and Eduardo Galvão (AMS Press, 1969). It discusses how this tribe's culture has adapted after more than 300 years of contact with outside cultures. Adrian Cowell's *The Tribe That Hides from Man* (Stein and Day Publishers, 1973) is an anthropological study of the Kreen-Akrore. A classic study of the conquest and exploitation of the Indians is *Red Gold* by John Hemming (Howard University Press, 1978). From 1500 to 1760 Europeans exploited the land and demoralized the tribes through forced removal from their homelands. Additionally, the introduction of European diseases caused many deaths among the native peoples.

C. R. Boxer's *The Dutch in Brazil 1624-1654* (Archon Books, 1973) is a scholarly study of the Dutch West India Company (founded in 1621) and Brazil. This is a fascinating aside to early colonial life in Portuguese Brazil and how the Dutch were finally driven out. A section deals with the conquests of John Maurits. *Conflicts and Conspiracies: Brazil and Portugal 1750-1808* by Kenneth R. Maxwell (Cambridge University Press, 1973) is a study of the shifting relations among Portugal, England, and Brazil. Special emphasis is placed on the Minas Conspiracy of 1788 to 1789 and its social, economic, and political impact. *Royal Government in Colonial Brazil* by Dauril Alden (University of California Press, 1968) presents the problems the viceroy faced governing Brazil during the Portuguese War with Spain. *Colonial Roots of Modern Brazil*, edited by Dauril Alden (University of California Press, 1973), is a collection of essays highlighting the political themes and economic background of modern Brazil. *From Colony to Nation*, edited by A. F. R. Russell Wood (The Johns Hopkins University Press, 1975), covers the time from 1775 to 1825. Political, social, and cultural aspects of independence as well as Brazil's relationship with the United States and Portugal are well presented.

The Brazilian Monarchy and the South American Republics 1822-1831 by Ron Seckinger (Louisiana State University Press, 1984) examines the relationships of the newly independent South American countries. How the countries defined and defended their national borders and the beginnings of international economic relations are discussed in detail. *Dom Pedro* by Neill Macaulay (Duke University Press, 1986) is a biography of the first monarch of Brazil. He declared independence from Portugal and set forth a new constitution. Harry Bernstein's *Dom Pedro II* (Twayne Publishers, 1973) treats the second monarch, who ruled until 1889. *Dom Pedro the Magnanimous* by Mary Wilhelmine Williams (Octagon Books, Inc., 1966) is a reprint of the 1937 edition. This biography covers Dom Pedro II's accomplishments in the fields of education, communication, agriculture, law and order, and international relations. Emilia Viotti da Costa's *The Brazilian Empire: Myths and Histories* (University of Chicago Press, 1985) is a study of the powerful segments of the population and how they influenced the political, economic, and social structure of nineteenth-century Brazil. *The Life of Joaquim Nabuco* by Carolina Nabuco (Greenwood Press, 1968) is a biography of one of the foremost leaders of Brazil at the end of the nineteenth century. For a slightly different look at nineteenth-century Brazil, see Frederick Luebke's *Germans in Brazil* (Louisiana State University Press, 1987), which presents the history of the German settlement from 1818 to 1918 and the social and cultural institutions developed during that time. The book concentrates on the attempts of the German community to keep Brazil out of World War I and the results of Brazil's declaring war on Germany.

Scott Mainwaring's *The Catholic Church and Politics in Brazil 1916-1985* (Stanford University Press, 1986) is an excellent analytical history of the Catholic church and Brazilian politics. The church's relationship with the state changed dramatically after the beginning of the military regime in 1964. *Politics in Brazil, 1930-1964: An Experiment in Democracy* by Thomas Skidmore (Oxford University Press, 1967) is an analysis of political and economic policy-making during this period. The problems that led to the overthrow of the João Goulart government by the military in 1964 began just after World War II. Another look at this turbulent period is offered by Carlos E. Cortés in *Gaúcho Politics in Brazil* (University of New Mexico Press, 1974). *Castello Branco: The Making of a Brazilian President* by John W.F. Dulles (Texas A&M University Press, 1978) is an informative biography of General Humberto de Alencar Castello Branco up to his becoming president in 1964. Also by Dulles is *President Castello Branco, Brazilian Reformer* (Texas A&M University Press, 1980), which deals with his presidential years. His views of nationalism, law, and justice led to a series of economic and political reforms that saw the stabilization of Brazil's government. *State and Opposition in Military Brazil* by Maria Helena Moreira Alves (University of Texas Press, 1985) is an in-depth analysis of the military rule from 1964 to 1984, covering the political, economic, and social systems developed under the influence of military power. Also discussed is the development of opposition political parties and their growing influence in the government. *The Politics of Military Rule in Brazil 1964-1985* by Thomas Skidmore (Oxford University Press, 1988) is another look at this time period. The author picks up where he left off in his previously cited book, presenting a fine analysis of this important era. Additionally, he presents a thoughtful assessment of the new democratically elected government of José Sarney.

John Dickenson's *Brazil* (Longman, 1982) treats economic development and includes maps and landscape photographs. *Victims of the Miracle* by Shelton H. Davis (Cambridge University Press, 1977) emphasizes the political and economic factors that are changing Brazil's economy. The seriousness of the economic changes on the human and ecological systems of the Amazon Basin is staggering. *The Economic Growth of Brazil* by Celso Furtado (University of California Press, 1963) is a good, general history of the economic growth of Brazil from the colonial era to the twentieth century. Winston Fritsch's *External Constraints on Economic Policy in Brazil, 1889-1930* (University of Pittsburgh Press, 1988) concentrates on the exportation of coffee. *The Roots of State Intervention in the Brazilian Economy* by Gustavo Maia Gomes (Praeger, 1986) is a technical discussion beginning with the development of the agrarian economy and including the development of industry.

Donald Pierson's *Negroes in Brazil* (Southern Illinois University Press, 1967) is a classic sociological study of race relations. Brazil's national policy of assimilation of blacks rather than segregation offers a different approach to race relations than that of the United States. *Neither Black Nor White* by Carl N. Degler (University of Wisconsin Press, 1986) is a comparative study of the history of slavery in the United States and Brazil. The historic similarity ends after slavery is abolished. The striking differences in the cultural evolution in contemporary racial patterns between the United States and Brazil are analyzed.

Douglas Botting's *Rio de Janeiro* (Time-Life Books, 1977) is a coffee-table book with color photographs. While it is somewhat dated, this short history of Rio de Janeiro and its relationship with Portugal is useful. *Samba* by Alma Guillermoprieto (Knopf, 1990) presents the social conditions and customs of areas in Rio as teams of Samba dancers prepare for the annual Carnival.

GUYANA. Charles Waterton's *Wanderings in South America* (Oxford University Press, 1973) was first published in 1825. Another personal account is *Climb to the Lost World* by Hamish MacInnes (Hodder & Stoughton, 1974).

On the Trail of the Arawaks by Fred Olsen (University of Oklahoma Press, 1974) is an account of the author's search for the first Indians encountered by Christopher Columbus. It offers insight into Arawak society, including their religion, thunderstones, tools and weapons, and their ballgame. Two books by Mary Noel Menezes provide information regarding Guyana. The first, *The Amerindians in Guyana 1803-1873: A Documentary History* (Frank Cass, 1979), is a scholarly presentation of a series of documents concerning the natives and Great Britain. Her other book, *British Policy towards the Amerindians in British Guiana 1803-1873* (Oxford University Press, 1977) is an excellent history of Guyana from the time the British took over the Dutch settlement in 1803. It discusses the tribes and their relations with the government, the economy (sugar, coffee, and cotton), customs and culture, and the role of Great Britain in Guyana. *Cultural Pluralism and Nationalist Politics in British Guiana* by Leo A. Despres (Rand McNally & Co., 1967) is an account of Guyanese society and its development during the last years of British rule. It is an anthropological study of the different ethnic groups and how they function together politically and socially.

Guyana Emergent by Robert H. Manley (G.K. Hall & Co., 1979) is a concise history of the first ten years after independence in 1966. Guyana's role in the Caribbean and the British Commonwealth is also discussed. Thomas J. Spinner's *A Political and Social History of Guyana, 1945-1983* (Westview Press, 1984) is a scholarly study based on original documents of the post-World War II development of a racially diverse country. Chaitram Singh's *Guyana* (Praeger, 1988) presents a short introductory history of British Guiana as background information to the recent history.

Sugar without Slaves by Alan H. Adamson (Yale University Press, 1972) is an excellent history of political and economic life in British Guiana in the nineteenth century. The importance of sugar to the economy and of slavery to governing the villages is presented in a thought-provoking manner. Kampe R. Hope's *The Post-War Planning Experience in Guyana* (Arizona State University, 1978) is a short analysis of economic planning. The development of public-works projects is described and their progress analyzed. Hope's *Development Policy in Guyana: Planning, Finance, and Administration* (Westview Press, 1979) builds on his previous book. *Guyana Politics, Economics and Society* by Colin Baber and Henry B. Jeffrey (Frances Pinter, 1986) is a comprehensive study of Guyana. The emphasis is on the twenty-year Marxist regime of Forbes Burnham, which ended With his death in 1985. There is a short section on the future of Guyana after Burnham.

SURINAME. John Gabriel Stedman's *Narrative of a Five-Year Expedition against the Revolted Negroes of Surinam* (The Johns Hopkins University Press, 1988) is a classic with more than twenty editions in six languages. Within the chronological structure of his diaries, written during the late 1700's, are descriptions of the flora and fauna, slave life, the relationships between slaves and planters, military campaigns against rebel slaves, his relationship with other soldiers, and his romance with a slave. This is one of the most interesting and informative books on South America. *Soldier in Paradise* by Louise Collis (Harcourt, Brace, World, 1965) is a biography of Captain John Stedman and nicely compliments his narrative.

First-Time by Richard Price (The Johns Hopkins University Press, 1983) presents the story of the Saramaka, descendants of African slaves who worked the sugar, timber, and coffee plantations in seventeenth- and eighteenth-century Dutch Guiana. The history of their escape and fight for freedom (won in 1762) has been passed down through storytellers to their descendants and is presented here as a series of interviews with the tribe's elders. *I Sought My Brother* by S. Allen Counter and David L. Evans (MIT Press, 1981) is the account of the authors' meeting with a tribe living deep in the jungle whose African culture remained intact. Peter Rivière's *Marriage among the Trio* (Clarendon Press, 1969) is an excellent anthropological study of the Trio tribe and their culture that concentrates on the ritual of marriage.

Edward Dew's *The Difficult Flowering of Surinam* (Martinus Nijhoff, 1978) is a study of the multi-ethnic, cultural and political aspects of society in the 1970's. *Surinam* by Henk E. Chin and Hans Buddingh (Frances Pinter, 1987) presents an analysis of the social, political, and economic developments that led to the military coup in February 1980. J. H. Adhin's *Development Planning in Surinam* (H.E. Stenfert Kroese N.V., 1961) presents many graphs and tables in the analysis of the economic history of Surinam. Its sections on the ten-year plan and future development planning and analysis are somewhat dated.

FRENCH GUIANA. Hassoldt Davis's *The Jungle and the Damned* (Little, Brown, 1952) is the story of a trip inland along the Maroni River. *Behind the Lianas* by Henry Larson and May Pellaton (Oliver & Boyd, 1958) is a story of exploration and travel, illustrated with many black-and-white and a few color photos. *The Petroglyphs in the Guianas and Adjacent Areas of Brazil & Venezuela* by C. N. Dubelaar (Institute of Archaeology, University of California Press, 1986) is a highly technical inventory of the rock inscriptions and paintings in Surinam, Guyana, and French Guiana. It contains many photographs and maps with site locations indicated.

French Guiana was used as a penal colony by France from 1852 to 1954. Of the 70,000 prisoners sent to French Guiana only one in ten survived. George John Seaton's *Isle of the Damned* (Farrar, Straus and Young, 1951) is the story of the imprisonment and escape from Devil's Island by the author. *The Man from Devil's Island* by Colin Rickards (Stein and Day, 1968) tells the story of a convicted murderer and his twenty-one years of imprisonment. It also provides a good history of French Guiana. Daniel de la Ravadière claimed the area in 1604 for France. Félix Milani's *The Convict* (St. Martin's Press, 1975) is the personal account of a small-time crook sent to the French Guiana penal colony in 1931, his nearly twenty-five years in prison, and his six escape attempts. *Papillon* by Henri Charrière (Morrow & Co., 1970) is the story of a fourteen-year imprisonment, escape to British Guiana, and eventual settlement in Venezuela. Alexander Miles's *Devil's Island: Colony of the Damned* (Ten Speed Press, 1988) discusses the history of French Guiana and the penal settlements. Interviews with the last of the survivors and other residents of French Guiana are illuminating.

FALKLAND ISLANDS. *Sovereignty in Dispute: The Falklands/Malvinas, 1493-1982* by Fritz L. and Olga Mingo Hoffmann (Westview Press, 1984) relates the long and complex history of these islands and provides information on the climate, wildlife, vegetation, society, and economy. Argentina lost the Falklands in 1833 to Britain and used force to try to regain them in 1982. For an account of the diplomacy leading up to the war, see Michael Charlton's *The Little Platoon: Diplomacy and the Falklands Dispute* (Basil Blackwell, 1989). Martin Middlebrook's *Operation Corporate: The Falklands War, 1982* (Viking, 1986) is an excellent military history although the perspective is British because the Argentine documents and personnel were not available for consultation. *The Falklands War*, edited by Alberto R. Coll and Anthony C. Arend (George Allen & Unwin, Press 1985), is a scholarly collection of articles that enumerates the challenges presented to international law; to diplomatic relations with Great Britain, the United States, and the other South American countries; and future implications of the Falklands War to the military and political climate in Argentina. *War in the Falklands* (Harper & Row Publishers, 1982) is based on the *Times of London*'s coverage of the war with additional information provided by many participants after the war. It discusses how many key decisions were made by the men in the field. Simon Winchester's *Prison Diary, Argentina* (Chatto & Windus, The Hogarth Press, 1983) is the personal account of his imprisonment in Argentina during the Falklands War.

Glossary

Selection of terms which appear in the maps: in Portuguese *(P)*, and in Spanish *(S)*.

agulha *(P)* needle
alegre *(P, S)* gay, lively
alto/a *(P, S)* high
arroyo *(S)* rivulet
asunción *(S)* assumption
avenida *(S)* avenue
bahía *(S)* bay
baía *(P)* bay
bajo/a *(S)* low
bello/a *(S)* beautiful
blanco/a *(S)* white
boa *(P)* good
boca *(P, S)* mouth
boreal *(S)* north, northern
branco/a *(P)* white
bravo/a *(S)* brave; intractable, savage
bueno/a *(S)* good
cabo *(P, S)* cape, headland
caliente *(S)* warm, hot
campo *(P, S)* field
casa *(P, S)* house
catarata *(S)* cataract, waterfall
cayo *(S)* rock, islet
cerro *(S)* hill, peak
chaco *(S)* jungle region
ciudad *(S)* town, city
colorado/a *(S)* red, colored
cordillera *(S)* mountain chain
costa *(S)* coast, shore, beach
cruz *(P)* cross
cuchillas *(S)* chain of mountains
cuenca *(S)* deep valley
dios *(S)* god
embalse *(S)* reservoir
estación *(S)* station
estado *(P, S)* state
estero *(S)* inlet, estuary; swamp
estrecho *(S)* strait
fortín *(S)* small fort
foz *(P)* mouth
franco/a *(S)* free
frontera *(S)* frontier
frío *(S)* cold
fuerte *(S)* sort
golfo *(S)* bay, gulf
grosso *(P)* big
hermoso/a *(S)* beautiful
ilha *(P)* island
isla *(S)* island
jardín *(S)* garden
lago *(P, S)* lake
lagoa *(P)* lagoon
laguna *(S)* lagoon
llano *(S)* prairie
mar *(P, S)* sea
monte *(P, S)* mountain
nacional *(P, S)* national
negro/a *(P, S)* black
nevado/a *(S)* snowy
norte *(P, S)* north, northern
novo/a *(P)* new
nudo *(S)* knot
nuevo/a *(S)* new
ojo *(S)* eye; spring
oro *(S)* gold
país *(P)* land
parque *(S)* park, zoo
paso *(S)* pass, strait
pedra *(P)* stone
peña *(S)* cliff, rock
pico *(S)* peak, high mountain
playa *(S)* beach
plaza *(S)* square
ponta *(P)* point, cape
ponte *(P)* bridge
porto *(P)* port
puerto *(S)* harbor
puna *(S)* desert plateau
punta *(S)* point, promontory, cape
real *(P, S)* royal
ribeirão *(P)* great river
rio *(P)* river
río *(S)* river
roca *(P, S)* rock, cliff
salado *(S)* salt
salar *(S)* salt pan
salto *(P, S)* waterfall
san *(S)* saint
santo/a *(P, S)* saint
são *(P)* saint
selva *(S)* wood, forest
seco/a *(S)* dry
serra *(P)* mountain range
serranía *(S)* mountain range
sierra *(S)* mountain range
sul *(P)* south, southern
sur *(S)* south, southern
territorio *(S)* territory
tierra *(S)* earth, land, territory
vale *(P)* valley
valle *(S)* valley
velho/a *(P)* old
verde *(P, S)* green
viejo/a *(S)* old
villa *(S)* country house, town
y *(S)* and
zona *(P, S)* zone, area

Index of Place Names

C

D

E

Q

R

S

Index of Persons